History of American Thought and Culture

Paul Boyer, *general editor*

Howard Brick

Daniel Bell
and the Decline of
Intellectual Radicalism

Social Theory and Political Reconciliation
in the 1940s

The University of Wisconsin Press

Published 1986

The University of Wisconsin Press
114 North Murray Street
Madison, Wisconsin 53715

The University of Wisconsin Press, Ltd.
1 Gower Street
London WC1E 6HA, England

First printing

Printed in the United States of America

For LC CIP information see the colophon

ISBN 0-299-10550-4

FOR MY MOTHER

JANET B. BRICK

Contents

vii

viii   Contents

Preface

This book began with an idea for a very different one. Looking at the history of the New Left, I was stirred by the movement's characteristic disavowal of theory to discover the latent social and political theory upon which it actually relied. So eager to declare its novelty, and to distinguish itself from preceding political generations, the New Left would have taken itself out of history if it could. It was not hard, however, to locate links between New Left thinking and tenets of conventional postwar American social theory, in its understanding of capitalism, bureaucracy, and mass culture.

Reading backwards in the history of recent American social theory, from the New Left to postwar liberal sociology, suggested some other intriguing historical problems, for the liberal theory itself was the product, in part, of ex-radical intellectuals, the remnants of the Old Left who had reconciled themselves with the order of power in the United States. The problem, as I saw it then, was one of understanding successive waves of deradicalization and radicalization in intellectual culture. In one respect, the liberal roots of the New Left were hardly surprising, for we might say, paraphrasing Lenin, that any attempt to deny the role of theory results only in an "instinctive" grasp of "the first available" theory, the prevailing ideology of the age. The construction of postwar theory by ex-radicals also pointed to the power of ideology, if we would understand "ideology" not so much as a self-contained set of "ruling ideas" but as a historical process that limits the compass of critical thinking and in time draws critical thought back into the closed circle of legitimations and sanctions for prevailing relations of power and authority.

The problem of a political "wave" among intellectuals and the social theory they generated meshed with my attempt to fashion a Marxist intellectual history which would examine the relation of intellectuals to ideology by trying to grasp processes of thinking under determinate historical conditions. In this pursuit, I would consider "ideology" neither a static body of propositions nor simply an explicit defense and celebration of the rulers in a society. While admitting change and even certain kinds of criticism within its orbit, ideology nonetheless remained, as Raymond Williams might put it, a structure of pressures and limits that, in time, channel the development of ideas.

In treating the history of intellectuals, and especially the history of intellectual deradicalization, it is important to avoid confusing Marxism with a utilitarian psychology of material self-interest, which would attribute deradicalization to the intellectuals' yearning for material comfort (the easy charge of "selling out"). Nor does a Marxist intellectual history require attributing a unique "class interest" to intellectuals. Intellectuals are best considered not a class but a "social category," determined by their role as creatures and creators of ideology. Indeed, intellectuals might be considered "free-floating" in the sense that they are relatively free of immediate dependence on class interests. They do, however, work within a prevailing framework of ideas characterizing a society as a whole, a framework shaped by the balance of power between dominant and subordinate groups. Since Marxism above all is a theory that attempts to grasp the historical conjunctures, or turning points, that alter the prevailing structure of class relations, a Marxist intellectual history would try to understand the course of ideas as they reflect significant changes in this overall configuration of forces.

Defined by their relation to ideology, in this sense, intellectuals do not have a vocational disposition to criticize or oppose prevailing social order. Conversely, political accommodation (as in the experience of the Old Left intellectuals) does not represent an unprecedented lapse of vocational responsibility. By seeking a historical understanding of deradicalization in terms of broad currents in ideology, I would hope to avoid reciting a jeremiad, like that aimed by the New Left against the Old Left intellectuals which obscured the common theoretical ground between the two camps.

The intellectual formation of Daniel Bell posed a historical case that promised to illuminate many of the problems—substantive and methodological—involved in this approach to recent American intellectual history. Bell's early intellectual biography centers on an experience of deradicalization, and his subsequent theme, "the end of ideology" (his definition of the term has little to do with my own), marked one point of debate where the generation of postwar liberal intellectuals came into contact, and conflict, with the young New Leftists. In fact, Bell's intellectual development, particularly his involvement with the "new radicalism" of the mid-forties, suggested more of an affinity with the New Left than either he or his young antagonists would easily admit. Considering this episode of his intellectual biography, it appeared that Bell's path to political reconciliation was a tortuous one, hardly a simple act of capitulation, and that significant remnants of radical ideas remained to enrich his thought. Thus, even politically conventional thought (lying within the bounds of ideology) allowed room for criticism, while the conventions of thought constrained, channeled, limited, or defused that criticism. Consequently, to show how a social theory, like Bell's, could be generated out of the experience of deradicalization was to demonstrate, very concretely, the workings of ideology, in the historical sense of the term I suggested above. My project then involved not only a case study of deradicalization but an attempt to elucidate, on that basis, the meaning of Daniel Bell's mature social theory.

Studies by Job Leonard Dittberner and Nathan Liebowitz helped to focus my attention on the early period of Daniel Bell's career, though their work has been limited largely to an examination of published work by Bell and his close associates in the "end of ideology" camp. By working with manuscript sources unexamined by earlier researchers, I have attempted to provide an account of Bell's early intellectual development which is both interpretive and historical, locating the fundamental elements of his work and situating them in a context of specific social and intellectual shifts marking the time of his coming of age.

My debts start with the original plan of study. That plan emerged from discussions with my friend Karl Pohrt on the relations between New Left thinking and the socialist tradition. Professor Alan Wald of the University of Michigan, who has led the way in recent studies of left-wing American intellectuals, eagerly supported my work from its earliest stages through completion of the dissertation on which this book is based. I am also very thankful for the supportive, critical attention given to me by Professor John O. King. My wife, Debra M. Schwartz, has offered me not only warm companionship but the most sound editorial advice at crucial points in the work. Also helping to spur me along in research and writing were regular discussions of U.S. intellectual history with my friend Daniel Halle Borus.

I have been fortunate to have a collegial relationship with Douglas G. Webb, of the University of Toronto, who has brought great erudition and scholarly rigor to the study of the "New York Sociologists," a group of academic sociologists, including Bell, who shared, in fact or in spirit, a common background in the New York Jewish community and the labor and left-wing political movements of the 1930s and 1940s.

Daniel Bell showed great generosity in several long interviews and a detailed correspondence. Sidney Hook, Lewis Coser, Philip Selznick, and Everett Kassalow were also very helpful in answering my questions in interviews and/or correspondence.

I appreciate the comments and criticism offered by Paula Rabino-witz, James Maffie, Robert Berkhofer, James McIntosh, Peter Railton, and Thomas Weisskopf, who read either prospectuses or early drafts of this study. Steve Fraser, Florencia Mallon, and Robert Westbrook made cogent criticisms that helped me improve the work. My editors, Paul Boyer, Peter Givler, and Jan Levine Thal, encouraged me to develop and refine the presentation of my argument. Naturally, neither these, nor any of the others who have aided my effort, are responsible for faults in the work.

The Program in American Culture and the Horace Rackham School of Graduate Studies at the University of Michigan provided financial support for much of my research. Linda Eggert of the Program in American Culture gave me invaluable technical assistance throughout. I deeply appreciate the help provided by Jeff Eichler, Peter Filardo, Ethel Lobman, and Dorothy Swanson of the Tamiment Institute Library at New York University.

My late father, Julius H. Brick, always warmly encouraged my academic work, and I know he was pleased to see the completion of my dissertation. I had him in mind throughout the preparation of this book. I do not know how to give him all the thanks he deserves. This book is dedicated to my mother, Janet B. Brick, in admiration for her ways of dignity, perseverance, and love.

Acknowledgments

Permission to quote unpublished documentary material is gratefully acknowledged:

Daniel Bell, for correspondence and for manuscript material in his files at the Tamiment Institute Library, New York University, and in other archival collections.

Rare Book and Manuscript Library, Columbia University, for excerpts from the Lewis Corey Papers.

Oral History Research Office, Columbia University, for excerpts from the Socialist Movement Project.

Manuscript Department, William R. Perkins Library, Duke University, for excerpts from the Socialist Party of America Papers.

Rare Books and Manuscripts Division, The New York Public Library, Astor, Lenox, and Tilden Foundations, for excerpts from the Norman Thomas Papers.

Tamiment Institute Library, for excerpts from the American Labor Conference on International Affairs papers.

Yale University Library, for excerpts from the Dwight Macdonald Papers.

Lewis Coser, for excerpts of personal correspondence.

Harold Isaacs, for excerpts of personal correspondence.

Harry Fleischman, for excerpts of personal correspondence.

Daniel Bell and the
Decline of Intellectual Radicalism

Introduction

It might seem anomalous that Daniel Bell published his signal book, *The End of Ideology*, in the year 1960. Conventional periodization marks that year as a pivot between distinct eras of apathy and upheaval, and critics sometimes claimed that Bell's views on the decline of the American left were outmoded almost immediately by the renewed vigor of political opposition and the radical imagination in the 1960s. Now, long after the demise of the New Left, it is easier to see Bell's book from another perspective. Not only did *The End of Ideology* pronounce the epitaph for one left-wing generation; it also challenged the leftists to come: after the demise of the "old" socialism, could a "new" radicalism fashion a coherent and convincing program capable of recasting American politics, a new and effective "ideology"? A quarter century after the publication of Bell's book, his skepticism does not seem quite so groundless as it did in 1965.[1]

The title of Daniel Bell's book took on a life of its own in the decade after its publication, a shibboleth in warring camps of intellectuals. Undoubtedly, for many in Bell's camp, the phrase connoted an overly simple confidence in the social stability of European and American welfare capitalism, along with a smug dismissal of "extremist" political doctrines. For Bell's opponents, the "end of ideology" bespoke a positivistic denial of evaluative biases in established social science, a technocratic program of scientifically managed reform, a vulgar-realist suppression of moral motivations in public life, and a repudiation of politics per se if politics were understood as an effort to reshape society according to valued ends. Together, C. Wright Mills suggested, these precepts robbed intellectual activity of its motivation and allowed it to lapse into acquiescence. To those student radicals who took up Mills's standard, the end-of-ideology doctrine came to

3

symbolize the older intellectuals' retreat from their responsibility for persistent and rankling social criticism, their surrender of vision and independent purpose, their unthinking celebration of American life, their bland support of official policy.[2]

The currency of the phrase, "the end of ideology," among American intellectuals in this period and the debate it stirred about their sense of duties and allegiances would, alone, mark Bell as a figure deserving the attention of intellectual historians. Since that time, Bell has maintained a distinguished position in U.S. intellectual life, if only for his ability to seize on a phrase or concept (after "the end of ideology," he propounded the idea of "post-industrial society") that focuses the attention of the intelligentsia, broadly speaking—the academic, literary, journalistic, and public-policy intellectuals. Yet, besides playing a highly visible role in the "events" of intellectual life, Bell deserves consideration as a social theorist. One cost of a penchant for phrase-making and public controversy is that ideas that are often quoted and questioned lose clarity of definition, as pictures lose resolution the more they are copied. Still, as I will show, Bell was one of the most sophisticated and complex thinkers of all those who embraced the concept of "the end of ideology," and I think intellectual history can recover the meaning of the idea, correct the misunderstandings perpetuated in tendentious intellectual discourse, and locate what might be called a social theory, proper, lying underneath or alongside the journalistic catchphrase.

This book is intended to illuminate the meaning of "the end of ideology" and of Daniel Bell's mature social theory by studying his intellectual formation in the context of his own "end of ideology," his experience of political deradicalization. The study focuses primarily on Bell's youth, his intellectual course through the 1940s leading to his first book, *The Background and Development of Marxian Socialism in the United States.* This critical phase of his intellectual development is examined closely, as a case study in the process of deradicalization among American intellectuals. I proceed, however, with the assumption that the central themes and motifs of Bell's mature theory were cultivated in this early period and that by reconstructing the early formation of his thought we can find the key to *The End of Ideology* and later works. I will justify this claim by providing a summary interpretation of Bell's most accomplished late works, *The Coming of Post-Industrial Society* and *The Cultural Contradictions of Capitalism,* showing the persistence of the structure of his early thought.

Granted, "the end of ideology" cannot be identified with Daniel Bell alone. At the same time, any *prima facie* attempt to identify the phrase with a particular, well-bounded, and coherent body of social theory will fail. Numerous variants of the theme can be unearthed from the long past of Western social theory—indeed, as far back as Frederick Engels, according to Seymour Martin Lipset.[3] The significance of the judgment, however, that "ideology" has, will, or might come to an end varies so greatly from writer to writer that a simple chronicle of usages sheds little light on the meaning of the idea in 1960 and the years that followed. At that time, "the end of ideology" was intimately associated with the Congress for Cultural Freedom (CCF), an international organization of liberal anticommunist intellectuals, secretly sponsored by the Central Intelligence Agency. Both Edward Shils and Seymour Martin Lipset used the phrase, "The End of Ideology," to report on the CCF's 1955 symposium in Milan on "The Future of Freedom."[4] Bell had participated in the symposium, and in fact held a number of official posts in the international organization and the U.S. affiliate of the CCF. For Shils and Lipset, "the end of ideology" signified the apparent consensus of the Milan meeting that market exchange and state intervention were no longer intransigently opposed, as unalloyed abstract principles of Right and Left, but could be pragmatically combined to maximize liberty and welfare. This view presupposed a convergence of all "normal" Western parties in the struggle against "totalitarianism" and suggested that Western intellectuals, by and large, had relinquished those apocalyptic visions of social change that tended, presumably, toward totalitarian outcomes. At the 1955 conference, however, there was even a hint of the desire to overcome the "ideology" of the Cold War, as Michael Polanyi, Bertrand de Jouvenal, and Raymond Aron spoke of the similarity of social problems encountered in the East and West as common features of "industrial society."[5] It is a sign of the doctrine's volatility that the impulse to deny polar political categories could express an anticommunist defense of mixed economy while suggesting a global convergence theory as well.

In the United States, Lipset, even more than Bell, shouldered the burden of defending and elaborating "the end of ideology" as a doctrine. There is some justice in attributing to Lipset a Panglossian philosophy of history, a narrative of social development ending in the present achievement of "the good society," where the working class was finally admitted to membership in the national community and bureaucratic norms increasingly limited the sway of arbitrary authority.[6] On the other hand, Daniel Bell, who tired rather quickly of the heated debates surrounding the title of his book, had a much more ambivalent estimation of the development of society in his time.

Indeed, it is hard to say how much of Bell's ambivalence was conscious. Trying to understand what he meant by "the end of ideology" is a difficult task because his book appears to be filled with so many unmediated contradictions, inconsistencies, and ambiguities. Undoubtedly he recognized a lapse of radical political opposition among American intellectuals like himself, who first assumed the intellectual vocation in the 1930s. Despite this underpinning, the book did not quite clarify what Bell meant by "ideology" and whether he intended to assert that it had actually ended. At one point in *The End of Ideology*, Bell emphasized the emergence of stable political compromise among "interest groups," yet at another point he noted "the 'ideologizing' of politics" as "symbol groups" like Labor, Business, and Farmers came to dominate public discourse.[7] Although the apparent decline in the appeal of apocalyptic ideologies gave society relief from the strains of extremism, Bell also suggested that "America in mid-century is in many respects a turbulent country."[8] In an essay that Edward Shils called a "gratified contemplation of American life," Bell dismissed the alarmism and despair inherent in theories of mass society, but Bell also borrowed the accents of mass society theory as he indicated the shift "from authority to manipulation as a means of exercising dominion," the tendency of an enervating work life to degrade leisure into "wildly aggressive play or passive, unresponsive viewing," and, implicitly, the contribution of *anomie* to the "rancor" of right-wing politics.[9] At one moment Bell applauded Western socialists for realistically accepting the role of the market in a mixed economy; at another, he criticized a market-based conception of socialism for accepting the imposition of utilitarian calculation on work.[10] Gradualist optimism about the prospects for rational political management of social problems mingled with postprogressive pessimism emphasizing "irony, paradox, ambiguity, and complexity."[11] And, not least, he seemed evasive in judging whether advanced industrial society in the West was distinctly "capitalist" or not. At one moment he approached a managerial conception of postcapitalist order, when he asserted that "private productive property" was "largely a fiction" and that professional managers were more interested in "performance" than profit rate; at another point he caustically challenged the ideological "rehabilitation of American capitalism."[12]

Any analysis and interpretation of Bell's ideas must attend to these contradictions. Bell's ambivalence, however, appeared also in more overt and conscious ways. The oft-forgotten subtitle of his book, "The Exhaustion of Political Ideas in the Fifties," hardly carries the celebratory ring most readers heard in the main title.[13] "The End

of Ideology" seems to connote not only the welcome lapse of absolute doctrines that Bell considered disruptive and nihilistic but also a
genuine frustration on his part with the vacuity of radical or critical
thought in his time. "One finds, at the end of the fifties, a disconcerting caesura," Bell wrote. He cited the argument by *Dissent*'s Lewis
Coser that the aim of the contemporary radical should be "fostering
the growth of the species 'radical'" as an indication of how difficult it
was to give content to a radical opposition once it no longer confidently asserted socialist ends.[14]

Only a superficial reading would construe Bell's point here as a
cynical and dismissive one. His yearning for sound principles of criticism was not too far below the surface. "The problem of radical
thought today," he wrote elliptically, "is to reconsider the relationship
of culture to society." He seemed to have in mind the fruitlessness of
investing the cultural avant garde with radical aspirations in a society
all too willing to embrace innovation for its own sake.[15] More clearly,
he marked the "cult of efficiency" in a mass-consumption economy,
embraced not only by corporate management but by the workers who
suffered the hierarchical regimentation of mass production, as a
proper target for criticism. Combating this "cult" in his essay "Work
and Its Discontents," Bell mocked the "scientific" approach of industrial engineers to conflict resolution and called instead for "new, hu-
manistic" approaches to work that would break down centralized controls and attack the alienation or estrangement induced by the gulf
between labor and meaningful activity. "For the unions to challenge
the work process would require a radical challenge to society as a
whole," Bell wrote, and for once he scattered any doubt of his own
inclinations: "The exploration of such a road is necessary." So much
for charges of technocracy or positivism. Bell needed no lessons about
the evaluative foundation of social analysis. "The idea that a scientist
simply studies 'what is,' as John Dewey has argued, is a parochial conception of science. . . . As Dewey said forcefully on another occasion:
'Anything that obscures the fundamentally moral nature of the social
problem is harmful.'"[16]

Certainly, all of these ambiguities make it difficult to discover a
precise, decided meaning, or a conscious, articulate theory, in the
phrase, "the end of ideology." I would suggest that the search for
meaning begin on a different plane, not merely with an interpretation
of finished works but with the historical phenomena that conditioned
their composition. At face value, "the end of ideology" concerned the
passage of a certain segment of the American intelligentsia from a
posture of radical opposition to American society toward an accom-

modation with its standing institutions and prevailing social relations. The "end of ideology debate" arose from divergent assessments of that passage. An understanding of "the end of ideology" in Bell's terms, then, should start with an examination of the phenomenon of intellectual deradicalization.

If nothing else Daniel Bell's *End of Ideology* spoke of his own passage, his own route to reconciliation, and his work has an unmistakable tone which identifies that reconciliation with maturation, a kind of personal progress. Anyone can see how the ideas that once enlisted youthful passions come to seem one-sided and formulaic in retrospect. Yet, if Daniel Bell was able to see his own development beyond youthful socialist politics as a welcome escape from doctrinaire rationalizations (one meaning of "ideology" in Bell's terms), we also know that his perspective at the end of the journey was not one-dimensional. Nor did it lack entirely that tension with its object (society as it is) that keeps thought at least potentially critical—despite the fact that many of Bell's opponents seemed to consider "the end of ideology" an abject capitulation to entrenched powers. For the New Left, "the end of ideology"—or the deradicalization of the Old Left— seemed a betrayal of vocation, but the transformation an intellectual generation underwent from the 1930s to the 1950s was not so simple as that. Objectively, the outcome of the Old Left decline was the collaboration of intellectuals—more or less consciously, more or less overtly—with existing powers; nonetheless, the *process* of deradicalization was mediated intellectually and took forms more complex than a collapse of will, failure of nerve, or vulgar-material quid pro quo.

The decline of the "Old" Left first became significant to historians at the moment a new radicalization commenced. Extant histories of deradicalization reflect the rise of the New Left and bear the burden of that conflict of generations which erupted in the 1960s. Indeed, it seems as if "the treason of the intellectuals" has become a refrain of modern intellectual life, adopted by one generation after another to mark it off from predecessors who failed to uphold some valued principle. So, in his cutting review of the political career of the American intelligentsia, *The New Radicalism in America* (1965), Christopher Lasch retraced the critique Julien Benda offered nearly forty years before. For Benda, the intellectuals had surrendered their critical "office" of upholding transcendent values and had adopted instead a debased "realism" subordinating thought to the imperatives of action. Similarly, according to Lasch, American intellectuals, in their longing for engagement, had refused to accept their tension-filled detachment from society at large. They were too anxious to escape the passivity of the "spectator," Lasch charged, and their peculiar "anti-intellectualism" culminated in the Cold War "realism" of the late 1940s and 1950s, the disabused concession to given facts of political and military power, advocated by thinkers like Arthur M. Schlesinger, Jr., and Reinhold Niebuhr. For Lasch, the 1966 disclosure that the CIA had funded the Congress for Cultural Freedom reconfirmed the judgment that the intellectuals had capitulated, "serv[ing] the interests of the state, not the interests of intellect." [17]

According to Richard Pells's *Radical Visions and American Dreams* (1973), the intellectual's capitulation was completed by the early forties. Echoing Lasch, Pells wrote that "the intellectual's century-long zeal to serve society and shape the course of history led him gradually to suspend his critical faculties." During the Depression decade, Pells found, the radical intellectual's desire to overcome the disintegrating effects of individualist competition, to reconstruct society as a vital community, melded into a drive toward order and security. "Under the inhibiting influence of the Popular Front, the search for community slowly became a celebration of conformity, the longing to be different became a hunger to fit in, the feeling of alienation became an excuse for adjustment, and the demand for a conflict of classes became an appeal for national unity." Another historian, Robert A. Skotheim, located the fulcrum of intellectual transition more specifically, in the "discovery of totalitarianism" in the late 1930s and 1940s. As left-wing intellectuals recoiled, Skotheim wrote, from the pragmatic politics of reform they thought were implicated in the rise of the new terroristic states, intellectual life came to be characterized by the "reembracement of America" and a "disinclination to probe [its] failings." [18]

Skotheim was mistaken, however, in assuming that the United States itself was exempt, throughout the forties, from the critique of totalitarianism. Dwight Macdonald's journal *Politics* (1944–49) persistently argued that American society, too, was victim of a universal trend toward militarist regimentation and hypercentralized bureaucratic organization of all social institutions under the control of a hegemonic state. Thus one intellectual historian has challenged "the erroneous conclusion that significant radical criticism disappeared entirely in the 1940s." Penina Migdal Glazer highlighted Macdonald's *Politics* as a center for "radical critics attempting to open new vistas," ideas in fact that prefigured tenets of New Left thought two decades later: designation of the centralized state as the source of authoritarianism and imperialism, doubt of the moral value of scientific and technological progress, the attempt to construct cooperative communities, insistence on decentralization as the basis of a radical program, repudiation of organized labor as the focal agent of change, the centrality of the issues of race and peace.[19]

Even here, however, the historical image of the forties fails to grasp the full complexity of intellectual process. For instead of recognizing the paradoxical interweaving of these radical tenets with the main drift of social thought, Glazer in effect portrays these radicals as a small coterie of estranged intellectuals who elaborated a self-contained, underground tradition of post-Marxist radicalism, hidden from view until the New Left resurrected it. This image is characteristic of those accounts—like Richard King's *The Party of Eros* (1972) and Martin Jay's *The Dialectical Imagination* (1973)—that have attempted to resurrect the radical heritage of figures like C. Wright Mills, the cultural critic Paul Goodman, or the intellectuals of the Frankfurt Institute of Social Research who were in exile in the United States during the 1930s and 1940s. The historical record shows, however, that such figures as these were not so isolated from the broader stream of deradicalizing intellectuals as their chroniclers suppose. The ideas of the unique "new radicalism" of the forties were bound up with emerging tenets of the new "realist" liberalism that would bring former radical intellectuals toward political reconciliation with American society.

Intellectual radicalism and deradicalization in the forties, I propose, were complexly intertwined, wrapped around a number of common and ambivalent concepts. The Frankfurt School, for instance, despite its appearance as a cloistered enclave of exiles at Columbia University, shared a number of themes with the broader milieu of New York intellectual life during the 1940s. Finding the source of social criticism not in a rebellious class but in the autonomous individual who seeks refuge from an increasingly organized collectivity was a theme current not only among Frankfurt School leaders like Max Horkheimer and Theodor Adorno but also in the *Politics* circle. The same can be said of the urge to reverse the "progress" of technological order rather than perpetuate it. *Partisan Review*'s equation of radicalism with the defensive struggle to preserve the conscience of the avant garde from the commercial juggernaut of public life resembled, in its "negativism," the Frankfurt School's conception of abstract thought per se as a kind of resistance, a negative critique of the functional social life that threatened to reduce reason to a mere instrument of production.[20] Both Herbert Marcuse and *Partisan Review*'s Lionel Trilling, a leader of the new liberalism, repudiated neo-Freudian revisionism as a therapeutic doctrine obscuring the ineluctable tension between the individual and society.[21] Even the Frankfurt School's resistance to

the "premature reconciliation of contradictions" (the harmonistic illusions of an administered society) found an echo in the work of
Reinhold Niebuhr, American existential theologian and new liberal. Niebuhr scorned premature resolutions on the grounds that the
source of moral aspiration lay outside reality (in the divine) and that
dilemmas of human spirit could never be resolved finally in history.[22]

Even those polar figures of the end-of-ideology debate, Daniel
Bell and C. Wright Mills, were friends and collaborators in the forties.
Bell offered Mills his first outlet for political journalism in the pages
of the social-democratic paper Bell edited, *The New Leader*.[23] Bell and
Mills started the decade with the shared conviction that socialism remained on the agenda as a liberating project, and both devoted their
popular writing to analyzing the growing fusion of politics and economy that moved beyond laissez-faire capitalism toward a new social
order tightly organized by a monopoly-dominated state. Both saw the
emergent order in terms suggested by *Behemoth*, the monumental
study of Nazism by Franz Neumann of the Frankfurt School. Thus
they hinted that the war, proclaimed as a struggle for democracy, so
fueled the concentration of power that a quasi-fascist domestic regime
could emerge from it.

When Mills moved to New York in 1944 to take a job at Columbia's
Bureau of Applied Social Research, he took an apartment upstairs
from Bell at 222 East 11th Street. Both had escaped the draft, and
during the war years they cultivated a sense of alienation which, they
believed, defined the role of the radical intellectual swimming against
the current. They both contributed to Dwight Macdonald's *Politics*,
and in the first years after the war, the specter of a "permanent war
economy," founded on the integration of business and military elites,
figured prominently in their publications. Toward the end of the decade, personal tensions intensified between Bell and Mills. Nonetheless
they both focused their energies on elaborating a new sociology of labor; they still hoped that the union movement would realize its progressive potential and break out of its alliance with the Democratic
Party toward political independence. In the late 1940s, moreover, Bell
wrote striking essays on the authoritarian bent of conventional sociology which were consistent with Mills's critical view of the profes-
sion.[24] As the decade wore on, both grew increasingly troubled by the
standardization of culture, its manipulative powers, and the apparent
foreclosure of possibilities for social change.*

* Another intellectual historian, Richard Gillam, found a similar sympathy between
C. Wright Mills, avatar of new radicalism, and Richard Hofstadter, a new liberal commonly associated with Niebuhr, Schlesinger, and the later Bell. In terms that sound
typically Millsian, Hofstadter wrote in 1950 of the manipulative control that concen-

It is important to capture the flavor of the new radicalism Bell and Mills shared in the mid-forties. It was dominated, first of all, by an acute sense of the end, or inversion, of progress. Such a perception on Bell's part grew from his experience of the war: rather than promoting the prospects of democratic planning, as he had hoped, the war appeared to consolidate the power of private monopolies over and within the state. By the end of the war Bell found himself in a political cul-de-sac, radicalized in his opposition to capitalist society yet dubious of imminent prospects for radical action aiming to create a new society. In the next few years he cultivated a radical analysis of the integration of all agencies of social action, particularly organized labor, into the self-reproductive whole of existing social order, and he came to consider a sociological critique of "mass society" more relevant to his purposes than a socialist critique of capitalism. The analytical poles of bureaucracy and alienation took precedence over the struggle between capitalist and proletarian. Increasingly marginalized and estranged from a monolithic order that could not, by its nature, realize his purposes, Bell opted for alienation, a role-defining sense of "otherness," that would sustain the values of community in the criticism of the communally disintegrative effects of rationalization.

Paradoxically, the "new radicalism" characteristic of this time figured as an intellectual pathway to political accommodation. Unable to find a sanction of success in history, but only a record of defeat, this postprogressive radicalism felt itself trapped by a reality that appeared intractable and stagnant. It was a radicalism lacking outlets, and its characteristic expression was intellectual estrangement—radicalism conceived as a transcendent critique rather than an immanent force. As such it was close to the tragic sensibility of German sociology, which combined a withering critique of modernity with a renunciation of the attempt to reclaim a morally meaningful social existence. Max Weber's Protestant Ethic summed up this syndrome, for as a kind of paradoxical "worldly asceticism," it bound up the radical rejection

---

trated power exercised over the community at large, defined the American order as a "genteel form of the garrison state," and agreed with Mills that responsible intellect properly assumed an adversary stance toward the surrounding society. Gillam concluded it was necessary "to rethink the common either-or assessment of two thinkers whose work has had a major influence on our time." It was no longer so easy to distinguish two camps:

In the 1945 to 1950 period, moreover, even their political conflicts remained a bit ambiguous. For in that time of intellectual retrenchment and reorientation—a confusing interregnum between wars—it was often hard to tell just who stood where on the murky battleground of ideology.[25]

of the world with a reaffirmation of that world. Thus the problem with Bell's perspective of radical alienation was that it steadily reduced radical opposition to a purely moral stance incapable of achieving an adequate political embodiment. Troubled by this disjunction, and driven by a concept of "responsibility" he borrowed directly from Weber, Bell finally accepted the limits of practice imposed by immediate political prospects and made his peace with society, proclaiming all the while his moral autonomy as "critic." Thus Lasch's model of intellectual vocation—Benda's "clerk," the marginal and estranged intellectual who keeps "criticism" alive in a sphere apart from politics—appears not as the antipode to intellectual deradicalization but as an essential element of the process of deradicalization.

Although this book repudiates the New Left depiction of deradicalization as the "treason of the intellectuals," it rejects no less decisively the liberal triumphalism of deradicalization, the view that portrays deradicalization as a story of progress, the end of illusion, the achievement of realism. It cannot be said, for that matter, that the left-wing intellectuals themselves surrendered radical politics out of a renewed conviction in progress, a discovery of the beneficent potential of ongoing developments in American society; it is just as true to say they surrendered radical politics out of an oppressive sense of how ongoing social development frustrated or blocked their aims. Indeed, Daniel Bell's social theory, in particular, draws its distinctive form and special interest from an odd blend of progressive confidence and postprogressive critique.

On the other hand, my critique of "the treason of the intellectuals" is not intended to exculpate the deradicalized intellectuals, to deny that this period witnessed their conversion from oppositionists to defenders of the status quo. Nor will it suggest, as Richard Pells does in his sequel to *Radical Visions*, that the writers of the 1940s and 1950s fulfilled after all the authentic critical "function" of the "free-floating" intellectual. Nor do I wish to point blandly, as Pells does in *The Liberal Mind in a Conservative Age*, to the "paradox" of postwar intellectual life where elements of criticism survived alongside apologia.[26] The New Left version of the "treason of the intellectuals" is not incorrect in assessing, ultimately, the role of the deradicalized intellectuals. The doctrine of "the treason of the intellectuals," however, is a markedly moralistic and ahistorical one, a common jeremiad mounted almost indiscriminately against various groups of intellectuals in diverse times and circumstances, focusing largely on the personal weaknesses, the corruptibility, of individuals. I seek a historical explanation of deradicalization that can surmount the contradictions and paradoxes of intellectual discourse in a synthetic understanding of a historically specific process of political reorientation—an explanation which can recognize how certain kinds of criticism, as well as the sincere pursuit of the intellectual vocation, can contribute to the absorption of intellectuals into the fold and the reconstruction of ideas that legitimize prevailing social relations.[27]

A word on method will help clarify the aims of the present inquiry. Unlike the "new intellectual history" of the 1970s—which was preoccupied with the institutional settings of intellectual life and the process of academic professionalization—I return in some respects to a more traditional history of ideas, while hoping to avoid an internalist preoccupation with the development of ideas solely in their own terms.[28] This study regards its principal subject, Daniel Bell, and his collaborators as intellectuals first rather than academics. Their ideas are seen not as the products of technically circumscribed (disciplinary) inquiries but as venturesome attempts to grasp the meaning of their times. I presume that focal questions or problems that motivate intellectual work are given first by history (and society as a whole) rather than by the bounded discourse of intellectuals themselves (a particular section of society). These questions or problems, however, never appear to the thinker directly or immediately; they are always appropriated in a form already conceptually shaped. Understanding how problems are constituted historically, and understanding the answers intellectuals propose, require locating the inquiry at the point of intersection between historical events and the intellectual apparatus contemporaries inherit and construct anew under the given conditions of their experience as they approach the task of rational reflection. This dialectical approach to the history of ideas strives to grasp "theory as the self-knowledge of reality," that is, to penetrate the point of articulation between subject and object and thus to find in the historical constitution of knowledge the real tensions and limitations of the historical reality.[29] In this sense, the enterprise of intellectual history, as I understand it, should attempt not to reveal the falsity of ideas but to understand their historical reality, that is, the way history determines how it will be seen and the way thought expresses the real aspirations and disabilities of the historical action it conceives.

Obviously, such a project of grasping the historical reality of ideas must move "beyond the author" in some sense (particularly in the "literary" presumption that texts in themselves have a reality apart from the overt consciousness and intentions of their individual authors). Still it does not dismiss the authorial subject entirely or deny the possibility of "interpretation," the location of "meaning." Contemporary literary theory, guided by poststructuralism, insists on breaking up the apparent unity of a work; my method, on the other hand, presumes that inquiry should at least culminate in a synthetic view of that which analysis finds to be distinct, disparate, inconsistent, and contradictory parts, discovering meaning, in fact, in those forces or devices that manage to hold the parts together, despite their differences.[30]

Locating contradictions (as in *The End of Ideology*), then, is not the goal of inquiry, but only its starting point. I accept Pascal's dictum which Lucien Goldmann cited as the basis of a dialectical method that ultimately grasps a totality:

> In order to understand an author's meaning, we must resolve all the contradictions in his work. Thus, if we are to understand the Scriptures, we must find a meaning which reconciles all the contradictory passages. It is not enough to have one meaning which fits a number of passages that already agree with one another; we must have one which reconciles even those that are contradictory. Every author either has a meaning which fits all the contradictory passages in his work, or he has no real meaning at all.[31]

The culminating meaning, however, cannot be discovered in a work, an *oeuvre*, or an authorial personality alone, but in a historical synthesis, in that historical conjuncture so formed that intellectual contradictions appear as real historical conditions that cannot, from the standpoint of the subject under study, be overcome. In such a study as this, historical inquiry aims at a conclusion, as Fredric Jameson puts it, that "maps the limits of a specific ideological consciousness and marks the conceptual points beyond which that consciousness cannot go, and between which it is condemned to oscillate."[32] The point is not, for instance, to debunk the end-of-ideology doctrine as but another "ideology," a distorted, interest-bound vision of reality, or a mask of hidden purpose, as many of its critics have done. The point is not to ascertain the falsity and fraud but the "truth" or authenticity of the end-of-ideology, the extent to which it knows itself and its situation.

How then can we define the historical conjuncture underlying the experience of deradicalization that formed Daniel Bell's thought? The question is made difficult by the need to take account of the diverse rhythms of social, ideological, and biographical elements and their complex combination. Essentially, that conjuncture must be defined in terms of the resolution of the crisis of world capitalism which opened in the 1930s. It is useful to examine the crisis and its resolution in both material and ideological terms.

During the Second World War and its aftermath, the crisis was resolved, for the most part, along two axes. First, the United States established worldwide hegemony, filling the vacuum left by the decline of British imperial power. The United States became the single force strong enough to manipulate the conditions of trade and finance and to serve as a balance wheel for worldwide accumulation.[33] Second, labor was incorporated into society en masse, as a result of wartime national unity and the official government recognition of and collaboration with the unions. The ensuing long wave of economic growth was sustained not only by the investment markets in war-devastated and underdeveloped regions open to American capital under the umbrella of U.S. military and political influence but also by the "intensive regime of accumulation" (as Michel Aglietta calls it) that unified for the first time high industrial output with mass proletarian consumption.[34] The two socioeconomic axes of crisis resolution found immediate ideological reflections in the dual images of the Cold War and the Welfare State, gradually knit together in the late 1940s: the justification of U.S. power mobilized against an external, aggressive totalitarian threat and of public economic management to control market instability and offer material security to all segments of society.[35]

A crucial political element in the resolution of crisis was the collaboration of social democracy in the West. In Europe, the collapse of tripartite government coalitions between Communists, Social Democrats, and Catholic liberals in 1947 coincided with a concerted effort by the United States to approach trade unionists and moderate socialists as guardians of stability in a left-leaning political environment.[36] As Christian Democrats sought popular support by promoting a strong "social policy," they forged an anti-Communist alliance with the Social Democrats in favor of welfare reforms under the auspices of U.S. reconstruction aid. In the United States where there never was an influential social-democratic force per se, a similar maneuver inhered in the majority labor endorsement of the Marshall Plan (and labor's civil war against Communist-led unions) and the application of labor's political muscle to reelecting Truman on a welfare platform in 1948. The Cold War and the Welfare State worked together to push and pull labor and social-democratic movements into involvement with the reconstruction of capitalism.

Alongside these economic and political developments ran a deep ideological crisis with its own process of resolution in the aftermath of the war. While the material rupture of capitalism in the 1930s cast doubt on traditional precepts of liberal individualism, economic growth, and progress, successive defeats of socialist attempts to plot a way out of the crisis drained confidence in a potential alternative. The late 1930s was marked dramatically by dual crises of bourgeois ideology and socialist theory. These dual crises were later resolved by an ideological convergence of the two poles. The disrepute of capitalism and the impasse of socialism were both accommodated in the image of the Welfare State: Western social democrats dismissed revolution and relinquished visions of wholesale socialist reconstruction while the defense of prevailing social relations shifted away from the beneficence of market competition and the inherent rights of property owners. Rather than profit, the rationale of the new capitalism was productivity and service. In the "politics of productivity," as Charles Maier puts it, labor surrendered its challenge of managerial authority in return for union recognition and a share of rising output.[37]

In this reconsolidation of capitalism, and the official concordat between labor and capital that ratified it, there was a diminishing social basis for intellectual radicalism. Still, there is no simple or automatic relation between this material basis and intellectual phenomena. Obviously, intellectual life is not immune to social and political developments at large, but its connection to them is mediated by terms of its own. Crucial to the course of intellectual radicalism in the 1940s, I propose, was the transformation of the content of modernism in the period bounded by the high pitch of social and ideological crisis in the late 1930s and the confirmation of welfare state capitalism in the late 1940s.

The cultural movements grouped under the rubric of "modernism" arose in the period 1890 to 1930 as an expression of multiple strains in social order. Perry Anderson has located the characteristic ambivalence of modernism—fascination with and fear of the new—in the uncertainty of a social impasse, marked according to Anderson by the tension between the residual power of precapitalist traditionalism and the hint of proletarian revolution on the horizon.[38] Certainly, modernism marked the disorientation of classic liberalism, namely the conviction that society manifested a natural tendency toward pacification following from undisturbed economic growth. If, as Paul Fussell suggests, the modernist sensibility, and particularly its irony, was reinforced by the experience of the First World War (the confrontation of civilized pretensions with barbaric destruction), it thrived in the 1920s and survived even through the 1930s (despite the movement at that time for political realism in the arts).[39] By the late 1930s, the impasse reached by capitalist crisis and socialist impotence drew taut the characteristic ironies of the modernist mentality, and the increasing salience of a theory of totalitarianism—an absurdist dead end where every meaning doubled for its opposite—led a young intellectual like Daniel Bell to write in *Partisan Review* that contemporary political rhetoric was a kind of "word surrealism."[40] The modernist mentality arose as a manifestation of ideological disruption, and it provided the intellectuals with a means of interpreting social developments in the wake of the crisis. Chapter 1 will examine the modernist mentality in this light, focusing particularly on the sociology of Max Weber as a species of modernism in social theory.

The modernist mentality proved not only a means of interpreting social developments but also a means of adapting to them. Oddly enough, historian Richard Pells, in *Radical Visions and American Dreams*, upheld modernist precepts as the antipode of intellectual collaboration. "At precisely the moment when the tension and turmoil of the depression years had grown intolerable," Pells wrote, radical intellectuals "could not live with ambiguity, paradox, and contradictions" and surrendered to the organicist appeal of the Popular Front.[41] Nonetheless, we know that the *Partisan Review* circle distinguished itself in its early days by vigorous attacks on Popular Front advocates of coercive solidarity, yet also played a leading role in intellectual deradicalization, becoming finally a center of orthodox liberal anticommunism in the 1950s. Even then it did not seek to burrow into the warmth of the social organism but maintained an arch modernist criticism of the insensibilities of mass culture.[42] The coincidence of political accommodation and cultural criticism should not be considered merely a perplexing contradiction but rather a complex unity manifesting its own cunning rationality. That peculiar unity may be sighted in the new radicalism that emerged at the end of the Second World War, a radicalism which bore the characteristic marks of modernism in its counterposition of the self and society, the individual and the organicist whole, the "critic" and "mass society." These marks of estrangement were intimately bound to the surrender of political visions of change at midcentury, as part of a tragic gesture of renunciation, in the Weberian mode. Thus modernism was transmuted from a posture of opposition at least potentially allied with political radicalism to a celebration, as literary critic Gerald Graff says, of "prevailing styles of powerlessness."[43] The decline of radicalism and the adoption of modernist arts as the society's sanctioned high culture were coincident phenomena.[44] Having helped to draw politically disabled intellectuals away from political radicalism, modernism lost the vitality it drew from the tensions of social crisis.[45]

The question remaining is how the thought of Daniel Bell in his formative years is articulated in this conjuncture. The question is, in the terms of this study, not really one of intellectual biography.[46] I do not seek individualistic explanations for the changes in Daniel Bell's thought but rather an explanation that properly situates his work in a broader force field of social change and ideological trends. The study will focus primarily on Bell's development as a social theorist during the 1940s—his recognition of the frustration of evolutionary progress during the course of the Second World War, his flirtation with the left-ism of Dwight Macdonald's *Politics* magazine and his work in the movement to build a new social-democratic party in the United States, his early encounter with the work of Max Weber and his attempt to fashion a critical sociology, his existential "choice" of the West and its welfare reforms at the high pitch of the Cold War. Finally, he is situated in that crucial concession of social democracy to the rehabilitation of Western capitalism.

The intellectual passage Bell took to reach this point is essential to understanding the full implications of his thought, both at the moment of his reconciliation and in his later work. As we have seen, the modernist sensibility—a feel for the fragmentation of the self in public life and an ambiguous assessment of technological rationality—contributed both to political reconciliation and to cultural alienation. That sensibility infused Bell's early formation. By the end of the 1940s, Daniel Bell wrote in a Weberian vein of the tragic demise of the socialist project in a bureaucratized order that seemed simultaneously to promise and prevent the realization of a rational society. The growing intervention of state control in the economy, it seemed to him, extended the sway of rational planning, while the common values needed to direct planning disintegrated. Thus Bell's social theory both spoke for the legitimacy of the Welfare State and revealed its internal contradictions—its structural inability to fulfill the promise that won it support in the first place. Such was the unhappy consciousness of social democracy at an impasse, trapped by its commitment to pursue socialist ends through the instrumentalities of the capitalist state: a static paradox of potential and frustration, a double bind of hope and hopelessness. The apparent contradictions of Daniel Bell's social theory—its oscillation between legitimation and critique, progressive rationalism and cultural despair—arose understandably from the limits of this situation. The fact that his theory "knew" these limits, that at some unconscious level it understood its own disabilities, kept a critical edge on thought otherwise bound to society just as it is.

1
The Stalemate of Politics
in the Late 1930s
Modernism as a Response to the Crisis of Ideology

The objective conditions for the overthrow of capitalism were ripe, Leon Trotsky wrote in 1937, though the subjective conditions remained immature.[1] In this formula the exiled revolutionist captured the definitive contradiction of the late 1930s, for despite the economic crisis of world capitalism and the political turmoil that followed it, no revolutionary socialist movement capable of wielding power achieved ascendancy among the working classes of industrially advanced states. On the ideological plane, the quandary Trotsky described might be reformulated in this fashion: given the abrogation of bourgeois progress on the one hand and the blockage of any escape from capitalist decline on the other, both liberal and socialist theory simultaneously entered a deep crisis. The doctrine that society naturally tended toward a pacified order with continued economic growth had little relevance to such a period of disruption, conflict, and political reaction; social-democratic theories of the gradual approach of collectivism suffered as much an eclipse as classic bourgeois theories of the market. On the other hand, revolutionary Marxism, which had reemerged after the First World War as a theory capable of understanding the dislocations of social order and responding to them in practice, was disgraced by the degeneration of the Russian revolution and disabled by the defeats suffered by the working classes of Italy, Germany, Austria, and Spain. This chapter will examine this dual ideological crisis and assess the intellectual influence, in this context, of modernist modes of thought. Broadly speaking, modernist modes can be identified by a special acuity for grasping static contradictions or antinomies—unconquerable polar tensions of being—a sensibility, I propose, which appealed to contemporary intellectuals who self-consciously inhabited a moment of historical stalemate. It is this historical context, too, which gives the essential coordinates of Daniel Bell's early intellectual development. It is here that an inquiry into the formation and constitutive structure of his social theory must begin. From the dual ideological crisis of the late 1930s to the watershed of postwar reconstruction in the late 1940s: these frame the historical moment of Daniel Bell's sociology.

Theodor Adorno once wrote that Kakfa's modernism was marked by the "dawning awareness of the approaching paralysis of politics."[2] What Kafka foresaw, the eerie stillness that reigned amid the furious activity of a controlled and terrorized existence, became awful reality in the last third of the 1930s, and the perceived paralysis of politics found expression in a new theory of totalitarianism. First hints of such a theory appeared the year after the Spanish Civil War and the Moscow trials began, and while it identified the poles of the political spectrum it also suggested the abrupt breach, and closure, of history. The image of totalitarianism allowed no room for the liberal theory of evolutionary progress: breaking the bounds of economic order and rational action, totalitarian society appeared immune to change, destined to last a thousand years. The theory represented a dead end of liberalism; it still spoke in the terms of liberalism, while negating them, for the end of steady, automatic progress appeared to it as the cessation of any historical dynamic at all.

Indeed, this was the time, in 1937, that Talcott Parsons was able to announce, "Spencer is dead."[3] The founder of evolutionary sociology had been under attack since the turn of the century, but now the new totalitarian phenomena seemed blatantly to reverse the tendency of development he described, bringing social evolution grinding to a halt in state-regimented "militant" societies that liberalism was supposed to have consigned to an ancient past. Of course, Parsons was not concerned immediately with the frustration of evolutionism, but his treatise introduced modern sociology to an American audience at a time when modern theory's grasp of the illusions of progress, the disharmonies of social organization, the inverse relations between purpose and effect in social action, and the ironies and contrarieties of social order gave it special force. These manifest the modernist mode, which according to writer Milan Kundera throve upon "terminal paradoxes," a play of opposites at the end of things.[4] Parsons' principal subject, Max Weber, provides a model study in social theory which bears the burden of the modernist sensibility. Since it is Weber's work, formed in the age of high modernism, that most influenced American social theory during the 1940s in the wake of the crises in liberalism and socialism, it deserves renewed attention in a study of postwar intellectual life. In the prehistory of Daniel Bell's work there is no more influential body of thought, aside from the evolutionism of traditional social democracy, than Weberian sociology, with its own unique sensitivity to "terminal paradoxes." The stalemate of the late 1930s accustomed Bell to the tension of political aspirations and impediments, depositing in his thought a permanent duality of idealism and skepticism. When he saw the intentions of progressive reform belied by the conservative outcomes of the Second World War, he was already primed to accept a social theory that probed the ambiguous effects of rational order and the discontents of the individual trapped by bureaucratic constraints. It is the task of the present chapter to examine the diverse rhythms of social change, ideological development, and intellectual history that established the constitutive conditions of Daniel Bell's thought and heightened the appeal at that moment of a social theory sharing the ironic sensibility of modernism.

The Dual Crisis of Liberalism and Socialism

The onset of coincident crises of liberalism and socialism in the late 1930s was evident to some of the leading left-wing intellectuals of the time. Three books of the early 1940s, well known for their reconsideration and repudiation of Marxian socialism, *presumed* the obsolescence of bourgeois society and bourgeois thought. In *To the Finland Station* (1940), Edmund Wilson marked the moment as "a time when the systems of thought of the West were already in an advanced state of decadence." At the beginning of *The Managerial Revolution* (1941), James Burnham asserted that "the bourgeoisie itself has in large measure lost confidence in its own ideologies"—which Burnham summed up in the essential elements of individualism, private initiative, natural rights, and progress. And in *The Children of Light and the Children of Darkness* (1944), Reinhold Niebuhr asserted that "bourgeois civilization is in process [*sic*] of disintegration."[5]

There may be no handier illustration of classic liberal social theory than the work of Herbert Spencer, which Talcott Parsons considered so lifeless in the late 1930s. Spencer's sociology is one of the classic formulations of bourgeois ideology, properly speaking. Indeed, sociology is congenitally a creature of bourgeois society. According to Göran Therborn, a "proto-sociology," focusing on property, labor, and social relations outside the bounds of governmental authority, emerged in the work of Adam Ferguson, a colleague of Adam Smith in bourgeois Edinburgh.[6] The very concept of "society," it seems, followed the discovery of the market as an object of inquiry. Hegel's image of "civil society," as Marx pointed out, was that sphere of private action apart from the state, the contractual relations among otherwise "isolated monads," or the sphere of market exchange.[7] For the German sociologist Ferdinand Tönnies, "society" or *Gesellschaft* also rested essentially on the cornerstone of the market, for its characteristic relation was that of the contract, the "resultant of two divergent individual wills, intersecting at one point."[8] Here, at its root, was the key problem the theory of sociology tried to address, the problem summed up in the title of Georg Simmel's seminal essay, "How is Society Possible?" That is, how does a whole cohere from a multitude of "divergent wills"?[9] It is essentially the same question that preoccupied classical and neoclassical economics—how an equilibrium is possible in an unguided market—and sociology's search for the central principle of social cohesion has been an attempt to define that mysterious principle that Smith called "the invisible hand." Sociology, it appears, is economistic at heart, insofar as its model of society is the market, an automatic system of order apart from voluntary, particularly political, means of action.

Thus it is mistaken to consider Spencer's theory a "biologistic" one. Although his depiction of differentiated partial structures knit together by interdependent functions in a coherent whole approximated models of organismic development, Spencer actually found his societal model in economics. He repeatedly cited the division of labor, a key discovery of Adam Smith's political economy, as the clearest instance of progressive differentiation-integration in society, an illustration of an evolutionary process yielding results that were distinctly *social* (hence the objects of sociology) insofar as they manifested yet transcended individual action. Fundamentally, the market—defined in pure terms by classical economic theory as an anonymous and autonomous mechanism, comprising multiple, interactive wills but issuing in results *no one willed*—provided a model for Spencer's portrait of social process. It is in this sense that Spencer insisted that "society is a growth and not a manufacture": the modern "social arrangement had neither been specially created, nor enacted by a king, but had grown up without forethought of anyone"—though it nonetheless issued from "the individual efforts of citizens to satisfy their own wants."[10]

The perfect market provided Spencer not only with a paradigm of analysis—structural determination, where events follow from an absent cause, or the combined self-action of the whole system of dispersed and unfocused interrelations—but with a model of the ultimate end of social evolution, the pure "industrial society." In Spencer's scheme this goal presumed the final liberation of economic organization from its domination by the state in "militant societies," where the prevalence and persistence of strife among peoples and nations made industry but a "permanent commissariat" to military forces, generalizing hierarchical domination and command throughout the order. Developing freely once loosed from political control, industrial organization itself generalized relations of exchange—voluntary, cooperative, and equal relations "in which the mutual rendering of services is unforced and neither individual subordinated."[11] To Spencer's mind a reversal in the relative predominance of public and private ends accompanied this development: in early forms of society, political institutions compelled individuals to make themselves agents of public ends; in highly evolved forms of society, public controls lapsed in favor of individual action according to private purpose. Spencer's ideal evolutionary end, the point at which human morality is wholly adapted to the social state, is that society wherein the private ends of individuals "naturally" imply unstated public order—as in the ideal market, where the pursuit of self-interest on all sides produces (objectively, for no one wills it) public welfare:

> The ultimate man will be one whose private requirements coincide with public ones. He will be that manner of man, who, in spontaneously fulfilling his own nature, incidentally performs the functions of a social unit; and yet is only enabled so to fulfill his own nature, by all others doing the like.[12]

The coherence of the coming order, however, already seemed elusive by the turn of the twentieth century. Spencer himself was forced to recognize "terminal paradoxes" in the age of modernism, for with the reemergence of the "strong state" and the apparent reversal of the progressive trend he had predicted, he wrote in 1902 of an emergent "process of re-barbarization." He disparaged the rise of imperialism as an approaching "era of social cannibalism." The "diffusion of military ideas" throughout the society resurrected the premodern principle of social order, "graduated subordination" or "status," and shattered the ideal of voluntary, cooperative equality sustained by the social bond of "contract." With the "recrudescence of barbaric ambitions, ideas and sentiments and an unceasing culture of bloodthirst," he wrote, resurgent militancy threatened "a bad time coming, and civilized mankind will be uncivilized before civilization can again advance."[13]

If Spencer's theory suffered a strong blow at this time, he was far from dead, in Parsons' sense. One of his sharpest critics—Emile Durkheim—was still deeply imbued with Spencerian premises. In Spencerian terms, Durkheim argued that the division of labor followed naturally from social evolution, particularly the increasing density of population, and that it held at least the potential of social order—the "organic solidarity" arising from the integral combination of specialized functions.[14] In his concept of an "abnormal" division of labor, whereby ethical standards were yet to be formed for the new regime of specialization, Durkheim recognized the deferral of the Spencerian promise of social pacification, but in effect only inserted in the evolutionary scheme the category of *lag*.[15] Thus, after Spencer, the new sociology stressed the need of mind to smooth the path of social evolution. Still, the naturalistic foundation of social evolution was evident. While British sociologist L. T. Hobhouse argued that social evolution itself had yielded the capacity to guide further development according to organized purpose, the Fabians argued along functionalist lines that the continuing process of differentiation-integration in society tended inevitably toward centralization and political hegemony.[16]

Essentially, social-democratic thought, gaining momentum in Europe at the end of the nineteenth century, remained within the confines of Spencerian thought—or liberal evolutionism—even though it reversed the valuation of Spencer's poles of analysis, declaring that the continued progress of civilization relied on the imposition of political controls over economics and the elevation of public purposes over private ones. Ostensibly, Eduard Bernstein's attempt to reformulate and modernize Marxist theory in his book *Evolutionary Socialism* (1899) came closest to the Spencerian paradigm. Bernstein replaced what he called Marx's "unorganic evolutionism" (the dialectic of movement spawned by the clash of opposites) with a concept of "organic evolutionism," claiming that disturbances and crises naturally abated as the social character of capitalist production emerged and "grew over" into socialism.[17] Still, the orthodoxy of Karl Kautsky, despite the ferocity of Kautsky's polemic against Bernstein, was no less evolutionist. Kautsky denied Bernstein's contention that socialism emerged gradually in the accumulation of partial reforms (asserting instead that socialism commenced with a distinct and decisive event, the proletariat's accession to political power) but his vision of the proletariat's progress was, like Bernstein's, a uniformitarian rather than catastrophic one. He assumed a steady maturation of social conditions and the corresponding instruments needed to realize their socialist potential, for these, he assumed, were functionally bound together. For Kautsky, the proletariat was the natural carrier of moral refinement in industrial society. By nature the proletariat was a collectivity, accustomed to disciplined, civil action and to the altruistic and rational understanding of society's general interests, he said. Its multifold organizational life cultivated all the technical and administrative skills it needed to assume leadership when the growth of its numbers, spurred by capitalist economic development itself, bequeathed the democratic state to its control.[18]

This path, Kautsky argued, was destined to be a smooth one, for he assumed, with Spencer, a tendency toward pacification immanent in industrial development. The establishment of democratic order in the nineteenth century, Kautsky said, effected the "humanizing of conduct"—the peaceable management of conflicting interests and the mutual respect of the rights of temporary majorities and minorities— and permitted elective, representative institutions to reflect clearly the "balance of forces" at work in a society, thus overcoming the key cause of the convulsive character of the bourgeois revolution—the fact that the absolutist state kept opposing classes "fighting in the dark." The socialist movement now could gauge its progress by objective measures, for the ascent to an electoral majority manifested the proletariat's social power and political maturity. Therefore the socialist revolution, Kautsky argued, was far more a rational and manageable affair than the bourgeois revolution had been: society's readiness for transformation spoke for itself.[19] If Kautsky denied Bernstein's claim that socialism emerged naturally within and beyond capitalism, he nonetheless envisioned a linear ascent implicit in capitalist development toward the threshold of socialism and its achievement. The proletariat grew as the child of capitalism into an adult prepared to assume its inheritance.

Thus social democracy shared with liberal theory its confidence in the evolutionary tendency of industrialism toward the pacification and moralization of social life, a tendency immanent in undisturbed economic growth and the emergent democratic state. As Cynthia Russett said of Spencer's model of social change, this depiction of development "has all the sedate and ordered pattern of the minuet."[20] Along with this temporal sense, social democracy borrowed the Olympian determinism implicit in liberal sociology, for just as Spencer believed that historical contingencies and willful action at most "precipitate [or] retard" the overpowering evolutionary drift that makes humans "merely the tools with which it works," so Kautsky believed "that natural phases of development cannot be precipitated" and would overrule the capricious will. This was the verdict Kautsky passed on the Bolsheviks, whose transgression of objective limits, he said, not only

wrought havoc but finally surrendered to necessity, as the real bourgeois content of their revolution forced them to "nullify" their rash
socialist measures.[21]

Furthermore, social democracy adopted the dissociation of politics and economics which lay at the foundation of liberal social theory,
even as it claimed to unite them. "We are Social-Democrats," some of
the Russian Mensheviks declared in 1921. "This means that socialism
as the economic order and democracy as the political order are our
double goal, the two parts of which are organically merged."[22] Despite
the supposed "organic" connection between them, economics and
politics appeared in this formulation to be analytically separable.[23] Social democrats in fact typically spoke of their project as the completion
of an evolutionary equilibrium, the mutually adaptive adjustment of
politics and economics: they aimed "to transfer democracy from politics to economics" or to "fill" political democracy "with social content"
in accordance with the social character of modern production.[24] The
notion of "extending" democracy from the political sphere, where presumably it was already established, to the economic sphere, where as
yet it was not, suggested that half the battle was already won. Thus
attempting to overcome evolutionary lag, social democracy took its
task to be that of furthering and fulfilling liberalism. Nowhere is this
clearer than in Bernstein, who defined socialism merely as the gener-
alization of democratic citizenship:

> Nobody has any idea of destroying bourgeois society as a civi-
> lized, orderly social system. On the contrary, Social Democracy
> does not wish to dissolve this society and to make proletarians of
> all its members. Rather, it labors incessantly at lifting the worker
> from the social position of a proletarian to that of a "bourgeois"
> and thus make "bourgeoisie"—or citizenship—univeral.[25]

Thus it appears that in theory social democracy was thoroughly
imbued with evolutionist premises shared with liberal sociology. Therefore, the obstacles and reversals thrown in the path of evolutionism
during the age of imperialism wounded classic social democracy no
less than it did Spencerian theory. If any event marked the obstruction of that path, it was the First World War, which undermined evolutionary confidence in the moral trajectory of modern society and
induced a profound cultural dismay, typified by the Henry James's remarks the day after Britain entered the war:

> The plunge of civilization into this abyss of blood and darkness
> . . . is a thing that so gives away the whole long age during which

we have supposed the world to be, with whatever abatement, gradually bettering, that to take it all now for what the treacherous years were all the while really making for and *meaning* is too tragic for any words.[26]

Social democracy was as incapacitated theoretically as Spencer was before the harsh contravention of pacific progress, perhaps even more so, since Spencer recognized the countertrend of "re-barbarization," while social democrats steadfastly held to a model of progress despite all. The war, Kautsky asserted limply, "interrupted" the path of progress, and socialists had the task of recreating the status quo ante, the "normal" civil regime under which the proletariat could properly resume its march.

Although at the onset of the war the Socialist International shattered into warring nationalist parties, it regrouped by 1923 as bourgeois society recovered a degree of stability after five years of postwar social strife. The signs of stabilization in the mid 1920s—the rise of worldwide cartels formalizing trade concessions among international business rivals, the vogue of scientific management as a means of bringing rational order to industrial production, and the first steps toward political integration of unions and workers' parties—gave a boost to the revival of evolutionary thought in social democracy and liberal sociology, as if the war had been a temporary disturbance in the way of orderly growth.[27] Writing a year after the German Social Democrats entered their second postwar coalition government, Karl Mannheim foresaw the imminent demise of disruptive messianic politics, the promise of social integration and economic planning, and the coming conquest of disorder in knowledge and action as functionalist analysis revealed the "complementary" roles of diverse standpoints given by the structural differentiation of "cooperative . . . group life."[28] At the same time, the Second International predicted that the new trends toward the cartelization of capital smoothed the way for public control over economic life. In 1927, Rudolf Hilferding, an Austro-Marxist who joined the German Social Democrats after the war, declared that "organized capitalism means replacing free competition by the social principle of planned production." Like Bernstein he believed the crises that followed from unregulated competitive commodity exchange receded as concentration of business tended to create a "single national capital"; like Kautsky he defined the socialist transformation by the proletariat's electoral conquest of the state. "The task of the present Social Democratic generation is to invoke state aid in translating this economy, organized and directed by the capitalists, into an economy directed by the democratic state."[29]

Very shortly, however, in March 1930, the center-left coalition that embodied Mannheim and Hilferding's hopes fell under the stresses of economic decline, giving way first to authoritarian presidential governments and finally to Hitler's ascendancy in January 1933.[30] It was here that the liberal theory of evolutionism met its greatest crisis.

Now, instead of political democracy, which according to the social democrats' economistic vision assured socialist ascendancy concomitant with capitalist growth, Kautsky confronted in the twin tyrants Hitler and Stalin an unheralded "epoch of dictatorships," a reversal of fortune equivalent in his own terms to Spencer's discovery of "rebarbarization." Kautsky's theory, however, was ill-equipped to explain the genesis or longevity of the new regimes, since neither fascism nor Stalinism, breaking the assumed natural, adaptive link between industry and democracy, was a "rational," or functionally stable, system in his scheme.[31] Kautsky shifted abruptly from economic determinism to voluntarism, for as he faced the reversal of all his expectations, his explanation of history relied increasingly on moral factors as the sole missing element in the necessary conditions of socialism. The First World War, he proposed, had unleashed spores of "ethical-political" degeneration that encouraged the Bolshevik revolution and the subsequent wave of fruitless risings—dangerous exercises of the will—by "undisciplined, disorganized elements" of the proletariat throughout Europe. The proletariat thereafter was split into political factions, and it was further demoralized and disintegrated by unrelenting unemployment, while petty bourgeois layers were declassed and disoriented. The fascist movement arose from this decay and met no resistance.[32]

The peculiarity of stalwart determinists leaping to purely subjective explanations of their frustration appeared also in the United States. When James Oneal, an American follower of Kautsky and member of the right-wing "Old Guard" of the Socialist Party, strained to formulate a "law of evolution from democracy to dictatorship," he produced the sheerest tautology:

> Back of it is a decaying economic system which registers in the decay of sober and intelligent thinking and which has provided an opportunity for the totalitarians of all stripes. . . . In normal periods of evolution the normal mind has an opportunity to function. In abnormal periods like the present the abnormal mind is in the ascendant. When the normal mind reacts on our material environment progress is assured; when the abnormal mind reacts on it progress is halted, reaction forges ahead.[33]

As far as Oneal was concerned, the "abnormal mind" was manifest among the young Socialist Party radicals who found the political crisis an occasion to challenge the old progressive party leadership. Here Oneal discovered a "depression psychosis":

> They have a morbid fear of fascism and in general believe that its rise in Europe could have been prevented if youth, with its vigor, enthusiasm and clearer insight into social and economic forces had been vested with leadership.[34]

Defending Second International legalism after the European defeats of 1933 and 1934, Oneal emphasized "the gigantic and complex forces that had overwhelmed" the European proletariat and denounced left-wing radicalism for adopting "the bourgeois philosophy of free will."[35] Seemingly, orthodox social democracy could not resolve its dilemma: defending its record amid unaccountable disasters it emphasized the limits of the will; explaining the disorientation of contemporary history it cited the force of rampant voluntarism. How could Kautsky account for the calamities of his day but as ill effects of voluntarist action, of utopian will, which then became a crucial historical cause despite, or paradoxically due to, its supposed insignificance in historical process? The ascendancy of fascism was to Kautsky an "irrational" and "anti-historical" event, since it controverted the evolutionary trend. What better demonstrated the theoretical crisis of Kautskyism than its designation of historical events as "anti-historical"?

Kautsky's judgment, however, shows how liberal theory was able, yet, to determine the way in which its own negation would be conceived. The late 1930s saw the emergence of a theory of totalitarianism, which marked a break in the chain of progress and gave voice to a profound sense of historical stasis. Indeed, the rise of the terroristic regimes of Stalin and Hitler rested on a political stalemate, the suppression of working class militancy which might have forged a way out of the crisis of world capitalism. Still, the theory of totalitarianism exaggerated the monolithism of the new order and the cessation of historical dynamics. With the overthrow of the old mechanisms of evolutionary change, it appeared that change was halted, *tout court*: thus the theory of totalitarianism was framed in the terms of liberal theory even as it marked the rupture of liberalism.

The hallmark of the theory of totalitarianism was the identification of the Soviet and Nazi regimes as a common political type. This identification was first proposed in two books published in 1937 by two German conservatives, former supporters of Hitler, Hermann Rauschning and Alex Emmerich. Their work appeared in the wake of the purge trials in Moscow, which devastated the original Bolshevik leadership, and the Four Year Plan announced by the Nazis in 1936, which appeared to mimic the statist measures of the Soviets. In fact, the common element of the two regimes, according to Rauschning and Emmerich, was their "planned economies." In large part it was the abrogation of the market that led liberal theory to see totalitarianism as a gross disruption of normal social development, to emphasize "the novelty of totalitarianism." Forming an "anti-Europe," as Rauschning said, totalitarianism inverted the Spencerian poles of analysis, for as politics subdued economics, so the will cut itself free of objective limits. By nature then, according to its observers, the totalitarian state manifested an unlimited expansionist drive.[36]

The social democrats contributed to the theory of totalitarianism along very similar lines, for the apparent primacy of politics turned their economistic theory of change upside down and made totalitarianism, to their minds, both uninterpretable (insofar as social policy did not flow from rational, economic interest) and perdurable. Totalitarianism, unlike classic capitalism, appeared to have no intrinsic contradictions or flaws that would disable or transform it, and instead of arising and passing away, it would, once established, perpetuate itself indefinitely. Hilferding recognized, for instance, that modern militarism overtaxed productive capacities, but he pointed out that the supremacy of politics broke the bonds of economic constraint, and the "idiotic overreaching" of dictatorial regimes tended toward a "vicious circle" of economic deterioration and territorial conquest.[37] Nothing inherent in the system broke the circle.

In his earlier work Hilferding had suggested that capital tended toward consolidation in a "general cartel," restricting the rule of free exchange and mitigating the business cycles that arose on the market. For the "general cartel" to be complete, for exchange to give way to plan, the capitalists would have to adopt the state as their proprietary organ; before that could occur, he believed, democratic representation would allow the organized proletariat to take over the reins of economic planning.[38] In a 1940 essay on "totalitarian state economy," however, Hilferding suggested that the "general cartel" had assumed the seat of power. The new regime leaped beyond capitalism while preempting the prospects of socialism. He wrote:

Once the state becomes the exclusive owner of all means of production, the functioning of a capitalist economy is rendered impossible by the destruction of the mechanism which keeps the life-blood of such a system circulating. A capitalist economy is a market economy. Prices, which result from competition among capitalist owners (it is this competition that "in the last instance" gives rise to the law of value), determine what and how much is produced, what fraction of the profit is accumulated, and in what particular branches of production this accumulation occurs.[39]

The survival in Nazi Germany of the forms of capitalist society—shares of ownership, profits and dividends, prices, and wages—did not prove to Hilferding the existence of capitalism: rather they had been reduced, by overriding political power, to the status of mere *means* for the execution of official policy, administrative implements. When Friedrich Pollock of the Frankfurt Institute of Social Research, writing in 1941, analyzed the political economy of the Nazi order, he echoed Hilferding's analysis almost entirely, though, oddly enough, he retained the term "state capitalism." Here in Pollock's essays were the decisive role of the state plan, the elimination of the market, the reduction of all residual capitalist elements to "tools" of policy which were easily discarded if they resisted political directives—and the conquest of crises:

> We are unable to discover any inherent economic forces, "economic laws" of the old or a new type, which could prevent the functioning of state capitalism. Government control of production and distribution furnishes the means for eliminating the economic causes of depressions, cumulative destructive processes and unemployment of capital and labor. We may even say that under state capitalism economics as a social science has lost its object.[40]

That is, the unique stability of this statist order stemmed from the willful political suppression of "economic laws" that hitherto operated objectively or automatically apart from human will and purpose: thus the immanent forces of change that defined the essence of classic capitalism were overcome, even if the formal appearance of capitalism in some respects survived, and the system overleaped all obstacles to its self-perpetuation. For Pollock and his colleagues at the Frankfurt Institute, the contradictions that motivated change were sealed and the dynamics of history ground to a halt. Here was located the "paralysis of politics" Theodor Adorno found in the modern age.

In this light the Kautskyan judgment of Nazism and Stalinism as "irrational," "abnormal," and "anti-historical" begins to appear not merely the mark of theory's incapacity but also a harbinger of the theory of totalitarianism later expounded by Hannah Arendt—a theory of crisis founded on the broken shards of liberal evolutionism. The theory of totalitarianism assumed the unprecedented character of the modern dictatorships, their radical departure from all hitherto comprehensible historical patterns and the gaping rupture in the course of Western civilization they represented. As Arendt wrote, totalitarianism was "entirely original," and thus in some sense apart from history, emerging from and opening a void, a caesura in the continuity of Western experience.[41] The political conventions of "left" and "right," or capitalism and socialism, of utilitarian class interests, had meaning in what Arendt would call the "normal" world but none in the world Kautsky called "abnormal." From the "normal" world, this cultural discontinuity precluded a fully rational interpretation of events on the other side, and the past in itself provided no understanding that penetrated the essence of the phenomenon.[42] The theory of totalitarianism suggested the breach—and closure—of history.

The theory of totalitarianism, however, not only marked the rupture of liberal theory and the models of evolutionary socialism based upon it but also helped reinforce the ideological crisis by disabling the theory that had provided an alternative to outmoded progressivism: revolutionary Marxism. By the late 1930s, the degeneration of the Russian revolution disgraced Bolshevism, but in the wake of the First World War, Bolshevism had signaled a profound theoretical departure. Resurrecting Marxism as a revolutionary theory of historical action, Bolshevism recognized the era of imperialism as a period of "sharp turns" and dispensed with the view of social development as an ordered and continuous process of growth. The "comparative equilibrium of the preceding epoch," Trotsky wrote in his 1920 polemic against Kautsky, had given way to "an epoch of crises and convulsions." At the same time Trotsky challenged the functionalist theory that society was, by nature, a coherent, integrated order. Of Kautsky's school, he remarked,

> The political worshippers of routine, incapable of surveying the historical process in its complexity, in its internal clashes and contradictions, imagined to themselves that history was preparing the way for the Socialist order simultaneously and systematically on all sides, so that concentration of production and the development of a Communist morality in the producer and the consumer mature simultaneously with the electric plough and a parliamentary majority.[43]

Lenin, too, in his analysis of imperialism, stressed "the uneven and spasmodic character of development" rather than the smooth course of evolution. Rather than developing the technique of produc-

tion generally, Lenin argued, monopoly capital throve upon dispari-
ties of productive efficiency and reinforced the underdevelopment of
backward regions and sectors, tending to dislocate rather than order
the world economy. Rather than conquering crises, monopoly capitalism rendered them more acute; and rather than salving social conflict,
it spurred it on and gave it new forms, particularly the struggle between imperial power and colonial movements of national liberation.[44]

Properly speaking, Marxism stood outside the liberal tradition of
sociological theory. Marx strove to overcome the theoretical distinction between civil society and the state: he proposed that the state was
actually rooted in social interests rather than abstracted from them
and that "political" relations of domination and subordination infiltrated the apparent equality of market exchange. Marx also overthrew the market paradigm of bourgeois theory: the object of theory
that emerged in Marx's critique of political economy was not the *market*, but rather *surplus value*—not a structure but a relation, a dynamic
principle, the practical embodiment of the struggle between capitalists
and workers over the terms of exploitation. And in rejecting the market model of society as an abstract, impersonal system which determined outcomes apart from purposeful action, Marx was able to escape the subject-object dualism that imposed on liberal theory the
antinomies, as Georg Lukács put it, of voluntarism and determinism.[45]
Hence Lenin's polemics against Kautsky characteristically referred not
to obdurate "objective conditions" apart from subjective will but to
"actuality," a changing field of contentious action that revolutionaries
inhabited, the real context of practice, of determined activity striving
to redetermine its reality.[46]

By the late 1930s, however, Bolshevism had lost its intellectual
standing. The Moscow Trials and the treachery of the Communists in
the Spanish Civil War seemed to deny that the Soviets offered any escape from the barbarism of capitalism in decline. At the same time,
the concepts developed in the early 1920s as part of the theoretical
apparatus of Bolshevism—the concepts of history, dialectic, and totality framed by Lukács—all came under attack in the second half of the
Depression decade, especially in the United States. In *Assignment in
Utopia* (1937), Eugene Lyons denounced "history" as a banner of false
messiahs, excusing present political atrocities; Edmund Wilson's *To the
Finland Station* (1940) probed the Faustian confusion of "writing history" and "making history," and Sidney Hook charged that Hegel
made of "history" an all-purpose sanction for existing power and
right.[47] Hook, the leading American Marxist whose early work, *Towards the Understanding of Karl Marx* (1933), acknowledged Lukács's in-

fluence and combined "dialectical materialism" with John Dewey's experimental social epistemology, turned against dialectics after 1935 as
the Soviet regime began to use it as another naturalistic guarantee of
socialist progress.[48] By 1941, Hook considered dialectics nothing but
obscurantism and anticipated Orwell in portraying it as mere double-
think, the equation of opposites that allowed totalitarians to invest
progressive terminology with reactionary meaning.[49] Totality, which
appeared in Lukács's reading of Marx as the unity of subject and object, politics and economics, struck Hook as an invitation to positivism,
eliminating contingency and judging all facets of social reality to be
necessary; likewise, James Burnham, as he bid socialism adieu in
1940, identified the Hegelian "vision of a block universe in which
every part is related to every other part" as "totalitarianism in philosophy." And Lewis Corey, once reportedly dubbed by Lenin "the first
American Bolshevik," "reconsidered" Marxism in 1940, declaring
that the unitary power of the totalitarian state compelled him to recognize the truth of the bourgeois principle that freedom lay in the
sure separation of politics and economics and the competition of multiple enterprises.[50]

The demise of Bolshevism's intellectual repute was demonstrated
dramatically in the movement of the intellectual circle that had grown
up in the United States around the person and political program of
Leon Trotsky. In the mid 1930s, Trotsky had appealed to left-wing intellectuals who were growing disenchanted with official Communism,
including figures like Herbert Solow, James Rorty, Lionel Trilling,
Elliot Cohen, Meyer Schapiro, Edmund Wilson, Burnham, and to
some extent Hook.[51] Not only Trotsky's critical analysis of the degeneration of the Russian revolution but also his image and his sensibility
attracted them. Knowing the defeat that followed victory, conscious of
the frustrating contradictions of historical process, Trotskyism repudiated facile optimistic faith in the course of events themselves,
while it upheld the struggle to bring revolution out of world crisis.
Still, the mounting debacle of the left in the 1930s—in Germany, Austria, Spain, and France—was too heavy a burden for the leftist intellectuals to bear. Viewing Stalin's purge trials as a watershed, Philip
Rahv, founder of the preeminent organ of anti-Stalinist Marxism in
the United States, *Partisan Review*, wrote:

We were not prepared for defeat. The future had our confidence, which we granted freely, sustained by the tradition of
Marxism. In that tradition we saw the marriage of science and
humanism. But now, amidst all these ferocious surprises, who has

the strength to reaffirm his beliefs, to transcend the feeling that he had been duped?[52]

Before long Trotsky's intellectual coterie began to fall away. In January 1939, James Burnham and his coeditor on the Trotskyist magazine *New International*, Max Shachtman, aimed a withering blast against the "Intellectuals in Retreat"—including Max Eastman, Hook, Lyons, Wilson, and John Chamberlain (who seven years before had pronounced the demise of liberalism)—for adopting a "theory of communo-fascism" that would lead them away from Marxism to social democracy and other political locales further to the right.[53] Trotsky's important distinction between the two regimes—considering Nazism a reactionary form of capitalism in decline, and the Soviet order an aborted form of the struggle for socialism—had until the mid-thirties won the assent of most anti-Stalinist leftists in the United States.[54] By 1941, however, even Burnham and Shachtman—in their analyses of "managerial society" and "bureaucratic collectivism"—virtually adopted the formula of "totalitarianism" and thereby lost the historical sense of tension and flux, of the potential for action and change, that remained in Trotsky's view of the contradictory Soviet order.[55]

In fact, the intellectuals' disenchantment with Trotsky had begun almost at the very moment of his seeming triumph. His vindication, by an American "Commission of Inquiry" formed under John Dewey's leadership to investigate Stalin's charges of treason and sabotage, coincided with the opening of a fierce debate over Trotsky's role in the suppression of the Kronstadt mutiny in 1921, the connection between the heroic age of Bolshevism and the Stalinist outcome of the revolution, and the importance of moral boundaries to political behavior.[56] What hung in the balance was the very possibility of a revolutionary Marxism, like that Trotsky and his followers espoused, which remained in principle distinct from repressive Stalinism. In fact, as Trotsky was tarred with proto-Stalinism in the Kronstadt debate, the left intellectuals began to surrender their hope of any radical political alternative to the black hole of totalitarianism. The dual crisis of liberal theory and the socialist alternative was sealed.

The Significance of Modernism in Social Theory: Estrangement and Reconciliation in Max Weber

In lieu of Marxism, what social theory could capture the contradictions within social action and order that disrupted the linear models of classic liberalism? The development of European sociology in the modernist era from 1890 to 1930 provided part of the solution, though the accumulated force of this intellectual trend reached the United States only in the late 1930s and afterward. At this point, in the wake of totalitarianism, modernist modes of thought offered an appealing sensitivity to "terminal paradoxes." The "revolt against positivism" that H. Stuart Hughes has located in the decades after 1890 had prepared the way: not only did it challenge the scientific monism of the Spencerian and Comtean tradition but also it broke the equation linking nature, reason, morality, and progress that characterized the classic liberal view of the market.[57] Nature was more likely to appear wasteful or wanton; reason and morality assumed the office not of discerning order in nature but imposing control on it; "progress," a suspect notion, suggested perhaps only a rush toward chaos. Nietzsche, perhaps the most influential thinker of the modern movement, disclosed a will to power, rather than an inclination to cooperative equality, in human nature. At the dawn of modern imperialism, social theory attended to the primacy of the state and the uses of power, the means of domination. Nietzsche's glorification of "noble" authority notwithstanding, the new emphases were not primarily results of resurgent aristocratic values;[58] as often as not, the new theorists spoke from within the tradition of bourgeois reform, and it was the perceived reversal of progress that gave modern social theory, in disillusionment, its most characteristic trait: the consciousness of paradoxical inversions in social order, captured in a new, mordant irony.

Modern social theory recognized the coexistence and interpenetration of contrary tendencies: instead of evolutionary development beyond relations of hierarchical "status" to those of equalitarian "contract," or from autocracy to democracy, each polar principle lived on within, and helped reproduce, its opposite. In *Political Parties* (1911), Robert Michels demonstrated that the "tendencies which oppose the realization of democracy" were immanent in democracy itself, that the very extension of democracy replicated the forms of its counterprinciple aristocracy, and hence that social evolution was not linear but "parabolic."[59] Max Weber's study of rationalization and the Protestant Ethic demonstrated no less ironically that individualism, carried out to its end, obliterated the individual.

Although some representative works of modern European social theory had reached the United States before the late 1930s, their impact was not great. By and large, indigenous social thought did not move in synchrony with the European trends. Indeed, Henry Adams had captured some of Europe's *fin-de-siècle* despair over the trajectory of scientific reason, but American social thought was dominated by the progressive liberalism of John Dewey. Certainly, in the aftermath of the 1894 depression, when his thought took its mature form, Dewey had recognized a deep crisis of culture, demanding "reconstruction" in philosophy as well as society: but the project relied, in Comtean fashion, on rooting out the stubborn survivals of traditionalism and overcoming evolutionary lag through the exaltation of the scientific temper. All of Dewey's thought assumed the essential unity of nature, reason, morality, and progress, to be realized in enlightened action. In fact, the persistence of liberalism in American social thought was so strong that when Talcott Parsons' translation of *The Protestant Ethic* appeared in 1930, a *New Republic* reviewer read it not as a pained discourse on reification but as testimony to the cultural valence of economics and the possibility of purposeful reform in mind and society.[60]

Only during and after the ideological crisis of the late 1930s did modern social theory emerge in the United States in its true guise. There had been a considerable delay in introducing European works to American audiences: Durkheim's *Division of Labor in Society*, originally published in 1893, was not translated into English until the end of 1933. Certainly the emigration of European intellectuals, in flight from Nazism and war, helped to bridge this gap. Alexander von Schelting, the key informant for Parsons' interpretation of Weber in *The Structure of Social Action*, lectured at Columbia University, and Daniel Bell studied mimeographed translations of Weber's introduction to *Economy and Society* with him in 1939 and 1940.[61] Hans Gerth, an associate of the Frankfurt Institute of Social Research, met C. Wright Mills around the same time, and the two collaborated on a translation that remained for decades the most influential English-language anthology of Weber's writings, *From Max Weber* (1946).[62] Michels' *Political Parties* became a canonic text in the late 1930s for a group of young New York radicals disenchanted by the centralist party norms of Trotskyism, and it inspired a brilliant treatment by the group's leader, Philip Selznick, of the self-defeat of liberal reform, *TVA and the Grass Roots* (1949).[63] The first concerted effort to bring the corpus of modern European social theory to the United States in translation was the founding of The Free Press in 1947.[64]

This growth in the influence of postprogressive European social theory coincided with the deepening of the influence of literary modernism in American intellectual circles. The significance of modernism for literary radicals in this period, from the late 1930s through the 1940s, is already familiar. In the midst of ideological crisis a circle of left-wing American writers destined to achieve prominence in association with their journal *Partisan Review* reasserted their debt to the modernism of the 1920s as a way of repudiating the political misuse of literature by the Communist movement and maintaining their resistance to capitalist society. Starting with the project of marrying Marxism and modernism, their political convictions gradually subsided, or were absorbed in the artistic *stance* of the modernists. Beginning with a critique of propagandistic applications of the arts in the service of wartime national unity—which they opposed initially on political grounds—they drifted toward a critique of the homogenizing tendency of mass culture, which could be resisted not by political action but by the perceptual acuity offered by the modern aesthetic.[65]

The significance of postprogressive social theory, during this same period and in allied intellectual circles, can be illuminated by considering it a species of modernism. The original age of the new social theory coincided with that of the modernist arts. Specifically, the years of Max Weber's greatest productivity, 1903 to 1914, coincided with the rise of the Expressionist groups, *Die Brücke* and *Der Blaue Reiter*, in Germany, the beginning of Cubism with Picasso's *Les Demoiselles d'Avignon* and the height of Futurist activity in Italy, the premiere of Stravinsky's key works and the development of atonal music by Schoenberg and Berg in Vienna, the composition of Proust's *A la recherche du temps perdu*, the publication of *Dubliners* and the commencement of Joyce's work on *Ulysses*, and the publication of Pound's early *Personae* and *Riposte*. By viewing the development of modern social theory as a parallel to the modernist aesthetic, the theory's most salient points come quickly into view and it is easy to understand its special appeal at a time when classic bourgeois ideology lost its legitimacy and no alternative appeared forthcoming. Fracturing the narrative plot line in literature (as the representative image in the visual arts or the centrality of key in music) is not unlike breaking the continuum of social evolution in theory. Estrangement from public life, the fragmentation of self and the dislocation of social existence, the elusiveness and ambiguity of meaning, the juxtaposition of incompatible artifacts to yield a new feel for irony and paradox, may be discovered in social theory as well as in the intentions and techniques of the avant garde arts in this time.

If a common denominator for various avant-garde movements named "modernist" can be found, it is a profound ambivalence towards modernity, its endorsement and repudiation intertwined.[66] Likewise, a paradoxical unity of estrangement and reconciliation is a key feature of Max Weber's social theory. A careful examination of the antinomies of Weber's sociology will illuminate the structure of modernist thought and help explain its renewed appeal in the wake of the ideological crisis of the late 1930s.

Clearly, Weber had as little use for the notion of "progress" as his younger associate Robert Michels. An image of linear progress explained little of the uneven development of the German social formation, where a prodigious engine of capitalist production developed under the tutelage of an authoritarian state bureaucracy and amid remnants of aristocratic elites. In intellectual terms, moreover, the German neo-Kantian movement of the late nineteenth century had spawned pervasive doubt about the significance of progress. The rapid centrifugal development of specialized sciences impressed upon German intellectuals a deep skepticism of the ability of reason to discern a comprehensive, coherent, and morally satisfying meaning in reality—and of the ability of morality to give an ethical sanction to the findings of intelligent inquiry.[67] As Nietzsche had written that "historical knowledge streams in on him [modern man] from sources that are inexhaustible," so for the neo-Kantians, the infinite multiplicity and diversity of event and experience in history overwhelmed the attempt to find a direction in it.[68]

Furthermore, the neo-Kantian separation of fact and value encouraged doubt of the meaning of progress. Kant's critical philosophy, concerned with the possibility and limits of objective knowledge, promised to preserve the valid achievements of modern science without threatening moral and esthetic judgments, which had a significance in themselves apart from scientific proof. Thus Weber wrote, "We cannot learn the *meaning* of the world from the results of its analysis."[69] Given the distinction of fact and value, Weber considered "progress" too "entangled" in value judgments to have any scientific validity. He agreed with the neo-Kantian philosopher Wilhelm Windelband, who judged, "Change is not progress."[70] Again, as Kant had suggested that objective knowledge was too limited for humans to ground their values in it, so the neo-Kantians emphasized the purely subjective source of moral motivations and denied that knowledge of what is could ever determine, by itself, what ought to be. For Weber, moral seriousness precluded opportunist "adaptation" to given "trends," which were ontologically uncertain in any case.[71]

Weber, however, had to face the difficult problem of demonstrating the interrelation of fact and value, since he defined sociology as a scientific inquiry into the realm of values.[72] The German idealist tradition had long opposed the use of scientific method in the study of society and history: the phenomena of this realm, the idealists asserted, were distinguished from the objects of the natural sciences by the active presence of human consciousness and will; consequently, these phenomena were irreducibly "individual" or unique, rather than regular and recurrent (conceivable in terms of general, covering laws). Weber found these arguments valid in themselves, but did not accept the conclusion the idealists drew from them, the denial of the scientificity of social studies. Indeed Weber's sociology was a *verstehende Soziologie*, founded on "interpretative understanding," the analysis of human action in terms of the subjective meanings attached to it by actors whose subjectivity was situated in a social complex of meanings.[73] In his renowned methodological essays, however, Weber sought to adjudicate the particularity of meaningful social action and the generalizing office of conceptual reason and thus overcome the gap between natural sciences and "cultural sciences" (*Geisteswissenschaften*) that German idealism supposed to be unbridgeable. He also had to adjudicate the combination of historical "relativism" (for the historian or cultural scientist was also a social actor, motivated subjectively by socially and historically unique values) and scientific "objectivity" (experimentally verified knowledge).

The basic terms of Weber's solution are familiar. "Historical individuals," the practices, situations, or events that comprised the objects of the cultural sciences, were artificial constructs drawn out of the illimitable diversity of human affairs through history and informed by the investigative interests rooted in the scientist's own cultural values.

"Ideal types" were likewise artificial—heuristic standards or guides, setting in relief anomalous aspects of the historical individual which became matters of significance to be explained. "Explanation" here involved not the subsumption of specific events under covering laws but the imputation of causal efficacy to particular elements of the constructed individual by an "imaginative" operation that hypothetically withdrew various elements from the construct, or altered them, and on the basis of generalizations gathered from historical knowledge, considered whether the actual course of events could have been expected to occur nonetheless. The results of the entire inquiry, subject to the critical observation of "all who seek the truth," would be "objective" insofar as they derived from the rigorous exercise of logic, *given* the particular value-relevant inception of the quest.[74] Thus cultural scientists (or sociologists) could justifiably claim to know a *part* of social reality, according to the experimental canons of their scientific peers, as long as they were conscious that they had no claim to absolute truth—not only because it was likely that their conclusions would be outmoded by further research, but because there was no guarantee that the reality they discovered, highlighted by very partial interests, was the essential or total reality of what existed. What any present culture could know of any past culture was based on the orienting values of the present, since as creatures of their own culture, investigators saw the past through the lenses of their culture's values.[75]

Therefore, for Weber, reason served at the behest of any value-relevant inquiry as a means of abstracting and organizing data and judging inferences from them according to the principles of formal logic. Weber considered reason as *formalizing reason,* in itself indifferent to, though crucially dependent upon and necessarily impelled by, nonrational values. He saw values as given and ultimate, matters of intrinsic meaning, wholly apart from the test of rational efficacy in action, though they crucially underpinned all human orientation, action, and knowledge. He recognized too that values varied widely and indefinitely in history, which could never be grasped as a meaningful whole:

> The belief which we all have in some form or other, in the meta-empirical validity of ultimate and final values, in which the meaning of our existence is rooted, is not incompatible with the incessant changefulness of the concrete viewpoints, from which empirical reality gets its significance. Both these views are, on the contrary, in harmony with each other. Life with its irrational reality and its store of possible meanings is inexhaustible. The *concrete* form in which value-relevance occurs remains perpetually in flux, ever subject to change in the dimly seen future of human culture. The light which emanates from those highest evaluative ideas always falls on an ever changing finite segment of the vast chaotic stream of events, which flows away through time.[76]

Weber had a dual commitment to both value and reason. He rejected the idealistic assumption that human free will made history a matter of chance and irrationality unassimilable by science; for action, he said, was only free when it was rational, when it could reliably predict its effects.[77] Consequently, however, Weber was caught in something of a double bind: reason, critically self-aware, knew its own limited, partial character and its dependence on values that, like the events they motivate, "flow away through time"; at the same time reason alone insured freedom of action. Reason then, too, knew its own fruitlessness, for by its self-criticism it undercut its own grounding values while it scanned history to find glinting reflections of them in the past. Reason offered only a very tremulous self-assurance, steadying contingent action in the chaotic flux of history, upholding and shattering at the same time the dignity humans claimed as free agents.

Weber's discourse on the problems of applying science to history, then, already manifested a peculiar pathos, for it recognized that reason and value combined in a tragic embrace—that reason secured value, or rendered humans free to act on its behalf, and destroyed value at the same time.

This conundrum—reason destroying value while attempting to secure it—informed Weber's analysis of the Protestant Ethic as well. According to Weber, the religious quest ending in Calvinism started with the problem of theodicy. The attempt to reconcile the perfect good of God with the presence of evil in the world, the attempt "to find a common meaning" despite "awareness of existing and un-bridgeable tensions," posed the theological dilemma of surrendering belief in either the omnipotence or benevolence of God. Calvinism chose the former while conceding that no coherent solution of tensions was possible. The doctrine of predestination, which asserted the unlimited power of God's free will over all His creation, a power indifferent to any human striving and inscrutable to human understanding, "renounces in a loveless clarity man's accessibility to any meaning of the world." Here was a theological expression of Weber's own conviction that meaning per se was unassimilable to the understanding. Indeed, the Protestant ascetic's "sharp distinction between things divine and things of the flesh" underlay the neo-Kantian distinction between value and fact, "the complete logical separation of factual and normative propositions," which according to Weber rendered questions of competing values "unresolvable" by human intelligence and ultimately a matter of "warring Gods."[78]

The Calvinist answer to the problem of theodicy, Weber suggested, had the specific effect of wholly devaluing the natural world, the world of the flesh and human relations, by locating value solely in the beyond, in God's will. This suggested on the one hand a radical rejection of the world and yet a reaffirmation of it, for its existence could only testify somehow to God's purpose. The devalued elements of the world, then, were objective and impersonal things serving as means of God's will, and as such were assumed to be organized perfectly to achieve His ends, necessarily obscure as those were. Bowing abjectly to hidden purpose in a solitary relation with God, the individual with a religious interest in salvation waited to be *called*, and one's *calling* indicated only that one was privileged to execute God's will. All earthly activity, then, permitted no satisfaction in the things of the world, but merely put them to use presumably as God intended. In the end, "The Christian proved . . . his state of grace by action in *majorem Dei gloriam*," action testifying to the greater glory of God. "The

active energies of the elect, liberated by the doctrine of predestination, thus flowed into the struggle to rationalize the world." [79] Here
Weber located the distinctive Protestant Ethic, the peculiar imperative
to action he summed up as "worldly asceticism." This ethos lay at the
base of "rational bourgeois capitalism," which elevated money-making
into an end in itself, not for the sake of material pleasures but solely
for the sake of *accumulation*, accomplished by the persistent rational
organization of materials and labor.

> The moral conduct of the average man was thus deprived of its
> planless and unsystematic character and subjected to a consistent
> method for conduct as a whole. It is no accident that the name of
> Methodists stuck to the participants in the last great revival of Pu-
> ritan ideas in the eighteenth century just as the term Precisians,
> which has the same meaning, was applied to their spiritual an-
> cestors in the seventeenth century. [80]

The distinctive feature of the Protestant Ethic, then, was the fact
that *rationalism itself was valued*. "It should be remembered that the belief in the value of scientific truth is the product of certain cultures
and is not a product of man's original nature," Weber wrote. In fact
Weber was "particularly interested in the origin of precisely the irrational element which lies in this"—and by "irrational" (Talcott Parsons
preferred the term "nonrational" instead) Weber meant not the ab-
surd or meaningless character of it but precisely its *meaningful* quality,
its rootedness in value apart from understanding. [81] Weber located the
Protestant Ethic's valuation of rationalism at the heart of modern
Western culture, tied to Descartes's *cogito ergo sum* (for "only a life
guided by constant thought [i.e., rationalized] could achieve conquest
over the state of nature," Weber explained) and to Kant's concept
of duty and categorical imperative (a definition of ethics by logical
consistency). [82]

The valuation of rationalism, however, created an intriguing conundrum. This rationalism was decidedly "formalistic," the work of
the categorizing understanding that strove toward the "most consistent and logical forms." [83] As an element of human action, reason connoted for Weber only instrumental or technical reason. [84] A recent
scholar writes:

> In his theoretical work Weber stresses repeatedly the view that ra-
> tionalization is the dominant experience of the modern West.
> This rationalization does not imply for Weber, however, a dimi-
> nution in the problem of finding meaning in the world. . . . In-

deed, an understanding of what rationality is and can be reveals the extreme importance and necessary existence of non-rational aspects of life in a way in which a less clear definition could never do. Rationalization for Weber does not eliminate the need to search for or to create meaning: it makes this need all the clearer. For rationality is restricted to means and not meaning.[85]

It appears, then, that the valuation of rationalism endlessly reproduced the problem it pretended to resolve, for instrumental reason devalued its objects at the same time that it offered itself as the sole avenue toward value or meaning. That is, reason discovered meaning by transforming it into means, thus dissolving meaning. Rationalism, valued in itself, tended inevitably to destroy value as it strove to realize it. When instrumental reason became itself the primary value, meaning was regularly reduced to means and ultimate ends of action retreated further and further from grasp.

Hence absolute commitment to service of an otherworldly reality tended to collapse into absorption with things as given. Under the reign of instrumental reason, "what is" threatened to conquer "what ought to be." The bureaucratic fate of modern capitalism realized this tendency. Weber knew that established capitalism no longer needed the support of ethical injunctions but operated now as a compulsive system, an "iron cage." "The idea of duty in one's calling prowls about in our lives like the ghost of dead religious beliefs."[86] For Weber, the bureaucracy predominating in the modern West was the *caput mortuum* of the Calvinist *calling*. Indeed, modern bureaucracy derived from this worldly asceticism: "office holding is a 'vocation'," he said.[87] The devotion of the individual to a specialized task, the "objective" orientation that ignored the particular qualities of things and people by grounding judgment and decision in abstract, formalized rules, the undisturbed continuity and regularity of action—all these bureaucracy inherited from the Protestant Ethic. Yet the routine and discipline of bureaucracy—behavioral traits founded subjectively in Protestant asceticism—were now imposed from without as inescapable constraints on the individual trapped within a rigidly integrated whole: they alone "remain after the 'ethical' qualities of duty and conscientiousness have failed."[88] The fierce moral imperative that drove the puritan saint—the conviction that one lived on earth to "do the works of him who sent him"—the sacrificial heroism of the individual bourgeois—all this had lapsed.[89] Weber echoed John Wesley: "So, although the form of religion remains, the spirit is swiftly vanishing away."[90] Now, on whose behalf did one pursue the "errand" first assigned by

God?[91] Bereft of transcendental motivation, the bureaucratic consciousness lost the sense of persistent tension with the world, and social action had no impulse but obedience to given rules and expectations. Therefore, Weber wrote:

> Imagine the consequences of the kind of bureaucratization and general rationalization which we are now approaching. Already today, the principle of rational calculation makes itself felt at every stage, in every enterprise of big private industry as well as in all other economic enterprises run along modern lines. Through such calculation, the output of each individual worker is mathematically measured, and each man becomes a mere cog in the machine . . . it is horrible to think that the world will one day be filled only with these cogs, only with small men clinging to small jobs and seeking to find bigger ones—a state of affairs which . . . plays a more and more important role in the thinking of our present administration system. . . . This passion for bureaucracy . . . is enough to bring us to the point of despair. . . . The key question is not how to further and stimulate this tendency, but how to oppose this machine-mentality and keep a part of humanity free from such fragmentation of the soul, from ultimate domination by the bureaucratic form of life.[92]

Weber's associate, Georg Simmel, likewise described a "tragedy of culture" in modern society, whereby the steady encroachment of relations of quantity on those of quality transformed reality into a realm of objects completely divorced from subjectivity, decimating culture as an expression of *persons* and making it merely an ensemble of things.[93] So it seems that the two sociologists inhabited the antimodern current of German thought which lamented the decline of culture incurred by the advance of industrial society; they nearly echoed the eighteenth century romantic poet Schiller, who wrote:

> Those many-sided natures of the Greek states, where every individual enjoys an independent life and, if necessary, can reproduce the totality, give way to an artificial clockwork, where, out of the piecing together of an unending number of lifeless parts a mechanical life of the whole is formed. . . . Eternally bound to only a single small fraction of the whole, man perfects himself only as a fraction . . . But even the mean, fragmentary participation that still ties the single members to the whole does not depend on forms which they create for themselves (for how could one entrust such an artificial light-shy clockwork to their

freedom?) but is prescribed to them with scrupulous strictness, by a formula through which their free insight is held in bondage. The dead letter replaces living understanding and a practiced memory is a surer guide than Genius and sensitivity.[94]

In fact, however, Weber did not belong to the tradition of conservative romanticism, for he was a member of the modernizing elite in Wilhelmine Germany, a "class-conscious bourgeois," as he put it himself: an advocate of free scientific inquiry, economic growth, and parliamentary constitutionalism, who disdained the self-effacing alliance the German bourgeoisie made with the aristocratic Junkers of the agrarian east for protection under a stolid, bureaucratic-authoritarian state.[95] As a rationalist, he repudiated all forms of vitalism, the apotheosis of the whole "personality," of natural spontaneity and esthetic intuition.[96] He scorned "that romantic-naturalist version of the 'personality-idea' which . . . finds the real sanctuary of the personal in the dark, undifferentiated, vegetative 'underground' of the personal life, i.e., in that . . . irrationality which the 'person' shares completely with the animal."[97] He refused to idealize the organic will of the communal man as Ferdinand Tönnies did, and he applauded industrial discipline, remarking on Germany's defeat in 1918, "One has seen all the weaknesses, but if one wishes, one may also see the fabulous capacity of work, the superbness and matter-of-factness, the capacity— not the attainment—of beautifying everyday life, in contrast to the beauty of ecstasy or of the gestures of other nations."[98]

The paradox of Weber's denigration and embrace of modernity was founded on his own embrace of the ascetic principle and his opposition to the "enthusiasm" manifested by radical romantic members of his prewar Heidelberg circle like Georg Lukács. The relation between the two men illuminates crucial aspects of each one's work. Simmel's tragedy of culture profoundly influenced Lukács and suffused his early work, *Soul and Form* (1910), which portrayed "empirical life," actuality, as "unliving," entirely destructive of the pure urges of the soul and thus of "real" or "authentic" life. Lukács drew a dichotomy between the world of the subject and that of the object so sharply that no exchange between the two was possible except on terms of total moral degradation—thus refusing to acknowledge the intercourse of fact and value that Weber so delicately probed. The "unbridgeable chasm between the reality that is and the ideal that should be" appeared to Lukács not as a methodological presupposition (that fact and value were unassimilable) but as a damning judgment, a repudiation of the valueless world.[99] Lukács's "radical rejection of the world," unlike Weber's Calvinist asceticism, would not accept the "renunciation" of meaning and the "reconciliation" of human being with the forms of a dehumanized society.[100] Instead, Lukács would demand "a total break with every institution and mode of life stemming from the bourgeois world."[101]

For Lukács, the ethical life, the exercise of the soul, was concerned with absolute imperatives, while actual existence was bound in the corrupting compromises of relative judgments, the calculation of effects that hamstrung and denatured pure intention. In his essay "On Poverty of Spirit" Lukács wrote, "Why should Goodness concern itself with the consequences? 'Our duty is to do the Work, not to try to win its fruits,' say the Indians. Goodness is useless, just as it has no foundation. Because consequences lie in the outer-world of mechanical forces—forces that are unconcerned with us." Weber, who had introduced Lukács to the mystic philosophy of India, could not disagree with Lukács's view of morals as wholly subjective, free of any truck with objectivity, and he excitedly championed the essay "as a striking confirmation of his own thesis that moral behavior should be judged not by its results but by its intrinsic value."[102] For Weber, however, this meant that social action could never be wholly moral; social reality—and especially political imperatives—excluded such an absolute principle of behavior.

Weber and Lukács agreed on the *transcendent* character of ethics, but Lukács would *realize* the transcendent. When he first approached revolutionary socialism in 1918, therefore, Lukács construed it in eschatological terms: "Make the kingdom of God come down to earth at once," he demanded.[103] Consequently, Weber identified Lukács's embrace of revolution with "enthusiasm," the theological *bête noire* of Calvinism which imagined it possible to manifest in life the actual presence of indwelling Spirit.[104] The messianic sects of radical Protestantism shared with Calvinism the repudiation of the world of the flesh, Weber had pointed out, but not its rationalism; in hoping to realize the biblical way of life in a special community of the saved, trusting solely in the inner testimony of the soul, this wing of Protestantism drifted away from asceticism, which insisted on man's role as "tool" of God's will, toward mysticism, which portrayed man as "vessel" of God's spirit.[105]

Mysticism, according to Gershom Scholem, arises as an attempt to bridge the abyss between humanity and God, to unify the finite and the infinite with a common symbolic meaning; but Weber braced himself for the impossibility of overcoming the transcendental disjunction of the two realms. In fact, with his focus on the peculiar anxieties summed

up in the Protestant Ethic, Weber approached the existentialist definition of modern life, the individual's solitary contention with meaning-
lessness. As William Barrett writes, "The more severely he [Protestant
man] struggles to hold on to the primal face-to-face relation to God, the
more tenuous this becomes, until in the end the relation to God Himself threatens to become a relation to Nothingness." In the early existentialist theology of Kierkegaard, faith appears as the "uncompromis-
ing and desperate wager it is," Barrett continues.[106] Weber too reflected
this existentialist emphasis on free self-constituting choice, ungrounded
in any certain knowledge; considering himself religiously "unmusical,"
he opted for the scientific vocation as his own wager on meaning,
though the urge toward pure value continued to contend with his rationalism. Hence the existentialist philosopher Karl Jaspers found in
Weber "a new type of man who had the poise to hold together in synthesis the tremendous tensions of his own self as well as the contradictions of external public life without resorting to illusions."[107]

Weber could not avoid embracing the Protestant Ethic as his own.
He wrote:

> The idea that modern labour has an ascetic character is of course
> not new. Limitation to specialized work, with a renunciation of
> the Faustian universality of man which it involves, is a condition
> of any valuable work in the modern world; hence deeds and re-
> nunciation inevitably condition each other today.[108]

Weber viewed "science as a *vocation*", and as a self-conscious scientist
he personally assumed the burden of that complex of problems bound
up with the Calvinist's calling.[109] Scientific investigation in itself remained incapable of creating values or resolving value conflicts; and it
manifested the same endless regress of meaning that the ascetic Protestant suffered and sustained. As scientists, Weber wrote,

> We cannot work without hoping that others will advance further
> than we have. In principle, this progress goes on *ad infinitum*. And
> with this we come to inquire into the *meaning* of science. For, after
> all, it is not self-evident that something subordinate to such a law
> is sensible and meaningful in itself. Why does one engage in do-
> ing something that in reality never comes, and never can come, to
> an end?[110]

For Weber there could be no answer. In its place, only the willful dedi-
cation to one's task responded to the apparent "senselessness" of science.[111] The problem remained unresolvable; it was merely *contained*
by the fiat of action. Weber would not deny the feeling of absence that

accompanied his commitment. Still, even "the inward interest of a truly religiously 'musical' man," Weber said, "can never be served by veiling to him and to others the fundamental fact that he is destined to live in a godless and prophetless time." Hence Weber's stoic counsel to the young radical intellectuals of 1918, who Weber believed "tarry for new prophets and saviors":

> Nothing is gained by yearning and tarrying alone, and we shall act differently. We shall set to work and meet the 'demands of the day,' in human relations as well as in our vocation.[112]

Science for Weber was precisely the ceaseless activity, valued for its own sake, of the ascetic Protestant bourgeois—activity absorbed with the manipulation of means that had, perforce, to be at the same time the reassurance of meaning that was distant and forever obscure.

For Weber, certainly, the Protestant Ethic, in its integrity, was by no means an acquiescent one. It was wholly distinct from vulgar *Realpolitik*, or the mere "'adaptation' to the possible" that characterized, he said, "the bureaucratic morality of Confucianism." Rather its dynamic opposition to the world made it a profoundly moral disposition. For the Confucian, on the other hand,

> any sort of transcendental anchorage of ethics, any tension between obligations to a supra-mundane God and the world of the flesh, any pursuance of a goal in the beyond, or conception of radical evil, was lacking. . . . The relentlessly and religiously systematised utilitarianism peculiar to rational asceticism, to live "in" the world and yet not be "of" it, has helped to produce superior rational aptitudes and therewith the spirit of the specialized man [*Berufmensch*] which, in the last analysis, was denied to Confucianism.[113]

Thus, in his judgment of asphyxiating bureaucracy, Weber stood apart from the world, as critic, conscious of evil and of the degradation implicit in the progress of capitalism. Still, in effect his ethical rigorism only reaffirmed the object of its disdain, for the only practical answer to the depravity of the world was vigorous action in it—the practice of the specialized *Berufmensch* who steadily wrought bureaucratic form out of the conditions of his labor that remained to be rationalized.

The double binds that emerged from the conflict of reason and value in Weber's thought figured in his social theory as the anxious consciousness of unresolved antinomies in social structure. Clearly his concept of bureaucracy went beyond Spencer by emphasizing the survival of "status" (the graduated subordination of rank, the obedience to authority, the "honor" accruing to place) amid the abstract, impersonal, and objectivist relations of "contract." [114] But this was only one of a whole set of polarities in modern life—ostensible opposites that coexisted permanently and that continually shaded off into one another—that Weber's analysis of bureaucracy revealed. He found that the rise of democracy stimulated bureaucracy, for the former demanded equality of conditions, free of all personal privilege and distinction, and this required purely formal means of estimating individual rights and opportunities; yet the "caste" consciousness of officialdom and the authoritative chain of command in the bureaucratic apparatus scandalized the democratic conscience. [115] Democracy spawned bureaucracy and perforce turned against it.

Furthermore, under the conditions of mass democracy in great states, centralized parties arose to corral votes and became organized, bureaucratic apparatuses staffed by professionals and officials expert in the regular work required by electoral and governmental efficiency. Yet such political "machines" required direction, too, and above the apparatus arose the demagogic leader, whose personality drew the affectual identification of the mass electors and assured the success of the party and fortunes of its retainers. [116] From mass democracy issued plebiscitarian Caesarism: that is to say, bureaucracy fostered the renewal of *charisma*, its opposite, which relied not on impersonal procedures, the rational conduct of efficient routine, but on the preeminence of "specific gifts of the body and spirit . . . not accessible to everybody." [117] The results, Weber said, might be called a "dictatorship resting on the exploitation of mass emotionality." [118] From rationality emerged irrationality—and the cyclic play of opposites was complete.

Although Weber considered bureaucracy the most efficient means of administration imaginable, because its strict system of differentiated duties achieved a mechanical reliability and expedience, he did not consider it an adequate means of *rule*. He believed the hypertrophy of governmental bureaucracy in Germany and the imperial suppression of professional political talent had left the state rudderless— for bureaucrats, efficient in their circumscribed bailiwicks, normally evaded individual responsibility and hence could not stipulate and enforce a line of action. Again, value, for Weber, imparted direction to instrumental reason *from without*. For the sake of controlling bureaucracy, submitting the apparatus to conscious direction, Weber sought parliamentary democracy: he hoped the play of parties would spawn prophetic political leaders of independence and vision. [119] Despite the centrality of rational action in Weber's system, he actually strained be-

yond fact and reason to value and meaning. Bureaucracy and charisma were but translations of these key terms in the persistent dualism of Weber's thought.

It was, precisely, Weber's tense sensitivity to oscillating antinomies
in social action and order that later made his sociology attractive, at a
time when historical prospects of change seemed closed. In fact, in
the wake of the ideological crisis of the 1930s, social theory generated
by left-wing intellectuals in the United States tended to revive dualist
disjunctures both as a sign of stymied action and as a hedge against
the repressive uniformity and harmony of totalitarianism. Both Sidney Hook and Lewis Corey emphasized their disconcerting discovery
that traditional socialist means (economic coordination) proved incompatible with socialist ends (liberation). While they sought new formulas for reintegrating means and ends in consistent democratic political practice, Will Herberg argued contrarily for acceptance of the
"dialectical" and "intrinsically contradictory" character of political action, the perpetual danger that effect might prove to be the opposite
of intention.[120] Meanwhile, Herberg's mentor, the ex-socialist Reinhold Niebuhr, developed an existential theology that studied the
tragic interweaving of human carnality and spirituality, of creativity
and destruction, of human liberation and domination—contradictions in perpetual tension, impossible to resolve or overcome—that
rendered political action by nature morally ambiguous, an inescapable field of aspiration and degradation.[121] And in the midst of these
American intellectuals there worked the exiles of the Frankfurt Institute of Social Research, who responded to the organicist sweep of
"state capitalism" by reverting to the disjunctions between theory and
practice, knowledge and will, moral critique and political action, the
private and public spheres, the individual and society that they hoped
would preserve the "memory" of resistance apart from the "false totalism" of the present.[122]

With the frank dualism of modernist thought, however, there
came an inner dynamic of estrangement and reconciliation. This paradox was evident in the tradition of German social theory we began to
explore with Weber. In the case of Robert Michels, concession to the
sociological necessity of organization and its antidemocratic consequences followed as the inverse of the intransigent idealism he upheld
as a revolutionary syndicalist in his youth.[123] For Weber, the two elements of idealism and concession stood side by side; their relationship
mirrored the paradoxical doubleness of the Protestant Ethic's worldly
asceticism. Weber's sensibility merged moral absolutism, which was opposed to reality as given, and practical reconciliation with that reality.

In part this syndrome rested upon the conception of morality in the German sociological tradition. As Georg Lukács pointed out in his pre-Marxist work, *The Theory of the Novel*, the "omnipotence of ethics" presupposed the "interiority" of the bourgeois individual driven to privatism by the social regime of market exchange—that is, the separation of personal motives from the organic mold of bygone communal life.[124] Of this, modern German sociology, as developed by Tönnies, Simmel, and Weber, was acutely conscious. Given the artificial, contractual associations of modern society, moral ends were inevitably sharply separated from the normal means of organized social life.[125] Moral discourse, in this guise, presupposed a painful sense of existential disjuncture, a riven world of experience. It certainly had little in common with the *immanent* morality of Spencer's market-based model of social evolution, where egoism and altruism naturally tended to converge. Arising from the rupture of private and public life, morality per se now resided apart from the public realm of material experience and lay not in effectual human acts but solely in consciousness, an expression of pure intention. Thus the realm of the subject and object, intention and effect, were drawn apart, and the gulf between "ought" and "is" grew to be unconquerable. The distinct problem of morality, then, was its self-defeating disposition, its affirmation of principles recognized as inapplicable to daily life, precepts understood to be ineffectual in organized social action. Thus the romanticism of German sociology decried modern society and conceded to it in a tragic gesture of renunciation.

In this sense, the Protestant Ethic made moral resistance to given reality a means of reproducing it. The suggestion of anticapitalist romanticism in Weber's withering critique of bureaucracy actually meshed with Weber's procapitalist rationalism. Weber found a great deal of value in the puritan rationalism he discovered at the heart of the capitalist spirit. At the same time, he portrayed the imminent capitalist future, the depersonalizing embrace of systematic bureaucracy, as the cold shell of social life left as the heroic will of the pioneering bourgeoisie ebbed. Looking backward, to the vigor and dignity of the classic bourgeois individual at the moment of his decline and eclipse, Weber finally valorized the trend of modernization even as less and less of value could be expected from it. In Weber we can recognize how the modernist critique of progressive thought assumes the function of a jeremiad, for as Sacvan Bercovitch puts it, the jeremiad thrives on a sense of "crisis," and from "cries of declension"—the conviction in historical degeneration—enacts a "ritual of progress."[126] Paradoxically, the embrace of progress lingers within the critique mounted by postprogressive thought. Thus, as we will see, it is the intimate association of estrangement and reconciliation, the contention of faith in progress with skepticism of it, that provides the key to Daniel Bell's thought. And it is, furthermore, the modernist sense of disabling antinomies which infiltrated Bell's thought as he came of age in a time of ideological crisis and which provided the intellectual medium for the accommodation he reached with American society.

The Beginnings of Daniel Bell's Thought:
The Tension of Idealism and Skepticism

Almost from the very beginning of his intellectual life, Daniel Bell's thought was double-sided, drawn on the one hand to moral absolutism and on the other to skepticism of professed political ideals, to determinist schemes of social evolution and to voluntarist conceptions of political purpose. The disjunctions in his youthful sensibility arose from the anomalous, stalemated political situation of his time, the combination of capitalist crisis and socialist impotence that posed difficult questions for the left in reformulating and recombining social theory and political practice.

At the age of 13, in the summer of 1932, Daniel Bell joined the Young People's Socialist League, youth wing of the Socialist Party of America. Such a precocious political commitment was not unusual at the time—for another New York intellectual, Irving Howe, avowal of Socialism came at the age of 14—and left-wing politics had a certain existential reality and traditional sanction in the Jewish community of the time. Bell's mother, a garment worker widowed when Bell was still an infant, belonged to the International Ladies Garment Workers Union (ILGWU), which was still allied to the Socialist Party in the early 1930s. The summer of 1932 was an election season, and the expert Socialist soapboxer Gus Claessens spoke on the streetcorners of Manhattan's Lower East Side for Norman Thomas, the party's presidential candidate. As the Depression sank to its depths, and the camps of the homeless unemployed along the East River testified to widespread misery, Bell read Upton Sinclair's *The Jungle* and was aroused by its portrait of corruption and abuse. "We were very poor," Bell later recalled, "and aware of the fact that something was wrong with the entire system." [127]

The Young People's Socialist League (YPSL), founded in 1913, was originally an educational and recreational organization for children just like Bell: at first its members were concentrated in New York, largely the offspring of Jewish workers in the needle trades who be-

longed to the Socialist Party. Like the Party and the unions, it suffered
a deep decline in the 1920s. After the party split with the Communists, the postwar red scare and repression, and the business prosperity of the Coolidge years, the Socialist Party was left with only 7,800
members in 1929, less than 8 percent of its membership a decade before. YPSL counted fewer than 700 members across the country. By
1933, however, the Depression had helped boost party membership
to more than 17,000. YPSL claimed 2,500 members in 1932, when
Bell joined, and 4,000 by 1933. That year, too, the limping ILGWU
called out all the workers in the New York dressmaking industry, and
the victorious strike brought the union's members at least to a level of
dignified poverty. Shortly before he died in October, Morris Hillquit,
head of the aging circle of right-wing social democrats who led the
party, wrote, "Now we are apparently facing a new Socialist uplift. . . .
The Socialist Party is getting a new lease on life. Its membership, vote,
and political influence are in the ascendant." [128]

Daniel Bell shared in this enthusiasm which grew from social crisis. Like others, he came to the Party, he said, "with a great sense of
devoting one's life to something which is pure and important." [129] Yet
events moved too quickly and tumultuously to leave such a passion
pure and unalloyed. At the time, the novelist John Dos Passos likened
the Socialist Party to near-beer, and the Communists importuned Socialist youth to come over to the only "fighting organization" daring
and forceful enough to overcome the danger of reaction. The Communists were practicing the policies of the "third period," the Comintern assessment that the imminence of revolution required its cadres
first of all to shatter the inhibiting illusions of reform sustained by the
Socialists, dubbed "social fascists" for their alleged collaboration with
the dying capitalist order. Under the constant stream of Communist
propaganda, stigmatizing the impotence or treachery of the Socialists,
Daniel Bell was one of many youths who considered switching their
allegiance, especially when Hitler's rise to power in January 1933
heightened the prevailing sense of emergency. [130] Bell was quickly dis-
suaded from joining the Communist camp, however, by a summer
visit to his mother's anarchist cousins, who lived thirty miles north of
New York City in the Mohegan colony, an offshoot of the renowned
anarchist settlement in Stelton, New Jersey. [131]

The Communists were quickly losing credibility in any case, due
to the gross errors and abuses of "third period" politics. In the United
States, "third period" policy reached the height of perversity on February 16, 1934, when Communists physically disrupted a Socialist
Party rally in Madison Square Garden called to honor the Social Demo-

cratic workers of Vienna. The incident led a group of intellectuals who had sympathized with the Communists in the 1932 election—including Lionel Trilling, Elliot Cohen, Meyer Schapiro, and Edmund Wilson—to publicly announce their break with the Communist Party, beginning their more or less tentative turn toward sympathy with Trotskyism.[132] By this point, Socialist Party youth who leaned leftward also tended to look toward Trotskyism, rather than the Communist Party, as the authentic revolutionary alternative to the outdated gradualism of the SP officials.[133] The pamphlets of Alexander Berkman and Emma Goldman, however, which Bell's relatives employed to tutor him on the history of the Russian revolution, clearly labeled Trotsky as a genius of Bolshevik repression. The anarchists and the SP Old Guard shared the view that Stalinism merely revealed the true nature of Bolshevism and that a return to the heritage of Lenin and Trotsky thus offered no alternative to Soviet enormities. Since anarchism had little political stature, and no organized expression in the United States by the 1930s, Bell responded to the sectarianism and brutality of official Communism by turning to the right wing of the Socialist Party.

Such critical choices are rarely made solely on intellectual grounds, especially for a boy of 14 or 15; personal associations weigh heavily in the balance. Having grown up without a father, Bell habitually attached himself intimately to older men, a pattern to be repeated later in his relationships with *New Leader* business manager Sol Levitas and philosopher Sidney Hook. On joining the Young People's Socialist League, Bell had quickly become a young protégé of Socialist Party elders Morris Hillquit, Algernon Lee, James Oneal, and Julius Gerber, and these ties were undoubtedly stronger than the appeal of more radical anarchist relatives who lived in a retreat outside the city.[134] The accoutrements of power, even on a small scale, may have also exercised some pull on an ambitious boy like Bell. These were the same men who had led the Party from the beginning: they left the Socialist Labor Party in the 1890s, alienated by Daniel De Leon's imperious style of leadership and his advocacy of dual "revolutionary unions," and they led the struggle against Wobbly syndicalism in 1912 and Bolshevik insurrectionism in 1919.[135] This Old Guard eliminated almost all its factional opponents by the mid 1920s, only to be left presiding over the party's declining fortunes. Then, with the party revival of the early 1930s, they faced a new leftist challenge. Eager and audacious, the young recruits were convinced that a socialist transformation of society was urgently necessary as well as imminently possible, and they threatened to overwhelm the old stalwarts.[136] They were inspired by the renewed intensity of the class struggle, manifest in the movement for industrial unionism, and the growing student antiwar movement, where young Socialists collaborated with young Communists.[137] Norman Thomas, who had moved up through the party during the 1920s as its leading candidate and orator, became the figurehead of the new activist current as he proclaimed his slogan of the 1930s, "Socialism in Our Time." In response the Old Guard prepared for battle. The factional dispute in the Socialist Party from 1934 to 1936, between the old leadership and the young radicals grouped loosely around Thomas in the "Militant" faction, was Daniel Bell's signal formative political experience.

The factional strife came to focus in a debate over the meaning of democracy at a time of intense social conflict. The Old Guard held to the classic Kautskyan view that modern industrialism throve only under the regime of democracy, which promised the political ascendancy of the proletariat as it grew, in step with capitalist development, to comprise a numerical majority of the population.[138] On the other hand, the Militants asserted that the victories of European reaction challenged the assumption that democracy was the "normal" political condition of capitalist society which permitted a legal and peaceful transition to socialism.[139] Hence, at the party convention of 1934, the party's left wing managed to pass a new Declaration of Principles that pledged militant and disruptive resistance to wars waged by the existing United States government, stated the party's willingness to seize political power in the event of a revolutionary crisis whether or not it could claim an electoral majority under the circumstances, and dedicated itself to "replacing the bogus democracy of capitalist parliamentarianism by a genuine workers democracy."[140] The Old Guard howled in rage, denouncing the Militants' "anarchistic, illegal, Communistic doctrine."[141]

While the Militants claimed the Old Guard had not learned the lessons of the European debacle, Old Guard pamphleteer James Oneal charged in turn that the young radicals had learned nothing since the days of street fighting in 1848, for their enthusiasm for extraparliamentary action "actually reverts to the force romanticism of that period which Marx and Engels abandoned." The issue for Oneal was scientific determinism versus utopian voluntarism. To suppose, for instance, that insurrectionary masses could combat the modern, technological might of the state was sheer "mysticism, not social science," he said. And to hold the European social democratic leadership responsible for the fate of the proletariat under the heel of triumphant reaction, as if a different policy of steadfast struggle could have wrought other results, ignored "the gigantic and complex forces that had overwhelmed these proletarians" and smacked of nothing but "the bourgeois philosophy of free will!" [142] Like previous outbursts of leftism in the party's history, the Militant tendency, Oneal charged, was motivated by non-Marxist middle-class adventurers who sought a "short cut" to socialism, unable to accept the discipline of an enlightened working class working its will through representative organs of state. [143] Oneal's argument echoed the Kautskyan critique of the Bolsheviks' utopian attempt to skip the evolutionary stage of capitalist democracy, and it was this anti-utopian determinism of orthodox social democracy which became a permanent deposit in Daniel Bell's thought. "The argument when I was a boy," he recalled, "was that the Communists had distorted Marxism, that Lenin was a Blanquist," that is, a middle class radical committed to the pure force wielded by conspiratorial cliques. And in *The End of Ideology*, he would remark that Bolshevism "can be considered as one of the few successful movements of pure will in history." [144]

At the time though, the "pure" political devotion of young Bell was scandalized by all the pulling and hauling of factional struggle. His moral sense was offended by the evident willingness of the contenders to seek political ends by deceitful means dressed in the rhetoric of lofty, humanitarian purposes. As a partisan of the right, most of his indignation was aimed at the left: there were reports that the Lovestonites (the right opposition expelled from the Communist Party in 1929) had infiltrated the Socialist Party under the auspices of a special left-wing caucus in the Militant camp; a member of Bell's own circle of the Young People's Socialist League on the Lower East Side was denounced at a national YPSL convention as a Trotskyist plant; a YPSL leader who unexpectedly announced he was joining the Trotskyist organization took the proceeds of a recent YPSL fundraising event with him, justifying the theft as a contribution to the revolutionary cause.

On the other side, Bell was not unaware of the cliquishness of the old-timers, who resisted turning over the party—by now more a social club to them than a political agency—to newcomers. [145] The members of the Old Guard, in fact, were roused out of their sloth, and showed a vigor belying their age, by factional contention for party rule rather than the struggle for socialism, which appeared to be much less pressing and less real to them. What mattered in the struggle for power was strategic organizational control more than debates and issues, and Bell saw that the secretary of the New York local, Julius Gerber, was a key source of power, despite his lack of stature as a theoretician and

orator, because he presided over a network of offices and personal relations that constituted, however modestly, a political machine.[146]

The distance between word and deed Bell sensed when he heard
socialist rhetoric masking the exigencies of power and organization
primed him for the appeal of Robert Michels, whose *Political Parties*
Bell read in a political science class at the City College of New York.[147]
Bell was profoundly influenced by the book, despite the fact that
Michels' argument was rooted in a radical critique of the Old Guard's
German comrades. Michels showed how the German social-democratic
and labor movement gave rise to an oligarchic leadership that used
revolutionary rhetoric to pander to a mass constituency while it appropriated all prerogatives of decision to itself, maneuvered to preserve its incumbency, and reached accommodations with the social
elites it professed to oppose. The anarchist critique of the authoritarianism implicit in political organization, however, a critique that
Michels learned from his days as a member of the left-wing opposition
to the International, merged into a kind of disillusioned sociological
realism that paradoxically led to common ground with social democracy. Just as Kautsky, in his evolutionary determinism, emphasized the
limits of human will, so Michels—who finally proclaimed the sociological doctrine that organization per se, necessary for any social action, precluded popular sovereignty—stressed the limits of political
aspirations, the impossibility of ever establishing a pure form of democracy. Kautsky himself had relied on a similar argument in polem-
icizing against anarchosyndicalist opponents like Michels: the image
of direct democracy conjured up in Marx's portrayal of the Paris Com-
mune, Kautsky argued, was obsolete in a modern, complex industrial
society, where parliamentary representation was the only form of democracy possible. Kautsky frankly identified proletarian rule with the
hegemony of the workers' bureaucracy cultivated in the party, the
trade unions, the newspapers and publishing houses, and the cooperative societies of the workers movement; and the promise of a
democracy of immediate, popular participation, he said, could be
nothing other than a mask for the ambitions of a ruthless elite striving
for power.[148] On this level, Kautsky and Michels were assimilable, even
if they evaluated the outcome of organizational exigencies by different lights.

Michels' warning of the inevitability of oligarchy seemed to Bell
an important insight into politics—and a more significant explanation
of the course of the Russian revolution than Trotsky's theory that the
Stalinist bureaucracy arose from backward economic conditions that
were inescapable as long as the rulers pursued the politics of "social-

ism in one country." Bell doubted that the revolutionism of the Trotskyist movement offered a genuine alternative to the political fate of Stalinism. Among the anti-Stalinist radicals who gathered at City College, Bell raised this challenge to Philip Selznick, a young Trotskyist who would become a leader in the sociology of organization in the 1940s and 1950s. "And you think," Bell asked Selznick, "that James P. Cannon [leader of the American Trotskyists] is immune to Michels' iron law of oligarchy?"[149]

Bell never accepted Michels completely, however, for he did not believe that all of social action could be reduced to terms of power and manipulation. Ideals in their own right sometimes motivated action, he thought.[150] Bell himself was an idealist, despite the political skepticism he learned from Michels. The defense of democracy, which was the root of Bell's adherence to the right wing of the Socialist Party, all but necessarily became an ideal, moral goal, as events of the time shattered the evolutionary argument that it was the given, fixed medium of natural progress. Bell also hewed strictly to the argument against force and violence in socialist politics, becoming something of a pacifist. He was active in the peace movement, and he organized the Student Strike Against War at the downtown campus of the City College of New York in the spring of 1937. Bell's perspective rested on a kind of ethical absolutism: having reason to doubt the utopian expectations of revolutionaries, he insisted that no future political goal justified the present sacrifice of human life; and even as European politics approached the breaking point of military conflict, he has recalled, "you couldn't accept the idea that war could be justified in any way."[151] His position was bolstered by his vehement anti-Communism, for the Communist Party—after 1935 committed to the Popular Front program of direct alliances with bourgeois liberalism—strongly supported collective security, which the radical peace movement considered a program of war mobilization. This posture, however, bound Bell closer to the student anti-Stalinist left, including the Trotskyists and the radical Socialists, than it did to his own political home, the Social Democratic Federation, which was founded by the Old Guard after it left the Socialist Party in 1936. Along with the right wing of the Socialist International, which favored antifascist alliances with liberal parties, the Old Guard like the Communists advocated collective security among the bourgeois-democratic states opposed to Germany and Italy.[152]

Bell was not entirely happy with his political choice for the right-wing social democrats. The best of his generation, he was willing to admit, went far to the left, and the most stimulating discussions of theory and politics took place in the Trotskyist milieu, where the "Russian Question" raised difficult issues of class and bureaucracy, state power and economic control, questions which set an intellectual agenda for a generation of young thinkers. Bell's isolation among his peers and his hankering to be with them and to be like them encouraged a certain modesty that was a counterpoint to his characteristic self-assurance. Bell typically shrank from acrimonious polemics, and he declined to break off cordial relations with his opponents on the left. Indeed, he was often ready to appropriate elements of theory from those on his left, and at several moments in the coming decade he would turn in that direction politically, radicalizing by shades, before returning to his social-democratic anchorage. In the 1930s he frequented the gathering places of the anti-Stalinist left at college, eager for conversation, and he grew familiar with the journals and bulletins of the revolutionary groups. Irving Kristol, a Trotskyist sympathizer in those days, later recalled Bell at City College: "He had an immense intellectual curiosity, a kind of amused fondness for sectarian dialectics, knew his radical texts as thoroughly as the most learned among us and enjoyed 'a good theoretical discussion' the way some enjoy a Turkish bath—so we counted him in." [153] Still, by the end of the decade, the "intellectuals in retreat"—left-wing writers stigmatized by Burnham and Shachtman for turning against revolutionary Marxism, such as Sidney Hook, Max Eastman, James Rorty, Edmund Wilson, Benjamin Stolberg, Louis Hacker, John Chamberlain, Eugene Lyons, and Ferdinand Lundberg—approached social-democratic positions, and many began writing for the Old Guard's organ, *The New Leader*.

The peculiarities of this turn—the new social-democratic allegiance of self-consciously modern intellectuals, who had none of social democracy's bland confidence in progress—helped to confirm the syncretism of Bell's thinking. Hook for instance, in *Towards the Understanding of Karl Marx* (1933) had defended Leninism against social democracy, propounding a theory that relied not on "laws" of objective social development but on the proletariat's revolutionary will and action. Now, the only thing left of the revolutionary will in Hook's theory was his assertion of the priority of moral intention in all social or political practice. Hook's mentor, the instrumentalist philosopher John Dewey, argued similarly at the time that democracy could not be preserved nor socialism achieved by placing trust in a fixed destiny: both were moral goals, the aims of imperative purpose, valued ends achieved by effort. Furthermore, Dewey argued in a 1938 exchange with Trotsky, the means and ends of political practice had to be integrated if moral purpose was to have any concrete significance. Hence political goals had little meaning except as implicit guides to current practice; the ultimate goal of a socialist society had to be present, implied in the commitment to an ongoing nonviolent and democratic process. The argument struck an old chord for Bell, and on the occasion of the Stalin-Hitler nonaggression pact, he wrote to *The New Leader*, assailing Trotsky with a combination of Dewey's argument and the old social-democratic critique of Bolshevism:

> The recent Stalin-Hitler pact has cleared the air of many confusions, but I deem it necessary to stress one aspect. Not only has Stalinism earned the world's contempt, but the whole theory of Bolshevism has been laid bare.
>
> The latest Bolshevik maneuver flows in a logical sequence from the Bolshevik theory that an end justifies any means, no matter how contemptible. It was Lenin who at the second congress of the Third International in 1919 said: You can lie and cheat, for honesty is part of a bourgeois morality, and the end justifies the means.
>
> Any party having that as a guiding beacon, plus a jesuitical belief in its righteousness which justifies, for it, the suppression of any other thought and other expressions differing from its own, will lead to the same swamp. Means are used, genetically linked with ends achieved; and dictatorial means can never lead to democratic ends.
>
> But Stalinism is only one wing of that church. There is a heretic who claims the true faith—Leon Trotsky. And of him, too, all those who are seeking a way to a better society, must beware.
>
> It was Trotsky who, as one of the rulers of the Third International, ordered the splits in the labor movement, throughout the world, and who pushed insurrectionary tactics in the early Weimar Republic. It was Trotsky, the Red Commander, who ordered the shooting of the Kronstadt sailors when, taking Lenin at his word, they asked for democracy and land.
>
> Socialism must be more than an economic collectivism. Socialism must be the extension of freedom of thought and conscience and lead to individual opportunity for culture and development. Trotskyism, as a derivative of Leninism, is alien to these and must be fought.[154]

The moralism of Dewey's position, however, was hardly a satisfactory solution to the dilemmas of the time; very shortly it foundered on the war issue. Like Bell, the anti-Stalinist intellectuals, even as they deserted Marxism, retained their opposition to collective security and the mounting threat of a new war in Europe. The Committee of Cultural Freedom, organized by Sidney Hook in 1939 as a political vehicle, in effect, for the "intellectuals in retreat," firmly declared itself against war while it endorsed Dewey's "democracy as a way of life" as the real alternative to totalitarianism. Dewey's doctrine of the necessary moral consistency of means and ends suggested that democracy could not be furthered through the instrumentalities of war: a war declared for democracy, in fact, would likely yield antidemocratic results, for it required the centralization of sweeping authority in the state and gave rise to totalitarianism. Yet only a year after the Committee for Cultural Freedom was founded, Hook announced a change of heart in the pages of *The New Leader*, declaring his support of the war by the democratic Allies against the Nazis, on the grounds that the military defeat of Hitler was the necessary precondition of any possible socialist advances in Europe. The war issue would impress a new view of morality on disillusioned radical intellectuals—a sense of the unavoidable dilemmas posed by counter-valued means and ends, rather than the imperative of rendering them consistent. Bell soon followed Hook's lead. After the United States entered the war at the end of 1941, when Norman Thomas dissolved his Keep America Out of War Committee and brought the Socialist Party around to a position of "critical support," only the dwindling Trotskyist movement and small circles of anarchists and conscientious objectors opposed the war from the left.

Growing up in the 1930s, Bell, it appears, constructed an uneasy perspective that straddled political currents of the left and right and combined elements of voluntarist and determinist theories. Indeed, the paradox of social-democratic theory in the 1930s was that its defense of democracy assumed a new moral urgency in the light of the decade-long decay of European politics, while the very crises and catastrophes of the period undermined the evolutionary foundation of the argument. And though Bell absorbed the anti-utopianism of orthodox social democracy, he learned about Marxism from Sidney Hook's *Towards the Understanding of Karl Marx*. He embraced John Dewey's philosophy of "democracy as a way of life" while he appreciated the arguments of Robert Michels, who denied the possibility of the participatory democracy Dewey imagined. Such contradictions were not merely personal pitfalls but manifestations of both the hope and despair aroused by the political experience of the 1930s. Daniel Bell experienced these years as a time, he would say, when a revolutionary situation seemed at hand and yet "almost all of socialist theory possibly was hopeless." Caught in a time marked by the combined crises of bourgeois society and the socialist movement, when the left faced acute difficulties trying to relate practice to theory, moral goals to political action, Bell's sensibility was strained between idealism and skepticism.[155]

The stalemate of the time was evident in domestic American politics. In 1936, Roosevelt won reelection in a landslide but immediately encountered stiff right-wing resistance in Congress. New Deal reform initiatives ground to a halt, Roosevelt's demagogic attacks on "economic royalists" notwithstanding.[156] The massive workers' movement that arose with the struggle for industrial unionism offered no immediate political alternative to the foundering regime. The union officials banked on support or at least forbearance from the government. The left committed its cadres to the organizing drive but failed to bring a socialist disposition to the leadership of the movement, and this failure was due at least in part to the Communist Party's Popular Front strategy of funneling labor and liberal support to Roosevelt on behalf of antifascist unity.[157] Soon, the recession of 1937 shattered a fragile recovery and left both government policy and conventional economic thought in disarray, bewildered by what appeared to be unprecedented, and perhaps epochal, stagnation.[158] But it also broke labor's momentum and disabled the unions, which lost dues payers steadily in the years approaching the war.[159]

Aside from the Communists, the left was near ruin. The Socialists had split at the 1936 convention and the right wing limped home to New York. Eager to build a labor party, the right wing acceded to the demands of the garment workers' unions to reward Roosevelt with labor votes; the result was the American Labor Party, a vehicle to support the New Deal outside of "old party" channels, which satisfied only in name the old socialist demand for independent labor politics.[160] Norman Thomas' Socialist Party, meanwhile, was preoccupied by continued factional strife; when it ended with the departure of the Trotskyists at the end of 1937, Socialist Party membership rolls fell to an all-time nadir, lower even than in 1929.[161] In turn, after losing its intellectual periphery, the Trotskyist Socialist Workers Party fell into a fierce dispute over the class character of the Soviet Union in the fall of 1939 and soon broke in two.[162] Finally, the group of former communists led by Jay Lovestone dissolved its organization, the Independent Labor League of America, at the end of 1940, declaring, "Present-day American radicalism finds itself in a hopeless blind-alley from which there is no escape along the old lines. All the organizations, parties and groups that have come out of the old socialist and communist movements have lost their very ground of existence."[163] Thus, when a

Republican victory in 1938 seemed to put Roosevelt's leadership and the Democratic Party in deep crisis, hopes for a nationwide labor-left realignment went unfulfilled.[164] In effect there was no left extant, ready to enter the breach.

Despite years of growing social polarization there was no innovative break in the structure of American politics. The unions, without ideological direction, grew preoccupied with organizational survival. In the summer of 1940, as the Nazi sweep of France led the intelligentsia to support Roosevelt's mobilization drive, the leaders of two of the most powerful blocks of industrial workers, Philip Murray of the steelworkers and Walter Reuther of the autoworkers, offered Roosevelt a deal, exchanging industrial peace for labor participation in planned military production. Despite the resistance of business to any such power-sharing schemes, the Murray-Reuther plans set labor on its course toward state patronage and an ideology of national unity during the war.

In the midst of the ideological crisis, at the beginning of 1939, Daniel Bell commenced a year and a half retreat in the graduate department of sociology at Columbia University. There he studied the work of Wilhelm Dilthey, father of the "revolt against positivism" in German social thought, the work of L. T. Hobhouse, and of Max Weber. He frequented the evening seminars conducted by the exiled scholars of the Frankfurt Institute of Social Research—Max Horkheimer, Theodor Adorno, Friedrich Pollock, Herbert Marcuse, Leo Lowenthal, and others—as they strove to define the socioeconomic character of the Nazi order and the future course of social development in the absence of a liberating revolution, which appeared to be blocked, rather than stimulated, by progress.[165] In the summer of 1940, Bell left Columbia to begin his writing career on *The New Leader*, preoccupied with the fate of socialism under the conditions of antifascist war.

2
The Politics of War
Estrangement and the Illusion of Progress

"It would almost appear," the editors of *Partisan Review* wrote in 1939, "that the peculiar function of the intellectuals is to idealize imperialist wars when they come and to debunk them after they are over."[1] The *Partisan Review* editors recalled the wave of disenchantment that swept over loyal writers, academics, and clerics in the wake of the Great War, and they predicted that the intellectuals who rushed once again to embrace official war policy would meet the same fate. The prediction was to be borne out more fully than subsequent historical myths, portraying the second war as an unqualifiedly popular crusade, would allow. Indeed, there did not emerge in the wake of this war that widespread resentment which followed the first, the grievous sense of having been manipulated and misled which became part of popular culture in the interwar years. Still, towards the end of the Second World War, many left-wing and liberal intellectuals—at least those who remained outside the Communists' Popular Front and immune to its triumphalism—came to recognize the "emptiness of victory," as they observed the betrayal of official democratic war aims by big-power settlements and the concentration of military-industrial power in domestic affairs. By 1944, even a prowar newspaper like *The New Leader* mourned the discovery that "the differences between this war and the last one are constantly being whittled down."[2]

This chapter observes in detail Daniel Bell's course through the war years, as it took the parabolic trajectory predicted in *Partisan Review*'s editorial, and it examines the impetus the war experience gave him to adopt a uniquely "modern" social theory. The First World War, we recall, had revealed how "treacherous" the appearance of progress had been, as Henry James put it, and according to the critic Paul Fussell, its startling juxtaposition of civilization and catastrophe helped

to confirm the ironic bent of the modernist mentality. The Second
World War, too, first elicited and then besmirched faith in progress,
thus refreshing the imprint of the modernist mode. In the United
States during these years, the modernist mentality throve anew among
a marginalized elite that rejected the false optimism and imperious
national unity of wartime. New modernist movements in the arts (abstract expressionism in painting, bebop in jazz) arose during the war
among underground, oppositional minorities. In politics and social
theory, the war spawned a new radicalism that set its face against an
order of concentrated power it imagined to be faultless.

At this time Daniel Bell was a young political journalist, a writer,
and by the age of twenty-three managing editor of *The New Leader*,
organ of the Social Democratic Federation, the right-wing socialists he
had joined in the 1930s. The war years marked the beginning of his
intellectual career. The problems he considered started with the politics of war (more specifically the politics of the left as it approached
the tasks of war) and advanced to the social roots and consequences of
the war regime. The questions he broached set an agenda for his intellectual future, particularly the problematic relations between capitalist economy and the state and the social functions of planning. Most
important for this study, however, was the broad pattern of change in
his thinking, his need to comprehend the frustration of his political
aims and the paradoxical relation of intention and effect in social
action.

Bell had grown up as part of a generation mesmerized by the image of the First World War. As a teenager Bell took part in the student
strikes, held each April 7 in the middle thirties to mark the anniver-
sary of Wilson's declaration of war and to pledge resistance to future
wars.[3] Bell opposed the program of collective security advocated by
liberals and Communists, and he supported the Keep America Out of
War campaign that Norman Thomas organized in 1938.[4] Even in the
first half-year of the European war, when relative inaction on the military fronts seemed to augur another protracted trench war of attri-
tion, Bell continued to oppose U.S. involvement. It was the rapid German conquest of France in May and June of 1940, suddenly making
the threat of continental Nazi domination real and imminent, that
wrought a major shift in U.S. public opinion and gave Roosevelt the
authority to commence military mobilization. Bell too finally swung
over to war support for the allied democracies. Perhaps Sidney Hook
had an impact, for after years of antiwar broadsides, the philosopher
used the pages of *The New Leader* to explain why socialists should give
political support to the war effort.[5] Hook later recalled that he had

difficulty persuading some of the younger people on *The New Leader* staff, so young Bell might have been a hold-out.[6] Nonetheless, by the fall of 1940, Bell was writing regularly as an advocate of the mobilization.

Then, regardless of any reservations he might have had, Bell's writings avidly pursued the argument that a successful war mobilization promised not only to defeat fascism but to fuel the advance of democratic socialism in the West. Later he would debunk this reformist ideal. By 1943, and through the end of the war, his view changed radically, and he warned, more stridently as time went on, that organized big business would preempt for its own purposes the very instruments of economic planning for war that social democrats had hoped would subordinate capital to popular democratic control. The "dialectics of war," as he put it in one article, reversed the direction and significance of social change. The dialectic Bell spoke of brought the negation of progress and—unlike Hegel's dialectic— quashed rather than motivated historical change. Bell found the contravention of social evolution as crushing as Spencer and Kautsky had in their day, and the society Bell saw emerging from the war—what he called the Monopoly State—had all the changeless monolithism that characterized the totalitarian model.

Interestingly, Bell never retracted his vigorous support for the war effort, even as he decried its outcome. By the end, the portrait of the war in Bell's writings resembled that drawn by the antiwar socialists at its beginning—a conflict of rival imperial powers which would more likely establish a fascist order at home than extend democracy abroad. Rather than reverse himself, however, Bell assumed an almost self-conscious "tragic" pose in recognizing the reversals of fortune—unanticipated consequences of purposive action, if you will—that constitute sociological reality. The problem was not an initial political error but the paradoxical inversions of social affairs. Here the modern temperament took hold, stirred by radical estrangement from the promises of progress. At the same time, however, the troubling ambiguities of social action and social order, disclosed by modern theory's sensitivity to persistent contradictions, would encourage a growing skepticism of radical political practice. This is the dilemma that would emerge in Bell's work in the wake of the war.

The Nature of Social-Democratic Prowar Progressivism

Daniel Bell's adoption of a prowar program in the summer of 1940 was influenced by two concurrent developments that seemed to promise a significant role for organized labor in leading the fight against fascism. As the Chamberlain government of Britain, disgraced by the inept policies of "appeasement," yielded to a coalition "people's government" of Labour and Tories, American labor leaders Philip Murray and Walter Reuther unveiled proposals for union participation in comprehensive industrial planning for war. The Union for Democratic Action (UDA), formed the next year by Reinhold Niebuhr and other prowar defectors from the American Socialist Party, sought to forge a transatlantic alliance between the "social unionism" of the CIO and the British Labourites. The UDA sponsored U.S. tours by Labour Party spokesmen, who declared that labor's program for the cooperative prosecution of the war augured "the economic reconstruction of the whole basis of society."[7]

The staff of *The New Leader* joined the UDA, despite the fact that the Social Democratic Federation (SDF) considered it a "rival organization" corrupted by "middle-class liberalism." Although formally a member of the SDF, Bell maintained a skeptic's distance from the party; he aligned himself with the business manager of *The New Leader*, a Menshevik emigré named Sol Levitas who strove to free the paper from the narrow limits of the SDF's entrenched sectarianism and make it a forum where liberal and left-wing intellectuals exchanged ideas with representatives of organized labor. With the rest of the small *New Leader* staff, Bell patiently submitted to, and weathered, a party hearing on the staff's lapse of political discipline.

Indeed, the program of the UDA was not explicitly socialist. Its declaration of principles, drafted by Lewis Corey, called for "economic democracy" as the domestic goal of a "two-front war" against fascism. Military mobilization, the UDA claimed, would require planning "our defense production on the basis of expansion and full use of productive capacity." The UDA encouraged organized labor to lead the drive for planning in order to protect the economy from the "anarchy and chaos" of private interest, and it warned that "unless an extension of economic democracy is allowed to solve the [economic] crisis *in time*, the resulting instability and dislocations will be seized upon by privileged groups as a pretext for imposing some form of dictatorship upon the country."[8] Briefly, in 1941 and 1942, Bell edited the monthly *UDA Bulletin*, and in one issue he printed an editorial declaring

that real democracy is not beaten yet, that the conditions of this war give progressives a fighting chance, that the war can only be won if it is fought democratically, that a people's morale is as

important as the number of tanks its army possesses . . . that
this war is not being fought by the people of the world for the
status quo.[9]

The prowar program that Bell advocated, in sympathy with the
UDA, paradoxically borrowed some classic arguments from the antiwar socialists of the late 1930s. Then, left-wing socialists opposed collective security not because they were indifferent to the threat of
European fascism but because they placed no trust in the capitalist
governments of Britain, France, and the United States as bulwarks
against it. The leftists had proposed the following argument: presiding over Depression-wracked economies, the bourgeoisie had neither
the ability nor the desire to fight the fascists and would desert democracy—and even patriotism—out of its fear of the proletariat. If on the
other hand the Western governments chose to wage war against Germany they would do so for the defense of imperialist interests, not democracy. In that event they would likely resort to fascist regimentation
themselves. Since fascism was a creature of decaying capitalism, the
leftists argued, only socialism could finally defeat it.

In the prowar position Bell adopted after 1940 many of these
arguments reappeared, turned on their head: bourgeois treachery
proved that the war against fascism was rightfully, and necessarily, labor's war in defense of its own interests; there was a contradiction between war mobilization and the capitalist interests that obstructed it;
and the democratic war to defeat fascism was the route to socialism.
The Social Democratic Federation, on the other hand, had little sympathy for the leftist suspicion of bourgeois democracy. Its support of
the war rested on the desire to preserve the "normal" conditions of
capitalist democracy, so that, in a world free of fascism, "the American
people can once more proceed with its orderly pursuit of greater security and freedom." The SDF, therefore, more or less uncritically
vested the leadership of the war in the Roosevelt regime; the prowar
position Bell promoted in the pages of *The New Leader,* standing
slightly to the left of the SDF, was more willing to criticize the regime
for restraining the progressive potential of the war effort.[10]

In *The New Leader,* Bell complained that the mobilization agencies
Roosevelt established were hamstrung by the representatives of big
business, the "dollar-a-year men," who headed them. Fearing an over-
expansion of productive capacity that would lead to another disastrous slump at war's end, the industrial chiefs sought to assure the
government that the nation's existing plant was adequate to produce
all necessary war materials. As Bell pursued this argument, the Union

for Democratic Action ran a pots-and-pans campaign to collect civilian donations of used aluminum, denouncing the "aluminum trust" for maintaining artificial scarcity of the metal. A few years earlier, Lewis Corey, the UDA's research director, had taken a new interest in Thorstein Veblen's work. He made Veblen's critique of business restrictionism the center of UDA ideology. Bell followed suit: the limitation of output by big business, Bell wrote, produced delays and bottlenecks that stymied the war effort; he rejoiced when government economists declared that phony business estimates of plant capacity were more responsible than strikes for shortfalls in production and when the Office of Production Management announced it would eject paid officials of trade associations from its staff. "There is an exodus from Washington," Bell wrote hopefully in July 1941, "and it isn't due to the summer heat. Going are many of the 140 dollar-a-year men who eagerly flocked to Washington some months ago to put 'business efficiency' into the government. They put 'business as usual' into the defense wheels; today much of our energy is being spent in releasing these brakes from the spokes." When the government seized a New Jersey shipyard, ostensibly to punish an antilabor management—leading *U.S. News and World Report* to mutter darkly about "how nebulous property rights can be"—Bell responded knowingly, hoping to confirm the magazine's worst fears. Indeed, the issue, he wrote, was "how far industry will be exempt from an all-out war against fascism," how far, that is, the government would go in subordinating private interest to the demands of organized war production. Bell wanted to get business out of government and he wanted government, on its own initiative, to get into business, to control production or build its own public industries that could serve as the basis of a planned economy after the war.[11]

Thus Bell considered a program of government initiative in war production a means of furthering labor's interests, and he saw the enhancement of labor rights, conversely, as the driving force of a full-scale mobilization. So, while left-wing socialists considered the repression of labor an integral part of the war drive, Bell asserted on the contrary that the Congressional attempt, following the strike wave of 1941, to clamp controls on organized labor hampered an effective military struggle against fascism. Regarding labor to be in the forefront of the antifascist struggle, Bell continued to harass the Office of Production Management for excluding union representatives from its Industry Advisory Boards. As the defense effort in the summer of 1941 remained "piece-meal," incoherent, subject to disabling dislocations, Bell promoted labor's demand for parity with business on unified industry councils that were empowered to plan the mobilization of industry-wide capacity as a unit. Such a necessary program, Bell believed, promised to carve deep inroads into the privileged sphere of private property rights. In one article, Bell remarked on Standard Oil's resistance to an army attempt to stockpile fuel, since the army program

> would have meant the complete pooling of the technical knowledge of the entire industry—with complete disregard for present and future patent structures. It would have meant the pooling of engineering processes, and the creation of standardized plants, instead of the present tailor-made plants. It would have meant additional manufacturing facilities and the destruction of the monopoly. Standard knew this and was afraid of this move. Consequently, it stalled and made promises.[12]

Labor's advocacy of planning strove to breach private property rights on behalf of pursuing total war; it seems in fact that Bell believed the tendency of the war to overcome the anarchy of the market made it part of historic progress toward a rational society. His progressive, rationalist standpoint led him to join Sidney Hook, by then a frequent contributor to *The New Leader*, in decrying the religious revival that accompanied the onset of war. Hook's landmark essays on "The New Failure of Nerve" in early 1943 combined a defense of rationalism against theology with a polemic against political leftists who, he said, evaded the responsibilities of war. In the late summer of 1942, Bell took the opportunity to make a similar argument, in response to a Catholic prowar manifesto by Jacques Maritain, which called for a renewal of religious faith to combat the ethically corrosive rationalism that allegedly spawned totalitarianism and the ensuing war. Bell, on the contrary, strove to put the Western war effort in line with socialism, which he understood as the fulfillment of Western tradition, the rational, scientific spirit of the Enlightenment.

> Reason, as exemplified by Deweyan instrumentalism, and by democratic socialism, may still reject a theological absolute and attack the "lying" absolutes of Stalinism and Hitlerism. The dictatorship of blind force came not out of reason, but out of a kind of social unreason. In holding to their goal of a democratic social order, the political movements stemming from the rational tendencies of the past four centuries inevitably fight totalitarianism, and all shares, Ignatius Loyola's, Stalin's or Hitler's.

Riled by Maritain's refusal to see the need for a socialist reconstruction of the postwar world, Bell went on to defend Marxism against Maritain's attempt to identify it with Nazism.

> The ethical motivation of the entire Socialist movement has been that the modern industrial system tears down the whole personality of man. The whole of Marx's analysis was that the "fetishism of commodities" conceals the fact that men are slaves of their productive forces; in his 1848 Manifesto, Marx—in almost theological fashion—raises the *key* problem of modern life-alienation: the fact that man is divorced from the satisfactions of his job, what Veblen in his more striking language called the "instinct of workmanship."[13]

War and the Analysis of Social Change

Was Bell's perspective a Marxist one? The appeal to Veblen was telling. Despite the politically protean character of his teachings, Veblen still had a high repute on the left. Four years before, in the short-lived but influential *Marxist Quarterly*, Lewis Corey had applauded Veblen as a "destructive critic of capitalism" and dubbed Veblen's concept of workmanship "his most enduring monument." In fact, Bell's view of capitalism rested more on Veblen's theory of business restrictionism than on Marx's analysis of the dynamics of capital accumulation. At that moment, it fit well with the social-democratic heritage Bell had absorbed from his years with the Old Guard. He was able to combine Veblenian theory with Karl Kautsky's theory of "ultra-imperialism," and on that basis discovered an anti-capitalist force immanent in the war drive, which required the high output of planned production freed from the limiting constraints that Veblen called business "sabotage."[14] The combination gave Bell a certain rationale for his political endorsement of the war, though it had the feel of a theoretical pastiche. Also, by raising questions about whether the social trends he identified under the war regime were progressive or reactionary, Bell's theoretical discussion revealed the contradictions that already hobbled evolutionary social theory, even as he tried to base his wartime politics on that theory.

During 1941 and 1942 Bell found that the "dollar-a-year" advice of risk-avoiding businessmen, intent on restricting production to maintain high prices and profits, was accompanied by a more sinister force jamming the drive toward effective production. This was the maze of covert relations between German and American corporations that had developed in the 1920s as a means of commonly managing the international marketplace. In a long string of muckraking report-age, Bell exposed the irradiating ties between the great German chemical combine I. G. Farben and U.S. firms like Standard Oil Company (New Jersey), E. I. du Pont de Nemours and Company, United States Rubber Company, Aluminum Company of America, and Dow Chemical Company, knit together by interlocking directorates and cartel agreements that allocated market zones, fixed prices, controlled patents, granted production licenses, and set royalty fees. Operative in the most advanced sectors of industry, Bell said, these bonds effectively constrained the diffusion and exploitation of technical advances in the fields of synthetic fuels, chemicals, and light metals—the very elements of a new twentieth-century industrial revolution. Furthermore, as Hitler established political controls over the German monopolies, Bell argued, the cartel agreements, originally intended for the mutual benefit of international businesses, became weapons of a national policy of economic warfare that kept its enemy's production tightly under wraps while mobilizing domestic resources on a massive scale. Since the new technology was crucial to constructing the modern tools of war, the willingness of the great U.S. firms to abide by the agreements was "sabotage" in a more literal sense than Veblen intended. In Bell's view it amounted to a criminal record of "putting profits before patriotism." [15]

From his investigations of the cartel patent deals, Bell concluded that the essential economic trend in the interwar years had been toward internationalism and the rationalized organization of world markets. The aggressive entrepreneurs of nineteenth-century capitalism had disappeared, replaced by the "administrators and fixers" of anonymous and institutionalized business management. On the world plane they sought not rivalrous expansion but stabilization, the timorous negotiation of mutually respected turf. In effect, Bell said, the trend toward cartelization bore out Kautsky's concept of ultra-imperialism. In its own way, the notion of ultra-imperialism was merely another example of evolutionary theory predicting the pacification of society. While Lenin claimed that the hegemony of finance capital in the epoch of imperialism compelled the capitalist nations to clash repeatedly and ever more fiercely in the struggle to divide and redivide the world, Kautsky suggested that other sectors of the bourgeoisie could subordinate the power of the financiers and initiate an era of peaceful capitalist coordination on a world scale. This development no longer seemed benign, though, as Bell concluded that ultra-imperialism had become the real social basis of the appeasement policy of leading bourgeois elements in the Western nations. Nonetheless, the analysis provided an ostensibly anticapitalist rationale for the war, for it suggested the war could not be considered, as it was by its left-wing opponents, a second installment of the great imperialist war of 1914–18: on the contrary, the defense of democracy against fascism required a decisive break with the capitalists' policy of ultra-imperialism.

Bell applied Kautsky's theory in this manner despite the fact that pro-Hitler sentiment in "respectable" Western circles was perhaps strongest, precisely among the financial establishment of Great Britain. On the other hand, Bell found grounds to support Kautsky's prediction of power passing from the hands of the financiers—to industrial corporations themselves. This undercut Veblen's emphasis on the role of absentee bank capital in restrictionism, but that was precisely the point. Bell suspected that a new order was emerging where economic consolidation was converted from a means of restrictionist international organization to a base of aggressive, expansionist national power. Bell found grounds to suggest that the transformation that had taken place in Germany, from ultra-imperialism to a new aggressive imperialism, might be occurring in the United States. Of course, that conclusion undercut the progressive rationale he had built for supporting the war. In fact Bell's investigation of the patent system led him, like the left-wing socialists of the 1930s, to warn that war might bring fascism home. In the September 1941 issue of *Common Sense*, he wrote,

> Whether we get in or stay out, the war gives cartelization a terrific impetus. And it will continue after the war. We are faced with the creation of a tremendous industrial bureaucracy—men who parcel sales territory, allocate raw materials, administer the contracts—a huge supernumerary government such as the one which grew in the Second Reich and which abetted the rise of Hitler. If we do not bend the monopolies to the government will—with government intervention and democratic controls—then we may have secured only an illusory "military" victory. The ground-swell of "business as usual," pushing on and creating an undertow to pull us off our feet, will leave us with the very system we fought to destroy.[16]

Evolutionary theory was revealing all its weaknesses as Bell tried to assess the trends of his time. Under analysis cartelization proved to be an ambiguous phenomenon. On the one hand, it tended toward the more or less passive stabilization of international business, but on the other hand, it operated within national bounds to fuel the centralization of massive monopoly power. Bell had relied heavily on two books by Guenter Reimann, a German exile and former Communist—*The Myth of the Total State* (1941) and *Patents for Hitler* (1942)—and he borrowed from Reimann the notion of the 'national monopoly,' a new social entity constituted by the direct fusion of cartels with state interests. In fact, Bell recognized 'national monopoly' as a possible outcome of economic development in the United States.

In 1941 *The New Leader* reported that the Temporary National Economic Commission, established by Roosevelt in 1938 to placate the left flank of his coalition after the second slump of the Depression decade, had discovered "the passing of economic power from the Wall Street interests, who in turn had supplanted the early entrepreneurial industrialists." In fact, Bell often noted, the trend of recent years had been toward self-sufficient industrial corporations, like General Motors, that financed expansion out of their own reserves. In late 1942, Bell put the spotlight on a massive billion-dollar loan General Motors Corporation garnered from a combination of four hundred commercial banks to finance a prodigious production effort to meet war orders worth four billion dollars: the significant aspect, he suggested, was not the return to bank resources but the fact that the loan was arranged by the government and undergirded by government guarantees. Bell implied that the finance sector remained the subordinate element in an incipient link of the state and industrial monopoly. By early 1943 it appeared, Bell wrote, that "all available investment funds are being funnelled into government financing efforts which may go over one hundred billion dollars this year, devoted in many cases to government plants that would likely be sold to the dominant monopolies in each branch of industry after the war." Furthermore, given the decline of Britain, the devastation of Europe, and the emergence of the United States as the strongest power after the war, Bell foresaw "the active alliance of capital and government in a new international world." The specter of "national monopoly" loomed.[17]

The notion of "national monopoly" did not originate with Reimann; it had figured prominently in early twentieth-century analysis by Austro-Marxist theorists—including Rudolf Hilferding, Otto Bauer, and Karl Renner—of a tendency toward "organized capitalism." Observing the German government's control of production during the First World War, Renner had claimed that the economy was gradually consolidating into a "single national capital" fused with the state, establishing a full-fledged "state economy." Renner and the other Austro-Marxists continued to consider this development transitional to the rational economic order of socialism. In light of fascism, however, it appeared that the trend led, conversely, to totalitarianism.[18] In his wartime journalism, therefore, Bell frequently criticized the German Social Democrats for their placid acceptance of economic centralization, their failure to perceive the danger posed by the power of the reactionary monopolies. In these years he frequently cited Hilferding's writings on "organized capitalism," but he also referred to Nikolai Bukharin, the Bolshevik who adopted the Austro-Marxist analysis but treated "state capitalism" not as a transitional route to socialism but as a brutal "New Leviathan" that revolutionaries had to oppose resolutely.[19] Undoubtedly Reimann, with his Communist past, filtered the Austro-Marxist heritage through Bukharin. If Bell's writings hinted at the profound shortcomings of evolutionary theory, and in fact joined with Bukharin in pointing at its outright reversal, Bell's prowar program at the same time relied in large part on that theory, for it was built on the premise, like that of the Austro-Marxists, that the organization of the economy for war production promised to induce movement beyond capitalism to socialism. The contradictions of Bell's position were becoming clearer. For his part, in attacking the big monopolies Bell recognized the virtue of the American Progressive tradition, the popular hostility to concentrated Big Business, and under his editorship, *The New Leader* warmly endorsed the frustrated attempts by Attorney General Thurman Arnold to enforce antitrust laws against some of the largest firms supplying the government with war materials. The trust-busting tradition, however, conflicted with the social-democratic premise of Bell's prowar program that the war-fueled trend toward economic organization was the basis of a future rational order. Indeed, it was not easy for Bell to escape the welter of contradictions embedded in evolutionary theory when it was already outmoded by the sharp stresses of the imperialist age; ultimately, even as he recognized the deep flaws in that theory, he resided within its bounds, and its contravention in practice could only appear to him like a dead end.

The Rightward Turn of the War

By the beginning of 1942, as the period of defense mobilization ended and the United States finally entered the war, Bell had begun to doubt that government policy would help to institutionalize and legitimate the progressive social and political power of organized labor. Despite the New Jersey shipyard seizure case, the government seemed reluctant to intervene in other cases on behalf of union security, and Bell concluded that Roosevelt sought merely to "freeze the labor status quo," a wholly inadequate exchange, he believed, for the no-strike concession that government and industry exacted from the unions. Later, as he reported that the Navy had given away newly discovered oil reserves to Standard Oil Company, and offered to pay inflated prices for the company's products, Bell caustically remarked that "Standard threatened nothing less than a sit down strike of capital, and the government had no means of 'freezing' Standard's commitment to Navy deliveries, as they froze wages."

The administration had taken sides, it seemed, and as Congress pushed antilabor bills for a forty-eight-hour work week and federal registration of union financial records, Bell warned against the "opening wedge for effective government control of unions, a step which in the long run means death to a free labor movement." When the administration gave the War Production Board the unchallenged authority to exempt war suppliers from antitrust action, and Congress suppressed a promised public investigation of the dirty cartel patent deals, Bell saw a monopoly rampage shaping up. He became increasingly convinced that the war government would not take the punitive measures he warned (in *Common Sense*) were necessary to subordinate monopoly to its will. He wrote on June 6, 1942, "we have taken a long step here in permitting industry to duplicate the practices of Nazi big business in the Weimar republic, actions that led to the rise of Hitler." Thus he was gradually reaching the conclusion that a war-induced social transformation tended not in the direction of social democracy but toward a new repressive order of consolidated monopoly control.[20]

The political shift in Bell's journalism was becoming clearer in the fall of 1942. At that time the political strategy of the Union for Democratic Action faltered, for the organization failed miserably in its strenuous effort to elect a contingent of New Deal Democrats to a new "Win-the-War Congress." Instead the 1942 elections saw the right wing surge ahead in Congress to harass labor and begin dismantling the last surviving New Deal relief agencies—and the only New Deal agency committed to exploring the possibilities of postwar economic control, the National Resources Planning Board. In New York that fall, Bell wrote the state platform for the American Labor Party; the UDA supported the party's independent gubernatorial candidate, Dean Alfange. Running against the traditional Democratic machine, Alfange drew minimal returns, deflating hopes that the American Labor Party could be the model of a national movement for a third-party realignment of liberals and the union movement. By March 1943, in fact, Reinhold Niebuhr, leader of the UDA, was prepared to close down the politically and financially ailing organization. During this period too, alarm grew over the antidemocratic direction of war strategy, as the Allies openly solicited the collaboration of second-rank fascist leaders in French North Africa and Italy.[21]

In the October 17 *New Leader*, Bell's friend, columnist Melvin J. Lasky, noted the outcry in the press that greeted Henry Luce's assertion that U.S. war policy need not honor Britain's worldwide imperial claims. Since the U.S. Press seemed insistent on respecting Britain's "rights," as a condition of the alliance, Lasky suggested:

> We may be witnessing an important shift in ideology and propaganda. We are moving from what only yesterday was everywhere called "a peoples war" or "a world-revolutionary war" to what almost everybody today is calling "a war of coalition." In this department's analysis it appears as a shift from left-wing to right-wing perspectives. And it is grounded in the apparent failure of liberal, labor and radical people to get a real foothold in the direction of state policy.

A week later, writing under the headings "Reading from Left to Right" and "Peoples' or Anti-Peoples' War," Bell agreed: "You can't put your finger on it and say this is it, yet for the past six months there has been the definite uneasy feeling that reactionary and conservative tides are setting in while the progressive tide is running out." Adding that war aims, still only vaguely stated, came "perilously close to a theme of Anglo-American world domination," he warned that solicitude for a variety of European authoritarians implied that "governments may be imposed on peoples in occupied Europe by the Allied victors." The first two years of war were dominated by "the theme of 'people's war' and 'democratic collectivism' . . . . a buoyant hopefulness, a confidence that the war meant the end of empire and exploitation, that a postwar world must lead to a planned, democratic society." But by late 1942, he wrote, "the flushed hopes are fading." The war for democracy, in other words, was becoming simply a war for restoration; to his mind, the right had usurped the left's war leadership.[22]

In the October 31 *New Leader*, fellow staff writer Ralph de Toledano argued for a "realist" conception of the war effort as a coalition of interested parties, while suggesting that Bell's and Lasky's socialist radicalism outweighed their prowar commitment. Two weeks later, Bell and Lasky replied in common: "To argue that 'a people's war' is less a reality than a wish is one thing. To compromise the progressive efforts in its behalf by denying its profound democratic mass impulse is playing the game of reaction." They sought to insure their prowar credentials, insisting that since "this is our greatest and perhaps last chance to create a genuinely human world civilization," it was urgent to remain "on guard against all deceptions." They restated their position:

> We meant that the dominant business interests of the status quo, both in Britain and America, were taking more of a hand in running things, that the labor movement was revealing itself to be somewhat politically discouraged and spiritless, that the mood of political and social ideas in which the ruling war administrations were moving was becoming less and less promising.[23]

C. Wright Mills and the American Behemoth

By this time, Bell had another comrade in the pages of *The New Leader*: C. Wright Mills. Bell solicited contributions from him after reading some of Mills's early essays in the *American Sociological Review*. Radicalized by the war, Mills published his early political writings in *The New Leader* during 1942 and 1943. In fact he developed his distinctive view of the order of American power in close sympathy with Bell's own emerging analysis of the coming "Monopoly State."[24]

One of Mills's earliest, and most striking, journalistic forays was his essay, "Collectivism and the Mixed-Up Economy." Bell first broached the issue in response to John Chamberlain's argument in *Common Sense* that planning per se promoted totalitarianism and that freedom was sustained only in the unregulated spaces of a loosely mixed economy. Bell dismissed Chamberlain as a "prophet of retreat" who failed to recognize that "the growth of large-scale relatively self-sufficient giant units" deprived the mass of people of economic autonomy to begin with. In his December 1942 article, Mills echoed Bell: advocates of mixed economy, Mills pointed out, forgot the reality of "dependent, collective work" in advanced industrialism, which meant modern democracy could only be reconstructed by providing new collective means "to *control* what you are dependent on."

Socialism, therefore, was the aim, while "mixed economy" tended away from, rather than toward, democracy. According to Mills, the model of mixed economy that economist Abba P. Lerner had decribed in an earlier *New Leader* article (a balance of private and public enterprise determined by the yardstick of productive efficiency) was based on an "ideal, abstract system," considered apart from "the *political* conditions and consequences" of its actual implementation: existing social relations, Mills insisted, were already bending a mixed economy to the detriment of popular freedom. In the balance of private business and government, the former already possessed the concentrated power to enforce its will. In the coming "mixed economy" Mills saw a government "subsidizing the rise and defaults of the private enterprise side" at the same time the business oligarchy "infiltrated into the bureaucratic cells of the government."

> The political condition and consequence of this would probably be a corporate-business State. Economic power may be in Washington to stay, but Washington is full of business men who aim to stay. . . .
> As government and business become increasingly interlocked, economic questions will more and more become: who is to staff the points of political decision in the governmental hierarchies and pinnacles? . . . for today "the political freedom of enterprise" means the power of Corporations over and within the State.[25]

Relying on the analysis of fascism presented in Franz Neumann's monumental study *Behemoth* (1942), Mills argued, "there are structural trends in the political economy of the United States that parallel those of Germany. . . . The unmistakable economic foundations of a corporative system are being formed in this country by monopoly capitalism." In fact, Neumann's image of National Socialism—the interlocking domination of party, ministerial, business, and military elites—laid the groundwork for Mills's conception of an American Behemoth, the Power Elite of big business, government executives, and military commanders.[26]

Bell too was influenced profoundly by Neumann's study. In his regular column, "Clippings and Comment," of August 29, 1942, Bell endorsed Neumann's depiction of "German National Socialism as economically little more than the extension of monopoly capitalism." His fascination with *Behemoth* lingered. As he anxiously awaited a draft notice on December 23 (he later received a medical deferment), Bell wrote to Lewis Corey, then editor of *Antioch Review*, to propose "an extended review of Franz Neumann's *Behemoth* with the problem of Bureaucracy and class as the locus of the discussion." Bell's review never appeared, but he had disclosed some of his ideas in a polemic against Stuart Chase published in *The New Leader* on December 5. Chase, a cantakerous Veblenian liberal, had argued that socialist politics were "dated" by the "decline of capitalism" and the rise of non-owning managers in Nazi Germany and in the war regime of the

United States. Bell brought Neumann to bear against Chase's managerialism, arguing that fascism had not eliminated the class of industrial workers unique to capitalism. Furthermore, he said, fascism had ground the middle class down to proletarian status, and had vested power not in the hands of autonomous managers but with the great bourgeois industrialists, active owners who were by no means sideline rentiers. "The year 1942," Bell wrote, "showed that within the economic sphere the German industrialists received freer power of action, while in the larger political sphere there has been a growing fusion of the Nazi party and Big Business." The subordination of market exchange to state imperatives, furthermore, did not mark the Germany economy as a new type, for this characterized any war economy, including that of Britain and the United States. The predominance of Big Business as the beneficiary of organized production marked the system *socially* as a capitalist one even if the suppression of self-acting market mechanisms meant it was *economically* noncapitalist, Bell suggested.[27]

With this clever formulation Bell in effect intervened in the debates on the nature of the Nazi order which he had witnessed at Columbia University among the radical intellectuals of the exiled Frankfurt Institute of Social Research. In the early 1940s the discussion was polarized between the theses of Neumann and Friedrich Pollock. While Pollock analyzed the order as an unprecedented kind of "state capitalism"—actually a post-capitalist statism in which an all-embracing economic plan obliterated the market and the power of the bourgeoisie per se—Neumann found that the Nazi state sustained and augmented the authority of the established capitalist barons and that competition among enterprises survived, despite all the controls on free exchange, in the cutthroat maneuvering for government orders and privileged access to supplies.[28] In effect, Bell's argument against Chase mediated between Pollock and Neumann by considering the dual face of fascism, capitalist in a social but not in an economic sense. This image became the model of Bell's "Monopoly State" and his answer to the question long debated within socialist circles: was such a thing as planned capitalism possible? In the early months of 1943, he answered this question affirmatively, as he declared that big business itself had unexpectedly embraced collectivist planning.[29]

As the tide of the war turned and an assured Allied victory seemed only a matter of time, Bell suggested, business stepped forward to fix the future in its own image. One sign of the shift was the new friendliness of business toward liberal economics. Bell noted particularly the Keynesian arguments of Harvard economist Alvin

Hansen favoring government's role as an economic balance wheel. At the end of 1942, Bell wrote, "Henry Luce's *Fortune* has entered the lists in the debate on the 'mixed economy'—or the mixed-up economy as C. Wright Mills puts it. . . . In a sense, what *Fortune* is proposing is an institutional merger of business and government. Historically, capitalism has been suspicious of 'the state.' . . . Now with increasing government controls becoming necessary under economic complexities, one section of industrial thinking proposes a merger." Throughout 1943, Bell kept a spotlight on the stirrings of the U.S. Chamber of Commerce and the National Association of Manufacturers, which began to contemplate means of controlling the economic instability that was expected to accompany the end of war. He also wrote about the corresponding proposals of British industry which favored officially sanctioned cartels that would collaborate with centralized unions to create a package of comprehensive social services. By the end of the year Bell remarked that the Commerce Department's sponsorship of the new Committee for Economic Development, a research and planning body comprising the chiefs of some of the foremost American corporations, suggested a "rising 'business collectivism' of class-conscious industry."[30]

Following Mills's argument very closely, Bell pointed out that the issues at stake in the new economic thinking were not abstract and theoretical but instead matters of the social sources of power. He summed up the problem in an essay in the March 20, 1943, issue of *The New Leader* entitled, "Planning by Whom—for What?" Here, and in other articles that year, Bell began to distinguish the dawning "Monopoly State" from fascism per se. The point, he suggested in his March 20 piece, was that business actually remained suspicious of the state—for in a liberal order, he said, the state was open to the influence of farm, labor, and small-business lobbies, and under fascism a monolithic party and volatile mass movement gave the state a threatening measure of autonomy. Therefore, progressive-minded business intended to preempt state planning for itself and keep it free of extraneous interests. The issue of "mixed economy," raised by New Deal efforts to extend government regulation, was now an illusory one, for the pressing question was no longer the relative size of private and public economic sectors but the extent of business intervention in government itself. In a *Partisan Review* piece that summer, Bell reasserted that "Politics . . . has become the new arena of struggle," though business intended to insure its own weight within the algebraic formula of the private-public mixture by insinuating itself into government: hence, " 'economics' will rule over 'politics.' "[31]

Thus Bell finally proposed his notion of the "Monopoly State," an analog of fascism with a crucial difference. In early 1944 he summed up his analysis: based on "the maturity of American industry and its new willingness to seek world domination," there emerged

> a proposed integration of industry and government, leading in the direction of a corporative economy, dominated by the huge monopolies, operating through large administrative business bureaucracies. What we have here is the industrial facade of the corporative state, without the brutal political connotations of a fascist party—which might get out of hand and dominate industry. These plans are industry's bid for the monopoly state within the structure of democratic capitalist society.[32]

With this conclusion Bell reached a crucial pass, for the specter of the Monopoly State implied the betrayal of progress: whether or not he was fully conscious of it, Bell's "Monopoly State" paradoxically signified the fulfillment and negation of the prowar social-democratic program he earlier endorsed. Economic planning had evolved naturally, as it were, but with antidemocratic effect. In the summer of 1941, it should be recalled, Bell applauded the progressive import of labor's proposal to organize whole branches of industry as single units for the sake of productive efficiency. Now, the same program seemed to speed the coming of the Monopoly State. In February, he wrote,

> The Times reported a war drive by WPB to "rationalize industry." The net result, if carried through, would be to make an entire industry function as a single manufacturer to end wasteful use of critical equipment, manpower, transportation, etc. An industrial rationalization program is an inevitable step of a war economy and a long step towards "big business collectivism."

Similarly, Bell found that the government's recognition of labor's legitimate interests (including the government's concession of "maintenance-of-membership" clauses that gave unions a limited guarantee of organizational continuity), violated his own social-democratic intentions. The displacement of labor-management conflict from free collective bargaining to arbitration by the National War Labor Board gave organized labor "a role subordinate to the state machinery." "It means the decline of the Labor union as an independent force," Bell wrote. "It turns the union into a quasi-governmental agency mediating between its membership and the government." In the emerging corporative system, "labor is considered an element whose support must be won to the program of an organized economy at home and organized trade abroad. Labor must be a stabilizing factor in the market at home and lend political support to the trade program abroad." In this context, "labor participation" in the war effort, advocated by the CIO, meant only that labor's hands were tied by co-optation.[33] All his purposes were realized in the war regime, it seemed, with meanings contrary to those he intended.

America's New Imperialism

Throughout 1943 and 1944 Bell argued that the object of business planning was a "permanent war economy" oriented toward a "far-flung American expansionism." Big business plans to take over government munitions plants gratis after the war, to suspend anti-trust laws and to allocate materials so new competitors could not enter the market, threatened to lock the economy into a monopoly vice and centrally regiment its operations. Along with a worldwide network of military bases and supply lines, huge permanent stockpiles of industrial war materials, quasi-public international aviation and communication corporations, and state-guaranteed investments in the client states of "backward areas," the monopolized order was part of a program to create what Henry Luce called the "American Century," a new imperialism under conscious, central, and official control.[34]

At the same time, Bell persistently pointed out how "power politics" dominated the arrangements for a postwar settlement. The division of the world into "spheres of influence," and the consensus among the Three Powers on containing the volatile forces of social revolution while vying for hegemonic rights over the territorial blocks of a partitioned Europe, evidently sank Bell's hopes that the abused peoples of Europe could build for themselves a democratic socialism on the basis of the integrated continental industrial apparatus the Nazis had forged.[35]

> It may be one of the paradoxes of our generation that World War I was an imperialist war, devoid of revolutionary aims, yet with revolutionary by-products, while World War II began as an ideological war with social-revolutionary pretensions and ended in the vise of a Three Powers' peace. . . . the war is being fought along the lines of *real-politik*. *Real-politik* is essentially a cynical amoralism which derides the hopes and aspirations of peoples and settles "fundamental" questions of power and antagonism in the light of historical and economic interests. Men do not willingly die in defense of economic interests, so during the early pe-

riod of the war official pronouncements are in terms of ideologies; as matters proceed favorably however the war becomes, in Mr. Churchill's words, "less and less of an ideological war."

As Bell put it elsewhere,

The ideological masks fall swiftly, once the crisis is past; when the system is on the shoals, capitalism sits penitent in the sinners' pew. So in 1940 it was "people's war," "the end of imperialism," "social revolution," etc. But today, the crisis is past and the men who run the world have slipped back to play with their Pandora boxes. . . . The war that the trade unionists and the common people of Europe are fighting is *not* the war that men who *run* the war are directing.[36]

Although Bell suggested here that the war had dropped its mask, showing its true face, he did not actually concede to the propositions of the antiwar left—that, from the start, the war was an inter-imperialist conflict and that the existing war governments were by nature unable to satisfy the interests of the working class.[37] Rather, in some way capital had usurped labor's war. Although opposed to the war's consequences, Bell appeared to evade a reassessment of the social-democratic intentions that led him to support the war in the first place. Upholding the validity of his original prowar program, he was prepared to accept the "paradox" of events. At the moment, the war's ironic inversion merely put new political choices on the agenda:

The implications of the Three Power Peace have not, I feel, been fully realized by those labor and liberal forces which split on the issue of the war. This writer was "pro-war," a position which I feel was correct. The inner dynamic of Nazism inevitably precipitated war. To adopt a passive or isolationist position would only have given Hitler a chance to consolidate Europe his way. *But the outcome of a war differs from its purpose. And that is why the war issue is no longer valid or meaningful in political analysis.* A realignment must take place on the real issue of the day: whether we will have an imperialist redivision of the world or a unified world system without exploitation of any peoples.[38]

Liberal disenchantment with the coming settlement of the war—the shocked recognition that democratic ideals did not govern foreign affairs—was not at all uncommon in 1944. In his final State of the Union address, Roosevelt himself apologized for the evident priority of "power politics."[39] After Roosevelt's death, liberals tried to preserve their image of a humanitarian Roosevelt—to blame the outcome of the war on Truman's short-sightedness, incompetence, and political cynicism—but Bell had already distinguished himself from this naive current.[40] In June 1944, Bell mocked Archibald MacLeish, "a weather-vane of the liberals," who "warned in pathetic angriness . . . that the peace we are making 'is a peace of gold, a peace of oil.'" Bell countered, "The pattern of organization here is no accident but deliberately created to become the bone structure of Three Power domination." Noting that "power politics" were merely a symptom of "the system of imperialist relations," and that Roosevelt's war policies were "writing a blank check for the next world war," Bell endorsed Norman Thomas for president in 1944. This step put him at odds with his own paper, *The New Leader*, which editorialized in favor of Roosevelt's reelection. Bell urged the Socialist Party not to identify him as *New Leader* managing editor if it chose to publish his declaration of support for Thomas. In the pages of *The New Leader* Bell's dissension manifested itself in part in columns appearing under one of his pen names, Murray Everett, where the coming electoral battle between Roosevelt and the Republican right was assessed: "The anxious liberals who think they play the realistic game of politics, tell us that if you don't work for one side, obviously the other will win, so join with the one who is more liberal. The only trouble with that theory is that the Big Boys thought of it a long time ago and play both sides."[41]

Indeed, Bell's analysis of the war-induced social transformation differed as well from the paper's editorial line, which stuck closely to the social-democratic progressivism it had begun with, asserting that the economic organization the war spawned promised rational progress. When it held a symposium entitled "Is American Going Fascist?" the paper, answering negatively, editorialized:

> We have the vast productive system of this war, which is an example of planning. No matter how much fulmination there has been against our present bureaucracy, the entire structure has been built in accordance with the popular will and is under the control of elected officials. It has about it not a single one of the characteristic marks of fascism. A similar concentration of power for peace-time purposes could give us an age of abundance.[42]

Indeed, *The New Leader* had also come to the conclusion that "the differences between this war and the last are constantly being whittled down," but it defined the similarity differently than Bell did: just as Wilson had gone to Versailles and "discovered a mare's nest of secret agreements," so in 1944, "though our part in the war is so immensely greater than it was last time," an editorial stated, "we are mere onlookers." In its view, Roosevelt appeared an innocent party abused by the schemers, Churchill and Stalin, who agreed to a territorial accommodation at Teheran before Roosevelt arrived. In an article entitled, "Will U.S. Join the Imperialist Grab?" *New Leader* Washington correspondent Jonathan Stout regretted Roosevelt's public disavowal of the democratic war aims announced in the Atlantic Charter of 1941. The President decided, Stout said, "to embark frankly on a course of American imperialism to match that of Russian imperialism and British imperialism," and, Stout concluded, "If I were Mr. Roosevelt, I don't know what else there would remain for me to do."[43]

Thus when Bell resigned from *The New Leader* in December 1944, his farewell note testified to some significant political differences. Bell was about to take a more lucrative post as managing editor of *Common Sense*, at a time when his wife's pregnancy made a larger income urgent. In large part, then, the move was purely personal, a career choice rather than a political split. But Bell's published statement on his departure was subtly caustic by implying that *New Leader* editorial solicitude for government apology violated the integrity of socialist anti-imperialism. He wrote,

> One cannot have worked more than four years at an absorbing job, giving it a large measure of intellectual and emotional identification, and leave without a sense of loyalty and some possible misgivings.
>
> For me the strength and promise of *The New Leader*, at its best, was not only that it was a free forum of left opinion, but that it withstood, to a great degree, the pressures towards orthodoxy which has given most magazines an *official* coloration. The purposeful effort to maintain a critical voice—not only on Stalinism but on *all* imperialism—is the Socialist task today.
>
> I shall continue to contribute to the paper so long as *The New Leader* adheres to that critical spirit and independence of "party lines" and "official apologies" which gives it its deserved reputation.[44]

The Marginalized Radical

Bell's caustic reference to "official apologies"—he would use similar language the following year in an article that condemned the "growing official quality of American life"—echoed the characteristic concerns of New York's modernist intellectuals. At the start of the war,

Partisan Review editor Dwight Macdonald had attacked the liberal advocates of intellectual mobilization, Van Wyck Brooks and Archibald MacLeish, for advancing "that *official* approach to culture" which would impose on art duties dictated by the state.[45] In this view, war mobilization augured a society in which all activities were coordinated by central command, with no space for intellectual autonomy. Thus in the late war years Bell wrote more often of a coming "era of integration" that denied not only the prospects of radical practice but even the possibility of maintaining critical thought.

The image of an "official" order, which, cut in the totalitarian mold, extruded independent thought, would become the dominant theme of the social theory associated with the Frankfurt Institute of Social Research. Exiled in the United States, the leading theorists of the Institute began to develop this image of social reality during the war years, by building on Friedrich Pollock's interpretation of "state capitalism" as an order of planned production which suffered no disabling contradictions. In *Dialectic of Enlightenment* (1944) by Max Horkheimer and Theodor Adorno, and especially in Horkheimer's *Eclipse of Reason* (1947), the theory came to the fore, portraying contemporary society as a faultless functional organism built on systematic economic behavior, an order secured from disruption by conformism and freed from critical challenge by the absorption of thought within the apparatus of production. This order, a kind of repressive corporatism which rendered obsolete the old criticism of social anarchy and privatism, permitted no role for the individual, except as a participant in the whole productive machine, "a mere cell of functional response," or for thought, except as a guide to efficient operation. "In order to prove its right to be conceived," Horkheimer wrote, "each thought must have an alibi, must present a record of its expediency . . . must be gauged . . . by its effect on production or its impact on social conduct." Since reason was, as they said, "wholly functionalized," Horkheimer and Adorno claimed that "the rulers themselves disavow thought as mere ideology."[46]

Their response to this hermetic, solidary social order was an attempt to reclaim those "loopholes" and "cleavages" that Horkheimer said characterized the "liberalist" era of classic capitalism—particularly the moral autonomy of the private individual—and to emphasize in theory, as the Frankfurt School's historian Martin Jay has pointed out, all the sources of nonidentity and difference that would resist or fracture the seamlessness of a "false totalism." Thus the dualism of self and society, of subject and object, of will and knowledge, action and contemplation, practice and theory, became a part of radical theory as hedges against the harmonizing pressures of society.[47]

In this view, the role of the radical was hardly that of a maker of history—for the motivations of change were quashed under the well-honed efficiency of economic operations, and social liberation, as Horkheimer said, required not "the acceleration of progress [but] jumping out of progress." Instead the role of the radical was that of a marginal critic holding out against the threat of absorption within mass society.[48]

Increasingly, Daniel Bell's writing moved in these currents of thought. If the Frankfurt School nursed its sense of marginalization under the conditions of exile, conscious of barriers of language and culture, Bell's sense of marginalization in the late war years was more directly political, shared with the anti-Stalinist left as a whole, frustrated by the wartime power wielded by the Popular Front of liberals and Communists which blithely trumpeted the virtues of Soviet democracy and predicted international collaboration and social peace in an organized postwar world. Against this power, the anti-Stalinist radicals retained a certain unity, ranging from the antiwar Trotskyists on the far left to the prowar social democrats on the right, coming together for particular campaigns, like the protest against *Mission to Moscow*, a 1943 Popular Front film which for the sake of solidary feeling put a Hollywood gloss on Stalin's purge trials. *The New Leader* placed the protest manifesto prominently in its pages, and Bell participated in two meetings called to plan the anti-Stalinist counteroffensive in April 1943, with Dwight Macdonald, Sidney Hook, Meyer Schapiro, James Farrell, Mary McCarthy, Albert Goldman, George Novack, and Melvin Lasky.[49]

The new American modernist movements throve also under these conditions of marginalization, as art historian Serge Guilbaut has shown. The forerunners of abstract expressionism, loosely allied with the anti-Stalinist left, came together for the 1943 American Modern Artists show with a manifesto condemning the national mobilization of art signaled by the huge "Artists for Victory" exhibit at New York's Metropolitan Museum. The Modern Artists' affirmation of esthetic autonomy and the critical function of pure form drew scorn from advocates of social responsibility: one opponent wrote in response to their show, "Such windmill jousting, morbid individualism, heroic gestures belong to remote romantic ages and not to our own. . . . Very certainly, with victory, artists will have to keep pace in every sense with world progress."[50]

It was this very set of oppositions that motivated Daniel Bell when he wrote a heated response to the prowar effusions of *The New Republic*. The magazine's editor, Bruce Bliven, had included *The New Leader* in the circle of "hang-back boys"—those "spiritual saboteurs" of the war effort, Bliven said, who preferred niggling criticism to action and who "deliberately cut themselves off from the two great centers of dynamic energy in the world today," Russia and the Roosevelt regime. Bell rejoined, "I'd rather not be a hangnail on the moving finger of 'dynamic energy' history." He added:

> At a time when the critical spirit and function have degenerated into official apologies, when bureaucratic regimes and monopolistic controls have closed the major channels of free thought Bliven says surcease to "complaining" and criticizing. Surely this is a prime example of the impotence of the modern critical spirit.[51]

A few months later Bell found the same dismal trend implicit in Harold Laski's glorification of the Soviet Union as a source of a new "unifying faith." In an essay published in Dwight Macdonald's new *Politics* magazine, "The World of Moloch," Bell wrote, "We seem to be approaching the 'era of integration,' an age where large economic and political units are massed power blocs, and culture is pulverized into *faith* to serve as a unifying concept and spiritual dress." Soviet Russia, in particular, he said, had obliterated "the dividing line which modern society strove to maintain between religious and social facts," that is, it reversed the Enlightenment's rational disenchantment of the world— as Weber put it—and resurrected myth to enforce social cohesion. As was typical of radicals recoiling from totalitarian holism, Bell was eager to reaffirm dualist cleavages, in this case the dualism of scientific rationalism (which would separate fact from myth) and moral value (which would protect principle from corruption in practice). Scorning the "desperate hunger to believe" of those, like Laski, eager to "submerge themselves in 'heroic action,'" Bell echoed Julien Benda's critique of "divinized realism," which mobilized mass action while violating the division of material and spiritual phenomena. Benda's authentic "clerk," who assumed the office of preserving moral ideas apart from material reality, was not an inapplicable model for Bell's notion of a critic on the margins of society.[52]

Bell's sense of marginality undoubtedly grew too from the war's rupture of progressive faith, the reversal of the direction of progress Bell had forecast at the beginning of the war, and from the new sense of paradox by which social action turned political intentions into consequences with opposite meanings. As he found war to be an engine of capitalist rather than socialist development, Bell empathized with Arthur Koestler's dejected essay of February 1943, "Knights in Rusty Armor." Koestler wrote:

> The nearer victory comes in sight, the clearer the character of the war reveals itself as what the Tories always said it was—a war for national survival, a war in defense of certain conservative nineteenth-century ideals, and not what I and my friends of the Left said that it was—a revolutionary civil war in Europe on the Spanish pattern. . . . Let us be frank: while we rejoice over the victory of our arms, let us recognize the defeat of our aims.[53]

Bell warmed to Koestler's mood: it aptly tapped the "psychological malaise of individuals," Bell said, the "torments and doubts . . . experiences and disillusionments" of left-wing intellectuals, "in a world where daily we inch our way through little compromise[s], fearful that these may, in the end, betray the things we claim to stand for."[54] Koestler hoped, at the least, for an "interregnum" of peace, when socialists could regroup and renew their struggle, but in light of the war's frustration, he conceded:

> We have maneuvered ourselves into a political vacuum—a vanguard cut off from its sources of supply. . . . And there we stand in no-man's land, dazzled knights in rusty armor, with a well-thumbed handbook of Marx-Engels quotations as our sole guide—the truest and profoundest social guide of the last century, but, alas! of modest use on this topsy-turvy battleground of today.

Consciousness of residing in a "political vacuum" marked Bell's mood as he started writing for Dwight Macdonald's *Politics* magazine at its inception in 1944. In fact, Bell anticipated the pessimist estrangement from modern industrial monolithism that a few years later would sour Macdonald's conviction in the viability of a politics rooted in Marxism. At the inauguration of his journal, Macdonald judged that "the forties promise to be a more turbulent decade than even the thirties," but Bell's radical critique of labor and left-liberal politics already hinted that the consolidation of ruling power would effectively block disruptive departures toward a new society.

In "The Coming Tragedy of American Labor" (March 1944), Bell argued that "the war has given labor great numerical strength, yet sapped it of its real strength," for labor linked itself to the administration without recognizing that the "dialectics of war" had turned the administration against it. The statist trend in social development required that the unions enter the political arena in an independent Labor Party to advance their own interests, but since the unions were officially pledged to Roosevelt, solicitous of "free enterprise," and tied ever more tightly to the tail of the imperialist tiger, it seemed unlikely they would take that step.

A year later, Bell published "The Political Lag of Commonwealth" (May 1945), a severe criticism of the Michigan Commonwealth Federation, which even Macdonald endorsed as the harbinger of independent labor political action. Bell charged the Federation with ignoring international politics at a time when all social issues were "linked to the drag anchor of foreign policy." The Federation, he argued, could not challenge Roosevelt's labor policies without grappling with the "permanent war economy" as a whole.

> The choice then is either to go along with the whole of Roosevelt's policies—an acceptance of the Big Power world and an imperialist role, with its ever constant provocation for war—or a political decision that rejects it completely and works out the only meaningful alternative, a program of democratic and internationalist Socialism.

If it failed to go beyond a meager program of Keynesian "mixed economy," the Commonwealth movement would be left behind with the old protest movements of the nineteenth century, "chipping at the scaffolding of capitalism while the towers of corporate America rose, untouched, from within." Indeed, American labor leaders were required "to stultify protest rather than direct it" because of their dependence on the administration. Thus the "conservative mold" of the whole social order hardened: that mold "strengthens further the growing 'official' quality of American life, the increasing bureaucratization of controls and the making of decisions on the top, with no opportunities for those below to challenge or alter those decisions." Thus if socialism assumed new urgency in Bell's writing—for now he declared socialism itself to be his goal, rather than the euphemism of "economic democracy" he had adopted in 1940 under the politics of war progressivism—he seemed to doubt whether in practice it stood on the agenda at all.[55] In a sense, the war radicalized him, but also turned him back upon himself, unconvinced that the levers of social change were available to him.

The Theory of the Monopoly State

Bell's theory of the Monopoly State emerged only in fragments, a string of occasional articles published throughout 1943 and 1944. In the spring of 1944, he began writing a book on the subject, having obtained a contract with the John Day company, in part through the intercession of his friend and polemical opponent, *New York Times* book reviewer John Chamberlain.[56] Bell never completed the book, and his only refined, synthetic discussion of the doctrine appeared in an essay he published in the July 1944 issue of *Socialist Review*, the theoretical supplement to the Socialist Party's newspaper, *The Call*.[57]

In the article, entitled "The Monopoly State: A Note on Hilferding and the Theory of Statism," Bell challenged certain current theses:

> (1) That we are entering a new stage in society where top-down centralized state planning and state control is the basic feature, [and] (2) that statism is anti-capitalist, giving rise to new class forms independent of the old social structure, ie. the relation of worker to capitalist deriving from the means of production.

Bell insisted that "statism is not a *social form*, but a *technique*." As a tool, its real significance was determined by who wielded it; that is, as the state intervened in the economy, the issue was "who interferes on whose behalf." Bell recalled Rudolf Hilferding's depiction in *Das Finanzkapital* (1910) of the "general cartel" that emerged along with "organized capitalism." He argued that the rationalization and bureaucratization of large-scale production, combined with the ultra-imperialist stabilization of the world market in the interwar years, confirmed Hilferding's suggestions "that capitalism was moving toward some form of a planned state." Yet, Bell believed, Hilferding's later discussions of a "totalitarian state economy" (which superseded rather than consolidated capitalism) unaccountably reversed the valid formulations of *Das Finanzkapital*. Bell accused Hilferding of the same fault he and Mills laid to advocates of mixed economy: working abstractly with "formal economic criteria," instead of understanding the context of social and political power. Hilferding could argue that "totalitarian state economy" was not capitalist only because he relied, Bell said, on "classical Marxist conceptions of capitalism"—the "law of value" working automatically in a free market—rather than "on any sociological analysis of who holds power and for whom."

Classical notions could not be used to define capitalism in any case, Bell indicated, because "under modern monopoly capitalism, the 'market economy,' like 'free competition,' is largely a myth. The growth of monopoly has meant abridgement of the market system." While Bell had, by this time, conceded "the anticapitalist nature of Russia and Germany," this stemmed he said not from the suspension of market mechanisms but from shunting aside the bourgeoisie from positions of social and political dominance. In the United States, however, the war had consecrated the state's "marriage with dominant capitalist groups" and confirmed the trend Hilferding had earlier recognized: "the non-market economy operating under the capitalist system." The coming Monopoly State realized the

> inherent drive of capitalism to organize the total market, to use the state apparatus directly to guarantee . . . profits and back up industrial groups in imperialist adventure. This is not merely an extension of the old processes in capitalist society but a direct partnership with the state.

Bell continued:

> as a general perspective, the rise of statism here poses more clearly the issue of the future: An organized capitalist society over-expanding its capital goods in the drive for markets and war or a democratic socialist society which will use our huge industrial capacity to create a consumption economy of plenty.

This issue, however, was becoming increasingly abstract to Bell, for the Monopoly State served the same function in his thinking that the notion of totalitarianism did in the general crisis of liberal evolutionism: a recognition of the failure of evolutionary thought without leaving its bounds, so that the frustration of progress appeared to halt any dynamic of change whatsoever. If the opposition between capitalism and socialism seemed to Bell more acute, the possibility of achieving socialism increasingly seemed less real to him.

Hilferding, it should be recalled, had argued that a "planned capitalism" was possible, but only as a transition to socialism. In 1927, as the leading economic theorist of the German Social Democratic Party, he had summed up the diagnosis:

> Organized capitalism means replacing free competition by the social principle of planned production. The task of the present Social Democratic generation is to invoke state aid in translating this economy, organized and directed by the capitalists, into an economy directed by the democratic state.[58]

The lynchpin of the program was a liberal theory of the autonomy of the state, which would overcome capitalist interests and democratize planned production. Implicitly this doctrine underlay *The New Leader*'s prowar progressivism, the view that only the intervention of the democratic state—under the urging of organized labor—was needed to realize the inherent socialist content of war-fueled economic consolidation. Bell found, however, that the effect of the war was the exact opposite: rather than the state conquering capitalism, capitalism conquered the state. The Monopoly State, theoretically leaving all the tenets of orthodox evolutionism intact, appeared as the simple inversion (or abstract negation) of the progressive transformation social democracy had expected. Practically, the result was a dead end, no less for Bell than for Hilferding in his view of "totalitarian state economy." To Hilferding that outcome signified nothing less than the seizure of the state by the general cartel before labor could use the state to subdue it. For Bell, too, leaving the social-democratic intention unquestioned as consequences belied it, capital's preemptive strike seemed to close the progressive avenue toward socialism—labor's majority representation in the democratic state. At this historic roadblock, Bell's theoretical assessment of the social consequences of war came to a close.

Overall, Bell's wartime writings had a certain empirical warrant. Subsequent historiography has confirmed that industrial corporations—notably in auto, steel, and aluminum—were slow to join the mobilization campaign.[59] Once war production began in earnest, the greatest beneficiaries of government contracts were the largest corporations: more than half the funding for military production between 1940 and 1944 went to a mere 33 corporations, and the 250 largest companies in the country operated almost 80 percent of federally built war plants.[60] Furthermore Roosevelt gave official roles to the business elite in organizing the militarized economy.[61] Indeed, the liberal historian John Morton Blum considers this record a mark of Roosevelt's "pragmatism": to mobilize the country's productive resources the regime relied on the people most practiced in managing them, was willing to concede the incentives—in contract administration and tax policy—that would enlist their support, and was unprepared to spur any political and social conflicts that might disable the effort. The effect, Blum's account concedes, was to further enrich and empower the already rich and powerful.[62] Granted all this, whether their exposure to the instrumentalities of government administration won businessmen over to economic planning or collectivism and prepared them to seek class-conscious unity in a strategy of political domination—the essence of Bell's "Monopoly State"—is quite another question. Even more, it must be asked, did the war transform the social order of American capitalism, by creating a new structure of organized economy founded on the immediate alliance of business and government? While Bell's journalism accurately assessed the personnel and political drift of the war administration, did his writing offer an adequate theory of social transformation? The answer is no.

Certainly, conspiracy in constraint of trade is as old in the United States as the rate differentials imposed on Southern industry after the Civil War, and Adam Smith knew of it long before that, making it virtually the original sin of capitalism. "People of the same trade seldom meet together, even for merriment and diversion," Smith wrote, "but the conversation ends in a conspiracy against the public, or in some contrivance to raise prices."[63] Still, American capitalists have not been known for their foresight or ability to unite in conscious, effective action. Price consensus was achieved in some of the major industries—Judge Gary's turn-of-the-century dinner meetings of steel chieftains stand as further evidence for Smith's suspicion—but cartelization properly speaking, explicit parceling of territory and output quotas, did not proceed very far. The National Industrial Recovery Act (NIRA) of 1933 moved clearly in that direction and called for the self-regulation of business under official auspices, with government sanctions at its disposal—which meets Bell's definition of monopoly planning within the state. The only problem with citing the NIRA as an instance of corporate collectivism, or capital's self-interested solicitude for government intervention as means of assuring profits, is—as Theda Skocpol has remarked in her pointed review of corporate liberal theories—that it *failed* and was abandoned.[64]

Of course, in contrast to the NIRA, business-government collaboration *worked* for prosperity and healthy profits during the Second World War—and yet the collaboration gave out quickly. Advocates of a corporate liberal interpretation of the war—essentially Bell's "Monopoly State" is such a theory—point to the reconversion controversy of 1944 as key evidence.[65] Here big business representatives on the War Production Board vetoed an early shift toward consumer-goods production even as war orders started to fall off, in part out of fear that the large corporations still absorbed in military production would lose market standing to smaller, aggressive companies. According to C. Wright Mills, this episode "most dramatically" revealed "the merger of the corporate economy and military bureaucracy" which created the power elite of the postwar order.[66] Nonetheless, a year after the War Production Board reconversion veto, all of business urged the rapid dismantling of wartime economic regulation.[67] The Board went out of business quickly. The Controlled Materials Plan, which Bell repeatedly cited as a key element of the Monopoly State's postwar program—the centralized allocation of means of production—was dropped immediately after victory. The clamor for a return to laissez-faire competition infected big and small business alike.

Certainly the war strengthened the capitalist class—made it strong enough, in fact, to dare going it alone, independent of official state management. The agency that represented the furthest advance of planning ideology in the New Deal, the National Resources Planning Board, had already fallen before the ax wielded by the right wing in Congress. At the same time, there is reason to doubt how faithfully that wartime vanguard of probusiness Keynesianism, the Committee for Economic Development, reflected general big business sentiment. The Committee has been treated, even after Bell, as evidence for a corporate liberal disposition among American business, but its special locus must be recognized. The Committee developed from cooperation between a few, atypical business intellectuals with academic backgrounds and representatives of advertising, journalism, and merchandising—hardly a delegation from the great industrial monopolies.[68]

This is not to suggest that business was prepared to return to economic action free of state entanglements. Part of the problem of the Monopoly State theory, in fact, was its presupposition that state and economy had hitherto been independent of each other. Actually, the state was never as *un*involved in capital accumulation, nor capital so unwilling to mobilize state resources on its own behalf, as corporate liberal theories presume was the case before the dawn of the new order. Marx's review of political measures in the era of "primitive accumulation" of capital—antivagabond laws and colonial plunder—testifies to that. In the nineteenth-century United States, land grants to the transcontinental railroads show the state acting to support the primary technical-economic impulse to a long wave of economic growth. Clearly, too, wars certainly boost the degree and extent of business-government collaboration: in this sense, all major wars in U.S. history have unleashed "state capitalist" tendencies, from the banking regulation of the Civil War to the War Industries Board in the First World War, which put aside antitrust enforcement and sanctioned market controls supervised by the large corporations.[69] Business-government collaboration, however, which properly speaking has been enhanced rather than invented by war regimes, does not lead to the *fusion* of capital and the state—a model which is simply the dialectical opposite of the classic liberal idea of some original disjuncture between economy and an autonomous state. The relation between capital and the state is much more mediated than either of these polar alternatives—disjuncture or fusion—allow.

Aside from the question of business-government relations, it cannot even be said that the war induced an objective process of increased consolidation in the American economy. Contrary to the impression of mounting monopoly power given by Bell's theory and other corporate liberal estimations of the war, there is evidence that the degree of the centralization of capital in the United States actually *declined* somewhat during the Second World War. Although the number of corporate mergers increased slightly during the war years, the percentage of total assets held by the 100 largest firms sank from 41.9 percent in 1939 to 37.5 percent in 1947. The reduction was not quite as steep if the top 200 firms are considered, holding 48.7 percent of total assets in 1939 and 45.0 percent eight years later.[70]

The point is not that the Second World War initiated no unique social change—only that the transformation cannot be understood either as an expression of the conscious, collective agency of a self-interested capitalist class or as the emergence of a cohesive, coherent order of regulative control.[71] The analysis of social change should not be based, first of all, on the terrain of a presumably self-contained national economy. The real context of social change in the United States is international, and the overwhelmingly significant social outcome of the Second World War was the extension of the sway of U.S. imperialism: the destruction of all significant rivals in productive power (Germany and Japan) and the elevation of the United States to the role of managing world trade and monetary resources, as the international balance wheel whose absence accounted for the world economic crisis of the 1930s. The consequences of this were manifold, though perhaps not immediately evident: one was the indefinite maintenance of a quasi-war regime to defend the new world stature of U.S. power. Liberal theory conventionally sees the economic stability of postwar America as an achievement of social reason—the recognition, albeit spurred by the forced march of war mobilization, that the state could act to modify the market and smooth the swings of the business cycle. This theory, however, turns things on their head. The new degree of state economic intervention was not a rational discovery fostered by war or the *cause* of economic stability; rather long-term economic stability and growth arose from the preeminence of U.S. imperial power, and business-government collaboration followed as the consequence and concomitant of the perpetual war-footing of U.S. regimes. If that's the case, business-government collaboration, which must be considered an exigency of new world power, cannot be seen as a conscious survival strategy originated by big business itself to balance the economy for the sake of monopoly profits.

Furthermore, it is also clear that the war *initiated*, but did not complete, the transformation of American society. The war, on the domestic plane, did not create a solidary social order. Paradoxically, at the time, Bell and most radical critics perceived the outcome of the war as a new, repressive organicism, while the war in fact spurred conflict and ended with increased social polarization in the United States. The capitalist class was strengthened—economically and politically—not only by the burgeoning profits of war production but also by its sway over a government that required "business confidence" in order to extend prosperity into peacetime.[72] In a sense, the working class was strengthened, by the disappearance of unemployment, the dead weight of the reserve army of labor. At the end of war, both classes were emboldened to struggle, and industrial strife, measured in number of strikes, workers involved, and days lost, reached new heights. Labor fought to insure full employment and to limit certain managerial prerogatives; employers sought state measures to limit labor power.

The struggle was not to be resolved for another two or three years. Yet, while the war did not found a cohesive order, it did create an *ideology* of national unity, the will to submerge conflicting interests in a common language and purpose. Nowhere was this will more clear or effective than in the wartime no-strike pledge and the dynamic the war unleashed toward the closer and closer identification of trade union organization with the state as the guarantor of its security.[73] On this point Bell was not mistaken. As a result, however, while theorists of repressive organicism, like Bell, mistook the ideology of the solidary nation for fact—and while disruptive social conflict continued in actuality—labor was in practice deprived of independent leadership. This did not yet defeat, but it did hobble, labor resistance. The completion of the social transformation the war initiated awaited the political incorporation of labor a few years later, concurrent with the full revelation, at the outset of the Cold War, of the military requirements of U.S. international power.

The transformation, as we shall see, was more protracted and mediated than Daniel Bell imagined in his theory of the Monopoly State. It is often said that revolutionaries, from Marx to Trotsky, were vocationally disposed to optimism in their "foreshortened" view of the pace of class conflict and historical change; at the end of the war, Daniel Bell manifested, on the other hand, a foreshortened pessimism.

3
Towards a Critical Sociology
The Homeless Radical in the Mass Society

In Daniel Bell's intellectual trajectory, the experience of war had one decisive effect: as he perceived the Monopoly State growing from the war regime, he recognized the harsh contravention of progress and concluded that the immanent development of society, rather than realizing his political aspirations, forced them outside the fold. Then, as he assumed the role of a marginalized critic, a modernist dialectic of estrangement and reconciliation took shape in his thought, working its way out in two successive periods of Bell's intellectual biography— one period lived self-consciously at a distance, in critical alienation from a society perceived to be wholly antipathetic, followed by an accommodation with that order of society which had hitherto seemed so intractable to his wishes. The first period concerns us here: the three years after the war which Bell spent at the University of Chicago, as an instructor in the College social science program. The College was his "cloister," he once remarked. In the summer of 1948, he emerged from it, returning to New York to become labor editor for *Fortune* magazine.[1]

Until 1948 the social transformation begun by the war—toward the political consolidation of an aggressive international capitalism supported by the high-wage sector of labor—remained unfinished. Given the U.S. military victory and the government's ideological management of national unity during the war, the forces tending toward this conclusion were both clear and powerful in 1945. The social concordat underpinning the worldwide extension of U.S. political and economic power was yet incomplete, however, as an aroused mass movement of labor held open the potential for creating a new, independent political force, a social-democratic movement in the United States that might have provided a vehicle for anticapitalist sentiment.

It was only the evaporation of this potential which brought on the final collapse of the intellectual left by 1948 and the entry of radicals like Daniel Bell into the mainstream—the end of a political generation, which led Michael Harrington, a few decades later, to see 1948 as "the last year of the thirties." The interim—the years between the end of the Second World War and the beginning of the Cold War—constitutes a peculiar historical interlude, in which the continued combativity of the working class paradoxically provided a space of two years or more allowing the intellectuals to elaborate their radical critique of monolithic social order. This was the historical "moment" of that "new radicalism" which found expression in Dwight Macdonald's *Politics* magazine, whose lifespan, 1944–49, lapped over the boundaries of the postwar interregnum.[2] When the political independence of labor disappeared, however, the conditions of intellectual estrangement lapsed. Only then, when the intellectuals themselves acceded to reconciliation, did their earlier, estranged image of faultless social cohesion approach actuality.

A sketch of the political terrain during the postwar hiatus indicates the real conditions of intellectual activity. The social effects of the war, in fact, were more profoundly ambiguous than radical critics of the war regime—newly convinced of the solidary strength of American capitalism—imagined. Under the ideology of national unity, some business and labor leaders had attempted to decree a postwar era of industrial peace;[3] actually, however, the war had polarized the classes, and the combination of strengths and weaknesses each side accrued from the war experience was, inevitably, an inducement to struggle.

Business was buoyed by profits, while its legitimacy was enhanced by the high visibility of corporate leaders as directors of war production. In contrast, however, business also was weakened by wartime labor regulation that made all of industrial procedure—including the fundamental management prerogatives of work discipline, hiring, and firing—a matter of *public affairs*.[4] The fact that work disputes were routinely handled by public administration suggested to workers that resistance to arbitrary workplace authority had attained some social legitimacy. In response, when the war ended, business made it a priority to reprivatize the administration of labor and property by removing the sanction that wartime government tacitly conferred on the actions of workers.

Thus, in the spring of 1945, the National Association of Manufacturers (NAM) indicated it would seek laws against strikes which were aimed at forcing decisions by government arbitrators.[5] This anti-union impulse did not come solely from hardbitten, backward-looking small businessmen. For the preceding twelve years, 63 percent of NAM's directors and 88 percent of its executive committee had come from 125 large corporations representing 1 percent of the companies affiliated with the association.[6] Hence it appears that the large corporate sector of business provided ideological leadership to the competitive sector and pursued an aggressive policy toward labor, not a liberal program of labor cooptation, as Bell's theory of the Monopoly State might have suggested. By the end of the war, indeed, NAM had dropped its habitual call for repeal of the Wagner Act, but this did not connote a new strategy of solicitude for organized labor, for NAM did not suspend efforts to "modify" the Wagner Act and bolster business power.[7]

On labor's side, too, the war experience yielded both benefits and injuries. While the no-strike pledge limited labor's power, the Roosevelt regime provided guarantees of union security, albeit grudgingly. Certainly, opting for government insurance, rather than for the power of mass action, weakened the movement as business took advantage of the wartime moratorium to press for the restoration of workplace authority it had lost with the rise of the CIO.[8] At first the workers struggle regressed, to the point where one of the most characteristic forms of anticompany sentiment was the "hate strike," or wildcat walkouts by white workers opposing the racial integration of the shops. Then, after the fury of the white riots in the summer of 1943, the frequency of racial workplace incidents declined, while the number of wildcats continued to mount, sparked variously by company harassment of union militants, revision of work rules, or even minor changes in shop regulations, like smoking restrictions.[9] In all, the number of strikes in 1944 exceeded the previous annual record set in 1919. The funneling of grievances to the National War Labor Board often let local tensions simmer, inciting strife; at the same time establishment of the Board as an authority standing above management lent workers' resistance some legitimacy. Even more important was the disappearance of unemployment under war production, which strengthened and emboldened workers as a whole.

Still, against the backdrop of hate strikes, and considering the volatility of the labor struggle (the variability of strike issues, the short term and local limits of strike action), the labor rebellion of 1944 could easily have appeared to contemporary observers as a kind of diffuse workers *jacquerie*. Union officials desperately tried to contain the restiveness of their membership. The willingness of union chiefs to become disciplinary agents of the state, in exchange for union recognition, tended to suppress the vital force of the workers movement;

yet the survival of the union was essential if workers resentment was to find an embodiment in sustained action and a *political* formula.

At the end of the war, that formula emerged in the demand for full employment, and here began the potential for a social-democratic movement in the United States. As the essential condition of workers' strength and a social check on management's authority, full employment became a paramount issue. In the three months between defeat of Germany and defeat of Japan, a million war-production workers were laid off, and by the next winter, a quarter of all war workers lost their jobs. To counteract the loss of overtime pay among their workers, leaders of Detroit locals of the United Automobile Workers asked 48 hours pay for 40 hours work; in June, 400 UAW local officers in the Detroit region voiced support for a 30-hour workweek with no reduction in pay. Rubber workers in Akron, Ohio, approved the same demand, and the United Mine Workers won a 35-hour workweek that spring. In the summer of 1945, mass demonstrations under official CIO leadership—50,000 in New York City, 25,000 in Camden, New Jersey, 30,000 in San Francisco and 20,000 in Detroit—pressed for full employment. CIO President Philip Murray told a Senate committee that without full employment, "the people will recognize the failure of private capitalism and vigorously call for government operation."[10]

To speak of a social-democratic potential in this movement is not to suggest that labor had adopted a socialist ideology. Here for the first time in American history, however, were stable mass organizations of the working class which could formulate demands that were all but political, insofar as they sublated local issues in planks of a national program for the working class as a whole, aimed at bringing business policy under the sway of a social policy. The attempt to negotiate product prices in addition to wages in the General Motors strike of 1946 was one modest indication of this reform tendency.[11]

The full employment demand, hardly a revolutionary program in itself, nonetheless placed a challenge before the capitalist order. As a March 1945 report by the National Planning Association pointed out, no level of government spending in itself could insure full employment; only shifting a portion of profits over to working class consumption could accomplish that.[12] Indeed, the only full employment program worthy of the name—"30 for 40," or a reduction in work time with no cut in pay—would increase that portion of total value which went to wages. In contrast, the Employment Act passed by the Truman administration in 1946, as one congressman noted at the time, gave workers nothing more than a license for job hunting.[13]

The strike wave assumed more massive and organized propor-
tions in 1946. The year following the U.S. defeat of Japan saw more
strikes than any other twelve-month period in the nation's history, and
featured a number of general strikes in small industrial cities like
Stamford, Connecticut; Lancaster, Pennsylvania; Rochester; Du-
quesne; and Pittsburgh.[14] Nor did the strikes disappear in 1947, as
hundreds of thousands of miners and telephone workers walked out.
It is this sustained combativity of the working class—in contrast to the
quiescence of workers in those countries that had directly suffered the
force of fascism, military occupation, and the devastation of battle—
that stands out as one of the key features of American history in the
two or three years immediately after the war. It was not until after the
middle of 1947 that the Taft-Hartley Act, the Marshall Plan, the inter-
necine struggle over the role of Communists in union leadership,
and—by 1950—a new pattern of long-term contracts trading away
full employment for productivity-based wage gains combined to de-
mobilize the working class and draw it toward political support for a
welfare regime based on domination of the world economy.

For Daniel Bell, the hiatus between the end of the Second World
War and the beginning of the Cold War was a period of personal disorientation. He suffered keenly from the loss of community occa-
sioned by his departure from New York, a loss compounded by the
breakup of his marriage while living in Chicago. And as he told
Dwight Macdonald in the summer of 1946, "Writing is too painful at
this stage when ideas are slowly changing." Indeed, the pace of his
writing slackened. Often, in these years, Bell promised essays that
went undelivered, and he often apologized to importunate editors.[15]
He resumed work on a Michelsian doctoral dissertation concerning
trade-union oligarchy, conceived years before at Columbia but sus-
pended during the war years because of the delicacy of his journalistic
relations with labor leaders.[16] Nonetheless, at Chicago, the project remained incomplete. While he commenced research in these years for
his monograph on the American Socialist Party, he published little
more than a string of book reviews in *The Progressive*, occasional *New
Leader* articles on current social trends, and a pair of accomplished essays for *Commentary* indicting positivist sociology for complicity in
maintaining the authoritarian mold of American institutions.

Still, Bell experienced his Chicago years as a heady intellectual
awakening; readings in philosophy and economic theory, as well as
seminars with fellow instructors Edward Shils, David Riesman, Philip
Rieff, Morris Janowitz, Barrington Moore, Milton Singer, and Robert
Redfield, provided him with what he came to consider his first real

education. Looking back later, he would say, "I became much more involved with Weber's thinking and became much more of a Weberian than a Marxist."[17]

Weber's impact on American intellectuals grew immediately after the war. Bell's friend C. Wright Mills had begun collaborating during the war with Hans Gerth, a German exile once affiliated with the Frankfurt Institute of Social Research, on a translation of selected essays by Weber. The collection was published in 1946. Other translations followed, including work by Bell's Chicago colleague Edward Shils.[18] Combining with the impact of Weber was the influx of French existentialism in 1946. Camus and Sartre toured the United States that year, and shortly afterwards *Politics* published essays of theirs along with work by de Beauvoir and Merleau-Ponty. *Partisan Review* recruited Hannah Arendt to explain German origins of the tendency in her essay, "What is *Existenz* Philosophy?"[19]

The French intellectuals in particular struck a chord in the sensibility of radical American intellectuals like Bell. Out of their association with the resistance movement, Combat, they cultivated a new style of radical humanism that seemed to surmount the deadlock of the old prewar left: still, as intellectuals who had endured military occupation, the French existentialists had a very concrete sense of being trapped by overweening power, which echoed the marginal sensibility of American left-wing intellectuals unable to share in the triumphalism of war. For Bell, the two new intellectual influences—Weber and existentialism—clearly meshed. The existentialist paradigm of aloofness and choice, as he put it, was akin to the dichotomy of conscience and responsibility that Weber elucidated in his essay, "Politics as a Vocation," which was featured in the Gerth-Mills volume and seemed to voice the enduring dilemmas Bell faced as a political man estranged from the realm of political action. Perhaps the central intellectual problem for Bell in the postwar years was the problem Weber discussed of relating morality and politics. Having assumed the role of the marginal critic, his radicalism steadily took on the cast of a moral posture, and he was frustrated by the difficulties of giving that moral disposition a political voice.

Bell's perception of the rise of the Monopoly State, marking the blockage of progress, left him facing an order that seemed integrated, stable, impervious to challenge. As Weber had written, "Where the bureaucratization of administration has been completely carried through, a form of power relation is established that is practically unshatterable."[20] Bell brought the postwar strikes into the equation, seizing one-sidedly on their function as safety valves, channeling formless discontent into support for the organizational dynamic of the unions. So, in the years after the war, Bell plied the theme of "the centralization of decision and the growth of dependence" in American society, and he foresaw a fifty-year interregnum of stolid social order before the possibilities of radicalism would flare again.

It is also clear that Bell shared in the mentality of modernism, for the confrontation with historical stasis at the end of progress intensified the taut dualism in his thought. The critical sociology he built on Weberian foundations focused on the experience of alienation and community, the force of rationalization and demagogic myth—shifting sands of existential paradox under the feet of the political actor he still wished to be. The tension between determinism and moralism that emerged first in his early experience of social democracy and antiwar radicalism continued to agitate him. This tension lodged itself in the very structure of his theory, as the two poles of *interests* and *ideals* that characterized any instance of social action; it found expression as well in the dualism of economics and politics, which in Bell's thinking bore toward each other the same external relation as that between reason and purpose, fact and value, in the thought of Max Weber.

The Monopoly State and the New Economics

Bell's shift from the engaged political journalism of the war years to the radical quietism of the postwar interlude was marked, oddly enough, by the surrender of the Monopoly State project. It was, after all, the image of the Monopoly State as a solidary order that signaled his retreat to marginality in the first place. Nonetheless, the theory of repressive organicism—of which the Monopoly State was only one instance—would remain part of his thought in other guises.

Writing the Monopoly State book, however, had become an awesome and frustrating task. During the summer of 1944 he troubled over two chapters, one on the economic position and role of organized labor before, during and (prospectively) after the war, and another on Britain's movement toward business collectivism as its stature in the world economy declined. Starting after his regular editorial duties at *The New Leader*, Bell's evening labors on the manuscript lengthened his work day to a wearying fourteen hours. Overwhelmed by a mass of detail, he struggled to bring the material into coherent literary form; by the end of October, the union chapter was only half complete, and the chapter on Britain—long before promised to Lewis Corey for publication in the *Antioch Review*—was persistently delayed.

Finally, after accumulating hundreds of pages of drafts, Bell suffered a crisis of self-confidence, struck by the absurdity of his pretensions to expertise at the young age of 25.[21] As he would tell it later, it was like a revelation interrupting his work in the New York Public Library reading room one night:

> I only know this second hand . . . and it's all silly. I suddenly realized I was very badly educated. I was educated in a vulgar Marxist framework, if you want to put it that way, making imputations about corporate behavior, and I never really knew what was going on. . . . [I had pictured] American business as somehow coming together in a central web with a small, controlling clique dominating society. . . . I'd say that what was happening was a greater awareness or feeling for the actual operational structures of the society; and inevitably one gets a more complicated view of them.[22]

In many ways, the conspiratorial view of business behavior in Bell's Monopoly State articles was closer to the antimonopoly tradition of Progressive-era muckraking than it was to Marxism. On the other hand, Marxist themes did not abruptly disappear from his work after this point, as his retrospective version of the episode suggested. His crisis of confidence, in any case, should not be considered only in psychological terms. He had, by 1945, good reason to doubt the empirical validity of many specifics in the Monopoly State thesis. Most significant was the resurrection in 1944 and 1945 of right-wing rhetoric in business and Congressional circles calling for unregulated free enterprise. As early as March 1944, in fact, Bell recognized the need to revise his forecast. He wrote to Lewis Corey, "More than likely, the buying boom that will come after the war will result in increased demands for hands-off from govt controls [sic] with a more disastrous depression afterwards and a more savage 'monopoly state' along fascistic lines." Bell's journalism in late 1944 and 1945 began to waver; he was uncertain whether the rulers of war indeed looked ahead to a new world order or whether they foolishly looked backward toward a reactionary utopia of nineteenth-century capitalism.[23] With the return to a vision of the free capitalist market an analysis of its inherent instability, conceived in roughly Marxist terms, became more prominent rather than less in Bell's writing.

Thus Bell reopened the question of whether capitalism itself, however reformed, could be stabilized, short of a transformation to socialism. He seemed to give several contradictory answers. In September 1944, reacting against Communist Party enthusiasm for a postwar Popular Front and a "people's capitalism," Bell pressed Dwight Macdonald to take the offensive in *Politics* against "this notion gaining ground in liberal circles that a capitalist economy can work *if* all social groups realize their *true* interests." Bell explicitly challenged the Keynesianism of Alan R. Sweezy, who had written in the Communist Party's *New Masses* that economic stability and social peace could be established by a high-consumption economy sustained by government spending. In August 1945, Bell took an orthodox Marxist approach in arguing that "capitalism can never achieve an equilibrium, and that is the major fact of our time." Urging an opponent to "read Marx," Bell explained in a *New Leader* article that the locus of capitalist crisis lay not in the sphere of distribution but in a system of production that is "constantly forced to expand or die." Yet Bell appeared to contradict himself in the same article by remarking that the planning proposals of English economist William Beveridge "can make capitalism work by introducing the state as the directing agency of investment; it also means that the ruling class loses a large part of its control." [24]

Similar twists and turns in Bell's postwar economic thinking can only be explained by Bell's tendency, from 1945 to 1948, to meld Marxism and Keynesianism together. In the social-democratic tradition, Marxism commonly appeared both as the culmination of classical economics—that is, a generally applicable abstract system of laws of production and exchange—and as a theory that emphasized the social and political conditioning of economic laws. [25] This approach, however, was never able to fully mediate economics and politics in the manner Marx intended; in fact it reduced Marxism to a kind of economic institutionalism. Essentially this was the foundation of the argument Bell and C. Wright Mills made against mixed economy during the war—distinguishing formal economics from its real context of political conditions. In the years after the war Bell took the same approach: casually merging Keynes's analysis of oversaving with Marx's theory of crises, he accepted the *theoretical* efficacy of Keynesian schemes of economic control while he asserted that real social and political conditions hindered their *practical* implementation—at least in any desirable form.

Bell's dicta on capitalist inequilibria referred to the workings of autonomous economic mechanisms—the possibility of state intervention was for him another, noneconomic, question—and on that ground he considered the Marxist analysis of the inherent capitalist disposition toward crisis superior to conventional bourgeois economics, which assumed the smooth self-correction of the market. On the same grounds Bell dismissed the minimal Keynesian program of compensatory spending as one that "aim[ed] at flattening out a business cycle" without addressing "the root problem of the cause of the cycles." On a deeper level, however, as Paul Sweezy had pointed out in his book *The Theory of Capitalist Development* (1942), the Keynesian critique of "oversaving" located a fundamental flaw in the capitalist accumulation process itself and thus, at least superficially, approached the Marxist paradigm. Hence in a November 1946 piece entitled "Notes on our Economic Prospects," Bell's summation of capitalism's *permanent* disability adopted the left-Keynesian view of oversaving as root of a secular tendency toward economic stagnation:

> Deflation has always been the permanent spectre of a capitalist economy. As corporate savings pile up and fail to find investment outlets, money gets dammed up which through undistributed profits taxes or higher wages should have been turned back in the functioning economic stream.[26]

But these alternative measures raised the question of political choices, which would ultimately determine economic fate. It was the ultimate priority of political conflict and decision that led Bell to agree with Hilferding's famous judgment that "a purely economic collapse [of capitalism] makes no sense." Despite the tendency toward stagnation, Bell wrote, there were any number of "counteracting forces" that "do not reverse the basic process of accumulation or meet the sources of crises [but] may represent an important brake against precipitous decline." Some of these counteracting forces were already naturally at work, such as the growth of "unproductive consumption" in the expanding sphere of marketing and services; others, like an extensive redistribution of consumer income or planned, government-sponsored development of backward regions, required policy initiatives. The "nub of the problem" was whether such initiatives could satisfy corporate demands for high profits or, if not, whether the government would have the strength to challenge or defy those demands. What was required, then, Bell wrote, was an understanding of "monopoly as a power and political problem rather than an economic one." Bell added that even the most thoroughgoing Keynesian program was vitiated by "its political and sociological unreality."

For Bell, the chief virtue of Marxism was not its analysis of crises but its status as a theory of *political* economy, by which Bell meant a theory that viewed economics embedded in a context of "the concrete power relations and the power mechanisms of society."[27] Referring to the best-known American spokesman of Keynesianism, Harvard economist Alvin Hansen, Bell wrote in 1946, the "orthodox Keynes-Hansen line" is

> an approach which is adequate in formal economic terms. But it needs to be supplemented with a realistic analysis of the institutional forces within the economy which work to block full employment and project imperialism outward as a substitute for adequate planning at home.

Again, a year later, he wrote,

> We *do* know how to solve depressions and assure full employment. There is the technical competence and "know how." The real problem is cutting across the strong vested interests that prevent the introduction and operation of these plans.[28]

Although Bell believed that capitalist class interests would resist surrendering that measure of power which they would have to turn over to the state in the Keynesian scheme, there was yet another ominous possibility. During 1946 and 1947 he continued to write about the "militarization of industrial life" that stemmed from the close ties between business and the armed services established during the war and surviving after it. The economic effect of this was not certain, because of the variability of state policy: the delicacy of alliances (particularly with Britain) required by an anti-Soviet world policy, Bell suggested at one point, might force the U.S. government to restrain the full-scale foreign expansionism that could fuel domestic prosperity;[29] on the other hand, state organization of domestic production in preparation for conflict with the Soviet Union could institutionalize a "permanent war economy" that might indeed bring economic stability. If so, the traditional socialist argument against capitalist anarchy was weakened, and the only issue remaining was the moral defensibility of buying economic health by militarist means. In an extended review essay on the work of Marxist economist Fritz Sternberg, published in the May 1947 issue of *Commentary*, Bell's thinking achieved a coherent formulation. The essay indicated how political issues increasingly had become defined, for Bell, by moral or "value" terms:

> We do know from Keynsian [*sic*] analysis how to prevent depression. . . . The real questions are what kind of state action is desirable, in what form, in what areas, and whether or not the price one may have to pay is too steep, as measured against a set of democratic values. . . . In an impending crisis, with a cry for increased state help, the economic area in which it would be easiest

for the state to step in and supplement private capital without competing with it is armaments. In fact, this is already being done. . . . And it is at this point that Sternberg's argument really loses its edge. For what he has spent most of his time proving is that in a laissez-faire capitalist economy a crisis is inevitable, and that under free enterprise the next one would be crucial. . . . Our present drift, accentuated by political tensions and given the present political constellation, is along the line of least resistance, towards a war economy. . . . It may be a type of stabilization unacceptable from a humanitarian and socialist point of view, yet it may find a ready acceptance on the part of large masses of workers, because they have jobs, just as in Argentina today the workers are following Peron into a militarized state capitalism. . . . If the political tension [with Russia] diminishes, progressive forces have a breathing space, for then an immediate war economy is averted and the chances for economic crisis *increase*, along with those for the mobilization of liberals for a non-militaristic economic planning program. If the political tension increases, then the chances for economic crisis probably will decrease and employment will be stepped up—for war. . . . Since we know the mechanisms of obtaining full employment and overcoming crises, our real analytical task is relating the consequences of different policies to sets of social values.[30]

Bell's economic thinking tended toward an abstract division of neutral economic form from the political purpose that gave it substance. It also construed politics as a question of competing *values* that orient rational procedure. The drift toward reducing politics to a *moral* enterprise marked Bell's postwar interlude. In large part, it resulted from his continued disappointment with politics as a kind of action.

The Appeal and Frustration of a New Politics

Bell's retreat from political practice was not fully completed with the frustration of his prowar progressivism. The contradictory reality lurking behind the theory of repressive organicism—the continuation of working-class combativity—sustained some hope that the backwash of war might loosen the structure of American politics and permit significant innovations. After the war Bell participated in a movement to create a new social-democratic party in the United States, though with a measure of skepticism and reserve that marked the distance he had

traveled since the enthusiastic days of "people's war." The dissipation
of the new party movement in fact compounded the frustration of
wartime progressivism and reinforced for Bell the kind of estrangement that throve on a sense of impotence.

The movement for a new party arose directly from the labor
strife that had emerged in the middle of 1943. A layer of middle-level
leaders of the United Automobile Workers, schooled in the pitched
battles for union recognition in the late 1930s and headed by Emil
Mazey of the militant Briggs plant local in Flint, spearheaded a drive
at the June 1943 CIO convention for repudiation of the no-strike
pledge and a break to independent political action. In March 1944,
Mazey and leading unionists from fifty other UAW locals met with
farmer and consumer-coop leaders, as well as various left-wing political activists, to organize the Michigan Commonwealth Federation
(MCF) as a state-wide third party dedicated to economic democracy.
In the new *Politics* magazine, Dwight Macdonald greeted the meeting
with enthusiasm. Although he criticized the MCF for failing to pro-
claim an explicitly socialist program, Macdonald predicted the movement would reshape American politics. If CIO leaders were forced to
yield to membership discontent and organize the national labor party
that radicals had long awaited, he wrote, "they will find it more difficult to keep it inside the framework of the *status quo* . . . than was the
case with the CIO. A political party is a more explosive mechanism
than a trade union, and the forties promise to be a more turbulent
decade than even the thirties."[31]

In its first year, Macdonald's *Politics* featured reports on the
movement from UAW militant Frank Marquart in Detroit. Despite the
members' lingering illusions in the promise of a Rooseveltian "mixed
economy," the magazine suggested, the MCF manifested a valuable
insurgent, antibureaucratic spirit at the grass roots. Macdonald considered the Mazey group in the UAW to be "articulate, aggressive and
infinitely disrespectful to its top officers." Marquart reported that the
new-party activists were "determined to put it over 'from the bottom
up and not from the top down.'" More than fifty people had attended
a recent meeting of the MCF program committee, Marquart wrote,
and were "eagerly talking about how to get public ownership without
allowing bureaucrats to take over—that's something you can no longer
do in the unions."[32]

The Michigan Commonwealth Federation derived its name
from Canada's Cooperative Commonwealth Federation, the social-
democratic party that won control of Saskatchewan's provincial government in 1944 and promised to become the leading opposition

party in the federal parliament in Ottawa, a success that inspired social democrats in the United States.[33] Lewis Corey, then teaching economics at Antioch College, believed the MCF pointed the way toward
the "basic reconstruction of economic institutions." He urged the
party not to fear appearing "too radical"; it should drop its call for
public "yardstick industries," Corey said, and adopt instead a bold
plan of socializing all monopolies in a rapid, concerted drive "beyond
capitalism."[34] Corey worked to build a parallel Ohio Commonwealth
Federation, while Maynard Krueger, a Socialist leader who was Norman Thomas' running mate in the 1940 presidential campaign, coop-
erated with transport and retail workers unions in Chicago to found a
short-lived American Commonwealth Party.

By the fall of 1945, a movement was afoot to bring all new-party
forces together on a national plane. Krueger, an economist at the University of Chicago who was responsible for bringing Bell there that
year, recruited Bell to the organizing effort.[35] Bell wrote to Corey in
November, inviting him to the Mid-West Exploratory Conference on
Independent Political Action to be held in Madison, Wisconsin, on
December 16. Bell told Corey he hoped "some audacity is shown"
there, and Corey agreed that "it must be socialism but socialism re-
defined in the light of the collapse of the old socialism [i.e., Second
International reformism] and the totalitarianism of communism."
Corey wrote in turn to A. Philip Randolph, who had organized a similar meeting in New York, and told Randolph "a socialist declaration"
was necessary. "We need to issue a challenge for a new social order,
but do it concretely, without sectarianism, in a convincing manner.
Any echo either of new dealism or socialist sectarianism will destroy
us."[36]

Organizers hoped to found a new national party that could run
Congressional candidates in 1946 and make a substantial bid for
President in 1948, preempting any attempt by the Communists to fill
the political vacuum on the left. They called a central Conference of
American Progressives for April 6 and 7, 1946, in Chicago. The Socialist Party was the strongest single force behind the move, but it
asked Bell, well known for his affiliation with *The New Leader* and
social-democratic politics in New York, to act as the Chicago-based co-
ordinator at the conference. Although representatives of the CIO's
Political Action Committee at the conference argued that a new party
was impractical as long as labor forces had not yet learned to vote as a
bloc, the delegates approved Randolph's call for a decisive repudiation
of all the "old parties." They also endorsed Corey's argument that the

decay of capitalism rendered inadequate the New Deal remedy of compensatory spending—and lent urgency to the need for a program of "socializing monopolies and the commanding heights of our economy," if progressives were to head off a fascist solution to the coming economic crisis.[37] Corey was appointed to draft a statement of principles, with Bell's assistance, and Bell agreed to edit the organization's newsletter.

The Chicago meeting ended, however, with a call for another national planning conference in December, ruling out a Congressional campaign that year. The delegates approved the formation of a National Educational Committee for a New Party (NECNP), which Corey pointedly defined as "a provisional national council to *promote* the idea of a party, *not* to organize one." Progress was slow: by October the first issue of the Committee newsletter had not yet appeared; fundraisers had collected only a few hundred dollars, and the national conference was postponed again to the spring of 1947. Corey's draft statement of principles, "Ideas for a New Party," appeared in the fall 1946 issue of *Antioch Review* with the endorsement of John Dewey, NECNP honorary chairman, but important potential allies, like the Reuther brothers of the UAW, remained hesitant to break from the Democrats: participants in an *Antioch Review* symposium "testified to growing recognition of the crisis of American liberalism and the urgent need for a discussion of ideas and policy for a new political realignment," the editor wrote, but progressive labor and liberal leaders still considered the moment inopportune, promising to join up, as a cynical observer put it, "if and when other national leaders will do so." Soon it appeared that the energies of the mass labor movement would not be channeled into a third party. In the summer of 1947, Bell wrote to Corey that the matter had become "quite academic."[38]

In any case, Bell had long had an ambivalent relation to the new party enterprise, in part because his growing sense of the accelerating trend toward a coordinated organizational order made him skeptical of labor-based reformism. His May 1945 essay on the MCF, "The Political Lag of Commonwealth," suggested that organized labor was bureaucratically integrated with imperialist state policy. Furthermore, the article suggested that institutional commitments bound second-rank labor leadership to their union chiefs, drastically narrowing the room in which they could maneuver, whatever their radical impulses. Bell also took exception to the strong emphasis in Corey's draft on liberating the forces of modern technology from business restrictionism, perhaps because he no longer considered those forces benign in themselves, or perhaps because, in light of the record of war production, he felt that restrictionism was an outdated issue. In the fall of 1946, Bell hinted at his reservations in a letter to Dwight Macdonald, who by this time had concluded that all party politics perpetuated the dehumanizing tendency toward an over-planned war-bound society. "Actually my heart is not in it," Bell wrote of his role in the National Educational Committee for a New Party, "but I'm going through the motions. The remnants of an ethics of responsibility still urges me on, and the feeling that this thing, however hopeless, is better than complete resignation, still guides me on." [39]

Bell's reservations about the new party movement stemmed also from his new interest in theories of mass society and authoritarianism. The combination of his involvement in the new party campaign and his growing suspicion of mass movements reflected the apparent ambivalence of the workers' struggle as a labor jacquerie. Wartime hate strikes had focused Bell's attention on the forces atomizing the working class. Perhaps he was influenced by the sociologists who warned that social forces unleashed by war would create "a nomadic way of life" and foster "sadistic, macabre" traits. In a letter to Macdonald, Bell noted in particular that "the changing nature of productivity" (intensive mechanization) helped create a "new proletariat—a permanent mass of unskilled and lumpen (*mass vs class*) elements," and he wrote to Lewis Corey that the new industrial plants were full of "green people, ex-clerks, hillbillies, etc." The result, he suggested, was the irruption of diffuse resentment. [40] Bell's view—implying that the hate strikes and the wildcats had a common basis, in newly proletarianized, untried strata—was probably mistaken. The most militant plants in the strike wave of 1943–45 were not the new war plants filled with migrant workers but the older plants where a union heritage survived among a more settled labor force. [41] Nonetheless, with his analysis of the devolution of workers into lumpen, Bell began to fear that a mass-society theory of totalitarianism might have a frightening applicability to American life. [42]

As the theory of totalitarianism later appeared in the work of Hannah Arendt, it supposed that totalitarian movements arose as "classes" gave way to "masses"; utilitarian interests—which presumed the individual's conscious membership in differentiated groups with practical, self-satisfying purposes—collapsed before the ideological appeal of a fused social whole to which the individual surrendered personal identity. [43] In this context the propaganda of "mass suggestion," as depicted in the apparatuses of indoctrination in Orwell's dys-

topia, assumed terrifying power.[44] Bell brought these elements together in a letter of August 1945 to Lewis Corey:

> I think the great lesson of fascism as a social and political move-
> ment is the importance of *masses* and the manipulation of *masses*.
> I think the debates on whether fascism won the middle class or
> didn't are much beside the point. . . . My hunch is that fascism
> was accepted by those who rejected classes and the older class sys-
> tems, by those, whether they were workers, intellectuals, lumpen
> elements etc who did not want to belong to any class and who ac-
> cepted fascism as a movement against *all* classes. In the United
> States where we do have, psychologically, a classless society, I feel
> that a revolutionary fascist movement will have more chance of
> winning over the working class than any other.

Furthermore, he wrote,

> The big problem of our time . . . is the manipulation of masses,
> or in the general parlance, of "public opinion." In this connection
> the concept of a new middle class is fruitful, but the new middle
> class I have in mind is not the technologist, but the social manipu-
> lator: the advertising man, public relations man, market re-
> searcher, pollster, etc. . . . In a bureaucratic society—towards
> which we are heading—the men who manipulate public opinion
> are coming to the fore.[45]

Bell's new outlook was influenced by his work as a consultant to a
1944 study of anti-Semitism in American labor, sponsored by the Jewish Labor Committee (JLC) and conducted by A. R. L. Gurland, Paul
Massing, Felix Weil, Friedrich Pollock, and Leo Lowenthal of the
Frankfurt Institute of Social Research. By various measures, anti-
Semitism rose markedly throughout the country in the late war years.
Based on 500 screened interviews of workers, the JLC study found
that "an embarrassing amount of prejudice existed among trade
union members" as well. The Frankfurt Institute researchers completed a massive four-volume 1300-page manuscript, but the JLC
never published it, apparently fearing that criticism of the labor
movement by European (and Jewish) intellectuals would only elicit an
ugly backlash. The study nonetheless served the Frankfurt Institute as
an exercise for the research project, "Studies in Prejudice," which culminated in the 1950 publication of *The Authoritarian Personality*. Bell
put his own conclusions into a 1944 essay for the labor-Zionist *Jewish
Frontier*, "The Face of Tomorrow" (featured on the magazine cover

under the title, "The Grass Roots of American Jew-Hatred"), which sketched the sado-masochistic character structure rooted in American culture.[46]

In Germany, Bell wrote, persecution of Jews assumed a cold, rationalized form, but "the country where anti-Semitism can emerge in the most violent shape and unabated fury," Bell proposed, "is the United States." He cited a set of unique cultural patterns—political cynicism, the urge to pacify public life, frontier vigilantism, xenophobia, and compulsive "joining" habits—as deep-rooted sources of a fearsome resentment. The urge to surrender individual identity by binding oneself to the imagined potency of the group—a yearning of "nobodies" to be "somebodies"—followed from the bitter frustration fueled by the false promises of American life, Bell wrote, and from the absence of vital symbols and solidarities that could motivate progressive change and sustain a satisfying social life.

> It is important to note that the American factory worker is less immune to the fascist virus than the European worker. Over there, held together by class solidarity, the European worker was able to offer some rudimentary opposition to fascism. Here, organized basically on "primitive" self-interest, the machine-dulled worker can be led more easily into lumpen channels.[47]

As yet, however, Bell's analysis of 'mass society' remained tied to some kind of a Marxist critique. Citing Erich Fromm's *Escape from Freedom*, he asserted that the social-psychological traits he discerned arose specifically from "the insecurities and fears generated by capitalism." The predatory character of capitalist society, "channeling various drives according to the premiums and sanctions of an aggressive and competitive world," had helped to make sadistic subjugation and torture a new symbol of the modern age. Furthermore, the disorientation of the popular mind was a creature of alienation, "a key concept to understand modern society, a concept utilized so well by Marx in showing how factory civilization divorces man from the sources and satisfactions of craftsmanship." Alienation, he continued in almost an existentialist vein, obscured concrete reality and evoked absurdity: "In this huge, complex world, motivations are unclear and ambitions petty, the sharpest perceptions have become dulled, the greatest words have lost their dignity and meaning." Hence politics was so often distorted, deluded, and misdirected. Even a progressive movement like American Populism turned darkly reactionary, as it "fail[ed] to understand the mainsprings of capitalism" and continued to denounce "money changers" and "international bankers." Bell warned that a mass fascist movement, "a people united against something they mis-understand or about which they are ignorant," might be made of re-turning soldiers and small-town workers. Truly progressive politics had to stand firm and militate against the surge of irrationality—and so, it seemed, Bell yet considered socialist politics and the socialist analysis of capitalism to be a rational hedge against "mass culture."[48]

New Roads in Theory and Practice

Still, Bell was steadily working his way from reformist Marxism to sociology, where "mass society," analyzed into the essential compo-nents of bureaucracy and alienation, supplanted an image of capital-ism grounded in the exploitation of labor. The image of the Monop-oly State as an economic order organized by a business clique gave way to a vision of stifling institutional integration: the two were not very different in their portrait of centralization and coordination, but in the latter case the motive force was not a conscious class but a generic tendency toward "increasing bureaucratization," whereby "more and more areas of living become organized, each organization deepening its own stake in the society."[49]

With all agencies of social action seemingly bound to the self-sustaining program of permanent war economy, prospects for change narrowed, and radicals commenced a frustrated search for new means of action. At the beginning of 1946 Dwight Macdonald's magazine be-gan publishing a series of articles, "New Roads in Politics," dedicated to a reconsideration of Marxism's potency as the foundation of radical politics. In his own contribution, "The Root is Man," Macdonald re-jected the prevailing optimism of the left and in effect buried his hopes for third-party politics. Despite the weakness of the old bour-geois parties in Europe and the continued growth of organized labor in the United States, Macdonald said, he foresaw no radical liberating renovation of modern society, for the traditional left simply called for those reforms that the elites of an emerging oppressive order were willing and eager to grant—full production, nationalization, and planning. "War and the preparation of war has become the normal mode of existence of great nations," he wrote, and he believed large sectors of the working class were content to lodge their desire for se-curity with a nationalist program of militarization implemented by a hegemonic state.[50]

Writers in the "New Roads" series proposed a new political para-digm for the left, one that counterposed the relentless organicism of society and the autonomy of the individual. Will Herberg announced the theme in his inaugural contribution to "New Roads." His essay, "Personalism against Totalitarianism," indicted the traditional socialist movement for its uncritical embrace of the "collective mystique"—the coordinated organizational life of a proletariat trained in the virtues of discipline and solidarity—that finally subordinated the individual to the "all-embracing machinery" of the state. Against this totalitarian way of life, Herberg emphasized the original "personalist" vision of Marx, who decried the bourgeois "degradation of the person into a thing, into a mere instrumentality or means" and longed to liberate the individual's creativity. Paul Goodman followed Herberg, condemning "the concern felt by the masses alienated from their deep natures for the smooth functioning of the industrial machine," a "mass attitude" of idolizing the social whole that Goodman termed "sociolatry." Another contributor, a conscientious objector and Socialist Party activist named Albert Votaw, aptly summed up the problem and the *Politics* paradigm:

> The most important single feature of contemporary society is that it reduces man to an entity, a certain minute quantity, which is bought, sold, transferred, aided, or crushed by vast amoral collectives over which he has no control and of whose functions he is completely ignorant. This is the primary wickedness of society today, not the fact that production is ordered by the managers with the capitalist's profit in mind instead of by the economist—read bureaucrat—in the interests of the people's stomach.[51]

In effect, Macdonald's own essay, "The Root," brought these themes into line with the principal preoccupations of modern sociology—the illusions of progress and the ambiguity of reason. Marxism, he wrote, shared the monistic evolutionism and scientism of nineteenth-century liberal culture, but contemporary events roundly defeated its hopes and expectations, for capitalism was in the process of giving way to the permanent-war regime of bureaucratic collectivism rather than to socialism, and science had proven vicious and destructive rather than liberating. Thus, he wrote, the values and aims Marxism professed were contradicted and suppressed by the very dynamics of economic organization it confidently claimed would realize them.

Then came the existential question of how contemporary radicals should act in the socialist pursuit of a classless and stateless society, when they could no longer trust in the culminating unity of fact and value Marxism had predicted. If, as Macdonald claimed, liberating values could no longer claim the sanction of either history or science, radical politics had to be recast on the basis of moral values regarded as absolutes—not in the sense that they were divinely given, but in the sense that they were meaningful in and of themselves and incontrovertible in practice. Thus, though Macdonald claimed to repudiate the rationalism of John Dewey, he actually embraced Dewey's doctrine of ends and means: valued ends did not permit counter-valued means, Macdonald believed, and no exigencies justified the use of violence and deception toward the ends of peace and truth. Philosophical questions about the origins and meaning of morals—the impact of historical determination, human nature, and free will—could be left aside, he said.

> The "trick" in living seems to me precisely to reject all complete and wellrounded solutions and to live in a continual state of tension and contradiction, which reflects the real nature of man's existence. Not the object at rest but the gyroscope, which harmonizes without destroying the contradictory forces of motion and inertia, should be our model. Perhaps the most serious objection to Marxism is that, in this sense, it is not dialectical *enough*.[52]

In fact, Macdonald's "dialectic" would better be termed a dualism that strove to keep fact and value apart in the face of "false totalism," a cohesive order that suppressed all ideals standing apart from given reality. His Kierkegaardian emphasis on asserting pure moral will, declining to embrace the security of progress, came in part from the influence of Nicola Chiaromonte, a representative of the Italian group *Giustìzia e Libertà*, who had injected the radical humanism of the European resistance into the pages of *Politics*.[53] More broadly speaking, Macdonald's argument reflected that nexus of existentialism and modern sociology which was based, broadly speaking, on some common tenets—the inaccessibility of the whole of society and history to sure (systematic) knowledge, the acute sense of experience riven into public and private spheres, the condition of otherness that was the only ground for an authentic sense of being in the contemporary world, a nonhistorical dialectic of inescapable and unresolvable tensions which followed the breach of progress, the "obstructed path" where, as H. Stuart Hughes said, existentialism resided.[54]

These conundrums conditioned the role of post-Marxist Radicals, as Macdonald outlined it. They were to embrace "negativism," by ridiculing, sabotaging, evading, and refusing the authority of the state, and "unrealism," by accepting the inefficacy of their program, if need be, rather than submitting to "lesser-evil" imperatives. They were to adopt "moderation," by recognizing "the tragic limitations of

human existence, the Nemesis which turns victory into defeat over-
night, the impossibility of perfect knowledge of anything" and by
agreeing "to live with contradictions, to have faith in scepticism, to advance toward the solution of a problem by admitting as a possibility
something which the scientists can never admit: namely that it may be
insoluble." Finally, Radicals opted for "smallness" and "self-ishness"
by pursuing political projects that could be implemented on a modest,
human scale and by choosing to act alone or in small groups, so that
they could insure the moral identity of experience and "preserve the
living seeds of protest and rebellion" as a moral example for other
"alienated and frustrated members" of society.[55]

Daniel Bell's Argument with Dwight Macdonald

Macdonald's editorial assistant, the young Marxist writer Irving
Howe, organized a series of contributions to the "New Roads" symposium which criticized Macdonald's new moralism. One of Macdonald's critics, David T. Bazelon, visited Daniel Bell in Chicago around
Christmas 1945 to give advanced warning that "Dwight has got religion." Howe would take up the argument of Bell's mentor, Sidney
Hook, against the "new failure of nerve": Howe claimed the vogue of
existentialism represented the intellectuals' "flight from politics." Bell,
however, was not so strongly married to his pragmatist heritage: he
wrote to Macdonald, "I suspect that I am closer to your new position
than to any enunciated by your critics."[56] Indeed, Bell was not immune to Howe's charge, for he later admitted to Macdonald, "my own
tendencies are increasingly apolitical." In one letter from his Chicago
cloister, concerning the scenario of erotic liberation drawn by *Politics*
writer Paul Goodman, Bell sounded almost plaintive, as he summed
up modest, very personal goals:

> The social liberation that I hope for does not involve moving vast
> institutions and "seizing power," but consists in the willingness of
> small groups of people to be themselves. I do not see that this re-
> quires great drafts of energy [as the liberation of Eros did], but it
> certainly requires freedom from anxiety and an independent
> sense of what is satisfying.

He was prepared, as well, to qualify his wartime endorsement of
Hook's old polemic against theology:

> I think one of the greatest intellectual crimes of the past few years
> was the attempt of the PR failure of nerve series to lump together

all rejections of pragmatism. Certainly, existentialism, with its emphasis on individual decision and aloofness is a far cry from the neo-Thomism here [the conservative thought of University of Chicago philosopher Mortimer J. Adler] which asserts a common core of morality created a priori from Aristotle and Thomas, which all men should share.[57]

Bell suggested to Macdonald that "Politics ought to examine more fully the kind of things Niebuhr has been writing." Niebuhr, a theologian with a political background as a left-wing socialist during the 1930s, had come into his own during the war years, with the publication of his principal theological treatise, *The Nature and Destiny of Man*, and his political formulation of UDA liberalism, *The Children of Light and the Children of Darkness*. He had in fact been one of Hook's principal targets in "The New Failure of Nerve" for his suggestion that progressive politics should rest on religious resources of moral conviction. If the affinity Bell suggested between Niebuhr and Macdonald is not entirely clear, it is not difficult to discover congruence between the perspectives of the two men. Niebuhr, too, began with a wholesale assault on the false optimism of "progress," the bourgeois (and allegedly Marxist) confidence in the beneficent potency of scientific reason and in the steady emergence of truth and justice out of a past of illusion and oppression. Niebuhr's argument that the individual's search for community and the spirit's yearning for fulfillment were resolved, paradoxically, in recognizing the necessity of ever-incomplete striving—and his depiction of values as both ahistorical and lived, immediate and transcendent—was largely consistent with the frank dualism of Macdonald's moralism. Yet there were significant differences between Macdonald's and Niebuhr's perspectives as well, for Niebuhr repudiated the Deweyan consistency of means and ends that underlay the moral *identity* of Macdonald's exemplary Radical. From a Niebuhrian perspective, Macdonald himself was "not dialectical enough," for at the last moment Macdonald denied the logical extension of his tragic sense of disjuncture and proposed that a whole personality could emerge from modern political experience.

The tension in his own thought between idealism and determinism allowed Bell to recognize this dilemma and play Camus to Macdonald's Sartre—denying that the exercise of free will could dislodge the personality from the given constraints of social conditions. The radical sociological perspective Bell had been developing—with its image of an institutional straitjacket—led him to political conclusions that were "moderate," as Macdonald had said, insofar as they assumed narrow limits of action. As he adhered to this perspective, Bell commenced an argument with Macdonald which asserted that the radical could not avoid being troubled by the disjuncture between his wishes and his possibilities, and that this disjuncture lay *within* the realm of any conceivable action. In pursuing his point, Bell implicitly denied the possibility of satisfying his own wish for an apolitical group life free of anxiety.[58]

The discussion with Macdonald began on common ground. Bell shared with the New Roads writers the desire to extricate individual being from the social organism. "There is a true distinction between society and the individual," he wrote to Macdonald.

> Most of our thinking, Marxist, and Deweyan is completely colored by an Hegelian conception of organic identity, a concept shared with the Catholic Church. To an Hegelian the proposition I am I is meaningless. There are no unique Is. I am a doctor, I am a teacher, I am a worker is meaningful in Hegelian terms because the individual is identified in terms of the social role he plays. . . .
>
> I would add a belief in a theory of natural rights, or personality rights if you will, so that no organic conception of society is permissible. I do not draw my rights from the social group and they cannot be taken away from me by the group. In this sense I would affirm Locke against Rousseau and Hegel.

Bell's defense of theoretical individualism was a reaction to the pressures of relentless organicism he discerned. He was working on a lengthy essay, intended for *Antioch Review* but never published, to be entitled, "The Centralization of Decision and the Growth of Dependence." He told Macdonald:

> I laid down the premise we are heading toward some form of bureaucratic society; that this bureaucratic society conceived of individuals as parts designed to serve the organizational and institutional structures of which the individual is a part, not as individuals in themselves (the Kantian notion of men as ends); that the root process which shapes the bureaucratic pattern is the process of rationalization; that the fundamental aspect of rationalization is in our machine technology and the rhythms of work created by the machine; that this rationalization extends into all areas. . . . I attempted to show how in technology the process works . . . then how labor becomes part of the pattern; politics; and the cultural realm.
>
> My main point was that at this stage, since the future is committed, the only constructive role we can play is that of critics, since

the men of action can only choose alternative paths within the dominant framework. That our role of critics should be such so that when some meaningful choices are possible say in fifty years, people shall have a truly relevant body of materials to draw upon.

Here he seemed to endorse Macdonald's view of a highly individual radicalism fashioned with the intention of keeping the flame of resistance kindled during an indefinite period of oppressive social stability. Bell recognized, however, the unsatisfactory quietist overtones to his tragic sense of a fifty-year interregnum. Even in Macdonald's sense of sustaining the radical flame, immediate political options were not irrelevant, Bell cautioned, for certain societies left at least small crevices open for the alienated while others eliminated all havens:

> Translating this in political terms, there is a real alternative as the kind of bureaucratic state possible: it can be a democratic bureaucracy, observing the forms of civil liberties; or a totalitarian bureaucracy; a state where unions can mitigate the basic evils of rationalization against a state where the situation is aggravated, a state which permits discussion, even if only in cloistered libraries against one that perpetuates Buchenwalds. In that respect the current struggles are not entirely meaningless.
>
> If I could, I would insist that the battle must be conducted on two levels; but how, I don't know.[59]

The "two levels" Bell sought were already explored in his key sources of moral reflection at this time—Weber and Niebuhr. The two "ethics" in Weber's discourse, "Politics as a Vocation," and the double vision of utopian and realistic motivations in Niebuhr's writing framed the issue. Both discussions, however, reveal the treachery of morality as a ground of political action.

I have already indicated that morality became acutely problematic in terms of the central paradigm of modern German sociology, the decay of organic communal life and the rise of a society founded on artificial interpersonal ties resting solely on rational calculation. The shift ruptured the traditional identity of private and public life, the integration of the individual's ends of action with those of the collective. By isolating the private self from the social whole outside it, "society" as such enforced a split between subject and object, between private consciousness and public activity.

This disjuncture underlay Weber's argument on the incompatibility of morals and politics in his 1918 lecture, "Politics as a Vocation." Speaking under the shadow of the German revolution, he warned that radical political enthusiasm implied the elusive ideal of reconstituting a morally whole social life. Weber pointed out, however, that morality was "one-sided, unconditional." It was, as Lukács had argued in his essay, "On Poverty of Spirit," wholly subjective: moral judgment ultimately concerned itself with the purity of intention, for the moral individual could not be swayed from commitment by any adverse effects of right action. So Weber repeated, "'The Christian does rightly and leaves the results with the Lord.'"[60] Politics, however, were carried on in the outer world, and necessarily counterposed the moral "ethic of ultimate ends" with the "ethic of responsibility, in which case one had to give an account of the foreseeable results of one's action."[61] In raising the issue of the practical aims and concrete effects of political action, Weber supposed, one also came to recognize the inappropriateness of the absolute, principled consistency of moral action. The difficulty in politics was precisely that means and ends were often inevitably *incongruous*—one could not rely, for instance, on peaceful means to render peaceful ends.

> No ethics in the world can dodge the fact that in numerous instances the attainment of 'good' ends is bound to the fact that one must be willing to pay the price of using morally dubious means or at least dangerous ones—and facing the possibility or even the probability of evil ramifications. From no ethics in the world can it be concluded when and to what extent the ethically good purpose 'justifies' the ethically dangerous means and ramifications. . . . Whoever wants to engage in politics at all, and especially in politics as a vocation, has to realize these ethical paradoxes.[62]

Reinhold Niebuhr's treatment of morality and its relation to politics approached Weber's view of the problem, resting likewise on the ineluctable disjunction between the individual and society, a disjunction that German sociology assumed as a given fact of postcommunal life. In *Moral Man and Immoral Society* (1932), Niebuhr had argued that society could never be moralized in full. In his view, morality operated on the plane of the individual, capable in part of living by love in immediate and intimate relations with others. But he considered the capacities of the human heart and mind too limited to allow people to recognize, accept, and honor all the interests that transcended their own primary collective identifications. While John Dewey sought to remake the "Great Society" as a "Great Community," Niebuhr asserted that cohesive community life could not be reconstituted.

This did not mean that morals were excluded from political concerns. The paradoxes of politics, though intractable, were equally inescapable, Niebuhr said, and any true morality had to face the demands of social amelioration while modestly recognizing the partial and insufficient character of all solutions. "We cannot purge ourselves of the sin and guilt in which we are involved by the moral ambiguities of politics without also disavowing responsibility for the creative possibilities of justice."[63] Still, the relation of morality to political criticism in Niebuhr's thought was highly ambiguous, for in his constantly shifting dialectic, it was extremely difficult to decide when one had reached the ultimate limits of the finite, stopping utopian aspiration, and when one could cross the line in pursuit of a far-reaching, but practical, aim. "The line between the creative and the inordinate" in human aspirations, Niebuhr wrote, could not "be simply drawn."[64]

> It is never possible to define the limits of the force of sin or of the ideal possibilities which transcend sin. One cannot, by definition, determine where and when an inequality of nature or history must be accepted as ineluctable fate and where it must be defied. . . . There are no precise distinctions either between relative and absolute natural law, as there are none between natural law and the law of love, for the simple reason that the freedom of spirit is so enmeshed in the necessities of nature, and the health and sickness of that freedom are so involved in each other, that it is not possible to make rules isolating certain aspects of nature and sin without having them disturbed by the claims of the law of love as the requirement of freedom.[65]

Hence Niebuhr's theory of politics offered no firm grounds of decision. The theory had an intrinsic tendency to vacillate between political resistance and reconciliation. Its theologically based skepticism could lead to political "realism," the acknowledgment of and adaptation to entrenched power, thus eschewing a critical ideal; on the other hand, the humility that knew that all human situations, nay, all moral achievements, were tainted with sin could inspire a persistent radical criticism that recognized the evil within every social order, no matter how healthy and stable it appeared.

For Bell in the years after the war, as for Weber and Niebuhr, a discourse of "two levels" constituted a double bind for the moral actor, driven to affirm central values while deprived of opportunities to express them. The definition of social order he offered—a self-reproductive whole integrating all agencies of social action—extruded radicalism into a posture of wholesale but hopeless opposition. The radical individual faced the social organism as a subject dirempted from its object. If under these circumstances radicalism assumed a distinctly *moral* stance, it also lost political relevance; its virtue lay in its unqualified, absolute hostility to society, but as such it stood at a far remove from any practical action. Hence the determinist and voluntarist (or moralist) elements in Bell's thought could not be resolved. The stringent limits of social structure incited opposition and ruled out its efficacy at the same time. Thus, for Bell, the same radical critique that denounced the integrative sweep of the new order—and mocked the "pathetic" liberals who could not recognize the determining "bone structure" behind official policy—also denied meaning to the exemplary moral action advocated by the radicals of Macdonald's camp. Bell wrote to Macdonald,

> I think the main value of Politics over its first year and a half period was to show how deeply rooted are these institutional pulls which are shaping our direction. Yet every proposed solution or re-evaluation [in the New Roads series] ignores these studies [from the early issues of *Politics* he cited Walter J. Oakes on the permanent war economy, himself on the bureaucratization of labor, Arthur Pincus on the "new imperialism"] and starts with the assumption of some free-will, and that if we only had the "right" road, then we could proceed ahead. I think the basic function of *Politics* as a magazine is to assess realistically the extent of the committments [*sic*] society already has because of the institutional structure and the role utopian values can play in terms of the politically relevant alternatives.[66]

The double vision of utopian and realistic politics was Niebuhr's idea. What Bell revealed of himself in the entire discussion was the conundrum of his thought in the postwar years, his persistent attempt to relate the two poles of moral absolutism and political practicality, utopianism and responsibility.

The troublesome tension between critique and action which arose in his sympathetic polemic against the New Roads writers, appeared again in Bell's review of Saul Alinsky's *Reveille for Radicals* in the March 1946 issue of *Commentary*, the only published piece that explored the argument of his unfinished essay on "The Centralization of Decision." Here he outlined the conditions of a highly industrialized mass society: the fragmentation of communal ties and the replacement of intimate personal relationships by functional coordination of anonymous individuals; the bureaucratization of all organizations and the distance between the grass roots and the loci of centralized power and decision-making; the widespread feelings of dependence and helplessness that resulted finally in "a life of ordered insecurities whose psychological concomitants are bewilderment and frustration." In this context, Bell said, the "sense of participation" that Alinsky sought to realize in activist "neighborhood councils" could be a vital hedge against fascist movements arising from the despair of atomized masses. But Bell wondered how Alinsky's "people's organizations" would relate to church, union, and other institutions already "rooted" in people's everyday lives and to the established power blocs exerting "pulls" on social affairs.

> The activities of Alinsky's Councils raise quite explicitly the questions of the limits of individual activity in a technologically organized and power-massed society, and yet fail woefully to define them. One of our crucial jobs is to explore the range of activities through which people can genuinely share in the basic decisions that affect them and in molding a society responsive to their economic and emotional needs. Otherwise the "people" and these "People's Organizations" may in their despair become another version of Italy's *L'Uomo Qualunque*.

Referring in this way to the protofascist "Common-Man Front," which arose in Italy amidst the frustrations of stymied postwar reform, Bell brought the issue full circle, suggesting that radical action against the effects of bureaucratization might end up compounding the problem.[67]

Alienation and the Critical Role of the Modern Intellectual

Bell further explored the role of values in radicalism in an article published in the November 1946 issue of *Jewish Frontier*, "A Parable of Alienation," which he considered a "companion piece" to the unfinished essay on centralization. It was, he told Macdonald, "a curious complement to your approach, yet because of its Jewish slant it may rub you the wrong way." But while Bell's essay focused on the peculiarities of Jewish experience (as illuminated by Isaac Rosenfeld's novel, *Passage From Home*) it actually summed up a coherent sociological analysis of the two complementary elements of mass society, bureaucracy and alienation, and delineated terms of being for the contemporary "homeless radical."[68]

In the tradition of German sociology, Bell's essay began with a discussion of "the divorce in our contemporary world between moral and secular conceptions," another way of phrasing Weber's notion of rationalization, "the disenchantment of the world." Bell presented

Weber's "rationalization" as a more general formulation of the process Marx found in the separation of the worker from the means of production, a thoroughgoing depersonalization of society. Bell summed up the tendency as the replacement of the principle of brotherhood by the principle of "otherhood." The old morality of kinship relations nonetheless survived in the atomized society as an ineffectual urge, a frustrated search for belonging that engendered the spurious communities of the fascist *Volk* and communist comradeship. This modern anxiety made the Jew the peculiar object of suspicion and resentment, Bell suggested. Approximating Horkheimer and Adorno's analysis of anti-Semitism, which proposed that the Jew represented to the popular mind both disintegrative Enlightenment rationalism and *mimesis* (the atavistic return to nature), Bell suggested that the rootless and isolated Jew represented the feared dissolution of community at the same time the "clannishness" of Jewish family life represented the fugitive ideal of wholeness.[69]

In Rosenfeld's novel, however, Bell found evidence that secularization invaded the heart of Jewish culture itself, as a young boy, having learned how tawdry are the appeals of city life at large, finds it impossible to consummate a reunion with his family. The dilemma was archetypal, Bell believed:

> The young Jew is left helpless, and aware. He is aware of a distance both from the Jewish culture from which he came and the Gentile culture into which he cannot or will not enter. He is helpless, for he cannot find his roots in either. Yet out of this tension of understanding and inhibition has been bred a new kind of Jew, the Jew of alienation, a Jew who consciously accepts this situation and utilizes his alienation to see, as if with a double set of glasses, each blending their perspective into one, the nature of the tragedy of our time. . . . The Jew cannot go home. He can only live in alienation.

Rosenfeld's story, Bell said, was the parable of the homeless radical—a socialist by conviction (Rosenfeld himself had been a Trotskyist) repelled by the futility and authoritarianism of a revolutionary party, yet hardly reconciled to the destructive values of existing society—"the increasing centralization of decision, the narrowing of the area of free moral choice, the extension into domains, particularly the cultural, of the rationalized, stilted forms of mass organization and bureaucracy, the rising sense of nationalism as a product of the war." What role could such a dissident play, if not as spokesman of critical thought frankly aloof from action—because all existing avenues, in active support of or opposition to the established order, "exact [their] own conformities." "All that is left is the hardness of alienation, the sense of otherness. And with a special critical faculty, an unwillingness to submerge our values completely into any 'cause' because of the germ cells of corruption which are in the seeds of organization." The calling of detached criticism, "the role of the prophet," Bell added, should not be considered deracinated, for "it means the acceptance of the Jewish tradition—its compulsion to community—and the use of its ethical precepts as a prism to refract the codes and conduct of the world."

> The plight—and glory—of the alienated Jewish intellectual is that his role is to point to the need of brotherhood, but as he has been bred, he cannot today accept any embodiment of community as final. He can live only in permanent tension and as a permanent critic.[70]

Thus Bell located two forms of alienation that emerge as counterparts of bureaucratization. The first, the frustrated search of masses for community, is only a spurious resistance, for it yields the fanaticism of ideology that fuels even more demonic advances of bureaucratization. The second, the alienation of skeptic-radicalism, the positive value of standing apart from dominant values, offers the only opportunity to oppose, challenge, restrain, and reform bureaucracy.[71]

The concept of "alienation" in Bell's article was clearly not a Marxian one. Although the concept's role in Marx's work, early and late, has often been debated, it is safe to say that it played an essential role in the discussion of commodity fetishism in *Capital*, where Marx showed how the exploitation of labor led to objectified and mystified economic relations. Lukács's treatment, in *History and Class Consciousness*, of the "phenomenon of reification" successfully elevated alienation to the center of Marxist philosophy, a reading that the late publication, in 1932, of the Paris manuscripts seemed to justify. In the United States Sidney Hook's book, *From Hegel to Marx* (1936), was based on the rediscovered early writings, but Hook, who was eager to discover a pragmatist social epistemology in Marx, sought to draw him away from Hegel. Thus Hook saw Marx's focus on alienation in 1844 as a sign of baneful dependence on the spiritual foundations of Hegelianism, which was anxious to bridge the gulf between humanity and God.[72]

Nonetheless, Bell was not unfamiliar with Marx's concept of alienation: in his 1942 polemic against Maritain he had cited it as the ethical foundation of socialism, i.e., the aim of overcoming the "divorce" of the laborer "from the satisfactions of his job," though he granted, in line with Hook, that it had "almost [a] theological" character.[73] In his 1944 essay on anti-Semitism, based largely on the work of Erich Fromm and other members of the early Frankfurt School, Bell reasserted that alienation was one of Marx's essential contributions to modern social theory. By 1946, however, Bell clearly sank Marx's "alienation" into the generic sociological concept of specialization, the fragmentation of all activity and the separation of the actor from the means of action. For him, then, "alienation" came to connote estrangement, an unconquerable sense of "otherness," rather than reification, the subordination of humans to their own objectified creations. Alienation then became a given fact of modernity, and Bell assumed the burden of Weber's and Simmel's tragic sense of life, as the peculiar role of the modern radical.[74]

By this time, too, there was more clearly a religious cast to Bell's discussion of alienation. In part the essay was spawned by the isolation he felt as a Jewish New Yorker in a largely Gentile midwestern environment;[75] he had, in fact, sought to salve his sense of deracination by joining a Judaic study group (including Daniel Boorstin and Benjamin Nelson) at the University's Hillel foundation. There may have been a specifically theological root to Bell's argument. As the liberal Zionist scholar Gershom Scholem wrote, "In *galut* [exile] there can be no Jewish community valid before God. And if community among human beings is indeed the highest that can be demanded, what would be the sense of Zionism if it could be realized in *galut*?"[76] In his essay, though, Bell explicitly stated that Zionism—at least in the sense of *aliyah*, or emigration—had no appeal for him or his kind. Hence exile would be a permanent condition and the need of community would remain urgent but unsatisfied. By refusing the personal relevance of Zionism, then, Bell could approach, in Jewish terms, Niebuhr's Protestant premise that moral values, rooted ultimately in the divine, constantly judged a human reality that could never concretize them fully or finally.

Even in earlier, more political times, Bell was hardly reticent about his Jewish identity. His conversation, even with non-Jewish associates, was from time to time lightened by Yiddishisms or casual references to the cozy atmosphere, the "latkes and herring," of Jewish home life.[77] Indeed, he always longed to recreate that familial intimacy with key figures in his life, with the elders of the Socialist Party or with Sol Levitas and his exiled Menshevik friends, Boris Nicolaevsky and Raphael Abramovitch, and thus to reclaim a "home," as Rosenfeld's protagonist wished to.

Nonetheless, it would be a mistake to attach undue importance to the specifically Jewish identity of Bell's model in "A Parable of Alienation." Although critics challenged Bell for suggesting that the salutary alienation he described was a privileged property of Jews, Jewishness was clearly parabolic, as his title suggested.[78] Parable aside, Bell's definition of the intellectual as a detached critic, in tension with mass society, had a clear modernist pedigree, certainly dating back as far as Matthew Arnold's *Culture and Anarchy* (1869), which called for a small number of creative "aliens" to nurture culture, in a struggle against the barbarity and philistinism of all the social classes. The Arnoldian project was renewed in the late 1920s and early 1930s by the circle around the British literary journal *Scrutiny*, who sought to fashion a "new social estate" of intellectuals combating "the systematic cultivation of conformism, quietism and . . . hostility to criticism of any kind."[79] The new role of the critic—not merely in a literary but in a general social and cultural sense—was in part based on the model of the "clerk" in Julien Benda's *Treason of the Intellectuals* (1927), the guardian of value confronting the "laymen" corrupted by the commercial and military life.

The modern "tradition" of the alien critic was intimately tied to the modern depiction of mass society. Almost at the same time as Benda's *Treason of the Intellectuals*, Ortega y Gasset's *Revolt of the Masses* (1926) described mass society as an "invertebrate" order of homogenized, faceless men threatening the integrity of rational, cultured elites. The existentialist philosophy of Karl Jaspers' *Man in the Modern Age* (1932) similarly lamented the facelessness, the "chronic lack of selfhood" and the pervasive sense of powerlessness characterizing contemporary mass society. Somehow, the intellectual, whose condition epitomized the deracination, the "essential homelessness" (as Jaspers' student, Hannah Arendt, put it), of the masses, was to check this levelling tendency toward a meaningless, passive existence. Karl Mannheim thus called upon the "free-floating" (or "unattached") intellectuals, recruited from all social classes and rooted in none, to act as "watchmen in what otherwise would be a pitch-black night."[80]

This modern tradition continued in the 1930s, even inflecting the Leninist notions of revolutionary leadership—at times misconstrued as the distinguished vocation of the intellectual—which were then current. It lived on at *Partisan Review*, which assailed intellectuals for failing to fight the forces that would reduce culture to a means of political control and artificial social harmony. Modern art, *Partisan Review* editor William Phillips said in an Ortegan vein, was an expression of an intelligentsia "thriving on its very anxiety over survival and its consciousness of being an elite." Through the 1940s, *Partisan Review* defined its politics by its commitment to protect that modernist elite from the threat of commercialism and cultural homogenization.[81] Thus Bell's view of the radical as both creature and critic of alienation inherited the modernist definition of the intellectual which was well entrenched in his cultural milieu.

Similar to Bell's treatment of the two sides of alienation and the double vision of the intellectual was C. Wright Mills's essay, "The Powerless People" (1944), written while he was collaborating with the exiled German scholar Hans Gerth on their anthology of Weber's work. The "tragic sense of life" that characterized his times, Mills said, reflected the prevalence of bureaucratic organization and the "irresponsibility" it bred. The modern structure of decision-making permitted an elite few, shielded from accountability in the intricate web of bureaucratic apparatuses, to make choices that determined the lives of the heteronomous and helpless many. Mills followed Weber by including the intellectual in this general process of expropriation from the means of self-determining activity: the rationalization of the modalities of intellect—the absorption of intellectuals within highly organized academic, communication, and government services—progressively cut the thinker off from avenues of significant action:

> We continue to know more and more about modern society, but we find the centers of political initiative less and less accessible. This generates a personal malady that is particularly acute in the intellectual who has labored under the illusion that his thinking makes a difference. In the world of today the more his knowledge of affairs grows, the less effective the impact of his thinking seems to become. Since he grows more frustrated as his knowledge increases, it seems that knowledge leads to powerlessness. He feels. helpless in the fundamental sense that he cannot control what he is able to foresee.

Mills's model intellectual, however, would recognize the fact of alienation without submitting to it, would "constantly shuttle between the understanding which is made possible by detachment and the longing and working for a politics of truth in a society which is responsible." Mills, like Bell, saw alienation as both the dehumanizing consequence of bureaucratization and the ground of critical insight combating it, and he depicted the role of the intellectual two-sidedly as the combination of detachment and engagement, following the two ethics, of conscience and responsibility, that Weber discussed in "Politics as a Vocation."[82]

Bell differed from Mills, however, in the interpretation of Weber's "ethic of responsibility," and his was closer to Weber's intention than Mills's was. In Mills's discourse, "responsibility," while evoking one of Weber's two ethics, actually carried a Deweyan meaning: a principle of action and a social goal, the establishment of a rational society wherein individuals directly and consciously decided their course of action based on the desirability of the effects they would consequently have to bear.[83] Bell, on the other hand, recognized that Weber's "responsibility" was not a principle of radical insurgency, as Mills would have it, but the principle that compelled concrete political action to recognize the narrow limits within which it had to work. It was this "ethic of responsibility" that led Bell to question his own radical quietism, to balance estrangement (existential aloofness) with action (choice), just as Mills said "responsibility" required the intellectual to come out of alienation into political engagement: but Bell recognized also that it meant qualifying, indeed reducing or limiting, the radical impulse in order to make it practical.

Bell's Weberian critique of utopianism (the ethic of conscience), however, was not at all motivated by a vulgar "realism" that restricted social and political affairs to the narrow bounds of self-interest and bare power. In the April 29, 1946, *Progressive*, Bell wrote disdainfully,

> Ours is a Machiavellian world. Each man is a 'realist' and woe betide the person who dares whisper some notion, especially a political one, which carries the taint of utopianism. And so, every one of the spate of books on world politics is a 'realistic' appraisal; and since politics is the 'art of the possible,' only the possibilities are discussed.

Geopolitical "realism," which Bell had earlier portrayed as the ideological correlate of the "power politics" that emerged with the Big Three war settlements, he still considered insidious.[84] Rather, Bell's whole effort was devoted to adjudicating the balance between moral purpose, which like Macdonald he increasingly saw as the source of radicalism, and the political impulse exercised on a terrain of concrete efficacious action that was woefully restricted in scope. In this effort, more than many of his contenders at the time, he grasped the essence of the sociological and existentialist mentalities. The existentialist philosopher Karl Jaspers found in Max Weber "a new type of man who had the poise to hold together in synthesis the tremendous tensions of his own self as well as the contradictions of external public life without resorting to illusions." This too was the model of Bell's unattached, but responsible intellectual.[85]

The Practice of Critical Sociology

The duality of moralism and skepticism that was fixed in Bell's mentality in the 1930s, and his continuing attempt to fashion a delicate balance of utopianism and realism, was reflected in the basic structure of his sociological analysis, the study of interrelated *ideals and interests* in social action and order. In a July 1946 review article, he found this intellectual paradigm in the classic republican thought of John Adams and James Madison.

> If one can draw a unified impression of the economic mind of America, it is that of the moral ambiguity of early liberalism's efforts to harmonize ideals and interests, its efforts to make freedom and wealth compatible by fusing ethics and economics into a unity. Yet the attempt, even if unsuccessful in practice, contained an important principle for a democratic philosophy. For it is in the interplay of ideals and interests that a free society strikes the necessary balance for survival. In Machiavelli's time, as possibly in our own, the dominance of material interests as a political force divorced from any sense of ideals, led to cynicism and corruption. The mere proclamation of ideals, detached, in the totalitarian pattern, from divergent or competing interests, can only lead to a fanaticism typified by the religious wars of the past and the cruelty of fascism and Stalinism today.[86]

The mediation of ideals and interests provided Bell with a model of social reform, for as we shall see his vision of the good society rested essentially on the goal of "fusing ethics and economics into a unity." The same mediation, to his mind, underlay any sociological analysis that would adequately grasp the real structural basis of ideology without denying the reality of subjective motivations.

The first major essay that manifested Bell's method of critical sociology was "Adjusting Men to Machines: Social Scientists Explore the World of the Factory," which appeared in the January 1947 issue of *Commentary*. Along with C. Wright Mills's essay two years later on "The Contribution of Sociology to Studies of Industrial Relations," Bell's piece was one of the earliest radical critiques of the school of industrial sociology founded by Elton Mayo at Harvard University in the 1930s, which sought to examine the factory as a social system, aiming to institutionalize those personal ties that knit it together as a common world.[87] For Bell, Mayo's goal was precisely the kind of spurious community that arose atop rationalized existence, and he considered

Mayo's work to be "a perfect picture of the benevolent bureaucratic state."[88]

The first striking feature of Bell's essay, "Adjusting Men to Machines," was its antipositivism, the critique of sociological practice that denies its own value-motivation. The industrial sociologists, Bell wrote, claimed "they are concerned with 'what is' and are not inclined to involve themselves in questions of moral values or larger social issues," sticking closely to problems they perceived as value-free technical ones.

> Many conceive of themselves as "human engineers," counterparts to the industrial engineers: where the industrial engineer plans a flow of work in order to assure greater mechanical efficiency, the "human engineer" tries to "adjust" the worker to his job so that the human equation will match the industrial equation. To effect this, the sociologists seek "laws" of human behavior analogous to the laws of the physical world, and by and large they give little thought to the fact that they are *not* operating in the physical world. And almost none among them seem to be interested in the possibility that one of the functions of social science may be to explore *alternative* (and better, i.e., more human) modes of human combinations, not merely to make more effective those that already exist.

The professed exclusion of ideals, Bell suggested, actually masked real interests. Taking "the present organization of industrial production, inhuman as it may be . . . as an inalterable 'given,'" specious "scientific objectivity" implied "the unstated assumption that mechanical efficiency and high output are the sole tests of achievement." This assumption was nothing less than the guiding principle of those at the top of industry's command structure, for whom the demands of the market, "the logic of cost, efficiency, and competition," were the only imperatives, regardless of the consequences borne by those who worked. Thus the sociologists' assertion that industrial tensions were resolvable by perfecting paths of communication between cooperative workers and management obscured the conflicting interests that made the implementation of technological advances and the distribution of their rewards a significant social problem to be resolved politically rather than technically. The sociologists' technical solution, denying the autonomous role of values, served only to reproduce the "given" situation and furthered "the increasing 'rationalization' of living (its organization for greater efficiency), pervading all areas and narrowing all choices."[89]

For Bell the motivation of ideal values had to be part of the sociological enterprise, and the overriding value to be realized in sociological research was simply the primacy of the human personality, the
direct opposite of the prevailing view of industrial sociology, which
treated workers "as *means* to be manipulated or adjusted to impersonal ends." "The belief in man as an end in himself has been ground
under by the machine," Bell continued, "and the social science of the
factory researchers is not a science of man, but a cow-sociology." In
contrast to the prevailing industrial sociology, Bell suggested, a valuable and value-motivated industrial sociology should try "to see what
kinds of jobs can best stimulate the spontaneity and freedom of the
worker, and how we can alter our industrial methods to assure such
jobs."[90]

In this essay Bell also introduced his analysis of changing class
structure, an analysis of interests which he supposed would substanti-
ate the subjective element better than the prevailing factory sociology.
Bell saw a new "class of technical and managerial employees" arising
from the rationalization of industry, the growth of research, and the
macroeconomic shift from manufacturing to services—accompanied
by the steady deskilling of labor and the emergence of a "general class
of semi-skilled machine tenders." "Thus a class of interchangeable
factory 'hands' is at last becoming a reality, and the 'promise' of the
factory system, as described by Marx, is only now being fulfilled." This
process of development, he said, also rigidified class boundaries, reduced easy vertical job mobility by placing a barrier of privileged credentials in front of the skill-less, and thus reinforced the "class consciousness" of workers who felt permanently "stuck" *as* workers. In
this class framework "status" and "solidarity" motivations were not
merely abstract categories of psychological traits, as the factory sociologists treated them. Rather "status" concerns of invidious rank distinctions probably characterized white collar, supervisory, and managerial employees, and "solidarity" concerns, driven by frustration
and resentment, probably characterized production workers. Consequently, Bell suggested,

> One might look for the development of certain types of militancy
> among workers—a militancy not necessarily political in its tone or
> motivation, but one just as likely to be anti-Semitic or anti-Negro
> or nihilistic. Again, one might look for the beginnings of an elite
> psychology in the technical and managerial groups, perhaps of a
> kind that has played such a significant role in statist movements
> and societies.[91]

With this approach, a quasi-Marxist class analysis yielded results Marxists had not expected. As in "The Face of Tomorrow," Marxist and mass-society analysis cohabited, but by this point, Bell no longer proposed that the socialist movement could act as a hedge against the totalitarian potential of mass society. Rather he attributed a privileged role to the critical sociologist, one "concerned with the social future of our democracy and not merely with increasing the productivity of its industrial machine," one who sympathized with the interests and plight of the worker but had little trust in him as a political agent.

Thus as Bell worried over the totalitarian propensities of frustrated masses, he saw the role of the critic specifically in terms of resisting the onrush of rationalization and the alienated resentment that resulted from it. Bell's continual critique of "mass culture" through this period clearly belies historian Robert Skotheim's assertion that the concept of totalitarianism in the 1930s and 1940s conferred on American society the privileged role as unquestioned defender of democracy in a Manichean world struggle with dictatorship. Echoing Horkheimer and Adorno's critique of the "culture industry," Bell considered his period "a time when our emotions are drained from us by the repetitiveness of horror and in their place is pumped the euphoric sentimentalism of the standardized entertainments." Mass communications pervaded common life, transformed their audience into a mass of passive spectators, and helped eliminate the preserves of privacy. The loss of privacy, a marked symptom of "the decay of our society," manifested itself in the proliferation of loyalty oaths and subversion tests, in functional home design, radio programing, the uses of psychiatry, and all "the mosaic of elements that go to make up what we call our culture and way of living."

> The stripping of man's privacy in the concentration camp is direct, stark and brutal. For most of us that is a nightmare world far away with little probability that it can affect "us." But the concentration camp is not an isolated act. It is the advance guard of the great transformation . . . on the road to a herd society.

Again contemporary social research was part of the problem rather than the solution. Bell remarked, for instance, that the corporate applications of Rorschach and Thematic Apperception tests helped "creat[e] standardized personality types," and "shap[e] bureaucratic monoliths."[92]

This was the subject of Bell's second major venture in sociological critique, "'Screening' Leaders in a Democracy: How Scientific is Personnel Testing," which appeared in the April 1948 *Commentary*. In this piece, Bell probed more deeply into the ambiguities of bureaucratized society, particularly the question of how leadership could be distinguished from authoritarian control. But his profundity here led increasingly toward paralysis, as the polar categories of sociological analysis maddeningly shifted position and melded into each other.

As in "Adjusting Men," Bell's "'Screening' Leaders" pursued an antipositivist tack. Sophisticated psychological exams became merely a means of screening applicants for an inventory of traits the corporations already valued in their management apparatus; the tests offered a specious "scientific" confirmation of given structures of social relations. "Far from providing scientific tests of leadership capacity, may they not merely place 'scientific' authority behind pre-scientific traditional leadership images?" Given the increasingly intimate relation between academicians and industry, he asked, "does not the tendency of much present-day social science, which is to fit people into a niche in a previously determined bureaucratic and hierarchical structure, violate the values of both free scientific inquiry and democracy?"[93]

But what is "democratic" leadership? Bell reviewed recent sociological studies of various "climates of leadership," which found that the "democratic" groups, permitting participatory discussion and planning, were more steadily productive, more resilient, and more immune to scapegoating than the groups characterized by "authoritarian" or "laissez faire" (unstructured) decision making. But if these studies suggested that people could be "educated in a non-manipulative way" to encourage self-reliance, Bell pointed out the manipulative potential of even the "democratic" concept of "participation," which even the industrial sociologists endorsed in their image of an illusory community of understanding between workers and managers. In fact, Bell wrote,

> participation as a goal in its own terms is meaningless. The fascist and Communist systems also emphasize participation. In the 1930s and even today the main attraction of the Soviet system for many liberals has been the sense of "belongingness" it created.

What, indeed, did "democracy" mean in the rationalized society, where inevitably complex technologies and organizations, binding large numbers of people in integrated tasks and responsibilities, rendered direct action, strictly speaking, impossible? And, given the powerful psychological disorientation produced by such a society, how was "democracy" shielded from its totalitarian inversion? In Bell's terms of analysis, these questions were all but unanswerable. The given social structure was all too integrated, self-reproductive, and perdurable. "Ultimately," he wrote, "the problem of leadership is shaped by the fact that while we live in a society of political democracy, almost all basic social patterns are authoritarian and tend to instill feelings of helplessness and dependence." The family, school, and factory all "impose the basic patterns of conformity" to the authoritarian leadership that pervades social life. "Within this inescapable context, will not participation appear as only another form of support for precisely those authoritarian economic and industrial structures which well-intentioned sociologists and psychologists wish to eliminate?"[94]

In part, Bell sought an answer by criticizing the unreal abstractions of most small-group social research, as he had criticized the abstract psychologism of factory research.

> The problem of bureaucratization can also be considered within the context of *power*, and, within that area, as a *conflict of interests*. These interests are . . . sociological—and political and economic—insofar as they are most intimately intertwined with the key problem of how our society intends to distribute the rewards and privileges at its disposal.
>
> It is rather curious that even among . . . democratically-motivated psychologists . . . there is no mention of the role of the trade union movement. A trade union exists in many areas, after all, largely because the need for belongingness and solidarity which the workers feel can only be fulfilled genuinely and independently outside the power structure of the factory hierarchy. And in the crucial morale test it is those unions which satisfy this need that are successful.

In earlier articles, however, Bell had already shown that the unions were themselves bureaucratic organizations integrated with the productive apparatus of industry—legitimated channels of resentment, as he said in 1945, that served to maintain order and constancy in industrial relations. If the ambiguity of "democratic" principles forced him here to return to the unions, as relatively independent and alternative structures of loyalty and obedience that could act as a check on the power of business management, he would also have to follow the dynamics of labor organization back into the closed circle of bureaucratic order. So it seemed that the subtle sociological analysis of the order and antinomies of society allowed the critic no exit. It was on such a "note of doubt" that Bell ended his essay.[95] Thus the practical limits of estrangement as a potent radical stance were revealed. For, from estrangement there was nowhere to go—but toward reconciliation with what was given and inescapable.

4

Choosing the West

The Death of Socialism in the Bureaucratized Society

Daniel Bell stepped out of his cloister at the University of Chicago in the summer of 1948, and the balance between estrangement and reconciliation tipped. Indeed, the intellectual and political perspective he had cultivated in the years following the Second World War—which showed society congealing into a monolithic bureaucratic mold, permitting radical opposition only in the form of critical values applied from the outside, or on the margins—posed a stark set of options. "The men of action can only choose alternative paths within the dominant framework," he had written to Dwight Macdonald. "The only constructive role we can play is that of critics." So conceived, opposition (criticism) rested on the suspension of action, and action demanded the surrender of opposition. The formula predetermined the outcome: if he was to assume again a public role, engaged with the social and political forces of his day, nothing was possible but an accommodation with prevailing structures of power. Thus, as his intellectual development reached a plateau with completion of his first major work, *The Background and Development of Marxian Socialism in the United States* (1952), Bell came to stand within the bounds of convention, looking outward from the cage of bureaucratic order.

In his monograph, written during 1949 and 1950, Bell filtered the socialist experience through his reflections on the dilemma of the "critic," who was morally bound to remain apart while the demands of responsibility and political involvement beckoned. The socialist movement, he claimed, had been drawn out of the political sphere of practical action by the intensity of its moral opposition: now was the time for socialists to follow organized labor and find a place *in* capitalist order. There was some justification for such a decision, Bell suggested, for the organizing tendencies of capitalism itself opened a path toward the political subordination of economics in a rational society. And yet Bell was too imbued with modern theory to let this evolutionist, social-democratic tenet go unquestioned. In Weber, we recall, the gesture of reconciliation involved "renounc[ing] . . . man's accessibility to any meaning of the world," and thus recognized the absence of value in the world it accepted. Absence, loss—a vacuum of values needed to achieve the political subordination of economics—was likewise the marked feature of the social reality that Bell accepted, and his mature social theory withdrew the very promise of progress it offered and recognized the obstruction of its aspirations. The standpoint of moral opposition hamstrung the Socialist Party, Bell suggested, since the practice of politics in a capitalist society required the party "to take stands on particular issues which arise out of it and thus get enmeshed within its web." Bell's language revealed his ambivalence: the political accommodation he advocated was, he recognized implicitly, as much a trap as an auspicious opening to reform.

That Daniel Bell turned toward accommodation after 1948 is neither surprising nor unique. His reconciliation was less a consequence of individual decision, motivated by private dispositions or traits of character, than a particular expression of a general ideological current shaped by a confluence of historical forces reaching a special intensity at this time. The context, most broadly speaking, was the full emergence of a solution to the prewar economic crisis, based on the preeminent American role in the reconstruction of the world market and on the realignment of social forces—particularly the entry of labor and social-democratic elements into an official compromise—under that umbrella. A set of events in domestic and international politics—signaling the first major eruption of Cold War tensions, the political weakness of the left, and the construction of welfare economies—marked the years 1947–48 as a crucial turning point in the revelation of this new synthesis. The push and pull of the Cold War and the Welfare State brought social democracy within the fold, and only within this condensation of historical determinations did the internal logic of Daniel Bell's thought—the conversion of opposites, from estrangement to reconciliation—take its course.

By 1948, it had become clear that the economic depression in the United States which was expected to follow the war would not materialize; rather than return to conditions of economic decline after the temporary prosperity of wartime, the downward spiral of crisis was reversed. The absence of a major postwar recession can be attributed to a concatenation of factors: the pent-up demand present in hoarded wages and profits at the end of the war, the strength of the working class in maintaining a high wage level in the postwar years and sustaining social consumption, the wide investment opportunities available to internationalized American capital, the erection of a new world monetary structure facilitating the free flow of trade and the settlement of debts.

The situation in Western Europe, however, looked considerably different. The economies of the war-torn countries worsened in the winter of 1946–47. In France, after two years without a major strike, the Renault workers struck for higher wages, initiating a broad-based strike wave and forcing the Communists, who had until this point urged austerity for the sake of reconstruction, to challenge government wage and price policy. As a result, in May 1947, the Communist Party was expelled from the tripartite government coalition, leaving the Socialists in the cabinet with the Catholic *Mouvement Républicain Populaire*. In Italy, tripartitism ended that same month, under the urging of American aid officials. Both the United States and the Soviet Union had embarked on political offensives. The consolidation of Russian control in the East—marked by the arrest of liberal political leaders in Hungary that summer and the Communist coup that overthrew the Czechoslovakian coalition government in early 1948—intensified anti-Soviet sentiment throughout the West. Meanwhile, the United States began a concerted campaign to win political sway over Western Europe. In the spring, as labor law was debated in Congress, Truman announced military aid to Greece and Turkey, adding a domestic loyalty program a week later. The Truman Doctrine did not work immediately to win broad political support, either in the United States or in Europe, for an aggressive American foreign policy. Yet, if the saber-rattling of the Truman Doctrine alienated Western European socialists, the Marshall Plan represented a slight shift leftward, putting a more benign face on American policy and winning wide social-democratic support.[1]

At this time, the State Department, recognizing the marked left-leaning political climate of Western Europe following Liberation, tried cultivating the friendship of socialists and trade unionists while placing a wedge between these forces and their left flank.[2] The Marshall Plan was motivated by U.S. fear that Soviet policy would benefit from the turmoil of Western Europe. It sought a political and social realignment, in which economic growth could bring labor and management together as partners in productivity.[3] Politically, the American campaign was successful, and its success was symbolized by the 1950 Berlin convention of the Congress for Cultural Freedom, where liberal and social-democratic intellectuals harped on the futility of third-force neutralism and called on the left and center to join unreservedly in a pro-American alliance.[4] Economically, the program worked as well, not merely in reviving prosperity but in facilitating the commitment of social democracy to take a place within capitalist order.

Thus, in France, after the departure of the Communists from the government, the Socialists worked to maintain their alliance with the liberal Catholics. They did so even though they were required to compromise with coalition partners who, despite the common anticapitalist rhetoric of the Liberation, increasingly resisted any reforms that suggested progress toward a socialized economy.[5] Postwar reform in France ground to an early halt, restricted to nationalization of banking and energy trusts and a formal plan, adopted at the urging of the United States and based on a consensus of businessmen, aimed at modernizing the industrial plant—a program fully shared by advocates of an entrepreneurial growth economy, who in the end set the purposes and limits of reform. The Socialists then limited themselves to trying "to make the search for profit and the search for utility coincide," or to manage the public welfare within the terms of a "mixed economy" rooted in a capitalist market.[6] Such compromises emerged throughout Western Europe, and by the early 1950s social democratic parties embraced the welfare potential of Keynesian management, dispensed with any attempt at public planning of a nationalized economy, and renounced even the program of accumulating reforms toward the construction of a socialist order.[7]

The fate of labor and social democracy in the United States was articulated with that of labor and social democracy in Western Europe. There the denouement of postwar reconstruction was the entry of social democracy, as political ballast, to the official apparatus of capitalist societies; in the United States, this was paralleled by the *suppression* of the social-democratic potential of a mobilized labor movement and the adoption of the labor movement within established party channels. The class conflict in the years immediately after the war issued in a disabled labor movement, outmaneuvered politically and compelled to surrender the most daring of its economic demands. By 1947 employers appealed to Congress for state aid in combating the labor power revealed in the mass industrial strikes and urban general strikes of the preceding year. Passage of the Taft-Hartley Act in the summer of 1947 was their reward, with a host of provisions that limited labor's opportunities to organize, hiked penalties for wildcat strikes, and legitimized federal coercion in labor disputes. Nonetheless, Taft-Hartley also marked the right wing's concession to the institutionalization of collective bargaining. As George Lipsitz has pointed out, Taft-Hartley, oddly enough, signaled a kind of class compromise, albeit an unbalanced one. If labor power had frightened the right into surrendering its dream of repealing New Deal labor legislation, so Taft-Hartley frightened labor into accepting collective bargaining as the limit of its aspirations.[8]

The resolution of social forces in this case was, as in Europe, interknit with the politics of the Cold War. After Taft-Hartley had imposed anti-Communist injunctions on unions seeking the protection of the National Labor Relations Board, Secretary of State Marshall appeared before the 1947 CIO convention urging labor to support foreign aid and repudiate subversives in its ranks. Domestically, the Truman administration was motivating Marshall Plan reconstruction aid as a key to domestic prosperity, and the officials of organized labor were eager to prove their "responsible" participation in maintaining economic health. Support for the Marshall Plan in fact became the crucial issue in the CIO purge of Communist-led unions in 1949. In turn, Marshall and other State Department officials nominated American labor leaders to serve as U.S. emissaries in Europe; American union representatives played an important role there in shielding the Plan from Communist criticism and encouraging noncommunist labor to accept the austerity of reconstruction.[9]

The social integration of American labor, and the eclipse of its political potential, was relatively complete by 1950. The 1950 United Automobile Workers contract with General Motors, written for an unprecedented term of five years, exchanged wage increases and pensions for stricter managerial enforcement powers and unhampered management control over work process technology. The mine workers also agreed not to oppose productivity increases if they were accompanied by higher pay. By thus failing to tie productivity gains to a program of reducing the work week, the unions formally buried the goal of full employment that had marked the high point of their postwar aspirations. Without such a provision, the unions could not hope to bring all of the work force into the high-wage sector of the economy; thus they became party to the fragmentation of labor forces, quashing the potential for social-democratic leadership by a united working class.[10]

The demise of labor's social-democratic potential in turn shattered the foundation for the political left consisting of articulate activists and intellectuals. That political formation found its final expression in the Normal Thomas presidential campaign of 1948. Supporters believed the Socialist Party would make a good showing that year, possibly opening the way for a labor party once Truman's expected defeat weakened the already-split Democratic Party. The role of Henry Wallace in the election, however, injected the anti-Communist issue into the campaign, helping Truman recement the Democratic Party coalition of liberal and labor forces. Norman Thomas' campaign foundered, gathering fewer than 140,000 votes when the party had hoped for a million. The left was now in a quandary. As an article in *The Progressive* said after Truman's victory, "Where does all this leave us independent progressives who supported Norman Thomas because we wanted to encourage the forces working for a new progressive party and a basic political realignment? Frankly it leaves us high and dry for the moment." [11]

With the demobilization and political incorporation of the working class, Western society began to manifest something of the social solidarity which radical intellectuals claimed to have seen in the outcome of the Second World War. Yet the political absorption of labor also withdrew the actual element of social discord that secretly provided the necessary condition for intellectual opposition, rendering the intellectuals just as susceptible to cooptation. Paradoxically, then, as their critical image of social consensus became somewhat more accurate, they would put their criticism aside. In the historic interlude of 1945 to 1948, Daniel Bell's thinking had been pulled taut between two poles of his being, between morals and politics, conscience and responsibility—in the existentialist paradigm, between aloofness and choice. In 1948 and the years that followed, priority swung from the former term to the latter. Essentially, "choice" meant involvement with the given order of things. When Dwight Macdonald announced in 1952, "I Choose the West," he evoked that sense of an existential choice which is ultimately unquestionable, less a rational than a willful option, an original action committing an actor to a chain of life consequences.[12] Obviously, as Macdonald rejected neutralism and took sides in the struggle between the United States and the Soviet Union, his choice was for involvement and commitment (taking Bell's sociological sense of the word) in American society. Like him, Bell and many other left-wing intellectuals opted for entry. That choice, though it could not put the fundamental tensions of his thought to rest, would lay at the heart of Daniel Bell's social theory. From his political reconciliation would follow the key terms of his mature thought, as it took shape around the problems of political alignment in the Cold War, the promise of the welfare state, the role of labor, and the fate of socialism.

Daniel Bell's personal course assumes a certain historical resonance when situated in the historical conjuncture sketched above, marked by the phenomenon of social-democratic entryism in the context of the Cold War. When he returned to New York from Chicago, Bell assumed the editorship of a socialist theoretical journal, *Modern Review*, which had just resolved a fierce intraeditorial dispute over third-force neutralism in favor of "choosing the West." At the same time, he assumed the editorship of *Fortune*'s new department of labor news. Lewis Corey told him, approvingly, that it was a significant "commentary on American life that an intellectual and socialist like you could get a job, and an important one, on a magazine like Fortune."[13] In fact *Fortune* had a leading ideological role in the transformation of American society, for its advocacy of a new capitalism—an engine of technological development and augmented industrial output—made it a mouthpiece for the "politics of productivity" that drew labor under the sway of management with the promise of mass production and mass consumption.[14] The magazine's recruitment of "a socialist like Bell" represented the same impulse to coalition-building that brought unions and social democrats into the political formula of reconstruction in Europe. Henceforth, Daniel Bell's theoretical efforts would be oriented toward solving this conundrum: what is the nature of modern capitalism and what is the role of the social democrat within it?

Socialist Unity and the Prospects of Socialist Theory at the Onset of the Cold War

By 1945, Daniel Bell had called for the American left to reunite in opposition to the consolidation of capitalist control in the United States and the imperialist settlement of the war in Europe and around the world. The growth of Cold War tensions, however, interfered with this project, for the anti-Stalinist left almost immediately fell into acrimonious debate over how to respond to the rise of Soviet power in world affairs. In the late war years, Bell considered the United States and the Soviet Union equally guilty, along with Britain, of seeking hegemony in expansive spheres of influence, equally complicit in setting the conditions for a new war. In contrast, Sidney Hook wrote an article for *The New Leader* denouncing Stalin alone as the spoiler of the peace, judging U.S. policy guilty only of impotence, confusion, and a willingness to appease Soviet ambitions.[15] This was the line *The New Leader* pursued in the postwar years, and *Partisan Review*, also under Hook's influence, concurred, attacking those leftists who put democratic capitalism and Stalinism "on the same plane" and refused to take a clear stand with the West. Irving Howe responded to the charge in an April 1947 article, speaking for Max Shachtman's Workers Party:

since the United States and the Soviet Union were both reactionary powers "lead[ing] humanity to barbarism of one kind or another," Howe wrote, a "choice" between them "would be necessary only if one abandoned the socialist perspective."[16]

Despite his quietude in the postwar years, Bell began 1947 still holding to his views of 1945. In March, he printed an article in *The New Leader* itself, condemning the war momentum of the time. "In many respects the political situation between the U.S. and Russia," he wrote, "resembles a paranoid situation where two delusional systems come into conflict." The Russians firmly believed that capitalist crisis led inevitably to war; the Americans believed totalitarianism necessarily spurred outward aggression to vent suppressed domestic tensions; both sides, he suggested, suffered from military fixations, expecting attack and mobilizing in response. A month after this article appeared, however, Bell was prepared to break his ties to *The New Leader* entirely, because of the war issue. The paper had sponsored a cable to the British Labour government, endorsed by conservatives like Henry Luce of *Fortune* and Stanley High of *Reader's Digest*, urging support for the U.S. policy of opposing appeasement of Russia. In a broadside printed in the Socialist Party newspaper, *The Call*, Bell denounced the cable as an unprincipled political alliance, for *The New Leader* should have known, he argued, that only a democratic socialist renovation of all Europe—a program that Luce and High did not support and U.S. policy did not promote—could effectively counter the sweep of totalitarianism.[17] Thus he suggested *The New Leader* had broken ranks with the rest of the left. Bell wrote to Dwight Macdonald:

> I've just sent off a piece to The Call attacking the New Leader for war-with-Russia position and that ends, on the whole, my collaboration with them. It was quite difficult to do for personal reasons, and I received a better understanding in this situation of the role of personal ties in politics. For all his faults and conniving [Sol] Levitas has been tremendously decent to me; in many ways a father, since I never had one as a child; so, writing as sharply as I did occasioned much personal pain.[18]

Bell's article in *The Call*, entitled "Fatalism of the Left," charged the *New Leader* with geopolitical determinism, for its "acceptance-in-advance-of-World War III." Bell proposed a lesson in sociology. Prediction in social affairs is difficult, he wrote in the fashion of Dilthey, precisely because humans, in their freedom, transcend the repetitions and regularities of nature—which marks the distinction between the physical and social sciences. As it evades natural determination, society is constituted and driven by the peculiar dynamics of subjectivity. Thus belief in something helps make it so:

> As with many such experiences in social action, the "*acceptance-in-advance*" *becomes a precipitating cause in its own right.* It becomes, actually, a "vicious circle" . . . It is a type of mentality to which the military is particularly addicted, whether Russian or American. . . . Psychologically, people begin to build the attitude that war is inevitable. Every sign of conflict in bargaining is taken as a fresh indication of the inevitability of that attitude. And so the inevitability becomes a crushing weight as a force in itself, and helps speed the war.

Bell doubted "that war will come." The Soviet Union "is on a political offensive," he wrote, prevented from launching a war by the damage inflicted upon it by the last one; in turn, the Truman administration was "whipping up a war hysteria here to assure support of its political counteroffensive." In any case, the Truman Doctrine, embraced by *The New Leader*, actually "shor[ed] up reactionary regimes" and was incompatible with a Socialist program of resisting Communism. The danger of Soviet-American sparring, however, was the creation of "a permanently militarized war economy on both sides," which would unleash a bureaucratic momentum toward war in the future.[19]

In some respect, Bell's argument was not too dissimilar from the "Third Force" manifesto released later that year in France by the existentialists and left-wing socialists, signed by Simone de Beauvoir, Maurice Merleau-Ponty, Jean-Paul Sartre, David Rousset, Marceau Pivert, and Claude Bourdet, the editor of *Combat*. Like Bell, they decried the fatalist expectation of war and called for a "reassembly" of the left dedicated to preserving peace by building a united socialist Europe: "When man allows himself to be convinced of his own impotence," they wrote, "the reign of necessity begins, and blood is going to flow."[20]

If socialist unity was thus the pressing need of the day, its fate could be seen in the case of *Modern Review*, a social-democratic project that drew Bell further into current disputes over Cold War choices. Sponsored by the American Labor Conference on International Affairs, a liberal-labor group founded in 1944 to promote postwar planning and reconstruction, the *Review* commenced publication in March 1947, under the editorship of the Menshevik emigré Raphael R. Abramovitch. The Socialist International, wrecked at the beginning of the Second World War, was not yet reconstituted, and Abramovitch hoped his journal would "serve international Social Democracy as an acceptable substitute for an ideological center." Abramovitch's managing editors, Travers Clement and Lewis Coser, understood their mandate more specifically as "attempting to span the gap between extreme right and extreme left in the socialist movement." The project failed, however, as the Cold War intensified: in fact, Abramovitch threw Clement and Coser off the editorial committee for refusing to back U.S. power in its conflict with the Soviet Union and endorsing instead a "third camp" between the two powers. A year later, Bell himself took their place as managing editor of the *Review*.[21]

Coser and Clement were somewhat surprised to find a young socialist like Bell, who they thought would be sympathetic to their views, join Abramovitch. But for Bell, despite his incipient break to the left in 1947, it was a matter of returning home. Through Sol Levitas's *New Leader*, he had warm relations, dating back to the early 1940s, with Abramovitch and with the other leading Menshevik exiles like David Dallin and Boris Nicolaevsky. Bell, in any case, had never broken cleanly with the right-wing social democrats: his letter to Macdonald notwithstanding, Bell's articles continued to appear in *The New Leader* throughout the spring and summer of 1947 (to excuse himself he told Travers Clement in June 1947 that they "were written months ago"). Furthermore, rooted in Bell's political thought since the 1930s were an anti-Soviet animus and a belief in the progressive potential of the democratic state, and thus he never quite embraced a "third camp" position wholeheartedly. Even in the postwar years, when he occasionally called upon socialism as an alternative to both great powers, he also felt that the force of socialism was withering away before the bureaucratization of society, and as he remarked to Macdonald in 1946, "there is a real alternative as the kind of bureaucratic state possible," democratic or totalitarian. While socialists like Howe, Coser, and Clement still saw hope in mass action, in popular movements free of capitalist or Stalinist control, Bell's theory of mass society saw primarily reactionary stirrings among popular masses. At the same time, while even the Mensheviks had expected some liberalizing reforms in postwar Russia, the years from 1948 to 1953 witnessed instead a particularly virulent repression, a sweep of purge trials and executions in Eastern Europe, leading to the ominous anti-Semitism of the "Doctors Plot" frame-up just before Stalin's death. So, the strong pull of personal ties that he noted in his letter to Macdonald, compounded by his recoil from Soviet atrocities, brought him back into the right-wing social-democratic fold and reinforced his own choice for the West.[22]

The original editorial coalition of *Modern Review* had never been a comfortable one. Coser and Clement were left-wingers. Clement, widower of Lillian Symes and with her a long-time leader of the radical left wing of the Socialist Party, had resigned his editorship of *The Call* in 1941 rather than concede to the party's shift toward "critical support" of the war; Coser, a refugee from Germany and Vichy France, had arrived in New York in the early 1940s, a left-wing opponent of the war who sympathized with the dissident Trotskyism of the Workers Party. A third managing editor was George Denicke, who had a long and "idiosyncratic" background in Russian Social Democracy, according to one of its historians: a Bolshevik sympathizer in 1905, a right Menshevik in 1917, a vehement anti-Communist thereafter, Denicke nonetheless "greeted with unflagging interest and hope the new currents that periodically emerged on the left of the international socialist movement . . . irresistibly attracted by the estranged, the downtrodden, the uprooted." On the other hand, Abramovitch's associates—the executive board of Sidney Hook, ILGWU functionary Max Danish, Liberal Party chairman John L. Childs, and sociologist Robert MacIver, along with a long list of contributors including William Bohn, James B. Carey, David J. Dallin, David Dubinsky, Louis Fischer, Harry Laidler, Algernon Lee, Jay Lovestone, and Bertram D. Wolfe—helped give the journal a liberal and right-wing social-democratic coloration that made it difficult for Clement and Coser to boost its credibility with the left wing. When Coser asked China expert and former Trotskyist Harold Isaacs to contribute, Isaacs responded,

> I am usually glad to be able to speak my piece anywhere and I assume I can do it in Modern Review too. But am I mistaken in my impression that your publication is associated with the New Leader? And isn't the New Leader an ardent supporter of support for Chiang Kai-shek in China on the theory of any-stick-against-Stalin? And a supporter to boot, of the notion that the US can do no wrong, or hardly ever?[23]

Isaacs nonetheless contributed a piece, "South Asia's Opportunity," for the December 1947 issue. He endorsed the battle for national liberation in Indochina and Indonesia, and called for a federated South Asia Union to apply socialist planning to the daunting problems of regional development. Isaacs urged South Asia to "keep clear" of both "super-states," the United States and the Soviet Union: "the issue [between them] is fraudulent because neither is pregnant with any decent promise for mankind. The one offers capitalist anarchy, the other totalitarian thraldom." So far, the region was not yet, as North Asia already was, a battleground between them.

In this indecisive interim, while the titans spar and skirmish, South Asia has the chance not to take sides. It has the chance to gather together its own resources for survival. It even has the chance to begin to build a world in some third image. . . . If some modified kind of socialism can still triumph in South Asia, if the best of South Asia's leaders are bold enough to work for it, they can create something new under the sun.[24]

This "third camp" position appalled Abramovitch, whose rebuttal was appended directly to Isaacs' piece. A close colleague of Rudolf Hilferding in the interwar years, Abramovitch had argued in an earlier issue of the journal that the Soviet regime had developed "from Utopian revolution to Totalitarianism": as "premature" revolutionaries, the Bolsheviks were doomed, as Engels had said of the proto-proletarian movement of Thomas Munzer, to serve an "alien class"—in this case the party apparatus itself. The system they established bore within it no "reversible" tendency to "a democratic collective" but followed a "totalitarian spiral," as the leading party accumulated ever more absolute power to enslave and exploit workers and peasants; with no hope of revolution from within, "the natural tendency of a totalitarian regime is to perpetuate itself ad infinitum—'for a thousand years to come.'" Compared to this static, monolithic, and self-perpetuating order, capitalism was by far preferable, since to Abramovitch's orthodox mind, natural evolutionary tendencies were there still at work. The optimistic mind of evolutionist social theory permitted Abramovitch to interpret U.S. cooptation of European social democracy as a sign of capitalist concession to the socialist tendency of development. In his response to Isaacs, Abramovitch wrote:

> I still hold to the Marxian diagnosis that capitalist society *is* pregnant with a new social order and thus historically viewed, does bear "a decent promise for mankind." . . . even America's "capitalism-in-one-country" is compelled by the force of events to maintain and strengthen, rather than destroy, the elements of planning and control in the economies of the countries to which, in its own interests, it must give assistance through the Marshall Plan. . . . So why place Stalinist Russia and democratic America on the same level? Why try to persuade colonial people that they have no stake in the struggle between the Soviet totalitarian bloc and the freedom-loving coalition of democratic states—materially led but not spiritually dominated by the U.S.A.?

Abramovitch added, "In the present world situation every country, every people, and every writer has to 'take sides.'" His piece was entitled, "Can the Choice be Evaded?" Since Clement and Coser themselves had publicly dissociated themselves from Abramovitch's position, they too were irresponsibles in his view. Abramovitch complained to Sidney Hook about "how increasingly difficult it was becoming for me to straighten out the general line of the magazine because of the rigid leftist leaning of Coser and Clement." The two editors resigned, and so, oddly enough, did Denicke, who had authored some of the most vigorously pro-American Cold War pieces in the magazine: he wanted at least to maintain an "open forum," but Abramovitch responded, "I am not in the least interested in maintaining a 'playground' for leftists of Isaacs kind."[25]

Hook had suggested to Abramovitch that he look for new help from Bell and Lewis Corey, who Hook had heard were hoping to start a new journal not too different from *Modern Review*. After the failure of the National Educational Committee for a New Party, Bell had suggested that intellectuals should concentrate on new socialist ideas rather than a new socialist party, and he proposed to Corey that they coedit a journal of "Fabian research and discussion." From this perspective, Bell considered the original *Modern Review* "too narrowly political" and insufficiently focused on central theoretical problems. Bell wanted a magazine based on a coherent, long-range program of inquiry, focusing each issue on a single "memorandum" followed by "expert" discussion. He and Corey both had some idea of integrating academic social science with social-democratic ends, and Bell thought the journal might be published under the imprint of the Free Press, the house just founded by his friend Jeremiah Kaplan to reprint the sociological classics of Michels, Simmel, Durkheim, and others. When Bell heard of the editorial shakeup at *Modern Review*, he thought he and Corey might pick up that franchise instead, but Corey demurred, suspicious of interference by old-line sectarians. "As I see our project—it must break new ground, it must have absolute freedom to evaluate the past, including the failure of socialism; and too much of the writing in MR has been an apologia, we were always right and still are!" Abramovitch's Second International orthodoxy certainly justified Corey's wariness, and Bell reported on Abramovitch's "intransigeance" [*sic*] in negotiations.[26] Probably Bell was referring to Abramovitch's insistence on his own ultimate editorial control, in light of the tussle with Clement and Coser. Bell, also, was uncomfortable with what he saw as the stodginess of the old Menshevik's political tradition.[27] The idea of joining forces lay fallow for months, while Abramovitch brought out the journal by himself and Bell began his job at *Fortune*. At the beginning of 1949, however, Bell took over the managing editorship of *Modern Review* (without Corey), intending to re-fashion it as a theoretical quarterly.

As Bell took the helm of *Modern Review*, he made it clear that he considered the contemporary crisis of the left to be primarily a conceptual crisis calling for theoretical renovation. The theoretical problems he cited in a prospectus distributed to potential contributors reflected interests that had guided his thought since the early 1940s—first the peculiarity of a planned capitalism, then the functions of bureaucracy, and the nature of mass culture. It was evident that Abramovitch's traditionalism would not hold sway in Bell's magazine. In the prospectus for a new *Modern Review*, Bell wrote,

> Editing a socialist magazine today is exceedingly difficult, for the theoretical prism that the socialist magazines of the past could conveniently focus on a variety of problems and obtain at least some refraction, whether adequate or not, is broken. Our major problem then is less an assured and doctrinaire analysis of contemporary events than one of self-analysis . . . the construction of some new theoretical spectacles.[28]

In particular, he wrote, he wanted to probe basic concepts of "capitalism" and "class," since new relationships between economy and the state qualified the autonomous "laws of motion" in an exchange economy, and the role of managers in bureaucratized corporations, he said, deprived a unified ownership class of control over policy. Manifesting the continued salience of "mass culture" in his thinking, Bell indicated he wanted to examine the concept of "ideology," and the links it drew between class structure and social action, in light of "the 'power of the word' in modern society and the role of mass communications."

Bell brought to his task the accumulated influences of the interdisciplinary social science program at Chicago. There he had seen a model of what he wanted his magazine to be, a short-lived journal called *University Observer*, which sought to consider the problems of politics from the perspectives of the social sciences, reprinted classic texts of Marx, Engels, and Weber, and solicited contributions from E. H. Carr, Erich Fromm, Hans Gerth, Karl Jaspers, Harold Lasswell, Georg Lukács, Franz Neumann, Meyer Schapiro, R. H. Tawney, and others. In his urge to combine socialism and the social sciences, Bell envisioned a magazine that could be many things to many people. When writing to social democrats abroad, Bell portrayed the new *Modern Review* as "a theoretical socialist magazine," whose search for "a more adequate body of theory" would help "extend our fraternal relations with our comrades abroad." To Milton Singer, an organizer of the Chicago program, he wrote that the journal aimed at "an integrating social science thinking," and to J. F. Wolpert he remarked that he hoped to cultivate "a vigorous sociology," bringing a serious "interest in ideas" to a discipline too narrowly restricted to statistical empiricism.[29]

Had Bell's magazine lived up to his intentions it would have been a fascinating forum of discussion. Vigorously soliciting contributions, he spread seeds of ideas for a wide range of articles, most of them never written. He asked a UAW labor intellectual to assay the historical and social conditions for the concentrated location of industrial plants and the new opportunities that advanced technology offered for decentralization. He suggested to his Chicago colleague Philip Rieff a curmudgeonly piece on "The Tyranny of Psychology," and Bell himself provided the argument: since psychology was now bound up with the bureaucratic ethic of "adjustment," it had become "the ideology of tyranny." Yet Bell had a hard time rousing writers to write. Sensing a retiring and sullen silence among politically minded intellectuals, he repeatedly urged upon his correspondents "the virtues of intellectual community and responsibility" in critical times. Philip Selznick complied with Bell's request for an essay on Michels' "Iron Law of Bureaucracy" but sent along a laconic cover letter indicating he was unsure the piece was worthy of publication. After only two disappointing issues—"between the reality and the shadow is a large gap," Bell wrote to his old friend Melvin Lasky, "although I am convinced more and more, that it is my memorandum which is the reality and the magazine which is the shadow"—*Modern Review* closed.[30] Bell's "editorial farewell" pointed to the exhaustion of political ideas as a sorrowful rather than salutary end of ideology:

> The sad truth is that the old socialist and liberal community in the U.S. is a tired one, and that few ways have been found to reach, awaken and excite the number of young people who in their natural idealism are searching for a moral community to sustain them. . . .
>
> Perhaps it was the language barrier; the words of the traditional left may have become, for some, trite and dull; or, as we believe, the words may have become for the greater [*sic*] indelibly corrupted by the Communists who through the years have succeeded in so besmirching the words "left," "liberal," "radical" and "progressive" as to confound all meaning and betray all sensibilities.

Perhaps it was the ideas themselves: the old categories may have lost their viability and resiliency in a world where unleashed destruction is on the prowl.[31]

Undoubtedly Bell was correct in considering the confidence of the old evolutionary socialism out of touch with a new world of power and violence that long ago had witnessed the end of progress in the Victorian sense. Nietzschean accents filtered into a note he sent to Columbia University historian Richard Hofstadter, whom Bell had met through C. Wright Mills. Nineteenth-century conservatives, Bell suggested to Hofstadter, "read much better today than many of the liberal contemporaries" not because their cynical view of human nature was correct but because they represented "an aristocratic traditon [and] were more aware of power and its exercise than those whose forte was largely value and symbolic appeals in the name of chiliastic and other utopian hopes." Hofstadter's response aptly summed up the melancholic mood then current among leftist intellectuals who knew not how to relate their values effectively to given social facts:

> I agree, in general, that the elite theorists make more sense, analytically, than the liberal propagandists—this in terms of their purely cerebral appeal. The conception of some kind of good society above and beyond ruling groups is very likely a utopian fiction. I think that it has a pragmatic justification, though, in that it keeps the elites somewhat on the defensive and keeps them from becoming rigid. That is, it does if it is widely believed, and acted on. That we accept the liberal and socialist values without being able to accept the liberal and socialist analysis *durchaus* [in its entirety] is a minor tragedy for us, but I suspect also a great source of insight.[32]

The Sociology of the Welfare State

By 1949 it seemed to Bell that the postwar left had grossly misconstrued the essential political and economic issues of the time. In May 1945 Bell himself had suggested that Truman might be the "Bruening" of America's "Weimar"; conventionally, the left believed that Truman's apparent retreat from the cutting edge of New Deal reform would only open the way for another disastrous business slump and a fascist reaction.[33] Yet there was no slump, and no fascist movement took hold of the directors of Big Business. Nor did the great corporations pursue a restrictionist policy leading to economic stagnation; growth was steady as technological innovation and productivity advanced. After his surprise victory in 1948 Truman nodded to his left flank with an endorsement of full-employment planning in the interests of "general welfare." Bell had supported Norman Thomas in the election, but now he was ready to see in Truman's declaration something he had not thought possible under capitalism—state management of the economy for civilian needs. In response, Bell sketched out a sociology of the welfare state he thought would help resolve the crisis of socialist theory broached in his *Modern Review* prospectus. Now he shifted clearly onto Weberian ground and made an "effort to backtrack on my simplistic Marxism."[34] In Weberian fashion, too, he was able to accept the society whose terms he delineated while marking its profound shortcomings in an understated, yet caustic, way.

In his most significant essay of the period, "America's Un-Marxist Revolution: Mr. Truman Embarks on a Politically Managed Economy" (*Commentary*, March 1949), Bell suggested that contemporary political thinking had been unable to grasp the nature of the social transformation induced under the Roosevelt regime because it was committed to an interpretation of politics as "only a bald class struggle." Bell indicated he was also skeptical of the New Deal's propagandistic self-image as the champion of human rights over property rights. Rather, he wrote,

> What has been emerging out of seventeen years of confused political pulling and hauling has been a definition of politics in terms of group rights and, more vaguely, an implicit theory of justice which sets limits to group prerogatives. This allows us to look at major social legislation in terms of interest blocs: in functional terms, labor, farmer, business; in social terms, the aged, the veterans, the minority groups; in regional terms, the Missouri Valley Authority, Columbia Valley Authority, St. Lawrence waterway. Equally important such a formulation provides a valid framework for political analysis of the past and future.[35]

Bell's last remark implicitly appealed to Weber's methodology, which assumed that society and history were irreducibly complex, interpretable only through a schema derived from the *Weltanschauung* of the present and applied, as a self-conscious artifice, to the objects of analysis. Furthermore, just as Weber's neo-Kantian epistemology posits that knowledge never conclusively and exhaustively grasps an infinitely variegated ontological reality, so Bell argued that a definitive social structure had never been stamped upon American social reality, that is, upon "the tremendous diversity of interests, sectional and functional, that have arisen successively in our history and the permutations possible in such multiplicity . . . in which identifications and loyalties shifted rapidly as the society expanded and became industrialized." Only now, he suggested, had American society assumed a determinate shape, due to governmental intervention that officially recognized "the particular collectivities created by the economy [as] the vital organs of the body politic." By so emphasizing the *political* reconstitution of social structure—the success of the New Deal in molding "an interest-group society"—Bell asserted, again in Weberian fashion, the priority of leadership (*Herrschaft*) in social analysis.[36] Furthermore, like Weber, Bell looked at "social action" from the subjective point of view, for his "groups" were aggregates constituted by voluntaristic affiliation ("identifications and loyalties") to organizations representing self-conscious interests.

Finally, in dismissing "class" as a "crude lens" of analysis, Bell implicitly tapped Weber's critique of the Marxian category. For Weber, Marx's concept of a ruling class fallaciously fused the distinct dimensions of class, power, and status or prestige. Corresponding to the analytical distinctions of economy, polity, and society, class in Weber's terms was determined by market function and accrued wealth, power by control over the administrative machinery of state, and status or prestige by the evaluative scale of social stratification. In certain specific historical circumstances these might coincide to constitute a full-fledged "ruling class"—as in feudal society—but such a convergence was by no means a social universal. For Weberian sociology, Marx's concept of class is an unsupple "single-variable" tool, with only historically relative meaning.[37] Bell brought this critique to play in his latest assessments of American class structure. In his *Modern Review* prospectus Bell suggested that class had as much to do with "divisions of manners, status and other 'badges of consumption'" as it did with relations to the means of production. The answer to the question he asked in a December 1949 review—"Has America a Ruling Class?"—depended, according to the three-part Weberian scheme, on whether a number of people performing a particular *economic* function were welded together *socially* by such status bonds to act *politically* on behalf of their own prerogatives. Bell doubted that "the American capitalist, without the social cement of a past, without a set of distinctive manners and morals, or a distinctive ideology" assumed the *class role* that Marxists attributed to him. The bureaucratization of the corporation, by producing a new type of business manager with functions and motives distinct from those of the traditional capitalist owner, further fragmented the "coherent *community* of interest among defined groups, and . . . *continuity* of interest" that sustained a ruling class.[38]

As he put it in "America's Un-Marxist Revolution," the "multiplicity" and "fluid combinations" of American society had long eluded the grasp of powerful, homogeneous class agencies. In a historical sketch, Bell argued that merchant capitalists and agrarians in the early republic as well as industrialists in the late nineteenth century had repeatedly fallen short of their political ambition for clear hegemony in the state apparatus, though he conceded that the business class had achieved at least *ideological* dominance by the turn of the century. In approaching the critical conjuncture of the New Deal, Bell drew upon two old themes, the "growth of dependence" in an "organized" (or as his friend Bert Hoselitz wrote for Bell's *Modern Review* in an Austro-Marxist vein, an "associative") capitalism.[39] As the industrial economy developed, Bell pointed out, the individual grew increasingly dependent on proliferating, far-flung relations and organizational combinations that infringed upon the market. "Today it is no longer individual men who are in the market but particular collectivities, each of which tries to exempt itself from the risks of the market." Thus Bell subsumed monopolization, unionization, and farmer cooperation under a single sociological tendency, a "convulsive drive to security." Administered prices and wages introduced a number of "rigidities" into the economy that undermined the self-corrective capacity of the market and called forth "sweeping government intervention" to impose some order on the self-protective controls implemented arbitrarily by private groups. Thus the politically managed economy emerged as an order that recognized and balanced the "group rights" that emerged from collective dependency.[40]

In Bell's interpretation, this political economy lent the society a clear determinate structure for the first time, knit it together as a single organized whole, and demanded that it be understood and planned comprehensively. In Bell's view, however, this outcome only set the stage for new problems. "Since in a managed economy, politics, not dollars [i.e., the market], will determine what is to be produced, the intervention of the government will not only sharpen pressure group identifications, but also force each to adopt an ideology which can justify its claims, and which can square with some concept of 'national interest.'" The major interest groups—business, labor, and farmers—however, had no effective "ideologies" with which they could seriously propose principles of common management, i.e., a way of expressing their particular needs and interests as a convincing general formula of "social decision." [41]

The promise of the politically managed economy was far from a reality in practice. "Washington remains today largely a giant pork-barrel," Bell wrote. As the state moved into a directive position, Bell was by no means uncritically sanguine, or convinced of its *social* commitment.

> We are floundering, both in practice and in analysis, because we no longer know what holds a society together. . . . where group relations amid the multiple identities created by varying allegiances are mediated largely through the mesh of politics, what is the basis of the over-riding unity of our social groups?

He wondered "whether transient majority coalitions can offer a convincing theory of social justice."

> The Fair Deal, in its own prosaic fashion, is . . . a reflection of the fact that modern industrial society can no longer be left to the direction of any one privileged interest group but has to submit to political management and political direction. It is a square assertion of the legitimacy of an economy managed by government. The question naturally arises, managed for whom? . . . just how is the managed economy to be managed, and how are we to achieve a popularly accepted definition of an over-all social interest? . . . A general theory as to how the satisfaction of varied group interests may be harmonized with the general welfare remains to be worked out. We have a managed economy, but the principles of management remain undefined. [42]

The process Bell described as resulting from the growth of dependence and the drive to security was essentially the same as that the historian Robert Wiebe later called "the search for order," the rise of a corporatist social structure in the United States. From a large and incoherent society of isolated local communities maintained by consensual morality and informal, personal relations, Wiebe proposed, had emerged a centralized and integrated national order based on new values of "continuity and regularity, functionality and rationality, administration and management," an order structured by a few large organizations (or syndicates) of business, labor, and agriculture recognized and coordinated by state authority. [43]

In sociological terms this depiction of social development indicated nothing more than the movement from *Gemeinschaft* (homogeneous community) to *Gesellschaft* (heterogeneous society). The problem Bell cited—"we no longer know what holds a society together"—arose precisely from the lapse of consensual moral order underpinning the old community. That is, Bell still focused on "the divorce between moral and secular conceptions," as he put it in his "Parable of Alienation," that marked the rationalization of the modern world. The question he posed now was whether a new moral bond, a public ethic holding society together, could be built in secular, that is, political terms. The problem that had preoccupied Bell as political actor and radical critic during his sojourn at Chicago—how to find a political embodiment for morality—now became the center of the social problem in his theory. He wanted "some new sense of civic obligation . . . strong enough to command the allegiance of all groups and provide a principle of equity in the distribution of the rewards and privileges of society."[44] If that could be done, in a society where politics and economics meshed, then it would be possible to achieve something like the good society, to Bell's mind—the ideal he inferred from the thought of the early American republicans, the goal of "fusing ethics and economics into a unity."

The terms of Bell's analysis also reached back to the problems he raised in the theory of the Monopoly State. Both the Monopoly State and the "politically managed economy" represented fusions of politics and economics, though in the former, economics ruled over politics as business usurped the state, and in the latter, politics (or the state) ruled over economics.[45] Still, as he had written in 1944, statism as such was merely a "technique": it had no purpose in itself, but had to be directed from the outside by certain valued ends. Who would posit those ends, and how? He was asking again the question he had posed in a 1944 *New Leader* article—"Planning by Whom—for What?" Now Bell in effect asked intellectuals, as the free-floating conscience of society, to take up the task of fashioning a genuine social universal, but to his mind they were bound by ritualistic formulas occluding their vision.

Nor did social conditions at large fructify new thinking for comprehensive planning. The old communal morality still lurked within the complex society, having now assumed a reactionary role.[46] Hence Bell wrote in 1949 that "the problem of American *politics* is (metaphorically) the small-town mentality," which, bound to static homogeneous localities, remained "crabbed, frightened by change, suspicious of ideas."[47] This reaction was not surprising, for the same force that organized the society for greater control—ongoing bureaucratization—made it more bewildering. Power was hard to locate, blame and responsibility hard to assess, because as Bell put it, "the area of manipulation is becoming so vast and the sources of authority so diverse." David Riesman, whom Bell knew from his Chicago years, argued similarly in *The Lonely Crowd* (1950) that the prevalence of manipulation rather than domination in modern society had rendered power increasingly "amorphous and indeterminate," spurring individuals who were frustrated by their diminished sense of "control and competence" to discover some hidden, conspiratorial force at work in affairs.[48] Thus, as Bell quoted Riesman, "There is an almost animistic feeling that since things run, somebody runs them." Scapegoating went hand in hand with the urge to impose the conformity of the town on the great society:

> Narrowness, anti-intellectualism, and prejudice find their greatest *articulation* in the small-town mind and particularly his broker, the small-town lawyer. If, as I think will happen, American society grows increasingly amorphous and undifferentiated, his sense of panic will rise, his readiness to violence grow all the greater.[49]

While purposeful order had to be imposed on the "technique" of state organization, it seemed that technical rationality in itself tended to disorient consciousness and interfere with the task of formulating supervening goals.

How did this sociology of the welfare state help Bell resolve the questions he asked about the nature of modern capitalism in his *Modern Review* prospectus? The answer he gave was profoundly ambiguous, and the question remained, was the society Bell described "capitalist" or not? In fact, despite his call for theoretical renewal, he had not gone far beyond traditional social democracy, for the corporatist order he described was much like the Austro-Marxists' "organized capitalism," and like Hilferding in 1927 he supposed it was possible to reach the socialist goal—in Bell's terms, a society of substantive rationality where economics was subordinated to values imposed by a coherent political plan—by working within and through that system. The Austro-Marxists themselves were never clear whether "organized capitalism" was, properly speaking, *capitalist*, since the market had virtually disappeared and production, they thought, was increasingly coordinated for rational efficiency rather than competitive private profit. Before the full realization of the potential of the politically managed economy, Bell seemed to say, economic order would remain elusive. Thus, in a 1952 review, Bell cast doubt on John Kenneth Galbraith's discovery of "countervailing powers" in the economy. The suggestion that there was a natural balance among these forces seemed to Bell as fictional as the smooth workings of a self-corrective market, and Bell reminded Galbraith that the present source of balance—and perhaps imbalance as well—was really the permanent war economy. "The intellectual rehabilitation of American capitalism," Bell remarked, "is being completed while the reality itself is rapidly changing; the newest ideologies may become outmoded and require new revisions long before they have had time to get themselves widely understood and accepted." [50] Bell still considered himself a critic of capitalism. As an evolutionist, though, he liked to think that capitalism was in transition and passing away; as a modernist he wondered what agency or impulse would or could bring that transition to its conclusion.

The Sociology of Labor

Bell had as yet high hopes for the political role of organized labor in the new order of controlled economy. Just as the Fair Deal culminated incomplete New Deal tendencies toward a political economy, so the election of 1948, he believed, finally unveiled a new type of labor political action that surpassed the old defensive formula of Samuel Gompers, "reward your friends, punish your enemies." To Bell's mind, the fact that the national mobilization of the labor vote supplied the crucial swing factor on election day meant that "labor came into its own as a third force." It was odd for this term to appear in a *Fortune* column. In the language of left-wing socialists the "third force" denoted an independent anticapitalist movement, and Bell's use of it suggested the radical possibilities he still ascribed to organized labor at the beginning of his tenure at Luce's magazine. Labor "will not again become a White House captive," Bell wrote: evidently he still held out the social-democratic hope that the labor movement would assume the vanguard of the politically managed economy, providing a new formulation of the social interest, the common values needed to guide the kind of comprehensive planning that yet remained merely a potentiality. [51] Within a few years, however, such hopes were defeated. In the end it seemed to Bell that the integration of organized labor into the national community subjected it to the general stresses and strains of a rationalized, but not yet rational, society, denying it the role of leadership. Bell's critical sociology helped him register the frustration of the potential for a rational society in modern life, the lapse of moral leadership in a bureaucratized order.

Evolutionary aspirations resided alongside the critique mounted by modern sociology. Again, Bell implicitly harked back to the social-democratic tradition. Hilferding's 1927 declaration, "The Tasks of Social Democracy," had proposed that industrial enterprises were increasingly managed rationally for planned production, that traditional class conflict consequently would naturally give way to enlightened cooperation and the integration of workers into the control apparatus, leading to economic democracy in the long run.[52] Similarly, Bell described how American unions and management had "matured" together, each accepting the legitimate role of the other, collaborating to fashion "an industrial government and a system of private law for the orderly protection of both."[53] In the long run, too, he saw the natural tendencies of social organization pressing toward fundamental revisions in corporate structure, with labor's power widening the area of its control over production. Bell's situation and perspective, however, were full of contradictions. His own reconciliation with American society coincided with the suppression of the social-democratic potential of the postwar labor movement, and while he advocated the institutional integration of labor as the means of social-democratic progress, it was precisely this political cooptation that undermined the unity and vitality of the movement, thus blocking the progress he sought. Still, whatever the consequences, he would not consider his political choice for reconciliation and advocacy of labor integration as errors; for him, intentions and consequences produced a set of double binds, a conflict of necessity and possibility. It was through the structure of his sociology—built in the modernist mode on a set of antinomies, probing the tension between the economic and political function of labor, the contradictory effects of bureaucratization, the competing pulls of centralization and decentralization, the discord between efficiency and democracy—that Bell rationalized the double binds he saw in the frustration of his aims.

Bell's *Fortune* columns, taken together, represent the formulation of a distinct sociology of labor. It was, above all, a theory of unionism. Bell did not attribute any significance to "class" in his analysis of American labor relations. His concern was not with the social class of American workers but with the functional organization, Labor, as one of several institutions in the corporatist order. He agreed with the Wisconsin school of labor theory, developed by John Commons and Selig Perlman, that American workers did not identify with their "class," though he denied the Wisconsin school premise that workers were bound by a narrow, individualist "job consciousness." Like the radical labor intellectual, J. B. S. Hardman, who conducted seminars on labor politics in New York, Bell saw in the rise of industrial unionism a new "consciousness of kind," an identification with the union body (as "auto workers" or "steel workers") more inclusive than job or craft.[54] If the Commons-Perlman school formalized the craft ideology of the AFL, Bell's labor theory represented the experience of the domesticated CIO.

To Bell, a fundamental paradox of American labor was that its achievement of legitimacy—the fulfillment of Samuel Gompers' "commitment to seek a secure place within the social structure of capitalist society rather than stand outside and fight it"—accompanied the rise of the new political order of group rights, which subordinated the market economy to central control and required labor to surrender its old Gompersian hostility to political action. The Gompersian tendency to ignore the state and rely simply on the economic force of combined workers—a rudimentary "class-struggle" unionism suited to "the tooth and claw of the economic jungle"—was outmoded, Bell believed.[55]

Yet, despite the new significance of political action, Bell put great weight upon the purely economistic functions of what he called "market" or "business" unionism. The private adjudication of interests between labor and management, apart from state intervention, had in itself a profound effect in reshaping economic institutions, Bell asserted, for "in seeking to share power, one necessarily transforms the way it is administered."[56]

Bell emphasized how collective bargaining had helped rationalize industry, by smoothing out market swings in pay rates, stabilizing the work force, and thus facilitating corporate planning.[57] More important, however, were the "social pressures [that] are [now] enlarging the definition of business unionism." As workers aged in the postwar years, and recognized they were "stuck" as industrial laborers, unions shifted from wage issues to demands for company-supplied pensions; the problem of job mobility would soon compel unions to bargain for industry-wide "pension pooling" and "interchangeability" of work tenure. Bell saw a "guaranteed annual wage" as an item imminently on the agenda. In the long run, too, the effects of technological developments in undermining employment, or drastically altering job classifications, would require unions to bargain for a voice in determining "production standards." Thus Bell asserted that the sociological function of unionism, its expression of workers' "security-consciousness," had the dual effects of levying "permanent responsibility on industry for a welfare economy" and making "striking inroads upon the decision-making powers of industrial enterprise." At this point Bell saw broad vistas of change: unionism connoted "a new industrial structure"—not merely the legal regulation of wage negotiations but an alteration in the relations of production.[58] The evolutionist side of Bell's theory was most evident in this argument that a "natural" development toward industrial democracy followed from economic functions alone.

On the other side of the analysis lay the separate sphere of politics. The forces leading the unions toward political action were as unavoidable as the tendency of market unionism to reshape the enterprise. Taft-Hartley, he suggested, was America's Taff-Vale, the anti-labor law that drove British unions to organize their own party: "Thus warned," Bell wrote, "labor leaders have begun to agree on one imperative—political action as a permanent part of the trade-union function."[59] It must have seemed to Bell that the social-democratic goal of a politically conscious labor movement was almost at hand. Again, Bell saw the forces tending toward social and political integration of labor as the impulse to progress. Just as Abramovitch had held a sanguine view of the Marshall Plan, so Bell believed even the Cold War furthered the political maturity of labor and hence the achievement of a social economy. When the AFL and CIO took a leading role in founding the anti-Communist International Confederation of Free Trade Unions, Bell wrote, they were swept "into the political vortex." Collaborating with the political unionists of Europe, he suggested, American labor leaders came under the influence of public-spirited European socialism, an influence that might encourage American labor finally to fashion those "long-range social goals" that could orient the managed economy. In this sense, labor's anti-ideological pragmatism was its failing, not its strength, as far as Bell was concerned.

> Ideology, long the weak point of American labor, rarely provides a wholly reliable clue to its actions. Lacking any long-range social goals, American labor moves pragmatically, assessing each consequence largely in terms of immediate objectives. But European problems are largely different from American; hence American labor in competition with the Communists and under the pressure of the Socialists, may find itself backing measures that it might not support at home. For example, Matthew Woll, in the name of the A. F. of L. has endorsed the demand of German workers for the socialization of the Ruhr industries. . . . At some doubtful time in the future, the American labor movement may face up to its intellectual dilemmas and make a conscious choice.[60]

Bell recognized, however, that the dual economistic and political functions of labor often worked against each other. In terms of market unionism, labor tied itself to the various specific interests of different industries and regions, he pointed out, often ending up at competitive cross purposes with itself. If economistic commitments blocked the coherent formulation of labor's general interests, there was still the additional problem of making labor's particular needs, as an interest bloc, relevant to the concerns of the whole society: "To the degree that the union takes on a political function it must take a stand on a variety of issues far beyond the scope of its immediate industry. Then it is forced to roughhew some ideological concept of the common good"—the key ingredient, that is, of an achieved political economy.[61]

Indeed, could labor stand forth as the exponent of the rational interests of society at large, and if so, how would labor as a particular interest group relate to labor as political vanguard of the public interest? For Bell, the issue rested on the difference between the *trade-union* and the *labor movement*: if "the former is an economic organization bargaining in market situations on wages and job security," he wrote, "the latter is a social conception, articulated largely by intellectuals, which assigns labor a specific historical role." Here Bell merely echoed the classic distinction, in social-democratic theory, between the "two arms" of the workers movement, the union and the party. Thus Lenin, following Kautsky, distinguished between the economistic consciousness of the trade unionists and the socialist consciousness brought to the working class "from the outside" by bourgeois intellectuals. Bell, in fact, invested much of his hope in the labor intellectuals who had come to union research departments from a background in the socialist movement. But while "this political experience broadened their view of the economy and often made them more socially conscious than the labor union leader whose view is limited by one industry," the labor intellectuals became "essentially . . . technician[s] rather than . . . policy maker[s]," frustrated by "their own powerlessness in the union movement." In this sense the bureaucratization of organized labor, the absorption of the intellectual in the technical apparatus, helped to frustrate the prospects of labor as a social movement.[62]

This was only one of the paradoxes of bureaucratization that Bell's sociology of labor analyzed. The achievement of labor peace in industrial government, he recognized, necessarily bureaucratized the union and supplanted internal democracy. As the rights and prerogatives of labor and management were negotiated and stipulated, labor action assumed a fixed, regulated, routine form, raising an administrative apparatus of expertise and authority above the membership to assure the stability and accountability of union behavior. As a consequence there arose "the problem of mass participation in the 'big organization,'" Bell wrote. Borrowing A. J. Muste's definition of the union as both a town meeting and an army, requiring the democratic participation of the membership as well as discipline and command, Bell wrote:

> The centralization of wage-fixing means the loss of control by the small local over the affairs of the union. As a result, the union becomes less a town meeting and more an army, with mandates supplied in advance by permissive strike votes and the generals in complete charge of strategy. As bargaining becomes more bureaucratized and the functions of office more complex, a greater need arises for continuity of administration. And with the union leader more in the role of the general, other officers become mere subordinates whose role is to carry out orders and check opposition.[63]

Consequently, though Bell heartily endorsed the CIO campaign against Communist Party-led unions from 1948 to 1950, he regretted that the factional struggle fueled extreme bureaucratization, "the tightening of union constitutions to allow incumbent regimes to centralize their control and more easily discipline opposition elements. . . . In the assaults on union democracy, both sides have been guilty."[64]

Bell found further sociological paradoxes in the ways that bureaucratization worked against the industrial stability of which it was cause and consequence. Centralization of authority in both corporation and union removed the agencies of adjudicating grievances far from the site of industrial tensions, letting local discontent smolder as the apparatuses of decision became more inflexible and untimely. The membership became bewildered by the size and complexity of the organization and lost an immediate "feel" for the problems the union faced and ways and means of their resolution. The demagogic leader arose to fill the void. Thus, like Weber, Bell saw that bureaucracy secretly fostered the renewal of charisma. Labor peace suffered, too, from the insecurity of plant managers. Distant from both the central decision makers and the workers, the managers were driven toward a reactionary, authoritarian posture, "more royalist than the king."[65] To Bell's mind industrial cooperation required the reinvigoration of intermediary organizational levels, tempering the pull of centralization with decentralizing strategies. Yet the drive toward rational efficiency in production inhibited such measures: while "many personnel people pay homage to 'participation,' [they] are unwilling to delegate authority and responsibility to work groups down the line that would allow them to work out different procedures—and so upset the neat blueprint."[66] Hence in the development of industry and labor, organization and disorder lay side by side.

In just a few years, by 1950–51, Bell was sorely disappointed in American labor's failure to live up to the hopes of 1948. At that time he seemed to share labor's enthusiasm for riding the wave of political success into a massive new organizing drive among white-collar workers that promised a second labor revolution. By 1950, however, Bell wrote that labor had "reached the crest of its advance": large manufacturing was virtually union-saturated, he calculated, and white-collar workers, more timid and status-conscious than the CIO strikers of the 1930s, resisted organization. And the entrenched bureaucratized leadership was less eager than it claimed to organize the unorganized, he suggested, for it feared that large boosts in membership would upset the status quo of internal power relations: so Bell recognized that bureaucracy granted the unions organizational security but inhibited their growth. Finally, as the elections of 1950 showed the Democratic Party intractable to labor interests, labor seemed stuck—since the Wallace campaign, he said, had discredited third-party initiatives—with "nowhere to go."[67]

"Which way, then, shall labor turn?" Bell asked. As labor seemed reluctant to lead the cause for comprehensive reform, Bell remarked on the "exhaustion of the left," the replacement of the old labor leadership by sedate administrators, the conversion of the CIO socialists to Fair Deal capitalism, the sidelining of the labor intellectuals in the technical apparatus. Consequently, "attempts to articulate a philosophy of labor have practically ceased."[68] In Bell's terms, that meant that labor could not meet its responsibilities in the politically managed economy. What happened, then, when the trade union entered the political arena yet still did not adopt "political unionism," as Bell defined it, that is, fell short of achieving the status of an articulate *labor movement*? In effect, labor became merely "a *pressure group* rather than a social movement."[69] Thus the vistas of reform Bell had imagined narrowed. He had once thought that security consciousness would force union economism to penetrate further into the sphere of managerial prerogatives, perhaps achieving something like the workers "co-determination" that developed in West German industries after the war. Now Bell thought the "unions have tended to reach the limit of their demands on the right to manage," far short of that goal. Having pressured government and business to establish "a series of floors under the economy," the unions were content.[70]

Unionism, Bell suggested, turned out to be nothing but a means of social assimilation. Its aspirations did not go far. It sought power, but only within the given structures, forms, and means of power.[71] Bell pointed out that labor's antibusiness rhetoric

> was not a language, like Veblen's, that bitterly satirized the whole society. It lacked any bite or mordancy. It never attacked the culture of the society, its canons of success and social standing. It was a language of protest against exclusion. It challenged the right to rule, but not the nature of the rule. That form of challenge has had a limit. In the deepest sense the present-day trade-union movement has accepted capitalist society.[72]

There was a deep note of melancholy in this conclusion of Bell's, for it meant that labor was unprepared to broach the difficult *value choices*—like the problem of efficiency as an unquestioned absolute—that had to underlie a new political philosophy for the managed economy. Labor's motives were too circumscribed, its vision too short. And its failure helped deepen the gloom Bell saw engulfing the socialist project.

The Sociology of Socialism

The demise of American socialism was the subject of Daniel Bell's monograph, *The Background and Development of Marxian Socialism in the United States*. More particularly the monograph was a long reflection on the frustration of the postwar left and the final eclipse of the Socialist Party. Published in 1952 as the centerpiece of the Princeton University symposium, *Socialism and American Life*, Bell's study was written in 1949 and 1950, while he was calling for a renovation of socialist thought and had begun to explore the sociology of the welfare state, though his research for the project had begun in 1945 at the start of his Chicago sojourn.[73] The book was composed in light of the failure of the 1948 Socialist Party campaign. In the fall of 1947, after the National Educational Committee for a New Party had died, Bell still thought the Socialist Party could mount an effective independent campaign. Given a choice between Truman and either Dewey or Taft, Bell believed, many people would look to the Socialist Party; furthermore, he suggested, "after '48 the trade unions would finally have to really canvas and explore the problem of labor political action realizing that the Messianism of a Roosevelt could not sustain them, and . . . a vigorous SP campaign would put the independent socialist forces in a bargaining position with labor."[74] Truman's election deflated hopes for a political realignment. Still, Bell tried to see the situation in the best possible light, presenting labor's new-found momentum as a "third force" in American politics. By 1950 even this hope evaporated.

Since American socialists had long avoided confronting their own impotence, by predicting that the classic Marxian model of crisis and class conflict would become a reality as American capitalism "matured," they now faced their day of reckoning, Bell suggested:

> The great depression was such a crisis—an emotional shock which shook the self-confidence of the entire society. It left permanent scar tissue in the minds of the American workers. It spurred the organization of a giant trade-union movement which in ten years grew from less than three million to over fifteen million workers, or one-fourth of the total labor force of the country. It brought in its train the smoking-hot organizing drives and sit-downs in the Ohio industrial valley which gave the country a whiff of class warfare. In the 1940s labor entered national politics with a vigor—in order to safeguard its economic gains. *Here at last was the fertile soil which socialist theorists had long awaited. Yet no socialist movement emerged*, nor has a coherent socialist ideology taken seed either in the labor movement or in government.[75]

Only then, in his own time, Bell suggested, was traditional socialist theory finally and decisively refuted, and the expectations of socialist activists denied. The conventional explanations for America's imperviousness to socialism—freely given political rights, the open frontier, the continuous stream of immigration, the lack of a "settled" working class—were adequate enough, Bell believed, but more or less irrelevant to the task he set himself. His book was not primarily a historical survey; instead, it was a sociological study, an attempt to understand, from the subjective point of view, the internal life of the socialist movement. "Most of the attempted answers to Sombart's question [Why is there no socialism in the United States?] have discussed not *causes* but *conditions*."[76] Bell had made the same point, less obscurely, in an earlier draft of the introduction to his book, an essay published in the January 1949 *Modern Review*:

> Such analyses deal largely with the external conditions of the American environment whereas the more immediate problem is the assessment of the Socialist movement itself. And while no decision can be taken without reference to the general context, pragmatically, the first question is: why did the Socialist Party fail to understand its environment and adapt accordingly?[77]

Better still, in a later revision of the introduction to *Marxian Socialism*, published in *The End of Ideology*, Bell asked pointedly, "How did the socialist see the world, and, because of that vision, why did the movement fail to adapt to the American scene? Why was it incapable of rational choice?"[78] In other words Bell sought to explore, in Weberian fashion, the sphere of voluntaristic action and to discover the non-rational orientations that steered it away from a rational standard of action (or, in pragmatic terms, from the norm of efficacious adaptation). In *Marxian Socialism* Bell suggested a number of root causes of the socialist movement's disabilities: its dogmatic ideological commitment to Marxism, its moral proclivities, its chiliastic or millenial temperament. Although these are interwoven in the book, I shall treat each of them separately in order to specify their meaning in Bell's discourse. As we unravel these themes, seeking a center to Bell's analysis, we will find that the essence of his argument settles on the issue of labor's involvement in the bureaucratization of society and the dilemmas that posed for radical intellectuals in his time.

Marxism

In part, Bell claimed that the orientation deflecting the socialist movement from rational adaptation derived from the ideological blinders of Marxist dogma and the sectarian practice it decreed. He pointed to the movement's "supreme confidence about the future" derived from "Marx's prophecy" of the decline of capitalism, which permitted socialists to consider "the particular issues of the day" irrelevant and ephemeral and to ignore real political setbacks as mere temporary disturbances in the onward march of History. Similarly the rigid dogma of class struggle led socialists to eschew any involvement with "capitalist government" in favor of autonomous workers action: since the former was real and present, and the latter so often absent and abstract, socialists too often "chose abnegation." In this sense too, Bell suggested that Marxist ideology was debilitatingly "utopian," committed to a world, wholly apart from the present one, that existed only in the imagination of socialists and could never provide "a standard of testing the immediate means" of action. This was one of the ways in which the socialist movement lived, as Bell put it, "*in* but not *of* the world."[79]

If we look more deeply into Bell's discourse, however, it becomes clear that his critique of Marxist ideology does not in fact carry the full weight of his argument. If it were indeed central to his argument, Bell would only be begging the question, for he posited the obtuseness of Marxist theory at the start: thus he would explain the inability of American socialists to see through the failure of the ideology by their commitment to it. In any case, the historical narrative Bell provides in *Marxian Socialism* by no means consistently demonstrates that the failures of American socialist movements stemmed from the doctrinaire and utopian character of Marxism. The disabling "utopia" of the nineteenth-century left, as Bell indicated, was not a Marxist image of socialism but the stubborn influence of nonproletarian schemes of communal colonies, money reform, and land reform. A labor movement weakened by workers' ambition "to escape their lot as workers" was repeatedly drawn into middle-class reform campaigns; thus the Socialist Labor Party allied itself with Henry George's single-tax campaign, despite Marx's "cogent criticisms" (Bell noted) of George's focus on the role of the landed proprietor rather than that of labor-exploiting capital. Likewise, Bell noted that the socialist sentiment of the 1890s grew more from antimonopoly Populism and the "evangelical fervor and moralistic tone" of the American West than from "European-flavored Marxism"; subsequently the short-lived Social Democracy of America (1897–98) foundered on the diversionary schemes of "Christian socialists, footloose rebels and middle-class romantics" who saw socialism as a step outside the stream of industrialization. The perspective that actually infused Bell's rendering of the history of nineteenth-century radical and labor movements was essentially the same Marxian critique he relied on in his essays of 1945 and 1946: failing to understand the mainsprings of the new industrial order, the old reform movements were, as he wrote in "The Political Lag of Commonwealth," "chipping at the scaffolding of capitalism while the towers of corporate American rose, untouched, from within."[80]

Bell's construction of socialist history did not in fact disclose such a clear dividing line between abstract ideology and practical realism as he would have liked. Samuel Gompers, whom Bell admired for his insistence on "ad hoc pragmatism and continual compromise," emphasized the primacy of labor's economic struggles and the futility of middle-class antimonopoly radicalism in part because his Marxist upbringing encouraged him to suspect the state and to consider the concentration of capital an unalterable tendency of development. On the other hand, Bell conceded, it was the arch "doctrinaire" Daniel De Leon who recognized at an early date that monopolization doomed "pure-and-simple" trade unionism and required a more inclusive political solidarity among labor than mere "job consciousness" allowed.[81] Bell illustrated the socialists' self-defeating abstentionism by quoting Debs:

> Although the American Socialist Party sought to function politically by raising "immediate demands" and pressing for needed social reforms, it rarely took a stand on the actual political problems that emerged from the on-going functioning of the society.

"What but meaningless phrases are 'imperialism,' 'expansion,' 'free silver,' 'gold standard,' etc., to the wage worker?" asked Eugene V. Debs in 1900. "The large capitalists represented by Mr. McKinley and the small capitalists represented by Mr. Bryan are interested in these 'issues' but they do not concern the working class." These "issues" were beside the point, said Debs, because the worker stood outside society.[82]

But what did Debs's agnosticism express but the antipolitical economism of Bell's prototype of practicality, Samuel Gompers? Indeed it was the "doctrinaire" De Leon who insisted that the proletarian movement address all significant "issues" agitating the body politic, especially the "issue" of "imperialism."[83]

Bell's version of the rise and fall of the prewar Socialist Party similarly escaped the frame of a dichotomy between ideological and practical orientations. Bell pointed out that the Socialist Party had its greatest strength in the rural and urban middle class, inheriting the remnants of Populism, tapping the social-welfare lobby, and attracting the declassed modernist intelligentsia. He indicated:

> In 1910 the whole country was going "progressive," and the "leftist" groups, including the socialist movement, were benefitting from the general trend. If the increasing vote was a product of a national swing to progressivism, equally relevant was the fact that the socialists were also tempering their dogmatism and widening their appeal. The socialist increase in great measure was probably due to the new appeal to the small middle class.

Yet this strength was also the party's weakness, for as Bell argued, the party rode the tide until 1912, its peak, after which Wilson's progressivism sapped the party base by drawing away the middle-class constituency. If so, it was precisely the immediacy and practicality of the party's propagandistic appeal that ruined its fortunes in the end. On the other hand, Bell's argument that the Socialist Party's "doctrinaire" opposition to the First World War finally killed the party by ostracizing it from American life is questionable, since the party's antiwar electoral campaigns drew a powerful protest vote in 1917, averaging 21.6 percent of the poll in New York and fourteen other cities across the nation.[84]

Finally, Bell's caustic portraits of the two great Socialist Party leaders, Eugene V. Debs and Norman Thomas, did not demonstrate that the political failings of either stemmed from adherence to abstract Marxist theory. Debs's leftism, in Bell's rendering, stemmed not from an ideological commitment to revolutionary socialism, but from the nineteenth-century sentimental romanticism of his namesakes, Eugène Sue and Victor Hugo. Similarly, Thomas's opposition to war in 1940 and 1941, which Bell wrote "exposed socialist thinking as the politics of irresponsibility," had, as Bell recognized, much less to do with socialist theory per se than with religious pacifism.[85]

Morals

Lacking a consistent argument about Marxist doctrine, Bell's treatise rested more firmly on the issue that preoccupied him throughout the 1940s, the relations of morality to politics. The socialist movement, he wrote, was compromised by "its inability to resolve a basic dilemma of ethics and politics." "It was trapped by the unhappy problem of living '*in* but not *of* the world,' so it could act, and then inadequately, as the moral, but not political, man in immoral society."[86] The socialist movement then was unable to adapt realistically to its environment because of its inclination to impose moral demands inappropriately on the political world, Bell suggested.

It seemed that Bell wished, in a "realist" fashion, to exclude moral concerns from politics per se. He wrote:

> In social action there is an irreconcilable tension between ethics and politics. Lord Acton posed the dilemma in a note: "Are politics an attempt to realize ideals, or an endeavor to get advantages, within the limits of ethics?" More succinctly, "are ethics a purpose or a limit?" In the largest sense, society is an organized system for the distribution of tangible rewards and privileges, obligations and duties. Within that frame, ethics deals with the *ought* of distribution, implying a theory of justice. Politics is the concrete *mode* of distribution, involving a power struggle between organized groups to determine the allocation of privilege. . . . The redivision of the rewards and privileges of society can only be accomplished in the political arena. But in that fateful commitment to politics, an ethical goal, stated as "purpose rather than limit," becomes a far-arching goal before which lies a yawning abyss that can be spanned only by a "leap." The alternatives were forcefully posed by Max Weber in his contrast between the "ethics of responsibility" (or the acceptance of limits) and the "ethics of conscience" (or the dedication to absolute ends). Weber . . . argu[ed] that only the former is applicable in politics.[87]

It is impossible, however, to conclude that Bell intended to argue that politics and morality were mutually exclusive. Since his youth Bell

had always been motivated by moralist concerns. In his earliest political experience—the contest between young Socialists and young
Communists—Bell recoiled from that baneful agnosticism about conventional moral values that turned into a casual nihilism. Reflecting
on that experience, he has said:

> The original motivation of course was a highly moral motivation.
> You come in with a great sense of zeal, and you come in with a
> great sense of party; you come with a great sense of pride, you
> come with a great sense of devoting one's life to something which
> is pure and important. And suddenly you find, not just petty ego,
> which I suppose is true of many situations, but the attempt—a
> sort of Bolshevik psychology, which was that the ordinary canons
> of what normally were called truth, decency, morality, were now
> 'bourgeois' ideas, and could be in a sense swept away in those
> terms.[88]

His subsequent alliance with the right-wing Old Guard followed from
his *moral* repudiation of revolutionary violence, and as an activist in
the Student Strikes Against War, he was moved by the "absolute" strictures of the play *Masse-Mensch* by revolutionary-cum-pacifist Ernst
Toller:

> Hear me: no man may kill for a cause.
> Unholy every cause that needs to kill.
> Whoever calls for blood of men,
> Is Moloch.
> So God was Moloch,
> The State Moloch,
> And the Masses—
> Moloch.[89]

In these same terms—the moral refusal to sacrifice a present good in
the name of a hypothetical future benefit, the moral priority of the
immediate over an obscure ultimate, the refusal to sanction killing today on behalf of the promise of peace tomorrow—Bell had embraced
John Dewey's argument against disjoining ends from means, on the
grounds that meaning inhered in immediate experience and that the
means of action, inseparable from the ends of action, had to assume
the weight of moral value if any good were to be accomplished in politics. Sidney Hook followed Dewey in castigating Marxism for failing to
recognize the centrality of democratic values in political practice, and
so radical intellectuals after the crisis of Marxism in the late 1930s
commonly argued not for the separation of morals and politics but

for the return to the *moral* foundations of the socialist project.[90] Indeed, in 1949, when Bell closed *Modern Review*, he castigated the left for failing to offer new recruits a "moral community."

In fact, the Deweyan argument—the morally corrosive effects of separating "ultimate ends" from immediate means—filtered into *Marxian Socialism* and muddied its meaning. Thus, in demonstrating the danger implicit in what Weber called the ethic of conscience, Bell considered the Bolshevik: "His is the ethic of 'ultimate ends': only the goal counts, the means are inconsequential."[91] But while Weber's term referred to any "absolute" principle of present action, the Deweyan argument against Bolshevism, which Bell implicitly cited, was aimed against the moral relativism, not the moral absolutism, arising from the Bolshevik's conviction in the coming of a revolutionary future: any crime was justified by its professed (but never effected) purpose. As a result, the anti-Bolshevik argument tended to circle back to the reassertion of moral absolutes, and had Bell pursued it, he would have found himself trapped precisely in the ethic of conscience that Weber repudiated. Thus a long, admiring note on Posadovsky, the Social Democrat who challenged Lenin in 1903 by counterposing transcendent moral absolutes to revolutionary expedience, was excised from the original manuscript of Bell's book, luckily for the logical consistency of his argument.[92]

The importation of the Deweyan argument, then, reduced the clarity of Bell's argument, for throughout his book Bell confusingly shifted back and forth between arguing on the one hand that the problem of socialism was its commitment to an "ultimate" (that is, distant) end, providing no effective principle or ethic for guiding present choices, and arguing on the other hand that the problem of socialism was the moral purism that interfered with practically effective action. The one suggested that socialist action was not moral enough; the other that it was overly so. For the most part, Bell's argument relied on the latter point, and therefore the arguments of Reinhold Niebuhr, rather than Dewey, were more relevant to Bell's purposes. But even Niebuhr, who denied that politics could be moralized in full, never intended to dichotomize morals and politics; rather he sought to determine the specific ways in which morality was relevant to politics. In his polemic against perfectionism, Niebuhr aimed his fire at "the error of regarding the transcendent norm as a simple possibility"; he condemned the "secular religions" that unreflectively identified political prospects and spiritual fulfillment.[93] Still, while Niebuhr insisted one could not abstain from realistically "choosing among possible alternatives" that were less than ideal, he also asserted one could not abstain from the perpetual struggle to concretize moral value.[94] History, and practical action in it, was the sphere of moral achievement, while it precluded moral completion. Consequently, Niebuhr's religious values applied to political action. Faith had to attend to the anomalies of experience, had to recognize both the possibilities and constraints of history; it situated man "standing beyond the contradiction [of history] and yet standing in it."[95] Of course, this Niebuhrian paradox signified nothing other than the Lutheran principle of living "in but not of the world," which Bell sought to repudiate.

Indeed, despite the strictures of *Marxian Socialism*, Bell himself had upheld precisely this paradoxical ethic in his 1946 essay on "alienation," which called on the "critic" to sustain the moral pressure on existence while standing apart from practical commitments. On the other hand, in a 1947 essay Bell criticized the dualistic Lutheran formula not because it proposed an impractical moral absolutism but because it denied the applicability of morals to political concerns. "The Judaic view affirms the value of the corporeal and the tangibility of the flesh," Bell wrote in his only religious essay of the period. "It is an earthly religion which insists that the problems of the world be solved in time, and by valuing life as the highest good, we deny anyone the absolute right to demand it." Consequently, Bell spurned all Manichean doctrines, including "the Lutheran distinction of being 'of the world but not in the world,' and the exemption of secular authority from moral commitment."[96]

The discussion in *Marxian Socialism* actually followed from his own experience of the mid-forties when his radicalism was expressed solely in moral terms that he could not render politically viable—the substance of his argument with Dwight Macdonald. His moralist predilections were too strong for him to jettison them in favor of political "realism." Bell learned from Weber's "Politics as a Vocation," however, that politics, by their nature, constituted a morally treacherous terrain; here the absolutist moral principles that Bell embraced as critic could not guide action reliably through bewildering ambiguities. Again, Weber did not suppose that morality was irrelevant but simply that moral and immoral means and ends constantly and confusingly interpenetrated. Weber wrote,

> No ethics in the world can dodge the fact that in numerous instances the attainment of 'good' ends is bound to the fact that one must be willing to pay the price of using morally dubious means or at least dangerous ones—and facing the possibility or even the probability of evil ramifications. From no ethics in the world can it

be concluded when and to what extent the ethically good purpose 'justifies' the ethically dangerous means and ramifications.[97]

For Bell this meant simply that the moral individual had to face the perils of politics without illusions. Such was the significance of "responsibility," which did not at all suggest the dismissal of moral motivations. In his January 1949 *Modern Review* essay, Bell stated,

> If one is to seek a redivision of the rewards and privileges of society . . . then it is only on the field of politics that such a struggle can take place. And if there is a genuine commitment to politics, *as a means of implementing the ethical ideal*, then one must accept the hazards of evil that are implicit in politics and shun utopianism.[98]

Hence, when Bell broached the subject in a November 1947 letter to Norman Thomas, he emphasized not the incompatibility of morality and politics but "the *moral dilemma* which a Socialist leader often is placed in"—that is, not the illicit combination of morals and politics but the given, inescapable tension between the two. Bell cited Thomas' vocal support of a union dissident named Kirschbaum who denounced the undemocratic leadership of the Amalgamated Clothing Workers at a time when the Party relied on a union subsidy. This example lacked the deceptive ease of other instances, such as support of the war against Hitler, where Bell implied that political "responsibility" conflicted with abstract dogmas yet still seemed to jibe with common decency.

> Here, seemingly is a situation in which the *moral* act (ie. protecting Kirschbaum) led to serious *political* consequences for the party as a whole (ie. loss of subsidy). As a Socialist leader and as a political leader, which was the wiser choice.
>
> This question is for me part of a larger canvas of similar tortures, for the SP position on many issues, if I can phrase it this way for metaphoric purposes, is of 'being in the world but not of it.' You reject capitalism as a social system but are called upon constantly to take stands on particular issues which arise out of it and thus get enmeshed within its web although formally rejecting the premises. It seems to lead, for example, to the situation where, as on Spain, the SP supports the Loyalist government, but fearing capitalist action creates the ambiguous formula of "workers' aid" but not capitalist aid. Yet in politics one must think in terms of the viable and if the victory of the Loyalist government is the prime objective then one must not blanch from the real alternatives at hand.[99]

In *Marxian Socialism*, Bell in effect charged that the leaders of the Socialist Party lacked the fortitude to confront these "moral tortures." It is here, in his character portraits of Debs and Thomas, that Bell's theme of living "in but not of the world" came alive. As an explanatory, historical thesis, the formula had a very limited value, for it was virtually tautological: Why couldn't the socialists adapt realistically to given conditions? Because their confusion of the moral sphere with the political forced them outside of time and place and rendered them unrealistic. Hence the socialists were not realistic—because they were unrealistic. Yet Bell's real concern was less with historical explanation than with outlining a *phenomenology of leadership*. As Weber argued, the essence of the political calling was leadership in the struggle for the power of the state, the "monopoly of the legitimate use of physical force." [100] "Real politics," Bell remarked in his notes for *Marxian Socialism*, required a "sense of power," and his critique of Debs and Thomas seemed to rest on an almost Nietzschean critique of their inability to handle and wield power and their choice of vague "symbolic appeals," as he put it in his letter to Hofstadter. [101] In his notes, Bell sketched a view of Debs that portrayed him, in effect, as leader of what Nietzsche called a "slave rebellion," an exponent of a morality expressing weakness and envy, a repudiation of force itself by those who are powerless to begin with. Bell considered Debs as both an "agitator" and an "evangelist," marking these traits in his notes:

> subconscious resentment against paternal authority
>
> refused to take positions of responsibility, unless they involved a fight against authority
>
> Strong suppressed sense of guilt
> skeptical appraisal of others motives
> hyperactivity, persistent policy of baiting authorities
>
> Self-conscious demands for punishment
> self-inflicted or otherwise
>
> While impatient with organized religion, freq. called attention to parallels between Jesus social ideals and his own
>
> His faith on the whole is simple and naive. God a sort of benevolent yet weak Father or Papa. [102]

Regarding Thomas, Bell also emphasized the *impotence* of leadership. At the end of *Marxian Socialism*, having recounted the denouement of the Socialist Party, Bell wrote,

> As a man whose instincts are primarily ethical, Thomas has been the genuine moral man in the immoral society. But as a political

man he has been caught inextricably in the dilemmas of expediency, the relevant alternatives, and the lesser evil. As a sophisticated modern man, Thomas has been acutely aware of his ambiguous role, and feels he has made the political choice. "One is obliged," he wrote in 1947, "to weigh one's actions in terms of relative social consequences . . . and the tragedy is that no choice can be positively good." . . . Thomas did learn the lesson of the lesser evil: instead of being an absolute pacifist, however, he became an indecisive one.[103]

Both Debs and Thomas, as Bell portrayed them, were primarily religious personalities, lacking "the hard-headedness of the politician." But Bell, like Weber, could not go all the way with Nietzsche. Morals were as necessary as power.

While Debs fully realized the messianic role of the prophet, he lacked the hard-headedness of the politician, the ability to take the moral absolutes and break them down to the particulars with the fewest necessary compromises. He lacked, too, the awareness that a socialist leader of necessity must play both of these roles, and that in this tension there arise two risks—the corruption of the prophet and the ineffectuality of the politician.[104]

Bell felt that Debs's "lonely grandeur," while defending the autonomy of the moral individual,

shirks the more difficult problem of living in the world, of seeking as one must in politics, relative standards of social virtue and political justice instead of abstract absolutes. It is but one pole—a necessary one—in creating standards of action. But as the isolated protestant refused to join the community of "sinners," so the isolated prophet, once said Max Scheler, stands on the mountain as a signpost; he points the way but cannot go, for if he did, no longer would there be a sign. The politician, one might add, carries the sign into the valley with him.[105]

Finally, what Bell held against both Debs and Thomas was that they were unable to balance the poles of political experience; they were not the existential men of the type Karl Jaspers defined by "the poise to hold together in synthesis the tremendous tensions of his own self as well as the contradictions of external public life without resorting to illusions." In the end the problem Bell saw in the Socialist Party was not that it chose morality over politics; it worked, as it had to, in the media of both morality and politics without ever adequately articulating them, and it exhausted itself in its oscillation between the two.

Chiliasm

Still, Bell suggested, the roots of socialist failure lay even deeper, in the peculiar conditions of modern consciousness, particularly the phenomenon of "chiliasm." Bell borrowed this portion of his argument entirely from Karl Mannheim's *Ideology and Utopia*, starting with an almost verbatim repetition of Mannheim's definition of modern politics:

> The distinctive character of "modern" politics is the involvement of *all* strata of society in movements of social change, rather than the fatalistic acceptance of events as they are. Its starting point was, as Karl Mannheim elegantly put it, the "orgiastic chiliasm" of the Anabaptists, their messianic hope, their ecstatic faith in the millennium to come . . .
>
> The characteristic psychological fact about the chiliast is that for him "there is no inner articulation of time." There is only the "absolute presentness." "Orgiastic energies and ecstatic outbursts began to operate in a worldly setting and tensions previously transcending day to day life became explosive agents within it." The chiliast is neither "in the world [n]or of it." He stands outside of it and against it because salvation, the millennium, is immediately at hand. Where such a hope is possible, where such a social movement can transform society in a cataclysmic flash, the "leap" is made, and in the pillar of fire the fusion of ethics and politics is possible.[106]

That is, as Mannheim argued, the disintegration of static, unitary medieval society unleashed, in this-worldly existence, passions hitherto restricted to privileged mystic experiences of the other-worldly; thus the eternal invades the present and obliterates time, while the chiliast awaits the apocalypse as an imminent prospect of real history.[107] Likewise, the socialist's atemporal consciousness, anxiously awaiting the revolution, abstracted him from "the here-and-now, give-and-take political world," Bell suggested.[108]

Perhaps this underlay the inability of socialist leadership to adequately temper moral purpose with an understanding of the exigencies of power, but Bell's point is quite tenuous. Certainly Mannheim did not consider modern socialism chiliastic: he considered the perspective of Marxian theory to have a very concrete "articulation of time," a sense of the determinateness of existence and the movement of history through past, present, and future. Furthermore, the modern social-democratic movement, Mannheim believed, steadily relinquished any "utopian" impulse to transform society as the party became increasingly absorbed in administering the "concrete details" of the modern parliament and union.[109] The best Bell could do to demonstrate the chiliastic temper of American socialism was offer a lame reference to Norman Thomas' slogan of the 1930s, "Socialism in our time"—which could as easily signify the collapse of utopian aspiration into administrative immediacy as the invasion of timeless ecstasy into the present.[110] When Bell amended the introduction of *Marxian Socialism* for inclusion in *The End of Ideology*, he added, as an example of the problem socialists face in disciplining chiliastic zeal, not an illustration of socialist activism but a reference to the anarchist in Henry James's *Princess Casamassima*, who believed "that a shot could transform the world in a flash and that he could command the moment when the shot would come."[111]

What then is the relevance of "chiliasm" to Bell's argument in *Marxian Socialism*? Actually, as Bell's argument develops, chiliasm has less to do with the Socialist Party per se than with the common condition of consciousness in mass society that socialism taps. In this sense *Marxian Socialism* is a continuation of the discourse on mass society that Bell began in his *Politics* essay of 1944, "The World of Moloch." There Bell scorned Harold Laski's adulation of the Soviet Union as an instance of the irrational "yearning for absorption" that arises among "atomized beings" in a rationalized, "pulverized culture."

> The source of Russia's strength is precisely that it is a religion, with an array of myths, seeking to satisfy a religious hunger. The dividing line which modern society strove to maintain between religious and social facts has disappeared in Russia. The lines separating state from religion, civil administration from 'priesthood,' profane art from sacred art, science from dogma has dissolved. Religious feeling—the veneration of the regime—is at the bottom of all institutions—artistic, literary and scientific. That is what gives it the unity and cohesion.

Bell added that "the Russian Revolution, for Laski, is a holy idea not bound in space in time." The image of the Russian revolution has become a "compelling myth" of the sort Sorel urged upon the workers movement. Thus revolution became, Bell suggested, a religious phenomenon, the realized apocalypse breaking upon temporal existence, a chiliastic experience impervious to rational analysis and practical tests.[112]

The modern "dividing line between religious and social facts," merely a clumsy way of phrasing Weber's "disenchantment of the world" or rationalization, came up again in *Marxian Socialism*: "In some periods of history, generally in closed societies, ethics and politics have gone hand in hand. But a distinguishing feature of modern society is the separation of the two."[113] Again, in *Marxian Socialism*, there appeared Sorel, who intended the revolutionary myth to be "'capable of evoking as an undivided whole' the mass of diverse sentiments which exist in society."[114] In Bell's discourse, then, it appears that "chiliasm" connotes the desire of masses, disoriented by the process of rationalization sundering meaningful communal life, to reclaim a lost sense of wholeness. In fact, Bell argued in *Marxian Socialism*, the apparent wholeness of the Bolshevik—the Bolshevik's complete identification of the self with the revolution, the Bolshevik's image as "the modern hero," "the man of no compromise, the man of purity"—gave Communism its special appeal, especially to intellectuals in the 1930s.

In response to the Sorelian myth of wholeness, however, Bell asserted that "in the here and now, people live 'in parts.'"[115] That is, as in "A Parable of Alienation," he called for the critical acceptance of otherness in order to resist the irrational temptations that react against rationalization but actually further it. Even Bell's rendering of the prewar Socialist Party is really a discourse on mass society, or mass sentiment in a rationalized society. (In draft, his chapter on "The Golden Age of American Socialism" was originally entitled "The Restless Masses and the Economic Man.")[116] The Party's strength derived from "anxious and distressed petty-bourgeois elements": the rural Populist base inclined to dark suspicion of obscure "plots" and "interests," as well as the urban base of the déclassé intelligentsia hostile to commercial philistinism and motivated by romantic longings for undivided experience.[117] These were the middle-class strata given to the "spiritual 'self-intoxication'" of chiliasm.[118]

Labor

So a note of old-line sectarianism crept back into Bell's analysis: As Old Guard leader Algernon Lee had complained of the "déclassés of various kinds" who invaded the Socialist Party, so Bell seemed to say that the American socialist movement failed because it was too middle-class—and hence too susceptible to the viruses of mass society that attacked, first of all, the archetypal "mass man," the rootless and isolated petty bourgeois. "But what of the proletariat itself?" Bell asked. He wrote:

In the fluctuations of socialist power within the American Federation of Labor, 1902 was the peak year, after which the socialist strength declined. This is an incongruous fact, for 1902 was the beginning of rising socialist political influence in the United States. The answer to this paradox is that the socialist vote was never drawn primarily from organized labor—a fact that was one of its fundamental weaknesses.[119]

It was indeed, Bell wrote, "its lack of commitments to the labor movement," the absence of "the strings of responsibilities which held the European socialists," that allowed the Socialist Party to stand out against the First World War, thus ostracizing itself from the national community and drawing upon itself the repression of the state.[120] The Socialist Party met its final defeat, though, in the ten years from 1938 to 1948, Bell indicated, when the organizational maturity of American labor made the gap between it and socialist ideologists almost impassable. The links the party strove to forge with labor led to its unraveling, as the activists it seeded in the CIO drive rose to positions of union responsibility and organizational exigencies demanded their support of prolabor Democrats in the quid-pro-quo alliance the union chiefs forged with Roosevelt. Socialist unionists quietly but steadily pulled away from the party, as it failed to find a way to tie up with the American political mainstream and satisfy defenders of socialist integrity at the same time. Bell quoted a letter from Socialist Party auto caucus head George Edwards to Thomas that summed up the conundrum:

> We are now faced with a very difficult situation on the political field. Our party here is growing in the unions in membership and influence. But our progress is jeopardized by the complex situation in the current political campaign. Some of the leading unionists cannot refrain from giving some support to Murphy [Democratic gubernatorial candidate] without sacrificing their own positions. This handicaps the party's campaign and even endangers the party organization at a time when there is a splendid chance to build the party and draw in many new elements from the entire labor movement here.

The Socialist Party would not support "old-party" candidates, however, and Bell wrote, "the doctrinaire stand on the election issues of 1938"—in his notes Bell recalled the Socialist Party's resistance to cooperating with garment unions that year in the pro-Roosevelt American Labor Party of New York—"completed the socialist isolation from the labor movement."[121] Thus, after the debacle of the 1948 Thomas campaign indicated "the demise of the party in the electoral field,"

Bell remarked in *Modern Review*, "the Socialist Party has not been a political party, certainly not for the past ten years."

The real problematic of *Marxian Socialism*, therefore, was the problem of the evolution of the American labor movement and the relation of socialists to it. In his *Modern Review* essay of January 1949, "American Socialists: What Now?" Bell pointed out that American society had already "matured" as Marxists said, as the instability of the early labor movement, the consequence of the worker's "attempt to escape the lot of being a worker," had been overcome. Now the rise of established industrial unions signaled that the worker was "settled" as such, knowing he was "stuck" as a worker; thus one of the key factors inhibiting the rise of socialism, the lack of a settled working class, no longer held sway. "Does that mean a new radical politics in American life?" Bell asked. Paradoxically, Bell answered, the crystallization of class in workers' consciousness, led to consequences that were the inverse of what socialists had expected:

> The growth of a "settled" feeling among workers has not led to a radicalization, but to an insistent two-fold demand for security: security in the shop through seniority systems, firing only for cause, resistance to technological change, etc.; and security in the larger society through unemployment insurance, old-age pensions, health insurance, etc. And the growth of the trade union as an instrument to realize that security has meant the development of an *institutional force that has had to, necessarily, grow integrally into the very fabric of society.* Whereas the fundamental outlook of nineteenth century utopian unionism . . . was to change capitalist society, the fundamental drive of twentieth century unionism is to assure a place and some weight in that social order.[122]

The development of the politically managed economy, Bell wrote in this *Modern Review* essay, had compelled labor to take on a new political role, and this in turn excited still new socialist hopes for the emergence of a labor party; but "while independent labor action is certainly in order," Bell commented, "it is a serious misreading of the American political scene to hope at this point to talk of a new *party*." The recent independent Congressional candidacy of his old friend and Chicago colleague, Socialist Maynard Krueger, had garnered disappointing returns. Hence Bell argued that the institutional framework of American politics made political fights in the Democratic primaries much more effective than initiatives outside them. The UAW's efforts to capture the Michigan Democratic party, he suggested, were testing out a new political orientation for labor. The tactic of entering old-party primaries was a common one for the prewar Socialists, and though Bell recognized some validity in the old warning that thereby "they won a party but lost their Socialism," he added that labor and its Socialist allies currently had few other options.[123] The big question for Bell, in other words, was *whether Socialists would follow labor where it seemed it had to go and face with it the inevitable political dangers that resulted.* At this point in his essay Bell broached the problem of "responsibility," the recognition of "the hazards of evil that are implicit in politics":

> Politics then becomes the acceptance of the relevant alternatives. One must in the practical sense live with realistic division of institutional forces as they exist. *It means operating within the labor movement, accepting its backwardness and the compromises it is forced to make.* In that sense the fundamental meaning of the British Labor party was not its function as an independent party but that the intellectuals in the Fabian Society and the Independent Labor Party went into it whole-heartedly.[124]

In this context the significance of *Marxian Socialism* becomes much clearer, for the problem of "getting enmeshed within the web" of capitalism, as Bell put it in his 1947 letter to Norman Thomas, now appears quite concrete. *Marxian Socialism* implied, first, a theory of social development marked by the bureaucratic involution of the historic agent of change, labor. The "maturity" of the working class, rather than leading it to mount a more intransigent opposition, led it, Bell posited, toward a place within the institutional mesh of society as it existed. This proposition in fact extended the themes Bell developed in his period of estrangement, the years 1945–48, when he saw society taking on an "official" cast, when all social agencies were made integral parts of a closed order. Second, the discussion of morality and the troubled sphere of political choice really pointed to one overriding contemporary problem: the choice American socialists now faced of *following labor into the Democratic Party* or remaining apart from it and impotent. *Marxian Socialism*, that is, was written in part as a rationalization of an unpalatable maneuver, the social-democratic entry that we have described as a key political element of postwar reconstruction. Bell concluded his *Modern Review* essay thus, trying to put the best light on the situation:

> Given the structure of American politics, it is likely that political unionism will operate largely within the Democratic Party. While it means an organizational tie to that party, no full ideological commitment is necessary because the American party system as a

brokerage house demands no ideological loyalties. In this sense, Socialists have a positive role to play. As intellectual catalysts, they could offer a comprehensive program and work for its adoption by the trade unions. A necessary first step in that direction would be a formal statement by the Socialist Party forsaking electoral activity on a national scale. It would free many of its own people and give them freer play to be effective. It would draw closer persons in the trade union movement who for practical reasons follow the political line of labor and have to eschew Socialist contact. . . . The demise of the Socialist Party as an electoral party in that situation is not a tragic event, but a clearing of the ground. It could allow for the emergence of a new intellectual leadership on the left which would attempt, working within the body politic of labor as a *political* force, to crystallize a new intellectual orientation. Such a one is long overdue.[125]

This optimistic portrait of the intellectual as the ideological leader of labor in the new politically managed economy was written still in the flush of 1948, when Bell hoped that labor, even within the Democratic Party, would emerge as a "third force" and that labor's commitment to politics on a national scale would steadily widen its horizons, galvanize its energies, and lead it by regular victorious steps to more audacious goals. But in his labor writings, as we have already seen, these hopes dwindled as unions remained rooted to parochial interests and intellectuals were unable to find a place for themselves as elaborators of a labor ideology suited to the political economy.

The End of Morally Meaningful Politics

Thus Bell's mood began to darken by 1949, and another undercurrent of *Marxian Socialism*, the mass society, assumed increasing salience. Bell had probed the impediments to a rational mass politics, in a mass society characterized by the two poles of *faith* and *apathy*. The first, which he had analyzed in "The World of Moloch," represented the compulsive drive by individuals who were both atomized and bound by the structure of rationalized bureaucracy to submit to a homogeneous collective sustained by myth. Yet the alternative to these feverish, grand fictions of mass faith appeared to be political indifference, distrust, and privatism.

Thus, following his judgment that "by 1950 . . . American socialism as a political and social fact was simply a matter for history alone," Bell's original manuscript of *Marxian Socialism* concluded:

And, if "modern" politics is understood (as defined in the intro-
ductory section of this paper) as the involvement of the masses of
people in the struggle for power, then western culture as a whole
is too at the end of an era. For out of the confusions and exhaus-
tions of war, a new non-political attitude is spreading, typified by
the French *je m'en fiche* (I don't give a damn) and the Italian *fanno
schiffo tutti* (they all stink), in which the sole desire of the great
masses of people is simply to be left alone. Conscripted, regi-
mented, manipulated, disoriented in the swirl of ideological warfare, the basic and growing attitude is one of distrust. And [for]
the intellectual, the seed-bearer of culture, the feeling is one of
betrayal, by power, and the mood is one of impotence.[126]

Bell's view struck a common chord with Hannah Arendt's theory
of totalitarianism, published in 1951. When the ideological furies subsided, she suggested, the result was not necessarily a return to a rational, democratic public world:

The moment the movement, that is, the fictitious world which
sheltered them, is destroyed, the masses revert to their old status
of isolated individuals who either happily accept a new function
in a changed world or sink back into their old desperate super-
fluousness.[127]

The problem for Bell, then, as for Arendt throughout the course
of her political thought, was how to reconstitute a viable public world.
Indeed, insofar as mass society denied any alternative to the poles of
mass faith and apathy, Bell's hopes of fulfilling the promise of the politically managed economy, which depended on elaborating a new
public philosophy of central democratic values to determine rights
and responsibilities within a planned order, were dead.

In its own way, Bell's *Marxian Socialism* was a reflection on a time-
honored problem of modern socialism, the relation between the "minimum" and "maximum" programs, the particular interests of the workers (the sphere of the trade unions and ameliorative reform) and the
"ultimate interests of the entire working class" (the sphere of the party
and the socialist goal). The problem of living "in but not of the world,"
the disjuncture of immediate means and ultimate ends, the distance
between labor and socialism, the strain between politics and ethics (especially when the ultimate goal, the realization of the politically managed economy, was essentially an ethical project), all reflected the
increasing difficulty of maintaining the link between minimum and
maximum programs. In fact, as the trade union and the minimum

program of welfare reforms were wholly absorbed within the institutional structure of a rationalized society, the maximum program disappeared almost entirely. Eduard Bernstein's slogan, "the movement everything, the goal nothing," took on a tragic meaning in Bell's Weberian analysis, for rationalization undermined the efficacy of meaningful values in the public sphere, degraded ends while concentrating solely on means, and precluded the fulfillment of moral purpose. Hence, Bell's analysis tended toward a dismal conclusion—the death of socialism in the bureaucratized society. In effect, Bell asked, how was a rational society possible in the modern world? As the reformed, organized capitalism of the welfare state offered opportunities for social planning, it simultaneously undermined the communal values that alone could motivate and direct planning. Thus, it seemed that any concession to the reformist possibilities inherent in capitalism had to be accompanied by a recognition of how capitalism also frustrated the reformist aim. Hidden within Bell's perspective at the end of the 1940s, then, was the unstated recognition that the Cold War absorption of social democracy within the structure of late capitalism effectively ended its ability to pursue socialist goals. Once he was firmly within the bounds of political accommodation, Bell knew, at some level beneath his professed aspirations, that he was trapped.

In a review of Orwell's *1984* in *The New Leader* on June 25, 1949, Bell gave a taste of his ambiguous and ambivalent reconciliation with American political reality.[128] The Greek word *utopia*, Bell noted, literally meant "nowhere," but "the frightening aspect of George Orwell's imaginary world is that it is somewhere—in and around us." "Apparently," he wrote, "there is nothing too extreme (either technically or psychologically) for the mind to contrive out of fantasy that is not already present today" (even in American culture), from the ruin of vital language by planners of linguistic efficiency to a two-way telescreen suited to continual surveillance.

What did Orwell's vision mean for democratic socialism? Bell asked. "Is, for example, the action of the British Labor government in creating a wage freeze the imposition of controls whose consequence is the acceleration of power concentration and the total state?" Or, what of the Congressional charter of a central intelligence agency empowered to infiltrate domestic voluntary associations? "Are not these irreversible steps, and hence, the danger that we are being warned against?" Bell could appreciate the appeal of taking an absolute and intransigent oppositional stand. Orwell, he knew, pointed to "the absolute truth that man is an end in himself"; but absolutes, Bell wrote, were no adequate guide to social action "in the *here* and *now*."

Obliquely, Bell suggested he assented to one or both of the "statist" measures he cited, though he shared the common trepidation over their ramifications. Perhaps, Bell said, the only security lay in skepticism and modesty, accompanied by the pragmatic test of proposed action "by its minimal infringement on the carefully defined set of values which stakes out man as the measure of man's things." "Colorless and unappealing," perhaps—but preferable to total withdrawal and nihilism, he said.

> One has to live in the world and accept it in all its frightening implications. One has to live consciously and self-consciously, in the involvement and in the alienation, in the loyalty and in the questioning, in the love and in the critical appraisal. Without that persistent double image, we are lost. At best we can live in paradox.

In the end, Bell had to leave all the key tensions of his sociological analysis—technique and purpose, bureaucracy and democracy—in suspension. The only "program" for politics and for moral action was "colorless and unappealing," purely a negative one of *checking* given social tendencies that could not be effectively refused or resisted. In the end, morality had indeed become only a limit, not a purpose, as he wrote in *Marxian Socialism*. And that, for a political man and a socialist, was very meager consolation indeed.

5

The Formative Moment of Daniel Bell

The Final Conundrum of Evolutionary Socialism

By the end of the 1940s, Daniel Bell had begun building a theory dedicated to probing social action in terms of the contradictions left by the demise of the socialist project in a bureaucratized order. With this problematic, drawn from his experience of deradicalization, the mature phase of his theoretical project commenced. Thus the survey of Bell's intellectual development through the 1940s will help illuminate the real content of *The End of Ideology*. It will also provide the kernel of meaning in his later work, the complementary *Coming of Post-Industrial Society* and *Cultural Contradictions of Capitalism*. The problematic of the late 1940s was the starting point for the construction—and hence, I suggest, the understanding—of this work. Here a brief encounter with these books will suffice to show the relevance of this problematic to their interpretation.

The process of deradicalization evident in Daniel Bell's early career involved a dialectic of estrangement and reconciliation following the obstruction or inversion of evolutionary progress. The moment of estrangement was manifest in the "new radicalism" of the postwar years, which left a certain permanent deposit in Bell's thought. The new radicalism reacted against the apparent closure of social structure and found a new warrant for dualist disjunctures. The marginalization that radical intellectuals suffered, as events consistently frustrated rather than realized their purposes, encouraged them to find a sanctuary for value in a special sphere apart from fact; in contrast, the identity of fact and value promised by holistic ideologies of progress seemed to mirror the bureaucratic pretension, the completion of a faultless whole of rationalized, efficient, and monolithic order.[1] Hence the disenchanted radicalism of the Frankfurt School, its antisystematic bias and resistance to "premature" syntheses, its cultivation of the ineluctably fragmentary and unfinished quality of thought that would resist the complete degradation of thinking to the status of a bureaucratic function. "Inasmuch as subject and object, word and thing, cannot be integrated under present conditions, we are driven, by the principle of negation, to attempt to salvage relative truths from the wreckage of false ultimates," Max Horkheimer wrote in 1947.[2] Critical integrity resided in the refusal to countenance the "premature closure" of problems, the insistence on keeping "the wound of the negative open," in Kierkegaard's phrase; the insidiousness of "ideologies" lay precisely in their intention to close the gap, as "secular religions" that sanctified the present and disallowed any critique that escaped its bounds. Furthermore, at least in the first few years after the war, this kind of criticism applied not only to Stalinism but to the new order of "massed power," as Bell put it, in the West.

The paradox of this critical disposition was its suspicion of strategies aiming to overcome the rationalization it assailed. Undoubtedly, the constitutive ambivalence in Bell's thought towards alienation and bureaucracy could give rise to one-sided misinterpretations, like the mistaken attribution to him of an undiluted validation of bureaucracy. What we find instead in Bell's mature thought is that peculiar circularity of modern social theory which responds to the obstruction of linear progress with an assessment of enduring contrarieties in social action and order. The antihistoricism of the "new radicalism" in the mid-1940s ushered in a social theory that played upon the continual interaction of opposites, the persistent tension of rationalization and ideology, bureaucracy and democracy. Thus any interpretation of Bell's work which perceives in it a prophecy of unilinear, unidirectional rational progress must be mistaken.

Critics have often viewed Bell's end-of-ideology theory as a doctrine testifying to the triumph of political moderation and stability, as bureaucratic management steadily displaced arbitrary class authority and political parties surrendered Weltanschauungen for the nonideological role of bargaining over compromisable interests. In fact, Bell's colleague, Seymour Martin Lipset, often presented the doctrine in this guise, for he tied it to an oversimplified version of Weber which presumed an evolutionary shift from substantive rationality (devoted to the attainment of valued goals) to functional or instrumental rationality, where ideology—or passionate commitment to absolute ends—was identified with the former.[3] Bell's work bespeaks too great a familiarity with the nuances of Weber's thought to coincide with such a formulation.

Actually, a literal construction of Bell's "end of ideology" to mean the final eclipse of destabilizing political passions falsifies his views and his intentions, for Bell believed that the impetus to ideology abided as a characteristic feature of mass society, despite, or indeed because of, the decline of substantive rationality.

Indeed, the mass society Bell described in the late 1940s was not, in his view, riven by the blunt, binary oppositions of class struggle as Marxists understood it. To his mind, a definite ruling class dominated the polity no more than a definite insurgent class challenged it. And in the absence of *class* action, motivated by a coherent program for administering power on behalf of class interests, substantive rationality did not guide politics. Rather, politics became a field for fluid combinations of multiple interests promoted by variegated organizational elites, and with the "practical," means-oriented rationality of politics, society achieved some measure of stability. Yet, at the same time, Bell suggested that the *amorphousness of power* tended to *disorient* individuals and groups insofar as the source and rationale of decision eluded popular consciousness. The disappearance of clearly defined and continuous power blocs in society stimulated a reaction-formation, as it were, the free-floating urge toward certainty that found satisfaction in suspicions of conspiratorial power and the fanatic hostility to a social whole of murky meaning. Hence Bell wrote, in a 1951 *Fortune* article, "The absence of stabilized power . . . increases the tendency to substitute ideological allegiances, which are rarely defined concretely, for traditional political compromise."[4] If ideology left the front door it returned through the rear, Bell suggested, evoking that ironic circularity characteristic of Weber's theory.

Thus, for Bell, the rationalization of political process yielded a new mystification of social reality, and despite the appearance that contending interest groups had reached a political accommodation, Bell could never be sure American society was, as he suggested in *The End of Ideology*, "a society where there is a shared consensus." Elsewhere in that book he remarked, "through the mass media we have the binding threads of a national community, and with it the *illusory* fabric of a national consensus" (emphasis added).[5] Bureaucratic integration, it seemed, could make a whole of society, in which no special groups were excluded from the organized process, but this did not necessarily produce a unity of consciousness, except negatively, in the common condition of depoliticized privatism, a shared lack of beliefs and bonds. A positive unity was absent, as Bell noted ruefully in his early essay on "the politically managed economy."

In similar terms Bell had often noted the unresolvable tension between bureaucracy and democracy. Democracy as an ethic of self-determination, of concrete participation in fashioning the conditions under which one lives and acts, opposed the immanent authoritarian tendency of bureaucracy that removed the locus of decision far from the field of ordinary social activity. Bell's critical sociology, however, recognized both the genuine appeal and the treachery of the popular impulse toward community and participation as a weapon against the depersonalizing order of bureaucracy—for the resentment of devaluing rationalism could lunge headlong toward the irrationalism of spurious communities that obliterate the autonomous self even as they promise to realize it, and the ethic of participation could issue in the manipulative control of the individual coopted into the illusory harmony of a repressive group. In these antinomies Bell recognized "the whole unsettled ambience" of modern society. Under the strain of structural tensions, interest conflicts, and social psychological disorders, society was far from a stable, self-adjusting system. The ambiguity of rationalization in Bell's theory determined the appearance of both welcome stability and threatening instability in modern society.

Recognizing Bell's sensitivity to contrariety and tension in social structure, however, does not yet yield the most fundamental component of his social theory, which is concerned with the nature of capitalism and prospects of socialism. At the beginning of his writing career, as the young managing editor of *The New Leader*, Bell troubled over the ambiguity of social change induced by the Second World War. Did the war spur the advance of social democracy, or the consolidation of a capitalist state? By the end of the 1940s, his theory of the emerging welfare state in effect synthesized the two alternatives: for him, the future of social democracy lay within the political order of an organized capitalism. In his depiction of the "politically managed economy," Bell demonstrated how the industrial economy had "grown over" naturally into a cohesive order ripe for conscious planning, and he justified the political accommodation of social democracy by the judgment that an organized capitalism stood on the verge of transformation to a social economy. Thus he remained close in spirit to Rudolf Hilferding's work, for in his 1927 declaration, "The Tasks of Social Democracy," Hilferding had proposed that socialists could accomplish their goals by working in and through the order of organized capitalism, a transitional phase of social development. In imagining this transitional phase, Bell also profited from current theories of statism and mixed economy which depicted a social order that was simultaneously capitalist and noncapitalist. In the 1930s, socialist economists like Oskar Lange and H. D. Dickinson had proposed making a mixture of markets and planning, and it was, paradoxically, just this vision of reform that Friedrich Pollock tapped in his essays on the efficacy of the new statist economy.[6] In such an order, the elements of classic capitalist economy—markets, prices, profits, wages—had lost their *autonomous* character: they no longer constituted a system that operated spontaneously, automatically, bearing certain effects that were uncontrollable by any of the participants therein. The survival of these economic factors did not by itself signify the maintenance of capitalism as a market process with its own inherent dynamic: they survived merely as the instrumentalities of policy. Hence it seemed modern social development promised the conquest of reification, for that which had appeared to be a self-subsistent objective reality—the mechanism of the market—was now recognized as *ours* to organize and deploy at will, for a purpose.

It was precisely the *purpose* that was missing, however, according to Bell's analysis in the late 1940s. In mass society, it seemed, rationalization had already paralyzed the moral intention that had to intervene to convert the organized order into a (substantively) rational society; reification had already frustrated the agencies that could overcome it. Bell's notion of the "politically managed economy" put a priority on politics as the sphere of central value decisions superimposed on technical administration, and the lapse of meaningful, or value-motivated, politics left unfinished the social-democratic project of economic control on behalf of the moral ends of society as a whole. Thus Bell's persistent problem—finding a political embodiment for morals—was left unresolved, an abiding question at the core of his thought.

In Bell's new Weberian terminology, the problem appeared as a disproportion between rationality and rationalization. Like Weber, Bell recognized the corrosive effect that instrumental reason had on meaningful values; and like Karl Mannheim, who worried that the capacity for central planning would coincide with "the relinquishment of utopias, [when] man would lose his will to shape history and therewith his ability to understand it," Bell saw that the prospects of a rational society were denied on the very threshold of their achievement.[7] For Bell, as shown in the critical reading of his book *Marxian Socialism* in chapter 4, the bureaucratic eclipse of rational collective purpose appeared as a tragic fact of modern society. But Bell's perception of that fact had its real basis in his situation as a social democrat entering the capitalist fold with mingled hope and dismay. For the impassable paradox his theory sighted—the persistence of reification, frustrating the real possibility of its conquest—reflected the ambiguous meaning of "capitalism" in a social-democratic theory of "organized capitalism," a moment when capitalism endured even as it appeared almost to pass away. Here was the final conundrum of evolutionary socialism, the unconquerable dilemma of social democracy at midcentury, absorbed within a capitalist order it saw evolving naturally toward socialism, yet powerless to break the bounds that capitalism imposed.

Thus the essential historical condition of the late 1930s—the impasse of socialism amid the decline of capitalism—remained a crucial reality at the heart of Bell's thought. His theory of the politically managed economy—its prospects and its disabilities—represented a particular inflection of the ideology of the welfare state, which resolved the ideological crisis of the late 1930s, the mutual weakness of bourgeois and socialist thought, by eliciting concessions from both. If socialism embraced mixed economy as the route to a rational society, so capitalism surrendered its traditional rationale of property and market freedom for the legitimacy of social reform, economic stabilization, and productive performance.[8] This was a peculiarly *negative* resolution, for it represented only a common default. The absence of any positive principle overcoming the ideological crisis makes entirely lucid the two title elements of Bell's later book, *The End of Ideology: The Exhaustion of Political Ideas in the Fifties*. Thus Bell implicitly points out the persistence of the open gap left from the stalemate of the late 1930s and the makeshift quality of the ideology of the welfare state. In fact, Bell's thought discloses the contradictions in the ideology of the welfare state even while conceding to it. By portraying rationalization simultaneously as the route toward, and the inhibition of, a substantively rational and morally directed society, Bell's theory offers the promise of a rational society and withdraws it at the same time, and in so doing expresses the presumption of progress in the ideology of the welfare state and undermines it as well.

The roots of "the end of ideology" doctrine, then, lie in a grudging theory of the welfare state which voices the conundrum of evolutionary socialism trapped in what it sees as a stymied transition within and beyond capitalism. This interpretation provides the clue to the meaning of the key contradictions in *The End of Ideology*: the definition of capitalism, the assessment of socialism, and the analysis of the condition of labor. At one point in *The End of Ideology*, Bell approached James Burnham's definition of a postcapitalist managerial society: with the separation of family ownership from corporate enterprise and the consequent disappearance of a cohesive ruling class, Bell wrote, "private productive property . . . in the United States is largely a fiction," and "performance" rather than profit per se "has become a driving motive for the American corporate head." At other points, however, Bell matter-of-factly referred to the American "capitalist order" and criticized the ideological "rehabilitation of American capitalism."[9] The contradiction resolves itself in a vision of a social order that is capitalist and noncapitalist at the same time, like Hilferding's "organized capitalism," which all but passes into socialism. For Bell, the noncapitalist character of the order stemmed from the fact that the classic conditions of an undisturbed autonomous market no longer prevailed; still, the residual capitalist character of the order (private, planless appropriation of revenue) survived until the full promise of the emergent politically managed economy was realized—a distant prospect. Such an anomaly conditioned Bell's simultaneous endorsement and critique of utilitarian socialism. He applauded the fact that Western socialists had come to terms with their society by accepting the mixed economy as the medium of progress and market mechanisms as means of economic rationality, but he criticized socialists for failing to challenge the imperatives of efficiency that market rationality imposed on production and on industrial workers. Again, the lure of progress and its frustration could only "trap" socialists in what appeared to Bell as a necessary, but fruitless, concession. Bell's portrayal of the stymied transition also underlay his severance of the categories of exploitation and alienation of labor. These two are intimately intertwined in Marxist theory but are sharply separated in Bell's discussion as "two roads" of analysis—for in an order that was both capitalist and noncapitalist, production seemed increasingly to be guided by consensual terms of rational cooperation, and yet labor was still unfree.

Bell's later work clearly manifests the growth of seeds planted in his thought during the 1940s, for the same ambiguity we have located here in assessing the contemporary fate of capitalism appears in Bell's major works of social theory, *The Coming of Post-Industrial Society* (1973) and *The Cultural Contradictions of Capitalism* (1976). In 1952, at the close of *Marxian Socialism*, Bell suggested the advent of an unheralded phase of social development. Then he fumbled for a definition—"whatever the character of that new social structure may be—whether state capitalism, managerial society, or corporative capitalism." By the 1970s, however, he found a name for the system: "post-industrial society."[10] Indeed Bell marked off 1945–50 as the "birth years" of postindustrial society and so matched the formative years of his social theory with the emergence of a new social order.[11]

Bell opens *The Coming of Post-Industrial Society* by reviewing the anomalies in Marx's schemata of social development, thus making it clear that postindustrialism arises as a theoretical problem from the ostensible obstruction of the path leading from capitalism to social- ism—a situation, that is, where a waning capitalism appears to yield something other than socialism. Dominating Bell's discourse is his sense of inhabiting a social interregnum which evades precise defini- tion. Although Bell insists that his concept of "post-industrial" society is not equivalent to "post-capitalist" society, his writing is fraught with telling contradictions: he both foresees the end of capitalism and re- fuses to pronounce its epitaph. Certainly Bell defines postindustrial- ism in terms that suggest if not the end of capitalism at least its wither- ing away.

It is the concept of transition that makes sense of one of the marked traits of Bell's book: the uncertainty and indeterminateness of his propositions. *The Coming of Post-Industrial Society* posits five dimen- sions of change—the sectoral predominance of services over manu- facturing in the economy; the growth of professional-technical oc- cupations; the social centrality of "theoretical knowledge" or science; the future-oriented outlook arising from attempts to assess the con- sequences of technological developments; and the dependence of decision-making on "intellectual technologies" of linear program- ming, game theory, and the like. Without a general theory that ex- plains the salience of these five dimensions of social analysis, and their relation to each other, however, Bell's argument appears principally to be a collage of social description. Each of Bell's five posits rests on a different kind of judgment: the service sector, broadly defined, out- sizes the goods-producing sector in a number of statistical measures; the professional and scientific occupations win their claim to preemi- nence not by absolute size but by their rate of growth; the "intellectual technologies" are cited, but their applications and efficacy are not ex- amined.[12] In place of a theory that relates these phenomena to each other and justifies varying ways of measuring their significance, Bell as- serts simply that the admittedly "speculative" character of the "post- industrial" concept precludes a "linear development of the argu- ment," permitting "only an exploration of diverse themes."[13] At the same time that the description of postindustrial society appears pecu- liarly disjointed, Bell's chronology of postindustrial society appears in- definite. The term seems to float in time, designating a dimly seen fu- ture (for the United States, Bell's theoretical model, yet remains an "industrial society," he says at one point), an emergent order (for, he writes, "we are now in the first stages of a post-industrial society"), or a structure already in existence (for the new society had its "birth," as Bell said, in the years after 1945).[14] In the end, these divergent assessments suggest, however, not confusion but a peculiar trait of the "post-industrial" concept: its elasticity, arising from Bell's "sense of living in interstitial time" which tries to comprehend both process and goal.[15] The fact that the concept stretches to accommodate these diverse meanings stems from the paradoxes embedded in Bell's thought, his attempt to define an ongoing process of social development in terms of an outcome that is both within reach and yet impossible to grasp. This problem, like that of Bell's descriptive collage, can be understood in terms of his discussion of capitalism and its fate. The sharp tension in the text between the suggestion that tendencies of social organization drive beyond capitalism and Bell's denial of his proximity to "post-capitalist" theories points to the abiding tension that characterizes the indeterminate transitional society Bell seeks to describe, the tension between evolutionary survivals and prospects which is the real theme of all his work.

Bell's principal attempt to extricate the concept of "post-industrial" society from the suggestion of postcapitalist society is evidently disingenuous. He argues that the former deals with the technological dimension of change, the latter with the economic, so that the move from industrial technologies of manufacturing to the postindustrial technologies of exchanging knowledge takes place on a plane apart from the system of property (private or collective, capitalist or socialist) in any given society.[16] Bell here refers to his overarching theory of society, which posits a "disjunction" of three "realms," social structure, culture, and politics, each examined according to its unique dynamics without presumption of their essential unity. He repeatedly ascribes postindustrialism to the "social structure," however, which he defines as "the techno-economic order,"[17] and nowhere but in this ad hoc apologia does he suggest that "social structure" may be analyzed further into distinct elements: technics and economics. In fact, the pastiche of social indicators Bell uses to define postindustrial society has unity only insofar as it points to those tendencies within the present that pass beyond the bounds of capitalism toward a collectivized order. The professional and scientific strata stand outside and beyond the classes of capital and labor. The centrality of theoretical knowledge sets at the heart of productivity a factor that cannot be accounted for in terms of discrete costs, which by nature escapes private control, offers little profit incentive, and thus must be driven by social commitment and control. The future orientation asserts the inadequacy of a market that "decides" after the fact of blind action, and the "intellectual technologies" provide the apparatus for rational planning.

Thus while Bell states, "the underlying system of the society . . . is still capitalist," he suggests that "post-industrial" society is at least in tendency noncapitalist, whether capitalism be defined by private property, the market, or the polarity of capital and labor: "If capital and labor are the major structural features of industrial society, information and knowledge are those of the post-industrial society. . . . In capitalist society the axial institution has been private property and in the post-industrial society it is the centrality of theoretical knowledge. . . . We in America are moving away from a society based on a private-enterprise market system." [18] Indeed, Bell suggests a wholesale shift away from the foundations of capitalism—the grounding of social action in individualism, utilitarianism, and the fortuitous order of the marketplace:

> Capitalism was not just a system for the production of commodities, or a new set of occupations, or a new principle of calculation (though it was all of these), but a justification for the primacy of the individual and his self-interest, and of the strategic role of economic freedom in realizing those values through the free market. This is why the economic function became detached from other functions of Western society and was given free rein.
>
> The political ethos of an emerging post-industrial society is communal . . . It is sociologizing rather than economic . . . as the criteria of individual utility and profit maximization become subordinated to broader conceptions of social welfare and community interest. [19]

Finally, the fifth dimension of postindustrialism—the sectoral predominance of services—suggests a profound shift in social reality to a new plane. Bell's triad of preindustrial, industrial, and postindustrial societies is paced by the relative economic predominance of extractive, manufacturing, and service sectors. Accompanying these economic emphases, Bell states, are distinct social ontologies: in the first case "reality was nature"; in the second, "reality became technics, tools and things made by men yet given an independent existence outside himself, the reified world." In postindustrial society, Bell writes,

> reality is primarily the social world—neither nature nor things, only men—experienced through the reciprocal consciousness of self and other. Society itself becomes a web of consciousness, a form of imagination to be realized as a social construction. [20]

Postindustrialism then promises nothing less than the conquest of re-ification, the subordination of things—human creations that formerly "rode men"—to the conceptions humans fashion in their social rela-tions. The outcome is nothing but the traditional goal of socialism: a rational society guided by collective purpose.

The difference, of course, is that the impulse to collectivization comes, in Bell's scheme, not from labor but from science. Bell's "post-industrial" society is not merely a technological society but a science-based society. Industrial society rested on the steady advance of pro-ductive technique, but postindustrial society motivates that advance not by trial-and-error tinkering but by codified "theoretical knowl-edge," or science. By this argument, Bell puts himself in line with the nineteenth-century positivism of Saint-Simon and Comte, for whom science was the *pouvoir spirituel* of modern society. Implicitly, though, Bell finds a more proximate influence in John Dewey's notion of a so-ciety rendered "scientific" insofar as it is constituted as a free commu-nity of discourse. Bell cites the communal ethic of science, based on free exchange of information and respect for the noncoercive author-ity of knowledge, and suggests that "the scientific estate—its ethos and its organization—is the monad that contains within itself the im-ago of the future society."[21]

Still, Bell has always been more Weberian than Deweyan, and he indicates that in the confluence of the scientific community and the great society, science is societalized, i.e., bureaucratized and thus robbed of its unity and self-conscious purpose. In Bell's view, the inte-gration of science and society levies a new responsibility on the state for determining the goals of research—another impulse toward plan-ning—but it also denies the positivist dream of a scientific priesthood imparting direction to the society as a whole, and thus "makes prob-lematic the utopian component of the post-industrial society."[22]

As a Weberian, Bell must repudiate all technocratic utopias. The advance of rationality does not in itself establish the principles of guiding a collective society. In fact, he points out, the progress of knowledge follows the course of intensive specialization, rupturing the unity of knowledge and rendering the whole of reality more intrac-table to any single, common perspective. Such, Bell writes, is the "cur-vilinear paradox," which denies rational order as rationality extends its sway. In this characteristic emphasis on paradox and circularity— "in the end is the beginning," Bell quotes—he posits and withdraws the promise of progress.[23]

After all, for Bell, rationality exists apart from value and hence cannot in itself posit ends. Technocracy, Bell suggests, inherits the utilitarian definition of rationality as efficiency, which never interrogates ends (assumed to be multifarious, given by private action in the marketplace) but only contemplates the efficacy of means towards those ends that are given. This "conception of rationality as functional, as rationalization rather than 'reason,'" as Bell puts it, obviously cannot suffice for social guidance.[24] For Bell, the impossibility theorem of Kenneth Arrow—which says that no optimizing formula can satisfy all private utilities and combine them in a common welfare at the same time—"undermines the application of rationality to public decisions."[25] Without a definition of ends justified in themselves—a kind of social "reason" distinct from technocratic rationality—no choices can be made to guide the conduct of society as a whole.

> In the end, the problems of the communal and post-industrial society are not technical, but political, for even though in the nature of the new complexities a large kind of new social engineering is involved, the essential questions are those of values.[26]

Thus Bell confronts again the old paradox of his thought, the steady emergence of collectivization and rationality—the infrastructure and apparatus of the planned society—and the absence of the spirit needed to bring it to fruition. "We now move to a communal ethic," Bell writes, "without that community being, as yet, wholly defined."[27] The problems of the communal society, which culminate his discourse on postindustrial society, are remarkably like those problems Bell posed in the 1940s, as he first tried to grasp the nature of the social transformation at work in modern capitalism. "If the major historical turn in the last quarter-century has been the subordination of the economic function to societal goals," Bell asks, "the political order necessarily becomes the control system of the society. But who runs it, and for whose (or what) ends?"[28] The language echoes that 1944 *New Leader* essay in which Bell outlined his "Monopoly State" thesis: "Planning by Whom—for What?" Later, in 1949, when describing the "politically managed economy" and problems it posed, Bell suggested, as he sought that secular ethic which could stand in for the bygone morality of the small community, "We are floundering, both in practice and in analysis because we no longer know what holds a society together."[29] A quarter century after he first posed it, this same question—as he put it once again, "What can hold a society together?"—is the motivation for Bell's inquiry into the "cultural contradictions" of modern society.[30]

The contradictions come to play in Bell's theory of the "disjunction of realms," the separate dynamics of social structure, culture, and politics, each moving according to a principle of its own, often antagonistic to the motivating principles of the other two. For all intents and purposes, however, the essential categories in Bell's theory come down to two: society and culture. In Bell's work, the polity appears integrally bound up with the other two spheres: the tendencies toward collectivization in postindustrialism increasingly vest the polity with the responsibilities of planning, and the tendencies toward hedonism in modern culture deprive the polity of the common philosophy needed to fulfill those responsibilities. In some sense the polity is Bell's repository of hope and frustration, but it has not received the sustained attention devoted to the other two "realms," a book of its own to complete Bell's triad of categories. Essentially, for Bell, the crisis he perceives—the troubling "contradiction"—stems from the blunt confrontation of two forces, society and culture.

It is, furthermore, the Weberian distinction between reason and meaning that draws the line between society and culture in Bell's thought. This basic dualism establishes the relation between *The Coming of Post-Industrial Society* (1973) and *The Cultural Contradictions of Capitalism* (1976). The latter book "stands in a dialectical relation" to the former, Bell wrote.[31] It is counterpart and companion, and the thrust of Bell's thinking cannot be understood apart from the way these two components relate to and interact with each other.

"The modern mind and modern sensibility unfold . . . in contradiction to each other," Bell wrote in his 1966 book, *The Reforming of General Education*.[32] The conflict, here framed in terms of the intellectual and affective faculties, connoted for Bell the strain between rationality and the impulse to escape the bounds of reason. In counterposing his two major books, Bell fixes on the conflict between a postindustrial society founded on science and a modern culture fleeing rationality in search of self-aggrandizing experience. If the two terms correspond to the dualism of reason and meaning, fact and value, each sphere external to the other though inevitably wedded together, then the strain between them, cited in Weber's theory, becomes the focus of Bell's work. Just as Weber's problem was the infinite regress of meaning and value in the face of accelerating rationality, so Bell's problem—the subject of *The Cultural Contradictions of Capitalism*—is modern culture's self-destructive dismantling of definite values as society rides the tide toward the "rule" of science.

And yet, Bell's book title immediately introduces some confusion. Rather than the contradiction between postindustrial society and modern culture, we have the "contradictions of capitalism." One wonders why "capitalism" has returned to Bell's analysis as a salient category of analysis, or—if as he suggests "capitalism" has lost meaning as a definition of modern society—why its contradictions are relevant to contemporary social problems. And it is unclear whether the "contradictions" Bell cites refer to tensions *within* capitalism or to some contrary force outside it.

At first Bell seems to intend the latter, an external contradiction. In this second book, his theme of the "disjunction of realms" cites the strain between a social structure identified with capitalist production, dominated by the economizing mode, and the "anti-bourgeois" animus of culture. Bell points to the rupture of the traditional identity of culture and social structure, whereby a character structure suited to the capitalist norms of productive activity is built upon a Protestant ethic of work motivations, frugality, impulse renunciation, and delayed gratification. Now, as culture in the wake of modernism repudiates impulse renunciation and seeks "immediacy, impact, sensation, simultaneity" in the boundless cultivation of the self, capitalism has proven "ideologically impotent," has lost the "transcendent ethic" that gave it legitimacy.[33]

Bell necessarily surrenders the argument for disjunction almost immediately, however. It would be better to read "contradiction" in the immanent sense. Seeing the "asceticism" of the Protestant ethic yield to the "hedonism" of modern culture, Bell concedes that the latter was generated by capitalism itself, first by the bourgeois impulse to liberate the individual and his private wants from social regulation, and second by the establishment of a mass-consumption economy in the twentieth century, which required the hedonist ethic to maintain a market flow of goods.

Bell concedes, too, that the classic era of the bourgeoisie was marked by its own contradiction—the emphasis on the autonomy of the self and the need to constrain it for fear of its excesses. In his own fear of the "demonic" thrust of the unbridled self, Bell seems to evoke that classic bourgeois personality as a model of social order, even as he condemns it for its genetic antisocial animus, but it would be an unwary reader who takes Bell's denunciation of the "adversary culture" created by modernism for a defense of bourgeois virtue and capitalist order. In *The Cultural Contradictions of Capitalism*, Bell's rendering of twentieth-century American cultural history finds the locus of traditional bourgeois character structure in the small town mentality, and since the 1940s that mentality always figured in Bell's thought as a disreputable source of reaction against the rational dynamic of modernity.[34] Bell cannot reclaim bourgeois order in any case, because, in his analysis of social structure, capitalism is on the wane:

> A capitalist order had historical strength when it fused property with power . . . [now] property is not private (but corporate) . . . [and] the political order becomes the place where power is wielded in order to manage the *systematic* problems arising out of that interdependence.[35]

Nor is modernism, strictly speaking, his enemy, for as he points out, "we have reached the end of the creative impulse and ideological sway of modernism."[36] If, then, capitalism and modernism are only the apparent poles of Bell's argument, in what terms can we understand the conflict which agitates his thought?

The real problem of culture, as far as Bell is concerned, lies not in modernism per se but in "post-modernism," the extension of the antisocial self-aggrandizing impulses of classic modernism to a mass attitude, sustained by the regime of mass consumption. The problem lies precisely in the absorption of modernism to the mainstream, which denies the tension that generated art when the self seeking liberation had to contend with a custom-bound culture. In sanctioning an insatiable search for innovative experience, as Bell's argument goes, mass culture turns nihilistic and disintegrates the bonds that tie a community together.

Curiously, Bell's critique of postmodernism echoes the critique of mass culture he shared with other intellectuals of the 1940s who proudly bore the label modernist. Two of the key traits Bell ascribes to the modernist arts in *Cultural Contradictions*—the "eclipse of distance" and the "loss of temporality"—recall his rejection of the "chiliastic" moment in mass culture. The "eclipse of distance"—or the closure of the gap between the spectator and the art product, the urge to envelop the culture consumer, to deny the distinction between subject and object—evokes the older criticism that mass culture obliterates the reflective autonomy of the viewer. The ultimate effect of the "eclipse of distance," for Bell, is the tendency to identify art and life. Just as chiliasm sought a fusion of the spiritual and the mundane, an ecstatic surrender to an undifferentiated whole of experience, so the "post-modernist" culture results in the "denial of necessary distinctions."[37] In its emphasis on immediacy, and hence the obliteration of time, so Bell's construction of postmodernism follows the mold of chiliasm, which fashions an "eternal present" freeing the devotee from the judgment of consequences.

Insofar as Bell attributes these traits to modernism proper, his definitions are at least partly suspect. One can point to Brecht's estrangement effects as evidence of a modernism devoted precisely to keeping the spectator at a distance and preventing any fusion with the artwork. The linguistic difficulty of modern literature also served consciously to make the art object strange and distant rather than enveloping. The adversary role itself was a mark of distance, insisting on a life of perpetual tension, and in fact, in his 1944 essay, "A Parable of Alienation," Bell pronounced a ringing endorsement of that adversary stance of modernism as a way of being.

By translating Bell's terms, we can read his argument in another way. It seems that Bell has sighted some of the effects wrought by the mainstream absorption of modernism which mediated the political deradicalization of left-wing intellectuals like himself.[38] Modernism, I have argued, answered estrangement with reconciliation, providing a framework for the discontents of radical intellectuals while denying the possibility of resolving them, hence smoothing the way for their surrender of political projects and their concession to given social reality. Bell appears to be conscious of this depoliticizing effect. In *The End of Ideology*, he pointed out the fruitlessness of grounding political radicalism in the cultural stance of modernism. The problem, as he sees it in *Cultural Contradictions* is that, with all its play on abiding tensions, modernism "leave[s] us without a resolution." It offers "no positive viewpoint."[39] Bell writes: "Political radicalism . . . is not merely rebellious but revolutionary, and seeks to install a new social order in place of the previous one. Cultural radicalism, apart from the formal revolutions in style and syntax, is largely rebellious only."[40] Bell's point can be reformulated in the terms used throughout this study: the ideological crisis opened in the 1930s was never adequately resolved, except negatively—with modernism standing in as a substitute for a program of action aiming to overcome it.

The antinomian culture Bell stigmatizes in *The Cultural Contradictions of Capitalism* is the banality of modernity. Its chief liability, for Bell, is its incapacity for mounting a positive program for societal action. Since culture needs to establish the principles for guiding the rationalized order of postindustrial society, postmodernism frustrates the potential offered by the social structure. The tendencies bequeathed by postindustrial social structure demand construction of a "public household," Bell's term for "an effort, in the realm of the polity, to find a social cement for the society."[41] But culture stands in the way:

> The interplay of modernism as a mode developed by serious artists, the institutionalization of those played-out forms by the 'cultural mass,' and the hedonism as a way of life promoted by the marketing system of business, constitutes the cultural contradic-

tion of capitalism. The modernism is exhausted, and no longer threatening. The hedonism apes its sterile japes. But the social order lacks either a culture that is a symbolic expression of any vitality or a moral impulse that is a motivational or binding force. What, then, can hold a society together?[42]

Finally, having understood Bell's critique of the political drawbacks built into postmodernism as the ethic of mass consumption, we can read his "cultural contradictions of capitalism" in this fashion: the detritus of capitalism in its senescence becomes the chief obstacle to creating the postcapitalist social order implicit in the postindustrial dynamic. Again, his theory settles on the stymied transition beyond the bounds of capitalism, the apparent evanescence of capitalism and its stubborn survival at the same time. The theory gives voice to the unhappy consciousness of social democracy at an impasse, trapped by its commitment to seek reform under the umbrella of capitalism.

The two components of society and culture, the promise and frustration of the rational society, are not really separate pieces of Daniel Bell's thought, counterposing fond optimism and dark despair. They are actually but complementary moments of a whole. It cannot be said, as Jürgen Habermas suggested in a recent review of neoconservative thought, that Bell accepts the social principle of modernism (scientific rationality) while rejecting the cultural principle of modernism (secularization and the dilution of morals).[43] Properly speaking, Bell endorses neither antinomian modernism nor a technocratic model of rational efficiency: there is a missing third term, a rational collective, a reason of common ends. His is a theory of an unconquered contradiction, an unfinished dialectic.

Throughout the above narrative of Daniel Bell's early theoretical development we have pointed out the dichotomous elements in his thought. The distinction of society and culture in Bell's later works, *The Coming of Post-Industrial Society* and *The Cultural Contradictions of Capitalism*, obeys the same dualism that structures his thought at its deepest level, falling into line with the poles of skepticism and morality, interests and ideals, objective structures and subjective purpose. Essentially these are so many expressions of the subject-object dualism which structured the tradition of sociology, in its analytical distinction of politics and economics, and imposed the antinomies of voluntarism and fatalism, as Lukács put it, on the heritage of bourgeois thought as a whole.

Lukács defined the antinomies as the unmediated combination of outward structural determinism and inward moral freedom. Indeed the antinomies come to play in the dichotomy of natural evolution and moral purpose that marks Bell's frustrated response to the welfare state. Throughout his early career, in fact, we saw how Bell continually vacillated between the two poles, on the one hand condemning the "fatalism of the left" that failed to recognize the role of human subjectivity in determining social affairs and on the other hand arguing, against the utopians of *Politics*, that imperious structural constraints denied radical intentions. The gulf between objective constraints and subjective purpose left Bell unable to integrate his wishes with his knowledge of reality, his conceptions of "ought" and "is." Hence he saw an unconquerable gap between minimum and maximum programs, the "movement" and the "goal" of socialism, which rendered the ultimate end of socialism a purely moral venture apart from immediate urgent realities and imposed on the socialist the torment of "living in but not of the world." Bell thus acknowledged a gulf between subject and object, a division that Lukács saw as the source of utopianism—a subjective venture unable to recognize itself in its objective conditions.[44] Despite those critics of the "end of ideology" who charged Bell with suppressing the motivation to reform that resided in utopian thinking, Bell's mentality was clearly a utopian one.[45] In politics, he was left with nothing but the persistent call for a moral act of will, ungrounded in any existent social force, that would fulfill the promise of the politically managed economy—a will he knew to be absent. The problem with Bell is not, as many of his critics suggest, a failure to recognize the strains within capitalist social order, nor even any sort of moral obtuseness. It is instead a strategic impotence in attainment of the goals—still, social-democratic ones—that motivate his thought.

At the beginning of the 1960s, Daniel Bell correctly challenged the New Left on the possibility of constructing a new radicalism on the basis of the modernist culture of estrangement. His own experience had demonstrated how weak a support of radicalism the ethic of estrangement is, how intimately bound up it is with its dialectical opposite, reconciliation. But as Bell awaits the public philosophy which yet has no embodiment in the society around him, it seems that the New Left, however confusedly, posed the more significant challenge: the problem of social change still rests on discovering and activating an agent of change. In this arduous task rests the possibility of bringing together the prospects for a rational collective, which lie unfulfilled within capitalist society, with the purposes of those political movements that continually arise among dispossessed groups seeking democratic rights of self-determination. In forging that link practically, radicalism must be rooted in society as it is while nurturing the historical tendencies that can break the mold of that society to create something new. Thus contemporary radicalism could strive to avoid the dichotomy that figures so prominently in Daniel Bell's thought—the choice of being "inside" or "outside" society, the choice of estrangement or reconciliation, the tendency to view society either as a changeless whole of repressive order or as the given means and limit of conceivable reform.

Notes
Bibliographic Note
Index

Notes

Introduction

1. Contrary estimations of Bell's book, as obsolete and prescient, are found in Peter Steinfels, *The Neoconservatives: The Men Who are Changing America's Politics* (New York: Simon and Schuster, 1979), 162, and Ronald S. Berman, *America in the Sixties: An Intellectual History* (New York: The Free Press, 1968), 3–4, 134–36.

2. For contemporary criticism of the end-of-ideology doctrine, see Henry David Aiken, "The Revolt against Ideology"; Joseph LaPalombara, "Decline of Ideology: A Dissent and an Interpretation"; Robert A. Haber, "The End of Ideology as Ideology"; Stephen W. Rousseas and James Farganis, "American Politics and the End of Ideology"; Dennis Wrong, "Reflections on the End of Ideology"; all in *The End of Ideology Debate*, ed. Chaim I. Waxman (New York: Funk and Wagnalls, 1968). Also see Thomas Hayden, "A Letter to the New (Young) Left," in *The New Student Left: An Anthology*, ed. Mitchell Cohen and Dennis Hale (Boston: Beacon Press, 1969), 4. Mills's broadside was his "Letter to the New Left," 247–59, in *Power, Politics and People: The Collected Essays of C. Wright Mills*, ed. Irving Louis Horowitz (New York: Ballantine Books, 1963). The intellectuals' flight from vocation, which critics associated with the end-of-ideology doctrine, was a dominant theme in Mills's later work, as he wrote in *The Causes of World War III*:

> Intellectuals accept without scrutiny official definitions of world reality. Some of the best of them allow themselves to be trapped by the politics of anti-Stalinism, which has been a main passageway from the political thirties to the intellectual default of our apolitical time. They live and work in a benumbing society without living and working in protest and in tension with its moral and cultural insensibilities. They use the liberal rhetoric to cover the conservative default.

C. Wright Mills, *The Causes of World War Three* (New York: Simon and Schuster, 1958), 143–45.

3. Seymour Martin Lipset, "Ideology and No End: The Controversy Till Now," *Encounter* 39 (December 1972): 17–22; also Lipset, "The End of Ideology and the Ideology of the Intellectuals," in *Culture and its Creators: Essays in Honor of Edward Shils*, ed. Joseph Ben-David and Terry Nichols Clark, (Chicago: University of Chicago Press, 1977), 15–42.

4. Edward Shils, "The End of Ideology?" *Encounter* 5 (November 1955): 52–58; Seymour Martin Lipset, "The State of Democratic Politics," *Canadian Forum* 35 (November 1955): 170–71; and Lipset, "The End of Ideology?" in *Political Man: The Social Bases of Politics* (New York: Doubleday, 1960).

5. Shils, "The End of Ideology?" See also Raymond Aron, "The End of the Ideological Age?", in *The Opium of the Intellectuals*, trans. Terence Kilmartin (New York: W. W. Norton and Company, 1955, 1962), 305–24.

6. See Lipset, "The End of Ideology?" in *Political Man*, 442–43, 452–53; Lipset, "Europe: The Politics of Collective Bargaining," in *Decline of Ideology?*, ed. Mostafa Rejai (New York: Aldine-Atherton, 1971), 85–86, 104–105; Lipset, "My View from Our Left," *Columbia University Forum* 5 (Fall 1962): 31–37; and the criticism of Lipset as Pangloss, in Irving Louis Horowitz, "Another View from Our Left," in *The End of Ideology Debate*, 167.

7. Bell, *The End of Ideology: On the Exhaustion of Political Ideas in the Fifties*, revised ed. (New York: The Free Press, 1962), 120.

8. Ibid., 103.

9. Bell, "America as a Mass Society," in *The End of Ideology*, 21–45; Shils, "The End of Ideology?" 56; Bell, *The End of Ideology*, 251, 259, 109–23.

10. Bell, *The End of Ideology*, 260–61.

11. Ibid., 300.

12. Ibid., 44, 94.

13. Elsewhere, in 1962, Bell again voiced his view that American political discourse was impoverished. He paid particular attention to the regrettable absence of a left wing political pole:

> There is no coherent conservative force—and someone like Walter Lippmann, whose *The Public Philosophy* represents a genuine conservative voice, rejects the right, as it rejects him—and the radical right is outside the political pale, insofar as it refuses to accept the American consensus. Nor does a viable left exist in the United States today. The pacifist and Socialist elements have been unable to make the peace issue salient. The radicals have been unable to develop a comprehensive critique of the social disparities in American life—the urban mess, the patchwork educational system, the lack of amenities in our culture. Among the liberals, only the exhaustion of the "received ideas," such as they were, of the New Deal remains. It is a token of the emptiness of contemporary intellectual debate that from the viewpoint of the radical right, the Americans for Democratic Action constitutes the "extreme left" of the American political spectrum.

Daniel Bell, "The Dispossessed—1962," in *The Radical Right: The New American Right Expanded and Updated* (Garden City, N.Y.: Doubleday Anchor, 1963), 30–31.

14. Bell, *The End of Ideology*, 404; Lewis Coser, "What Shall We Do?" *Dissent* 3 (Spring 1956): 156–65.

15. Bell, *The End of Ideology*, 308–14.

16. Ibid., 391, 386–87, 249, 237.

17. Julien Benda, *The Treason of the Intellectuals*, trans. Richard Aldington (New York: William Morrow and Company, 1928); Christopher Lasch, *The New Radicalism in America, 1889–1963: The Intellectual as a Social Type* (New York: Vintage Books, 1965), 289, 299–310; Lasch, "The Cultural Cold War," in *Towards a New Past: Dissenting Essays in American History*, ed. Barton Bernstein (New York: Pantheon, 1968), 323, 330, 339, 344–48, 354.

18. Richard Pells, *Radical Visions and American Dreams* (New York: Harper and Row, 1973), 367; Robert Allen Skotheim, *Totalitarianism and American Social Thought* (New York: Holt, Rinehart, and Winston, 1971), 7–9, 94–96, 124.

19. Penina Migdal Glazer, "A Decade of Transition: A Study of Radical Journals of the 1940s" (Ph.D. diss., Rutgers University, 1970), 1, 302.

20. James Gilbert, *Writers and Partisans: A History of Literary Radicalism* (New York: John Wiley and Sons, 1968), 253–82, 188–220, 234–52.

21. Lionel Trilling, *Freud and the Crisis of Our Culture* (Boston: Beacon Press, 1955). See Richard King's discussion of "The Uses of Freud," in *The Party of Eros: Radical Social Theory and the Realm of Freedom* (Chapel Hill: University of North Carolina Press, 1972), 43–50.

22. Reinhold Niebuhr, *The Nature and Destiny of Man* (New York: Charles Scribner's Sons, 1941, 1943).

23. On Mills in the 1940s and his personal relations with Bell, see Richard Gillam, "C. Wright Mills 1916–1948: An Intellectual Biography" (Ph.D. diss., Stanford University, 1972).

24. Daniel Bell, "Adjusting Men to Machines: Social Scientists Explore the World of the Factory." *Commentary*, May 1947, 79–88; "'Screening' Leaders in a Democracy: How Scientific is Personnel Testing?" *Commentary*, October 1968, 29–51.

25. Richard Gillam, "Richard Hofstadter, C. Wright Mills and 'The Critical Ideal,'" *American Scholar* 47 (Winter 1977–78): 69–85. See also, Gillam, "C. Wright Mills and the Politics of Truth: *The Power Elite* Revisited," *American Quarterly* 27 (October 1975): 461–79.

26. Richard H. Pells, *The Liberal Mind in a Conservative Age: American Intellectuals in the 1940s and 1950s* (New York: Harper and Row, 1985), vii, x, 185–88.

27. Edward Shils recognizes a dynamic of this sort in his essay, "The Intellectuals and the Powers." He writes:

> The rejection by intellectuals of the inherited and prevailing values of those intellectuals who are already incorporated in ongoing social institutions . . . supplies the important function of moulding and guiding the alienative tendencies which exist in any society. It provides an alternative pattern of integration for their own society . . .

Shils, "The Intellectuals and the Powers," in *On Intellectuals: Theoretical Studies, Case Studies*, ed. Philip Rieff (Garden City, N.Y.: Doubleday, 1969), 32–33.

28. Exponents of the new intellectual history are well-represented in John Higham and Paul K. Conkin, eds. *New Directions in American Intellectual History* (Baltimore: The Johns Hopkins University Press, 1979).

29. As Lukács summed up the lesson Marx learned from Hegel: Lukács, *History and Class Consciousness: Studies in Marxist Dialectics*, trans. Rodney Livingstone (Cambridge: The MIT Press, 1971), 16.

30. I draw my emphasis on totalizing and historicizing as the necessary ultimate aim of criticism from Fredric Jameson, *The Political Unconscious: Narrative as a Socially Symbolic Act* (Ithaca: Cornell University Press, 1981), 9–102.

31. Pascal, quoted in Lucien Goldmann, *The Hidden God: A Study of Tragic Vision in the Pensées of Pascal and the Tragédies of Racine*, trans. Philip Thody (New York: The Humanities Press, 1976), 13.

32. Jameson, *The Political Unconscious*, 47.

33. Charles Kindleberger explains the economic crisis by the lack of an international balance wheel in *The World in Depression 1929–1939* (Berkeley: University of California Press, 1973). See also Charles Maier's argument that the Second World War culminated a thirty-year effort to integrate the world economy and subordinate rival capitalist powers to U.S. leadership of it. Charles S. Maier, "The Two Postwar Eras and the Conditions for Stability in Twentieth-Century Western Europe," *American Historical Review* 86 (April 1981): 327–52.

34. See Michel Aglietta, *A Theory of Capitalist Regulation: The US Experience*, trans. David Fernbach (London: NLB, 1979).

35. The ideology of the Welfare State attributes economic recovery primarily to state control of market instability, rather than to the extension of U.S. imperial power and the consolidation of a class compromise based on new norms of mass consumption. Welfare State ideology, furthermore, portrays the regime as a generic stage of evolutionary development, an achievement of ascendant social rationality. It is, in other words, an ideology of progress. I treat the "welfare state," however, as a historically specific order of social relations and political organization stemming from the war and the class struggles in its wake. In fact, the historically transient character of the "welfare state" has been highlighted by the propagandistic attack on it by ruling administrations in the advanced industrial countries since the late 1970s. Certainly, no pure-market atavism will succeed in eliminating the economic role of the state, but the specific contours of the regime—the kinds of state intervention, the nature of labor relations, and the norms of social provision (relief and social security measures)—may change enough to yield an order significantly unlike the "welfare state" of 1945–75.

36. Maier, "The Two Postwar Eras and the Conditions for Stability in Twentieth-Century Western Europe," 345–47.

37. Charles S. Maier, "The Politics of Productivity: Foundations of American International Economic Policy after World War II," in *Between Power and Plenty: The Foreign Economic Policies of Advanced Industrial States*, ed. Peter Katzenstein (Madison: University of Wisconsin Press, 1978), 23–49.

38. Perry Anderson, "Modernity and Revolution," *New Left Review*, no. 144 (March-April 1984), 103–6.

39. Paul Fussell, *The Great War and Modern Memory* (New York: Oxford University Press, 1975).

40. Daniel Bell, "Word Surrealism," *Partisan Review* 11 (Fall 1944): 486–88.

41. Pells, *Radical Visions*, 326, 367.

42. See James Gilbert, *Writers and Partisans*, 221–23; Alan Wald, "Revolutionary Intellectuals: *Partisan Review* in the 1930s," in *Literature at the Barricades: The American Writer in the 1930s*, ed. Ralph F. Bogardus and Fred Hobson (University, Alabama: University of Alabama Press, 1982), 187–203; Linda Kaye Kirby, "Communism, the Discovery of Totalitarianism, and the Cold War: *Partisan Review*, 1932 to 1948" (Ph.D. diss., University of Colorado, 1974).

43. Gerald Graff, "Radicalizing English," *Salmagundi*, no. 36 (Winter 1977), 114–15.

44. See Lewis Coser, *Men of Ideas: A Sociologist's View* (New York: The Free Press, 1970), 263, 266–67.

45. See Perry Anderson's argument that modernism is no longer viable once the historical conditions that spawned it are surpassed, given the displacement of traditional aristocratic elites in postwar bourgeois regimes and the effective suppression of proletarian insurgency. Anderson, "Modernity and Revolution," *New Left Review*, no. 144 (March-April 1984), 106–8.

46. There have been several studies of Daniel Bell and "the end of ideology," among them Job Leonard Dittberner, *The End of Ideology and American Social Thought: 1930–1960* (Ann Arbor: UMI Research Press, 1979), Allen Paul Fisher, "Ideological Continuities in 'The End of Ideology': An Analysis of the Thought of Arthur Schlesinger, Jr., and Daniel Bell, 1940–1976" (Ph.D. diss., Purdue University, 1977), and Nathan Liebowitz, *Daniel Bell and the Agony of Modern Liberalism* (Westport, Conn.: Greenwood Press, 1985). Basing a chronicle of Bell's career almost entirely on his published writings, these works do not provide a sufficiently supple account of the *process of thinking* that led Bell to his mature perspective. Dittberner, however, provided an invaluable service by publishing the transcript of an extended interview with Bell, perhaps the most thorough commentary available from Bell on the course of his career through the 1960s. Fisher's study seeks to show that Bell and Schlesinger both maintain a set of evaluative presuppositions that guide their interpretation of events—and thus each has an "ideology," despite the doctrine that ideology had ended. It is hardly surprising that the work of these writers is not without presuppositions; furthermore, Fisher's suggestion that his demonstration disproves the "end of ideology" thesis unjustifiably identifies that thesis with the most vulgar positivism. Liebowitz's study is the best of these, for its attempt to locate a definitive tension within Bell's thought: in his terms, the contradiction between Bell's "Deweyan optimism" and "Niebuhrian pessimism." I think, however, that these poles are misconstrued: my own examination finds the two elements of social-democratic evolutionary theory and Weberian critique much more significant in Bell's theory. Furthermore, the contradiction Liebowitz cites remains, in his portrait, both unrelated to a constitutive historical contradiction and unresolved in a more inclusive meaning that gives Bell's work unity.

Chapter 1

1. Leon Trotsky, *The Transitional Program for Socialist Revolution* (New York: Pathfinder, 1977).

2. Theodor Adorno, in Ernst Bloch et al., *Aesthetics and Politics* (London: NLB, 1977), 194.

3. Talcott Parsons, *The Structure of Social Action: A Study in Social Theory with Special Reference to a Group of Recent European Writers* (New York: McGraw-Hill, 1937; reprint, New York: The Free Press, 1968), 3.

4. Milan Kundera, "The Novel and Europe," *The New York Review of Books*, 19 July 1984, 15–19.

5. Edmund Wilson, *To the Finland Station: A Study in the Writing and Acting of History* (Garden City, N.Y.: Doubleday, 1940), 431–32; James Burnham, *The Managerial Revolution: What is Happening in the World* (New York: John Day, 1941), 36; Reinhold Niebuhr, *The Children of Light and the Children of Darkness: A Vindication of Democracy and a Critique of its Traditional Defense* (New York: Charles Scribner's Sons, 1944), 5.

6. See Göran Therborn, *Science, Class and Society: On the Formation of Sociology and Historical Materialism* (London: Verso, 1980), 156–63.

7. Karl Marx, "On the Jewish Question," in Karl Marx and Frederick Engels, *Collected Works*, vol. 3 (New York: International Publishers, 1975), 146–74. Indeed, Hegel's term "bürgerliche Gesellschaft" translates into English as both "civil society" and "bourgeois society." For Marx's critique of Hegel's abstract separation of civil society and the state, see also "Contribution to the Critique of Hegel's Philosophy of Law," in *Collected Works*, vol. 3, 5–129.

8. Tönnies, quoted in Salvador Giner, *Mass Society* (New York: Academic Press, 1976), 94.

9. Georg Simmel, "How is Society Possible?" trans. Albion Small, *American Journal of Sociology* 16 (1910–11): 372–91.

10. Spencer, "The Social Organism" (1860), in *On Social Evolution*, ed. J. D. Y. Peel (Chicago: University of Chicago Press, 1972), 53–55.

11. Spencer, *On Social Evolution*, 149–61.

12. Ibid., 26.

13. Herbert Spencer, "Re-barbarization," 172–88, *Facts and Comments* (London: D. Appleton and Co., 1902), reprinted in Spencer, *Structure, Function and Evolution*, ed. Stanislav Andreski (New York: Charles Scribner's Sons, 207–13; Spencer, quoted in J. D. Y. Peel, "Introduction," *On Social Evolution*, xxxvii.

14. Emile Durkheim, *The Division of Labor in Society*, trans. George Simpson (1933; reprint, New York: The Free Press, 1964), 250, 353–409.

15. On the significance of evolutionary lag in the French sociological tradition, see Therborn, *Science, Class and Society*, 115–44, 163–86.

16. L. T. Hobhouse, *Development and Purpose: An Essay Towards a Philosophy of Evolution*, 2nd ed. (London: Macmillan and Co., 1927; reprint, Grosse Pointe, Michigan: Scholarly Press, 1969). On the functionalist basis of socialist evolution in Fabianism, see Willard Wolfe, *From Radicalism to Socialism: Men*

and Ideas in the Formation of Fabian Socialist Doctrine, 1881–1889 (New Haven: Yale University Press, 1975), esp. 262–66.

17. See Eduard Bernstein, *Evolutionary Socialism: A Criticism and an Affirmation,* trans. Edith C. Harvey, with an introduction by Sidney Hook (New York: Schocken Books, 1961), and Peter Gay, *The Dilemma of Democratic Socialism: Eduard Bernstein's Challenge to Marx* (New York: Columbia University Press, 1952).

18. S. K. Padover, "Kautsky and the Materialist Interpretation of History," in *Medieval and Historiographical Essays in Honor of James Westfall Thompson,* ed. James L. Cate and Eugene N. Anderson (Chicago: University of Chicago Press, 1938), 439–64; Massimo Salvadori, *Karl Kautsky and the Socialist Revolution 1880–1938,* trans. Jon Rothschild (London: NLB, 1979); Kautsky, *Social Democracy versus Communism,* ed. David Shub and Joseph Shaplen (New York: Rand School Press, 1946), 93.

19. Karl Kautsky, *The Dictatorship of the Proletariat,* with an introduction by John H. Kautsky (Ann Arbor: University of Michigan Press, 1964), 35–36, 24–26; Karl Kautsky, *Terrorism and Communism: A Contribution to the Natural History of Revolution,* trans. W. H. Kerridge (1920; reprint, Westport, Conn: Hyperion Press Inc., 1973), 146–47.

20. Cynthia Eagle Russett, *The Concept of Equilibrium in American Social Thought* (New Haven: Yale University Press, 1966), 169.

21. Spencer looked at social development "as upon other natural phenomena, which work themselves out in a certain inevitable, unalterable way. . . . These changes are brought about by a power far above individual wills. Men who seem the prime movers, are merely the tools with which it works, and were they absent, it would quickly find others." Spencer, *On Social Evolution,* 23–24. The Russian social democrat, George V. Plekhanov, argued similarly in "The Role of the Individual in History," appendix in *Fundamental Problems of Marxism* (New York: International Publishers, 1969), 139–77. It was a common theme in classical sociology. Auguste Comte wrote, "The progress of the race must be considered susceptible of modification only with regard to its speed. . . . It is absolutely necessary to understand the natural laws of harmony and succession which determine, in every period, . . . what the human evolution is prepared to produce, pointing out, at the same time, the chief obstacles which may be got rid of." Comte, quoted in Russett, 36. For Kautsky on necessary stages, see Kautsky, *Terrorism and Communism,* 198, 204, 217, and *Dictatorship,* 136. For a secondary review of Kautsky's debate with the Bolsheviks, see Fernando Claudin, "Democracy and Dictatorship in Lenin and Kautsky," *New Left Review* no. 106 (November-December 1977), 59–78.

22. A statement by the Right Mensheviks, quoted in *The Mensheviks: From the Revolution of 1917 to the Second World War,* ed. Leopold H. Haimson (Chicago: University of Chicago Press, 1974), 275–76.

23. The analytical distinctions between the economic and the political, the private and the public, were embedded not only in the theory of Kautskyan social democracy but in its practice as well, particularly in the orthodox conception of the "two arms" of the workers movement—the trade union and the

party. These were presumably "fraternal" and cooperative but ideally obedient to the principle of mutual noninterference. In Kautsky's terms, they reflected, respectively, the private and the public dimensions of the workers movement: the economic organization of the workers furthered special, sectoral interests, while the party inculcated the "grasp of large social relations and ends . . . the habit of regarding things as a whole." [Kautsky, *Dictatorship*, 29–30.] In fact, Kautsky commonly charged his opponents—anarchists, syndicalists, Bolsheviks, and Spartacists—with *economism*, the immature preoccupation with private ends; they all, he claimed, appealed to the unskilled elements (or "mob proletariat") that were given to spontaneous and unsustained protests on behalf of immediate, local, sectoral interests and were unable to generate the *political* formulation of demands corresponding to broad social needs.

In *What is to be Done?*, Lenin borrowed from Kautsky the orthodox division of the movement's "two arms" in order to defend the special role of the party as agent of revolutionary consciousness against the "Economists" who relied solely on the elemental force of "trade-union consciousness." In later work, however, particularly *State and Revolution* and *Left-Wing Communism*, Lenin overcame this orthodox dichotomy and stressed the interpenetration (not the amalgamation) of political and economic agencies in the struggle for socialism.

24. Kautsky, *Dictatorship*, 23; see also, for instance, Algernon Lee, "Social Democracy Points Way to Modern Freedom," *New Leader*, 10 December 1938, 2.

25. Bernstein, quoted in Gay, *The Dilemma of Democratic Socialism*, 210–11.

26. Henry James, quoted in Paul Fussell, *The Great War and Modern Memory* (New York: Oxford University Press, 1975), 8.

27. On the postwar restabilization of European capitalism, see Charles S. Maier, *Recasting Bourgeois Europe: Stabilization in France, Germany, and Italy in the Decade after World War I* (Princeton: Princeton University Press, 1975).

28. Karl Mannheim, *Ideology and Utopia: An Introduction to the Sociology of Knowledge*, trans. Louis Wirth and Edward Shils (New York: Harcourt Brace, 1936), 149, 29.

29. Hilferding, quoted in Franz Neumann, *Behemoth: The Structure and Practice of National Socialism* (New York: Oxford University Press, 1942), 15–16. See discussion of Hilferding's *Das Finanzkapital* in Paul Sweezy, *The Theory of Capitalist Development* (New York: Monthly Review Press, 1942, 1979), 258–69; see also discussion of Hilferding in Tom Bottomore's introduction to *Austro-Marxism*, trans. and ed., Tom Bottomore and Patrick Goode (Oxford: Oxford University Press, 1978), 22ff.

30. On the "Great Coalition" of 1928–1930, see Richard N. Hunt, *German Social Democracy 1918–1933* (New Haven: Yale University Press, 1964), and Richard Breitman, *German Socialism and Weimar Democracy* (Chapel Hill: University of North Carolina Press, 1981). On Mannheim's Weimar optimism, his view of Weimar as a "Periclean age" of ascendant prosperity and reason, belied by the rise of Nazism, see Gunter W. Remmling, *The Sociology of Karl Mannheim* (London: Routledge and Kegan Paul), 64–65.

31. Salvadori, *Karl Kautsky and the Socialist Revolution*, 364; Kautsky, *Social Democracy versus Communism*, 121. See Salvadori, 343: "For Kautsky, fascism and Bolshevism alike remained exceptional governments incapable of developing into organic systems of political-social management."

32. Kautsky, in Salvadori, 354–55.

33. James Oneal, "Social Democrats Now Have Greatest Chance," *The New Leader*, 18 February 1939, 10.

34. James Oneal, "To the Secretariat of the LSI," Socialist Party Correspondence, Tamiment Library, New York.

35. James Oneal, *Some Pages of Party History* (New York, 1935), 23–24.

36. On the development of the totalitarianism thesis among American intellectuals, see Robert Allen Skotheim, *Totalitarianism and American Social Thought* (New York: Holt, Rinehart, and Winston, 1971); Thomas R. Maddux, "Red Fascism, Brown Bolshevism: The American Image of Totalitarianism in the 1930s," *Historian* 40 (November 1977): 85–103; Les K. Adler and Thomas G. Paterson, "Red Fascism: The Merger of Nazi Germany and Soviet Russia in the American Image of Totalitarianism, 1930s–1950s," *American Historical Review* 75 (April 1970): 1046–64; Stephen J. Whitfield, "Imagination of Disaster: The Response of American Jewish Intellectuals to Totalitarianism," *Jewish Social Studies* 42 (Winter 1980): 1–20; Stephen J. Whitfield, *Into the Dark: Hannah Arendt and Totalitarianism* (Philadelphia: Temple University Press, 1980); Pierre Ayçoberry, *The Nazi Question: An Essay on the Interpretations of National Socialism 1922–1975* (New York: Pantheon, 1981). The significance of the shift implied in the Nazis' 1936 Four-Year Plan was emphasized in two analyses of statism, Dwight Macdonald, "The End of Capitalism in Germany," *Partisan Review* 8 (May-June 1941): 198–217, and Guenter Reimann, *The Myth of the Total State: Europe's Last Bid for World Rule* (New York: William Morrow, 1941). The first two works to identify Nazi Germany and Soviet Russia as totalitarian were Alex Emmerich's *Der Mythus Hitler* and Hermann Rauschning's *Die Revolution des Nihilismus*, cited in Ayçoberry, 35–40. The "novelty of totalitarianism" was the topic of a 1939 symposium sponsored by the American Philosophical Society, cited in Whitfield, *Into the Dark*, 17; Rauschning quoted in Ayçoberry, *The Nazi Question*, 40–41. On the expansionist nature of totalitarianism, see, for instance, Hans Kohn, "Two Revolutions," in *Whose Revolution? A Study of the Future Course of Liberalism in the United States*, ed. Irving DeWitt Talmadge (New York: Howell, Soskin, 1941), 3–41.

37. Rudolf Hilferding, "State Capitalism or Totalitarian State Economy," and "The Modern Totalitarian States," reprinted in *Modern Review* 1 (1947): 267–69, 597–605.

38. See Paul Mattick, Jr.'s discussion of Hilferding's "general cartel," in his review of *Finance Capital*, by Rudolf Hilferding, *Telos* no. 54 (Winter 1982–83), 199–212.

39. Hilferding, "State Capitalism or Totalitarian State Economy," *Modern Review* 1 (1947): 266–67, 269.

40. Friedrich Pollock, "State Capitalism: Its Possibilities and Limitations," *Studies in Philosophy and Social Science* 9 (1941): 217.

41. Hannah Arendt, *The Origins of Totalitarianism* (New York: Harcourt Brace, 1973), 357.

42. On political conventions inapplicable in the totalitarian world, William Ebenstein, *The Nazi State* (1943), quoted in Arendt, 347. The critique of the historiographical inadequacy of "totalitarianism" theory, as in Ayçoberry, *The Nazi Question*, 41, sometimes forgets that the theory by its nature posits the inadequacy of historical studies.

43. Leon Trotsky, *Terrorism and Communism: A Reply to Karl Kautsky* [1920] (Ann Arbor: University of Michigan Press, 1972), 16–18.

44. V. I. Lenin, *Imperialism: The Highest Stage of Capitalism: A Popular Outline* [1916] (New York: International Publishers, 1939).

45. Georg Lukács, *History and Class Consciousness: Studies in Marxist Dialectics*, trans. Rodney Livingstone (Cambridge, The MIT Press, 1971), 110–149.

46. See, for instance, V. I. Lenin, *The Proletarian Revolution and the Renegade Kautsky* (Peking: Foreign Languages Press, 1975), 136.

47. Eugene Lyons, *Assignment in Utopia*, quoted in Les K. Adler and Thomas G. Paterson, "Red Fascism: The Merger of Nazi Germany and Soviet Russia in the American Image of Totalitarianism, 1930s–1950s," *American Historical Review* 75 (April 1970): 1048. Eugene Lyons in *Whose Revolution?*, 130. Edmund Wilson, *To the Finland Station: A Study in the Writing and Acting of History* (Garden City: Doubleday, 1940). Hook, "Reason and Revolution," *New Republic*, 21 July 1941, 90–91.

48. Sidney Hook, *Towards the Understanding of Karl Marx: A Revolutionary Interpretation* (New York: John Day, 1933), xii. Hook states his indebtedness to Lukács's *Geschichte und Klassenbewusstsein* for stressing the dialectical element in Marx. Hook remarked later that the phrase, "dialectical materialism" was "incurably ruined" by Soviet abuse of it, in "Experimental Naturalism," in *American Philosophy Today and Tomorrow*, ed. Sidney Hook and Horace Kallen (New York: L. Furman, 1935), 205. See also "Dialectic and Nature" and "Dialectic in Society and History," in Hook, *Reason, Social Myths and Democracy* (New York: The Humanities Press, 1940), 183–226, 250–66.

49. Hook, "Reason and Revolution," *New Republic*, 21 July 1941, 90–91.

50. Hook, *Reason, Social Myths and Democracy*, 192–93; James Burnham, "Science and Style: A Reply to Comrade Trotsky," in Trotsky, *In Defense of Marxism*, 196–97. See Lewis Corey, "Marxism Reconsidered," *Nation*, 17 February 1940, 245–48; 24 February 1940, 272–75; 2 March 1940, 305–307.

51. The influence of Trotsky in American intellectual life, and the contours of the Trotskyist intellectual circle, are treated most thoroughly in the work of Alan Wald. See *James T. Farrell: The Revolutionary Socialist Years* (New York: New York University Press, 1978); *The Revolutionary Imagination: The Poetry and Politics of John Wheelwright and Sherry Mangan* (Chapel Hill, N.C.: University of North Carolina Press, 1983); "The Menorah Group Moves Left," *Jewish Social Studies* 38 (Summer-Fall 1976): 289–320; "Herbert Solow: Portrait of a New York Intellectual," in *Prospects: An Annual of American Cultural Studies*, ed. Jack Salzman (New York: Burt Franklin, 1977), 419–60; "Revolutionary Intellec-

tuals: *Partisan Review* in the 1930s," in *Literature at the Barricades: The American Writer in the 1930s*, ed. Ralph F. Bogardus and Fred Hobson (University, Alabama: University of Alabama Press, 1982), 187–203.

52. Philip Rahv, "Trials of the Mind," *Partisan Review* 4 (April 1938), 3, reprinted in Philip Rahv, *Essays on Literature and Politics 1932–1972*, ed. Arabel J. Porter and Andrew J. Dvosin (Boston: Houghton Mifflin, 1978), 284.

53. James Burnham and Max Shachtman, "Intellectuals in Retreat," *New International*, January 1939, 13, 16. Chamberlain's study of the obsolescence of liberalism was *Farewell to Reform* (New York, 1932).

54. Leon Trotsky, *The Revolution Betrayed: What is the Soviet Union and Where is it Going?* trans. Max Eastman (Garden City, N.Y.: Doubleday, Doran, and Co., 1937; reprint, New York: Pathfinder Press, 1972).

55. James Burnham, *The Managerial Revolution: What is Happening in the World* (New York: John Day, 1941); Max Shachtman, *The Bureaucratic Revolution: The Rise of the Stalinist State* (New York: The Donald Press, 1962).

56. See Alan Wald, "Memories of the John Dewey Commission: Forty Years Later," *Antioch Review* 35 (Fall 1977): 438–451. Key documents in the Kronstadt dispute are collected in V. I. Lenin and Leon Trotsky, *Kronstadt* (New York: Monad Press, 1979). See also Isaac Deutscher, *The Prophet Outcast: Trotsky: 1929–1940* (New York: Oxford University Press, 1963), 436–38. The debate over political morality appeared, among other places, in "Violence, For and Against: A Symposium on Marx, Stalin, and Trotsky," *Common Sense*, January 1938, 19–23.

57. On the "revolt against positivism," the intellectual turning point at the end of the nineteenth century that opened a new era in social theory, see H. Stuart Hughes, *Consciousness and Society: The Reorientation of European Social Thought 1890–1930* (New York: Knopf, 1958).

58. Arno J. Mayer attributes turn-of-the-century European intellectual trends to an antidemocratic, revanchist aristocracy, in *The Persistence of the Old Regime: Europe to the Great War* (New York: Pantheon Books, 1981), 275–329.

59. Robert Michels, *Political Parties: A Sociological Study of the Oligarchical Tendencies of Modern Democracy*, trans. Eden Paul and Cedar Paul (New York: The Free Press, 1962), 6, 70.

60. Benjamin Ginzburg, "Money-Making as a Religion," review of *The Protestant Ethic and the Spirit of Capitalism*, by Max Weber, *The New Republic*, 8 October 1930, 212–13. Ginzburg wrote, "What really emerges from a reading of Weber's essay is the feeling that economic facts and institutions are cultural phenomena, more or less responsive to the ethical aspirations of men" (213).

61. Interview with Daniel Bell, 20 May 1982.

62. Max Weber, *From Max Weber: Essays in Sociology*, ed. Hans H. Gerth and C. Wright Mills (New York: Oxford University Press, 1946). On Mills' collaboration with Gerth, see Richard Gillam, "C. Wright Mills 1916–1948: An Intellectual Biography" (Ph.D. diss., Stanford University, 1972).

63. Philip Selznick, *TVA and the Grass Roots: A Study in the Sociology of Formal Organization* (Berkeley: University of California Press, 1949). On the influence

of Michels on Selznick's circle in the late 1930s, see Seymour Martin Lipset, "Socialism and Sociology," in *Sociological Self-Images: A Collective Portrait*, ed. Irving Louis Horowitz (Beverly Hills, Calif.: Sage Publications, 1969), 143–75; Douglas G. Webb, "Philip Selznick and the New York Sociologists," paper presented at the Annual Convention of the Canadian Historical Association, 9–11 June 1982; Lewis Feuer, "Ideology and No End," *Encounter* 40 (April 1973): 84–87.

64. Among the titles announced by The Free Press in its first three years were *The Sociology of Georg Simmel*; Sorel's *Reflections on Violence*; Michels' *Political Parties*; Durkheim's *The Elementary Forms of the Religious Life, The Division of Labor in Society, Le Suicide*, and *Rules of the Sociological Method*; Weber's *General Economic History, The Religion of China*, and *The Methodology of the Social Sciences*. Listed in *Publishers Trade List Annual*, 1948–50.

65. For the relation of modernism and radicalism in the trajectory of *Partisan Review*, see James Gilbert, *Writers and Partisans: A History of Literary Radicalism* (New York: John Wiley and Sons, 1968), and Linda Kaye Kirby, "Communism, the Discovery of Totalitarianism, and the Cold War: *Partisan Review*, 1932 to 1948" (Ph.D. diss., University of Colorado, 1974).

66. See Marshall Berman, *All That Is Solid Melts Into Air: The Experience of Modernity* (New York: Simon and Schuster, 1982).

67. Jeffrey Bergner, "The Epistemological Origins of Modern Social Science 1870–1914," (Ph.D. diss., Princeton University, 1973), 42–45. Later published as *The Origins of Formalism in Social Science* (Chicago: University of Chicago Press, 1981).

68. Bergner, "The Epistemological Origins of Modern Social Science," 31–32.

69. Max Weber, *The Methodology of the Social Sciences*, trans. and ed. Edward A. Shils and Henry A. Finch (New York: The Free Press, 1949), 57.

70. Windelband, quoted in Bergner, "The Epistemological Origins of Modern Social Science," 36.

71. Weber, *Methodology*, 22–27, 51–52.

72. "The scientific investigation of the general cultural significance of the social-economic structure of the human community and its historical forms of organization is the central aim of our journal," Weber wrote in his inaugural statement as coeditor of the *Archiv für Sozialwissenschaft und Sozialpolitik* in 1904. "The concept of culture is a value-concept. Empirical reality becomes 'culture' to us because and in so far as we relate it to value ideas." Weber, *Methodology*, 67, 76.

73. On the role of the subjective orientation in "verstehende soziologie," see Weber, *Economy and Society: An Outline of Interpretive Sociology*, ed. Guenther Roth and Claus Wittich (Berkeley: University of California Press, 1978), 3–24; Parsons, *Structure of Social Action*, 635–42; Therborn, *Science, Class and Society*, 278–94; Ted Benton, *Philosophical Foundations of Three Sociologies* (London: Routledge and Kegan Paul, 1977), 108–29.

74. See Weber, "Objective Possibility and Adequate Causation in Historical Explanation," in *Methodology*, 164–88.

75. Scientific inquiry, Weber wrote, is "determined by the evaluative ideas which dominate the investigator and his age." *Methodology*, 84. Hence, Weber himself makes "rational action," the priority value of modern Western culture, the central ideal-type concept of his general sociology, applying it as a comparative standard to all his objects of analysis.

76. Weber, *Methodology*, 111.

77. Ibid., 124–25; Parsons, *Structure of Social Action*, 584.

78. *From Max Weber*, 358, 359; Max Weber, *The Protestant Ethic and the Spirit of Capitalism*, trans. Talcott Parsons (New York: Charles Scribner's Sons, 1958), 164; Weber, *Methodology*, 8; *From Max Weber*, 153.

79. Weber, *Protestant Ethic*, 224.

80. Ibid., 104.

81. Weber, *Methodology*, 110; *Protestant Ethic*, 78; See Talcott Parsons' introduction in Weber, *The Theory of Social and Economic Organization*, trans. A. M. Henderson and Talcott Parsons (New York: Oxford University Press, 1947), 15–17, and Parsons' development of the concept of the "nonlogical" (or nonrational as opposed to irrational) in his discussion of Pareto, in *Structure of Social Action*, 200–18.

82. *Protestant Ethic*, 118. On the Kantian ethic as a matter of logical consistency, see Reinhold Niebuhr, *Moral Man and Immoral Society* (New York: Charles Scribner's Sons, 1932), 29.

83. *Protestant Ethic*, 270, 98. Weber points out "the decided propensity of Protestant asceticism for empiricism, rationalized on a mathematical basis." Ibid., 249.

84. See Jeffrey C. Alexander's argument, in Weberian fashion, for the necessarily technical definition of rational action in sociology, *Theoretical Logic in Sociology*, Volume 1: *Positivism, Presuppositions, and Current Controversies* (Berkeley: University of California Press, 1982), 65–89.

85. Bergner, "The Epistemological Origins of Modern Social Science," 47.

86. *Protestant Ethic*, 181–82.

87. *From Max Weber*, 198.

88. Ibid., 255.

89. *Protestant Ethic*, 157.

90. Ibid., 175.

91. See Perry Miller, *Errand into the Wilderness* (Cambridge: Harvard University Press, 1956), 1–15.

92. Weber, quoted in Michael Löwy, *Georg Lukács—From Romanticism to Bolshevism* (London: NLB, 1979), 41–42.

93. On Simmel's "tragedy of culture," see Löwy, 43–44.

94. Schiller, quoted in Arthur Mitzman, *Sociology and Estrangement: Three Sociologists of Imperial Germany* (New York: Knopf, 1973), 18–19.

95. On Weber's politics, see Hans H. Gerth and C. Wright Mills, "Introduction: The Man and His Work," in *From Max Weber*, 32–44; Anthony Giddens, *Capitalism and Modern Social Theory: An Analysis of the Writings of Marx, Durkheim and Max Weber* (Cambridge: Cambridge University Press, 1971), 191–92. On Weber as a member of modernizing elite, see Mitzman, 33. Weber's

liberalism shone brilliantly in contrast to the reactionary cast of the imperial academy. On the latter, see Peter Gay, "Weimar Culture: The Outsider as Insider," in *The Intellectual Migration: Europe and America 1930–1960*, ed. Donald Fleming and Bernard Bailyn (Cambridge: Harvard University Press, 1969), 11–93.

96. On Weber's disdain for the "cult" of "personality" and "personal experience," see "Science as a Vocation," in *From Max Weber*, 137, and Weber, *Methodology*, 6.

97. Weber, quoted in Mitzman, 11.

98. Mitzman, 11; *From Max Weber*, 30.

99. Georg Lukács, *The Theory of the Novel* (Cambridge: The MIT Press, 1971), 78.

100. According to Michael Löwy, Kantian dualism suggested to Lukács the Kierkegaardian "either-or": "the 'either-or' principles of absolute opposition between the authentic and the everyday, good and evil, the ethical ideal and the existing world's 'total sinfulness.'" Löwy, *Georg Lukács*, 146.

101. Lukács, quoted in Löwy, 157.

102. Löwy, 105.

103. Lukács, quoted in Löwy, 125.

104. Michels quotes Weber's remarks on the absence of "genuine revolutionary enthusiasm" at a Social Democratic congress. *Political Parties*, 283.

105. See Weber's discussions of Pietism, Methodism, and Baptism, *Protestant Ethic*, 128–49.

106. William Barrett, *Irrational Man: A Study in Existential Philosophy* (Garden City, N.Y.: Doubleday, 1962), 28–29.

107. Karl Jaspers, quoted in H. H. Gerth and C. Wright Mills, "Introduction," in *From Max Weber*, 26–27.

108. *Protestant Ethic*, 180.

109. Just as the name "Methodism" aptly expressed the tendency of worldly asceticism, so a "precisianist" concern for stipulating the terms of *methodology* in social science dominated Weber's work.

110. *From Max Weber*, 138.

111. Ibid., 355.

112. Ibid., 153, 156.

113. *Methodology*, 24; Weber, *The Religion of China*, quoted in Giddens, *Capitalism and Modern Social Theory*, 177–78.

114. On "status" and "contract," or graduated subordination and exchange, see Spencer, *On Social Evolution*, 149–66.

115. On relations between bureaucracy and democracy, see *From Max Weber*, 224–28.

116. *From Max Weber*, 105–11.

117. Ibid., 245.

118. Ibid., 107.

119. Roth, *The Social Democrats in Imperial Germany*, 296–304; Weber, "Parliament and Government in a Reconstructed Germany (A Contribution to the Political Critique of Officialdom and Party Politics)," appendix 2 in Max

Weber, *Economy and Society: An Outline of Interpretive Sociology*, ed. Guenther Roth and Claus Wittich (Berkeley: University of California Press, 1978), 1381–1469.

120. Sidney Hook, *Reason, Social Myths*, 140; Lewis Corey, "Marxism Reconsidered," *The Nation*, 17 February 1940, 247, and "Socialist Fundamentals Reexamined: Recreating Socialism," *Workers Age*, 23 and 30 March 1940; Will Herberg, "Socialist Fundamentals Examined: The Basic Dilemma of Socialism," *Workers Age*, 8, 15, and 22 March 1940.

121. Reinhold Niebuhr, *The Nature and Destiny of Man*, 2 vols. (New York: Charles Scribner's Sons, 1941, 1943).

122. See Martin Jay, *The Dialectical Imagination: A History of the Frankfurt School and the Institute of Social Research, 1923–1930* (Boston: Little, Brown, 1973), 52.

123. See Arthur Mitzman, *Sociology and Estrangement*, 265–344.

124. Georg Lukács, *The Theory of the Novel*, 66.

125. Salvador Giner, *Mass Society*, 92–94.

126. Sacvan Bercovitch, *The American Jeremiad* (Madison: University of Wisconsin Press, 1978), xiv–xv.

127. Transcript, Daniel Bell interview, Socialist Movement project, Oral History Research Office, Columbia University, New York.

128. Patti Peterson, "The Young Socialist Movement in America From 1905 to 1940: A Study of the Young People's Socialist League" (Ph.D. diss., University of Wisconsin-Madison, 1974); on Socialist Party membership, see Daniel Bell, *Marxian Socialism in the United States* (Princeton: Princeton University Press, 1967), 177; on YPSL membership: 1932, Peterson, "The Young Socialist Movement," 132; 1933, *Challenge* (official organ of YPSL), October 1933. Morris Hillquit, *Loose Leaves from a Busy Life* (New York: Macmillan, 1934), 325–27.

129. Daniel Bell, Socialist Movement project, typescript, 8–10. Bell, "First Love and Early Sorrows," *Partisan Review* 48 (1981): 532–51.

130. M. S. Venkataramani, "United Front Tactics of the Communist Party (USA) and Their Impact on the Socialist Party of America, 1932–6," *International Studies* (New Delhi) 1 (October 1959): 154–83.

131. On the Stelton and Mohegan colonies, Laurence Veysey, *The Communal Experience: Anarchist and Mystical Counter-Cultures in America* (New York: Harper and Row, 1973), 77–177.

132. Daniel Aaron, *Writers on the Left* (New York: Avon Books, 1965), 363; Alan Wald, "The Menorah Group Moves Left," *Jewish Social Studies* 38 (Summer-Fall 1976): 301–304; Wald, "Herbert Solow: Portrait of a New York Intellectual," *Prospects: An Annual of American Cultural Studies* (1977): 435–36.

133. Interview with Daniel Bell, 20 April 1982.

134. Ibid.

135. For a summary of the Old Guard's view of its heritage of struggle against leftism, see James Oneal, *American Communism: A Critical Analysis of its Origins, Development and Programs* (New York: Rand Book Store, 1927).

136. On the development of the Socialist Party factions in the early and

middle thirties see David A. Shannon, *The Socialist Party of America, A History* (New York: Macmillan, 1955), esp. 238–48; Frank Warren, *An Alternative Vision: The Socialist Party in the 1930s* (Bloomington: Indiana University Press, 1974); Daniel Bell, *Marxian Socialism in the United States*, 157–72.

137. See Hal Draper, "The Student Movement of the Thirties: A Political History," in *As We Saw the Thirties*, ed. Rita J. Simon (Urbana, Ill.: University of Illinois Press, 1967), 151–89.

138. See, for instance, the Old Guard's "Proposed Declaration of Principles," Socialist Party Minutes, Tamiment Collection 6, Tamiment Library, New York.

139. See, for instance, Haim Kantorovich, "Towards Reorientation," *American Socialist Quarterly* (hereafter *ASQ*) 2 (Autumn 1933): 13–19; Andrew J. Biemiller, "Socialism and Democracy," *ASQ* 3 (Spring 1934); 20–28; Maynard Krueger, "Problems Facing the Party," *ASQ* 3 (Summer 1934): 6–12; Reinhold Niebuhr, "The Revolutionary Moment," *ASQ* 4 (June 1935): 8–13; and *Towards a Militant Program for the Socialist Party of America*, May 1934 (pamphlet).

140. See "Declaration of Principles," reprinted in *ASQ* 3 (July 1934), special supplement: 3–6.

141. Louis Waldman, quoted, in Waldman, *Labor Lawyer* (New York: E. P. Dutton, 1944), 264.

142. James Oneal, *Some Pages of Party History* (New York, 1935), 18–19, 23–24.

143. See James C. Duram, "Algernon Lee's Correspondence with Karl Kautsky: An 'Old Guard' Perspective on the Failure of American Socialism," *Labor History* 20 (Summer 1979): 420–34. As early as 1930 Lee wrote to Kautsky of a growing minority in the party:

> The tendency of almost all these well-meaning folk is to prefer Bolshevism to Social Democracy, just as, some fifteen to twenty years ago, they preferred Anarcho-Syndicalism to Social Democracy and the I. W. W. to the trade unions. And this is, of course, just what you or any good Marxian would expect of them. Not being actually engaged in the prolitarian [*sic*] struggle and disciplined by its experience, they get a thrill—in American slang, "get a kick"—out of playing with what they conceive to be the most extreme left of the revolutionary movement.

And as the split neared in the summer of 1935, Lee said he looked forward to "a dissolution of partnership with the ex-preacher [Thomas], college professor, theological students, déclassés of various kinds—in a word, the egotistic adventurers and their sentimental following."

144. "Interview with Daniel Bell, May 1972," in Job Leonard Dittberner, *The End of Ideology and American Social Thought: 1930–1960* (Ann Arbor, Mich.: UMI Research Press 1979), 331; Daniel Bell, *The End of Ideology: On the Exhaustion of Political Ideas in the Fifties*, rev. ed. (New York: The Free Press, 1962), 333.

145. Interview with Daniel Bell, 20 April 1982.

146. Interview with Daniel Bell, 20 April 1982; Daniel Bell, Socialist Movement project, Columbia University, New York.

147. Interviews with Daniel Bell, 20 April 1982 and 10 December 1982.

148. Salvadori, *Karl Kautsky and the Socialist Revolution*, 237–38; on the role of the workers' bureaucracy, see Kautsky, *Social Democracy versus Communism*, 93.

149. Selznick was a Trotskyist at the time and, according to Bell, had not heard of Michels until that moment. Selznick does not recall the incident but does not find Bell's account implausible. Interview with Daniel Bell, 20 April 1982; letter, Douglas G. Webb to Howard Brick, 2 May 1983; on "Alcove No. 1," the CCNY home of the anti-Stalinist left, see Irving Kristol, "Memoirs of a Trotskyist," *New York Times Magazine*, 23 January 1977, 83, 90–92.

150. Interview with Daniel Bell, 10 December 1982.

151. Interview with Daniel Bell, 10 December 1982; Bell, "First Love and Early Sorrows," 540.

152. On the politics of antifascist coalition within the Socialist International, see Julius Braunthal, *History of the International 1914–1943*, trans. John Clark (London: Thomas Nelson and Sons Ltd., 1967), 399–400, 417–18, 474–78.

153. Interviews with Daniel Bell, 20 April 1982, 10 December 1982; Interview with Sidney Hook, 18 October 1982; Interview with Lewis Coser, 17 April 1983; Kristol, "Memoirs of a Trotskyist," 91.

154. Daniel Bell, "Trotzkyism Echoes Stalinite Hypocrisy" *The New Leader*, 9 September 1939, 8 (letter to the editor). Bell, who wrote a lengthy college paper on the history of the Comintern, evidently took Lenin's remarks out of context: in *Left-Wing Communism: An Infantile Disorder* Lenin urged Communists to join the existing conservative unions, rather than found dual "revolutionary unions," in order to address workers directly and intimately. Should labor bureaucrats harass, victimize, or expel Communist activists, Lenin said, Communists had the right to resort to subterfuge to keep their union membership.

155. Interview with Daniel Bell, 20 April 1982.

156. Richard Polenberg, "The Decline of the New Deal," in *The New Deal: The National Level*, ed. John Braeman, Robert H. Bremner, and David Brody (Columbus: Ohio State University Press, 1975). A Democratic Congressman defeated in the 1938 midterm elections reflected, "Truly has it been said, 'The Republicans wrecked the country and the Democrats are at a stalemate with reference to the problem of recovery and reconstruction.'" The historian William E. Leuchtenburg adds: "A year after his overwhelming triumph in the 1936 election, Roosevelt appeared to be a thoroughly repudiated leader." Further, "The recession [of 1937], which might have bred a radical movement of discontent with the workings of capitalism and liberal reform, served instead to strengthen the conservatives." William Leuchtenburg, *Franklin Roosevelt and the New Deal* (New York: Harper and Row, 1963), 271, 251, 254.

157. James Weinstein, *Ambiguous Legacy: The Left in American Politics* (New York: New Viewpoints, 1975), 57–86.

158. Paul M. Sweezy, "Why Stagnation?" *Monthly Review* 34 (June 1982): 1–10; "Listen, Keynesians!" *Monthly Review* 34 (January 1983): 1–11; Dean L. May, *From New Deal to New Economics: The American Liberal Response to the Recession of 1937* (New York: Garland Publishing, 1981).

159. Nelson Lichtenstein, *Labor's War at Home: The CIO in World War II* (Cambridge: Cambridge University Press, 1982), 8–25.

160. Throughout the 1930s the Old Guard looked forward to the formation of a national Labor Party on the British model. In 1935, after the heads of the railway unions called for railroad nationalization, Algernon Lee wrote to Kautsky that he saw a real possibility of an independent union-based party forming by 1936. At the time the Old Guard left the Socialist Party in 1936, the New York garment unions were preparing to organize their own party, but they were intent on backing Roosevelt. The Social Democrats balked: they still resisted affiliation with a politician of the capitalist parties. But they finally had their chance for a labor party and could only grasp it if they acceded to the unions' wishes. The American Labor Party was formed to support the New Deal outside of "old party" channels. The Communist Party, under the program of the Popular Front, turned in the same direction. In 1944 the American Labor Party split between its Communist and anti-Communist wings after years of intraparty contention: the Communists kept the American Labor Party name through the 1950s, while the Social Democratic Federation went with the new Liberal Party.

See Duram, "Algernon Lee's Correspondence with Karl Kautsky," 429–30; Louis Waldman, *Labor Lawyer*, 284–86.

161. David A. Shannon, *The Socialist Party of America: A History* (New York: Macmillan, 1955), 250.

162. For the record of the dispute, see James Thomas Burnett, "American Trotskyism and the Russian Question" (Ph.D. diss., University of California at Berkeley, 1968); Leon Trotsky, *In Defense of Marxism* (New York: Pathfinder Press, 1973); James P. Cannon, *The Struggle for a Proletarian Party* (New York: Pathfinder Press, 1972); Max Shachtman, "Twenty Five Years of American Trotskyism," *New International*, January-February 1954, 11–25; Max Shachtman, *The Bureaucratic Revolution: The Rise of the Stalinist State* (New York: Donald Press, 1962).

163. "Towards a Genuine American Democratic Socialism!" *Workers Age*, 25 January 1941, 1.

164. On the weakness of the Democratic Party, see Leuchtenburg, 272. Labor historian Mike Davis writes, "It has, in fact, been the traditional view of certain Marxist currents that 1938 was the most advantageous opportunity for revolutionary politics in the twentieth century. The puzzle, however, is how to explain why 1938 was actually a year of unmitigated disaster for third party and labor party hopes, which instead of growing at the expense of the New Deal's crisis, virtually collapsed." See Mike Davis, "The Barren Marriage of American Labour and the Democratic Party," *New Left Review* no. 124 (November-December 1980), 57.

165. Interview with Daniel Bell, 20 April 1982.

Chapter 2

1. The Editors, quoted in Dwight Macdonald, "War and the Intellectuals: Act Two," *Partisan Review* 6 (Spring 1939): 9.

2. Ed., "The Curse of Realism," *Common Sense*, March 1945, 4, quoted in William L. O'Neill, *A Better World: The Great Schism: Stalinism and the American Intellectuals* (New York: Simon and Schuster, 1982), 114; "An Editorial—The Division of Europe," *The New Leader*, 23 December 1944, 1, 3.

3. On the antiwar movement of the 1930s, see Eileen M. Eagan, *Class, Culture, and the Classroom: The Student Peace Movement of the 1930s* (Philadelphia: Temple University Press, 1981); Hal Draper, "The Student Movement of the Thirties: A Political History," in *As We Saw the Thirties*, ed. Rita J. Simon (Urbana, Ill.: University of Illinois Press, 1967), 151–89; Ralph S. Brax, "When Students First Organized Against War: Student Protest During the 1930s," *New York Historical Society Quarterly* 63 (July 1979): 228–55; Lawrence S. Wittner, *Rebels Against War: The American Peace Movement, 1941–1960* (New York: Columbia University Press, 1969).

4. Bell, "First Love and Early Sorrows," *Partisan Review* 48 (1981): 532–51; Letter, Daniel Bell to Howard Brick, 16 January 1982.

5. Sidney Hook, "Socialism, Common Sense and the War," *The New Leader*, 31 August 1940, 7.

6. Interview with Sidney Hook, 18 October 1982.

7. On the Reuther "500 planes a day" plan, Philip Murray's "industrial council" plan, and the CIO leadership's sympathy for British Labour's coalition role, see Nelson Lichtenstein, *Labor's War at Home: The CIO in World War II* (New York: Cambridge University Press, 1982), 41–42. On the British Labour Party's view of the transformative impulse of the war, see, for example, "In War and Peace Labour's 'Price' is a Socialist Britain," *New Leader* [hereafter cited as *NL*], 1 June 1940, 5; "In War and Peace British Labor Demands Socialist Economic Program to Meet War Strain," *NL*, 8 June 1940, 5; Alfred Baker Lewis, "British Labor's Post-War Program Supplies Motif of Anti-Nazi Fight," *NL*, 19 October 1940, 5; Boris Shub, "Britain's Bloodless Revolution Holds Key to World's Future, Laski Predicts," *NL*, 18 January 1941, 2; Walter Citrine, "Revamped Production Set-Up Gives British Labor New Powers," *NL*, 6 September 1941, 10; and an American endorsement, Ferdinand Lundberg, "Profits Against Tanks: 'Money Mentality' of U.S. Industrialists Slows Defense," *NL*, 19 October 1940, 4, 6.

8. *UDA Bulletin*, June 1941; Robert Clayton Pierce, "Liberals and the Cold War: Union for Democratic Action and Americans for Democratic Action" (Ph.D. diss., University of Wisconsin-Madison, 1979), 30, 47–48; also see Adam Clymer, "The Union for Democratic Action: Key to the Noncommunist Left" (Honors thesis, Harvard University, 1958). On *The New Leader*, the UDA, and the conflict with the Social Democratic Federation: "Report of the Sub-Committee on Relations of the S.D.F. and the New Leader," "Statement of New Leader editors and Board of Directors, September 28, 1942," "Report of Sub-Committee on the U.D.A.," all in Social Democratic Federation Rec-

ords, Tamiment Library, New York University; "Union for Democratic Action," *NL*, 10 May 1941; "Minutes of Board of Directors Held Sunday May 10, 1942," UDA organizational file, Tamiment Library, New York.

9. "Why the UDA," *UDA Bulletin*, October 1941, 2.

10. On the official position of the Social Democratic Federation, "SDF Resolution Backs Democracies," *NL*, 30 September 1939, 1; "Active Anti-War Socialists of 1917 Urge Fight on Nazis," *NL*, 14 June 1941, 2. On the left-wing critique of collective security and the popular front in the 1930s, see "Radicals and War: A Debate, For Sanctions: Ludwig Lore, Against Sanctions: Sidney Hook," *Modern Monthly* 10 (April 1936): 12–17; Hook, "Thoughts in Season," *Socialist Review* 6 (May-June 1938): 6–7; Norman Thomas, "Collective Security and Socialism," *Socialist Review* 6 (May-June 1938): 4–5; Hook, "The Anatomy of the Popular Front," *Partisan Review* 6 (Spring 1939): 29–45; Macdonald, "War and the Intellectuals: Act Two"; "War Is The Issue," *Partisan Review* 6 (Fall 1939): 125–27.

Sidney Hook, a featured contributor to *The New Leader* in these years, criticized the SDF's uncritical reliance on Roosevelt and quipped, "Few things are more amazing than the sight of those who are social determinists . . . wallowing in the euphoria of hero-worship." Sidney Hook, "Failure of the Left," *Partisan Review* 10 (March-April 1943): 172.

11. On the industrialists' reluctance to undertake a full-scale mobilization, see Richard Polenberg, *War and Society: The United States 1941–1945* (Philadelphia: J. B. Lippincott, 1972), 4. On the pots-and-pans campaign of the Union for Democratic Action, see *UDA Bulletin*, August 1941, 3. Picketers in New York's Times Square held signs reading, "Give Pots and Pans for Democracy—But No Gravy for the 'Aluminum Trust.'" On business and mobilization: Daniel Bell, "U.S. Seeks to Fix Prices to Halt Inflation," *NL*, 29 March 1941, 3; "Business Plans to Defy Gov't Efforts to Control War Industries," *NL*, 28 June 1941, 2; "'Business as Usual' Dollar-a-Year Men Fired by OPM to Spur Production," *NL*, 12 July 1941, 1; "Industrialists See Material Shortage Halting Defense Soon" *NL*, 26 July 1941, 1; "Defense Monopoly Hits Small Business, Chokes Production," *NL*, 2 August 1941, 1, 7.

12. Daniel Bell, "Labor Wants 'Win the War' Congress; Tory Drives Hit Production Morale," *NL*, 25 April 1942, 1, 7; "Standard Oil Tactics May Ground 40% of U.S. Air Force, Monopoly Practices Balked Output of Vital Aviation Octane Fuel," *NL*, 1 August 1942, 1, 7.

13. Daniel Bell, "Where the News Ends," *NL*, 22 August 1942, 8, 7. "Jacques Maritain Replies to Bell Column on Catholic Manifesto" and "A Reply," *NL*, 5 September 1942. Bell, "Where the News Ends: The Catholic Cauldron," *NL*, 26 September 1942, 8, 7. Sidney Hook, "The New Failure of Nerve," *Partisan Review* 10 (January/February 1943): 2–23.

14. See Veblen, *The Engineers and the Price System* (New York: B. W. Huebsch, 1921; reprint, New York: Augustus M. Kelley, 1965); Lewis Corey, "Veblen and Marxism," review of *What Veblen Taught*, ed. Wesley C. Mitchell, in *Marxist Quarterly* 1 (January-March 1937): 162–68.

15. Bell, "Monopoly Can Lead to Fascism: 'Business as Usual,' Unchecked,

Will Mean 'the Usual Business.'" *Common Sense*, September 1941, 267–69; Bell, "Standard Oil-Nazi Firm Tie-Up Halted Rubber Production; I. G. Farben Patents Held by Jasco Balked U.S. Efforts—Full Story Told," *NL*, 31 January 1942, 1, 7; "Urge Congress Probe 'Sale' of Nazi I. G. Farben Patents To Standard Oil, Justice Dep't Files Hold Evidence of Tie-Up," *NL*, 7 February 1941, 1, 7; "Nazis Seek To Hide Reich Control of U.S. Magnesium Supply," *NL*, 22 February 1941, 1; "Urge Probe of Int'l Cartels Balking Production, Foreign Ties Of U.S. Firms: Farben Patents Worth Millions Sold To Standard Oil for Song," *NL*, 4 April 1942, 1, 7; "Arnold Starts Quiet Probe to Break Alcohol Trust, Rockefeller Interests Hold Key to Explosives, Rubber, Sugar Markets," *NL*, 16 May 1942, 1; "Senate to Probe Hi-Octane Sales to Axis," *NL*, 27 June 1942, 1, 7; "Sterling—A Story the Senate Fears to Hear," *NL*, 8 August 1942, 1, 6; "Tales from the Record: German Contract Stopped Remington Arms (Dupont) From Selling Bullets to the British in 1941," *NL* 15 August 1942, 1; "Tales From the Record: Nazi Contract Set Remington's Price on Sale of Arms to U.S. Gov't," *NL*, 22 August 1942, 2; "Reveal 'Oil International' Behind Allied Aviation Fuel Shortage," *NL*, 3 October 1942, 1, 6. Daniel Bell and Melvin J. Lasky, "WPB Firing May Reveal 'Scandals', Sterling Fights Efforts to End Quinine Monopoly," *NL*, 19 September 1942, 1. Popular Front journalists I. F. Stone and George Seldes also pursued the German-American business links vigorously. For a more recent historical review of the matter, see Gabriel Kolko, "American Business and Germany, 1930–1941," *Western Political Quarterly* 15 (December 1962): 713–28.

16. Bell, "Monopoly Can Lead to Fascism," 280.

17. Guenter Reimann, *The Myth of the Total State: Europe's Last Bid for World Rule* (New York: William Morrow, 1941); Reimann, *Patents for Hitler* (New York: The Vanguard Press, 1942); Interview with Bell, April 20, 1982; Bell, "The Secret International" (review of *Patents for Hitler*), *NL*, 7 November 1942, 3; "3, Not 60, Families Run U.S., Says TNEC," *NL*, 11 October 1941; Bell, "Clippings and Comment," *NL*, 31 October 1942, 2; "Clippings and Comment," *NL*, 7 November 1942, 2; "Clippings and Comment." *NL*, 26 November 1942, 2; "Clippings and Comment," *NL*, 9 January 1943, 2.

18. See Karl Renner, "Problems of Marxism," in *Austro-Marxism*, trans. and ed. Tom Bottomore and Patrick Goode (Oxford: Oxford University Press, 1978), 100.

19. In *Imperialism and World Economy* (1915), Bukharin depicted unitary, crisis-free "state capitalist trusts" competing among themselves on the international terrain of imperialist politics and war. In contrast to the Austro-Marxists, Bukharin used his depiction of an organized capitalism—"an iron organization which envelops the living body of society in its tenacious, grasping paws"—as further ammunition for the Bolshevik argument that the capitalist state could not be used for progressive ends but had to be smashed. Nonetheless, Bukharin's view of solidary state capitalist trusts had little in common with the description of monopoly capitalism in Lenin's *Imperialism*. See Nikolai Bukharin, "Toward a Theory of the Imperialist State" (1916), cited in Stephen F. Cohen, *Bukharin and the Bolshevik Revolution: A Political Bi-*

ography, 1888–1938 (Oxford: Oxford University Press, 1980), 28–31. Bukharin, *Imperialism and World Economy* (New York: Monthly Review Press, 1973), esp. 144–60; Bukharin, *Imperialism and the Accumulation of Capital* (with Rosa Luxemburg, *The Accumulation of Capital—An Anti-Critique*), ed. Kenneth J. Tarbuck (New York: Monthly Review Press, 1972), 226.

20. Bell, "This Week in Labor," *NL*, 30 August 1941, 1, 6; "Captive Mine Decision to Settle Lewis Role at CIO Parley," *NL*, 8 November 1941, 1, 7; "Anti-Labor Bills Flood Congress as Strike Wave Hits New Peak," *NL*, 15 November 1941, 1, 7; "Labor in 1941: Gains and Setbacks," *NL*, 3 January 1942, 2; "Labor Wants 'Win the War' Congress; Tory Drives Hit Production Morale," *NL*, 25 April 1942, 1, 7; "Byrnes Halts 'Teapot Dome' Deal, Moves to Probe Elk Hills Oil Scandal," *NL*, 5 June 1943; "Monopolies Move Quietly to Suspend Anti-Trust Law," *NL*, 6 June 1942.

21. John Morton Blum, *V Was for Victory: Politics and American Culture During World War II* (New York: Harcourt Brace Jovanovich, 1976), 221–45; Polenberg, *War and Society*, 73–93; Bell and the ALP, Interview with Daniel Bell, May 1972, in Dittberner, *The End of Ideology and American Social Thought 1930–1960*, 313; on UDA's crisis and its close ties to ALP, Pierce, "Liberals and the Cold War," 68–78; and "Memorandum to UDA Executive on ALP," UDA file, Tamiment Library, New York; Blum, 244, 258–59.

22. Bell on the rightward drift of foreign policy, "Anti-Fascists Assail Radio Propaganda to Italy," *NL*, 17 October 1942, 1, 6; "Anti-Nazi Germans Score Radio Propaganda to Reich," *NL*, 24 October 1942; Bell and Leon Dennen, "Pro-Fascists Seek to Control Polish Exile Gov't," *NL*, 31 October 1942; Melvin J. Lasky, "The Time of Day," *NL*, 17 October 1942, 2; Bell, "Clippings and Comment," *NL*, 24 October 1942.

23. Ralph de Toledano, "A People's War and the British," *NL*, 31 October 1942, 8; Bell and Lasky, "War, Politics and Confusion," *NL*, 14 November 1942, 2.

24. Richard Gillam, "C. Wright Mills, 1916–1948: An Intellectual Biography," (Ph.D. diss., Stanford University, 1972), 174.

25. See Carl Dreher, "John Chamberlain, Prophet of Reaction," and John Chamberlain, "Carl Dreher: Totalitarian Liberal," *Common Sense*, November 1942, 366–72; Bell, "Clippings and Comment," *NL*, 31 October 1942; Abba P. Lerner, "Collectivism and Freedom: An Attempt to Resolve 'the Conflict' By a Modern Economic Approach," *NL*, 28 November 1942, 4; Mills, "Collectivism and the Mixed-up Economy," *NL*, 19 December 1942.

26. Gillam, 218–20, 226. See Mills, "The Conscription of America," *Common Sense*, March 1945, 15–17, for an early description by Mills of the tripartite structure of power growing out of the war. Daniel Bell was managing editor of *Common Sense* when this essay by Mills was published.

27. Daniel Bell, "Clippings and Comment," *NL*, 29 August 1942, 2; Letter, Bell to Corey, 22 December 1942, Lewis Corey Papers, Columbia University, New York; Bell, "The Strange Case of Stuart Chase," *NL*, 5 December 1942, 2.

28. See Friedrich Pollock, "State Capitalism: Its Possibilities and Limitations," *Studies in Philosophy and Social Science* 9 (1941): 200–25; Pollock, "Is Na-

tional Socialism a New Order?" *Studies in Philosophy and Social Science* 9 (1941): 440–55; Franz Neumann, *Behemoth: The Structure and Practice of National Socialism* (New York: Oxford University Press, 1942), 291–92; see Martin Jay's treatment of the dispute between Pollock and Neumann in *The Dialectical Imagination: A History of the Frankfurt School and the Institute of Social Research, 1923–1950* (Boston: Little, Brown, 1973), 143–72.

29. Just as Bell rejected Chase's arguments, he dissented from James Burnham's definition of the planned order dawning in the United States as a post-capitalist "managerial society." See Burnham, *The Managerial Revolution: What is Happening in the World* (New York: John Day, 1941). The planned coordination of the new order followed, in Bell's scheme, from the collective class consciousness of the capitalist class (or the vanguard monopoly sector of it) and not from a new managerial class.

30. Bell, "Clippings and Comment," *NL*, 12 December 1942, 2; "Clippings and Comment," *NL*, 23 January 1943, 2; "Clippings and Comment," *NL*, 6 February 1943, 2; "Planning By Whom—for What? Business Menaces FDR Schemes, Vested Interests Plan Own Boards for Economic Control," *NL*, 20 March 1943; 5, 7; "Clippings and Comment," *NL*, 20 March 1943, 2; "Clippings and Comment," *NL*, 13 May 1943, 2. Bell's main piece on the Committee for Economic Development, "Business Plans for Business," *Common Sense*, December 1943, 427–31. On the CED's adoption of Hansen's Keynesianism, see Robert M. Collins, "Positive Business Responses to the New Deal: The Roots of the Committee for Economic Development, 1933–1942," *Business History Review* 52 (Autumn 1978): 369–91.

31. Bell, "Planning by Whom—for What?" Bell, "Business and Politics," review of *Business as a System of Power* by Robert Brady, *Partisan Review* 10 (July-August 1943): 377–80; Bell, "The Coming Tragedy of American Labor," *Politics*, March 1944, 42.

32. Bell, "Washington '44—Prelude to the Monopoly State," *NL*, 29 January 1944, 4. See also Bell, "Clippings and Comment: Notes on the Monopoly State," *NL*, 30 October 1943, 2, 7; "Monopoly Groups Seek to Smash Anti-Trust Laws After the War," *NL*, 25 December 1943, 1; "Two Steps Toward Monopoly State," *NL*, 26 February 1944, 5.

33. Bell, "Clippings and Comment," *NL*, 6 February 1943, 2; "Clippings and Comment," *NL*, 8 May 1943, 2, 7; "Tory Socialism in Britain," *NL*, 19 February 1944, 5.

34. Bell, "'Air Empire' Battle for Skyways Hits Post-war Unity," *NL*, 6 March 1943, 1, 7; "US Moves to Realize Business Dream of 'American Century' in Hemisphere Pacts," *NL*, 27 March 1943, 1, 6; "Clippings and Comment," *NL*, 1 May 1943, 2; "'The American Century'—Imperialists Plan Post-war Mobilization," *NL*, 30 October 1943, 2, 7; "Washington '44—Prelude to the Monopoly State," *NL*, 29 January 1944, 4; "Pipeline to Imperialism," *Common Sense*, April 1944, 130–33.

Henry Luce had called for the United States "to assume the leadership of the world" in a 1941 editorial, "The American Century," in *Life* magazine. The theme of a "new imperialism" was one that Bell shared with Dwight Macdonald's *Politics* magazine in 1944. This "new imperialism" was distinguished from classic imperialism because it did not consist merely of government action backing up prior private business initiatives abroad. Rather "new imperialism" was a calculated, state-orchestrated intervention in world economic affairs to establish the conditions for the hegemony of the "national capital" of the United States. The "new imperialism" relied especially upon direct state-to-state arrangements, for instance massive loans to Latin American governments, underwritten by Washington, that would further the penetration of North American capital into the southern continent. See the series in *Politics*: Frank Freidel, "The New Imperialism, I: The Haitian Pilot-Plant," *Politics*, March 1944, 43–45; Arthur Pincus, "Twenty and ONE: The New Imperialism in Latin America," *Politics*, April 1944, 74–80; George Padmore, "The Anglo-American Condominium," *Politics*, May 1944, 113–16.

35. On the Nazi-forged industrial unity of Europe and the danger that a restorationist peace would redivide it, Bell, "Clippings and Comment," *NL*, 30 January 1943; Daniel Bell and Melvin Lasky, "On the Eve of New Europe," *NL*, 24 July 1943, 2.

36. Bell, "Politics for Power," *NL*, 24 June 1944, 5, 7; "Mood of Power Politics," *NL*, 18 December 1943, 5.

37. The clearest analysis of the second World War as an interimperialist struggle was presented by Leon Trotsky in May 1940, "Manifesto of the Fourth International on the Imperialist War and the Proletarian World Revolution," in *Writings of Leon Trotsky (1939–40)* (New York: Pathfinder Press, 1973), 183–222.

38. Bell, "Politics for Power," *NL*, 24 June 1944, 7.

39. John Lewis Gaddis, *The United States and the Origins of the Cold War, 1941–1947* (New York: Columbia University Press, 1972), 17–18.

40. Alonzo L. Hamby, *Beyond the New Deal: Harry S. Truman and American Liberalism* (New York: Columbia University Press, 1973), 73.

41. Bell, "Politics for Power." Bell's declaration of support for Norman Thomas, typescript, Socialist Party papers, undated correspondence 1944, Duke University, Durham, N.C. *NL's* endorsement, "Roosevelt Without Illusions," *NL*, 15 July 1944, 1. Murray Everett, "Inside and Out," *NL*, 1 July 1944.

42. "Is America Going Fascist? A Symposium on John T. Flynn's Thesis," *NL*, 1 April 1944, 7; "A Statement by John T. Flynn and a Reply by the Editors," *NL*, 15 April 1944, 9.

43. Jonathan Stout, "Will U.S. Join the Imperialist Grab?" *NL*, 23 December 1944, 1, 3; "An Editorial—The Division of Europe," *NL*, 23 December 1944, 1, 3.

44. "Daniel Bell to Leave," *NL*, 16 December 1944, 11; "A Note from Bell on New Leader," *NL*, 23 December 1944, 11.

45. Dwight Macdonald, "Kulturbolschewismus is Here," *Partisan Review* 8 (November-December 1941): 442–51.

46. Max Horkheimer, *Eclipse of Reason* (1947; reprint, New York: Continuum, 1974), 28, 50–51; Max Horkheimer and Theodor Adorno, *Dialectic of Enlightenment*, trans. John Cumming (New York: Seabury Press, 1972), 37.

It is possible to contextualize the Frankfurt School's concern over the disappearance of space for the individual and for contemplative thought by pointing out the ideological preeminence of collectivist and action-oriented themes not only in Nazi Germany but in New Deal America as well. In his history of New Deal, William Leuchtenburg selected two contemporary remarks that illustrate the cultural disposition of the time. Writer Edgar Kemler commented,

> We no longer care to develop the individual as a unique contributor to a democratic form. In this movement each individual sub-man is important, not for his uniqueness, but for his ability to lose himself in the mass, through his fidelity to the trade union, or cooperative organization, or political party.

Stuart Chase gloried in the "live stuff" of a government report: "wheelbarrow, cement mixer, steam dredge, generator, combine, power-line stuff; library dust does not gather here." Both quoted in Leuchtenburg, *Franklin Roosevelt and the New Deal* (New York: Harper and Row, 1963), 340–41.

47. Horkheimer, quoted in Martin Jay, *The Dialectical Imagination*, 155. On the Frankfurt School's return to Kantian dualism in reaction to "false totalism," see Jay, 52.

48. Horkheimer, quoted in Martin Jay, "The Frankfurt School in Exile," *Perspectives on American History* 6 (1972), 347.

49. "A Statement by 66—'Mission to Moscow' Exposed," *New Leader*, 29 May 1943, 2. Bell's participation in the campaign is recorded in minutes of meetings held in New York, 6 April 1943 and 16 April 1943, in Dwight Macdonald Papers, Yale University Library. The episode is recounted in O'Neill, *A Better World*, 75–78.

50. Serge Guilbaut, *How New York Stole the Idea of Modern Art: Abstract Expressionism, Freedom, and the Cold War*, trans. Arthur Goldhammer (Chicago: University of Chicago Press, 1983), 69–79. Although it had an entirely different social base from the American Modern Artist movement, and lacked the political affiliations of the left-wing painters, the rise of bebop in jazz music can be interpreted likewise as a "modernist" reaction against integrative, organizational constraints threatening individual autonomy. Furthermore, the new music partook of that spirit of underground rebellion in the black community which also nurtured a kind of resistance to absorption in the war effort, as illustrated, for instance, in the memoirs of Malcolm X. Bebop took wing in Harlem jam sessions during 1942–43, the period of a musicians' union ban on recording. As one commentator wrote,

> Bebop is music of revolt: revolt against big bands, arrangers, vertical harmonies, soggy rhythms, non-playing leaders, Tin Pan Alley—against commercialized music in general. It reasserts the individuality of the jazz musician as a creative artist, playing spontaneous and melodic music within the framework of jazz, but with new tools, sounds, and concepts.

See Gilbert Chase, *America's Music, From the Pilgrims to the Present*, 2nd ed. (New York: McGraw-Hill, 1966).

51. Bruce Bliven, "The Hang-Back Boys," *New Republic*, 6 March 1944, 305–307; Bell, "Bruce Bliven—Don Quixote of Liberalism," *NL*, 4 March 1944, 4.

52. Bell, "The World of Moloch," *Politics*, May 1944, 111–13. Writing at the time under the pseudonym J. R. Johnson, C. L. R. James responded to Bell's essay on Laski and suggested Bell's proximity to Benda. "Laski, St. Paul and Stalin: A Prophet in Search of New Values," *New International*, June 1944, 186.

53. Arthur Koestler, "A Challenge to 'Knights in Rusty Armor.'" *New York Times Magazine*, 14 February 1943, 37.

54. Daniel Bell, "A Note on Arthur Koestler," *NL*, 20 November 1943, 2.

55. Dwight Macdonald, "The MCF," *Politics*, April 1944, 65–66; Daniel Bell, "The Coming Tragedy of American Labor," *Politics*, March 1944, 37–42. Daniel Bell, "The Political Lag of Commonwealth," *Politics*, May 1945, 139–43.

56. Interview with Bell, April 20, 1982.

57. Daniel Bell, "The Monopoly State: A Note on Hilferding and the Theory of Statism," *Socialist Review*, July 1944, in *The Call*, July 14, 1944.

58. Hilferding, quoted in Franz Neumann, *Behemoth*, 15–16.

59. Barton J. Bernstein, "The Automobile Industry and the Coming of the Second World War," *Southwestern Social Science Quarterly* (June 1966), 22–33.

60. *Economic Concentration and World War II*: Report of the Smaller War Plants Corporation to the Special Committee to Study Problems of American Small Business, U.S. Senate, 1946, 29, 40, cited in George Lipsitz, *Class and Culture in Cold War America* (South Hadley, Mass.: J. F. Bergin Publishers, 1982), 7.

61. Polenberg, *War and Society*, 89–91.

62. Blum, *V Was for Victory*, 117–46.

63. Smith, quoted in Robert Nisbet, *History of the Idea of Progress* (New York: Basic Books, 1980), 192.

64. Theda Skocpol, "Political Response to Capitalist Crisis: Neo-Marxist Theories of the State and the Case of the New Deal," *Politics and Society* 10 (1980): 164. Bell himself later criticized precisely this presumption of his "Monopoly State" theory, that capitalists formed a cohesive class, self-conscious, as a whole, of its purposes. Then, because he could conceive of class in none other than these voluntaristic, instrumental terms, Bell concluded that there was no "ruling class" in the United States. See his essay, "Has America a Ruling Class?" *Commentary*, December 1949, 603–7. The concept of class, and of "ruling class," in Marxist theory, however, does not depend on an identifiable corporate consciousness. In fact, according to Hal Draper, Marx's writings on the political action of classes often referred to the bourgeoisie's historically unique incapacity as a ruling class, in part because the regime of competition undermined formulations of collective interest. Likewise, according to Fred Block, the overall irrationality of capitalist society prevents capitalists, as the dominant class, from "ruling" in the sense of exercising conscious, collective, and effective dictation. See Hal Draper, *Karl Marx's Theory of Revolution, vol. 1: State and Bureaucracy* (New York: Monthly

Review Press, 1977), 321–26, and *Karl Marx's Theory of Revolution, vol. 2: The Politics of Social Classes* (New York: Monthly Review Press, 1978), 266–70; Fred Block, "The Ruling Class Does Not Rule: Notes on the Marxist Theory of the State," *Socialist Revolution*, no. 33 (May-June 1977), 6–28, and "Beyond Corporate Liberalism," *Social Problems* 24 (February 1977): 352–61.

65. Barton J. Bernstein, "The Debate on Industrial Reconversion: The Protection of Oligopoly and Military Control of the War Economy," *American Journal of Economics and Sociology* (April 1967), 159–72. The analysis of corporate liberalism was promoted in the 1960s by New Left historians like Gabriel Kolko, James Weinstein, Ronald Radosh, and James Gilbert. These historians found that liberal reform, particularly the development of government's regulatory capacity, arose not so much from efforts of the opponents of big business as from far-sighted plans of big business leaders themselves. The rise of the great corporations as large units of organized production, so the argument went, fueled the collectivist mystique, the priority of planning over competition, of "social responsibility" over irresponsible individualism. See Gabriel Kolko, *The Triumph of Conservatism* (New York: Free Press, 1963); James Weinstein, *The Corporate Ideal in the Liberal State* (Boston: Beacon Press, 1968); Ronald Radosh, *American Labor and United States Foreign Policy* (New York: Random House, 1969); James Gilbert, *Designing the Industrial State: The Intellectual Pursuit of Collectivism in America, 1880–1940* (Chicago: Quadrangle Books, 1972); and Ellis W. Hawley, "The Discovery and Study of a 'Corporate Liberalism,'" *Business History Review* 52 (Autumn 1978): 309–20.

66. C. Wright Mills, *The Power Elite* (Oxford: Oxford University Press, 1956), 273.

67. Blum, *V Was for Victory*, 234–38.

68. Robert M. Collins, "Positive Business Responses to the New Deal," 369–91.

69. See Robert D. Cuff, *The War Industries Board: Business-Government Relations during World War I* (Baltimore: Johns Hopkins University Press, 1973), and James Weinstein, *The Corporate Ideal in the Liberal State*, 214–54.

70. Michel Aglietta, *A Theory of Capitalist Regulation: The US Experience*, trans. David Fernbach (London: NLB, 1979), 222–23.

71. Skocpol, "Political Response to Capitalist Crisis," 160–81.

72. See Block, "The Ruling Class Does Not Rule," 16.

73. This trend is documented by Nelson Lichtenstein, *Labor's War at Home.*

Chapter 3

1. Bell referred to the University of Chicago as his "cloister" in a letter to Dwight Macdonald, n.d. [late 1945, early 1946], Macdonald Papers, Yale University Library, New Haven.

2. Richard Gillam, in his biography of C. Wright Mills, used the term "new radicalism" to identify the postwar, post-Marxist social theory that characterized Mills's work. See Gillam, "C. Wright Mills 1916–1948: An Intellectual Biography" (Ph.D. diss., Stanford University, 1972). I have borrowed the term from him.

3. Art Preis, *Labor's Giant Step: Twenty Years of the CIO* (New York: Pathfinder Press, 1972), 257.

4. Michel Aglietta, *A Theory of Capitalist Regulation: The US Experience*, trans. David Fernbach (London: NLB, 1979), 193–94. Consider, for instance, the Kelsey-Hayes strike of August 1945, which led the War Labor Board to overturn the previous dismissal of nine workers, recounted in George Lipsitz, *Class and Culture in Cold War America: "A Rainbow at Midnight"* (South Hadley, Mass.: J. F. Bergin Publishers, 1982), 38.

5. Preis, *Labor's Giant Step*, 257.

6. Lipsitz, *Class and Culture*, 117.

7. Preis, *Labor's Giant Step*, 258.

8. Nelson Lichtenstein, *Labor's War at Home: The CIO in World War II* (New York: Cambridge University Press, 1982), 119.

9. Racism, however endemic in the white working class, had not always assumed such a virulent form as that of the hate strikes. Although during the war whites in some factories would walk out if a black sat on the next work stool, at other times and in other workplaces shop politics were entirely different. For instance, according to August Meier and Elliott Rudwick in *Black Detroit and the Rise of the UAW*, at the Midland Steel plant in late 1936, blacks accounted for one-third of the work force, "and because they worked in an unusually broad range of job categories in close interaction with white workers, the setting was conducive to interracial cooperation." Given this historical variability in racial politics, the hate strikes need to be explained, rather than attributed simply to a given, racist disposition of white workers. Thus Mike Davis suggests that the labor movement's lack of political leadership, at a time when workplace tensions were high, let resentment loose in spontaneous, backward ways that fell far short of the high level of consciousness and organization achieved during the CIO union recognition drives. Also, it seems that once the initial shock of integration was overcome, interracial shop work continued largely without incident. By the end of 1943, black participation in war work had increased to 8 percent, from 3 percent two years before, and, as Nelson Lichtenstein writes, "Although the number of wildcat strikes over other issues increased after the spring of 1943, hate strikes almost vanished." There were still occasional outbreaks of racist labor action, like the Philadelphia streetcar strike in August 1944. See Meier and Rudwick, *Black Detroit and the Rise of the UAW* (Oxford: Oxford University Press, 1979), 35; Davis, "The Barren Marriage of American Labour and the Democratic Party," *New Left Review*, no. 124 (November-December 1980), 66–68; Lichtenstein, *Labor's War at Home*, 126; Lipsitz, *Class and Culture*, 1, 18, 23–24.

10. Preis, *Labor's Giant Step*, 258–60.

11. On the General Motors strike, see Lipsitz, *Class and Culture*, 45–53; Lichtenstein, *Labor's War at Home*, 224–32.

12. Lipsitz, *Class and Culture*, 121–22.

13. Barton J. Bernstein, "America in War and Peace: The Test of Liberalism," in *Towards a New Past: Dissenting Essays in American History*, ed. Bernstein (New York: Vintage Books, 1969), 301.

14. Lipsitz, *Class and Culture*, 56–86.

15. Letter, Bell to Macdonald, June 1946, Macdonald Papers.

16. Letter, Bell to Lewis Corey, 22 December 1942, Lewis Corey Papers, Columbia University, New York.

17. Interview with Daniel Bell, 20 April 1982; "Interview with Daniel Bell, May 1972," in Job Leonard Dittberner, *The End of Ideology and American Social Thought: 1930–1960* (Ann Arbor, Mich.: UMI Research Press, 1979), 319.

18. *From Max Weber: Essays in Sociology*, ed. H. H. Gerth and C. Wright Mills (New York: Oxford University Press, 1946); *The Theory of Social and Economic Organization*, trans. A. M. Henderson and Talcott Parsons (New York: Oxford University Press, 1947); *The Methodology of the Social Sciences*, trans. Edward A. Shils and Henry A. Finch (Glencoe, Ill.: The Free Press, 1949).

19. William Barrett, *The Truants: Adventures Among the Intellectuals* (Garden City, N.Y.: Anchor Books, 1983), 99–130; *Politics*, July-August 1947; Hannah Arendt, "What is *Existenz* Philosophy," *Partisan Review* 13 (Winter 1946): 34–56.

20. Max Weber, *From Max Weber*, 228.

21. Letters, Bell to Macdonald, 19 July 1944, Macdonald Papers; Bell to Corey, 7 August 1944, Corey Papers; Corey to Bell, 12 August 1944, Bell's Files; Bell to Corey, 30 October 1944, Corey Papers; Interview with Bell, 20 April 1982.

22. "Interview with Daniel Bell," in Dittberner, 319, 321–22. In retrospect Bell exaggerated the callowness of his wartime writing. In journalistic circles, it was prized enough to win him an offer in 1945 to join the reporting staff of *Time*'s business and finance section. Letter, Bell to Macdonald, n.d. [November 1946], Macdonald Papers.

23. John Morton Blum, *V Was for Victory: Politics and American Culture During World War II* (New York: Harcourt Brace Jovanovich, 1976), 234–38; letter, Bell to Corey, 29 March 1944, Corey Papers. See also Bell, "The Balance Sheet of the War: The Record on the Political Front," *New Leader*, 21 October 1944, 8; Bell, "Cartels, Fascism and Peace: The Kilgore Report Adds Confusion on What do Do With Postwar Germany," *New Leader*, 18 November 1944, 5; Bell, "Labor and Peace Table—Has It a Program?" *New Leader*, 24 November 1944, 1, 8; Daniel Bell [Murray Everett], "The Future of Monopoly in America: ALCOA Decision Affects Entire Postwar Economy," *New Leader*, 7 April 1945, 4; Bell, "Notes on Our Economic Prospects," *New Leader*, 9 November 1946, 6.

24. Letter, Bell to Macdonald, n.d. [September 1944], Macdonald Papers; Daniel Bell, "Economic Heresy and Capitalism: Some Notes on Social Credit— Brooks Adams and Marx," *New Leader*, 25 August 1945, 11.

25. Paul Mattick, Jr., finds this combination of formalism and institutionalism in Hilferding's *Das Finanzkapital*, the distinguished work of Second International economic theory. Mattick defined Hilferding's perspective as an "attempt to combine political economy with its critique," that is, bourgeois "economic science" with Marxism. Paul Mattick, Jr., Review of *Finance Capital* by Rudolf Hilferding, *Telos* no. 54 (Winter 1982–83), 199–212.

26. Daniel Bell, "What is Our Economic Future?" *The Progressive*, 2 June 1947, 8; Bell, "Notes on Our Economic Prospects," *New Leader*, 9 November 1946, 6. Also see Bell, "What is Labor's Role From Here On?" *The Progressive*, 13 January 1947, 10, on capitalism as an "economic jungle" without the smooth self-corrections classical economics attributed to it. On Keynes's approximation of Marx by focusing on the built-in inhibition of the accumulation process, see Paul Sweezy, *The Theory of Capitalist Development: Principles of Marxian Political Economy* (New York: Oxford University Press, 1942; reprint, New York: Monthly Review, 1979), 52, 348; and the Editors, "Listen, Keynesians!" *Monthly Review* 34 (January 1983): 1–11. The Keynesian argument on the chronic stagnation of modern capitalism appeared in Harvard economist Alvin Hansen's *Full Recovery or Stagnation?* (New York: W. W. Norton, 1938).

27. Rudolf Hilferding, *Finance Capital: A Study of the Latest Phase of Capitalist Development*, ed. Tom Bottomore (London: Routledge and Kegan Paul, 1981), 366. Bell, "Preventing Economic Breakdown," review of *The Coming Crisis* by Fritz Sternberg, *Commentary*, May 1947, 492–93; Bell, "What is Our Economic Future?" *The Progressive*; Bell, "The Political Economy," *Common Sense*, January 1946, 35–36.

28. Bell "American-British Ties and Tugs," *The Progressive*, 20 May 1946, 10; Bell, "What's Our Economic Future?" *The Progressive*.

29. Bell, "Notes on Our Economic Prospects"; Bell, "The Militarization of Industrial Life," *New Leader*, 1 March 1947, 6; Bell, "American-British Ties," *The Progressive*.

30. Bell, "Preventing Economic Breakdown," 494–95. Bell's *Commentary* essay shows that while he repudiated his theory of the Monopoly State Bell held to the concept of "permanent war economy" which was closely linked to the Monopoly State in his early *New Leader* articles. "Permanent war economy" was a concept current in left-socialist circles by the end of the Second World War. In *Politics* there were two key articles on the topic: Walter J. Oakes, "Toward a Permanent War Economy?" *Politics*, February 1944, 11–17, and Walter J. Oakes, "Reconversion—to What?" *Politics*, November 1944, 299–303. Oakes argued that production and maintenance of military stockpiles had become economically necessary for American capitalism, in order to absorb "surplus labor." The permanent war economy thesis also figured in Paul Sweezy's *Theory of Capitalist Development* (1942), which pointed to the role of state expenditures on arms in resisting the capitalist tendency toward crises of underconsumption, by withdrawing a certain proportion of surplus value from circulation and insuring the purchase of the product from it. Sweezy, *The Theory of Capitalist Development*, 233–34, 342–46. In the late 1940s, Max Shachtman's Workers Party in particular pursued the analysis and critique of the "permanent arms economy." See Michael Kidron, *Western Capitalism since the War* (London: Weidenfeld and Nicolson, 1968) and Martin Shaw, "The Making of a Party," in *The Socialist Register 1978* (London: Merlin Press, 1978), 100–45.

31. Lichtenstein, *Labor's War at Home*, 148, 153, 155, 194–95; Davis, "The

Barren Marriage of American Labour and the Democratic Party," 65–67; Dwight Macdonald, "The MCF," *Politics*, April 1944.

32. Macdonald, quoted in Lichtenstein, 144; Frank Marquart, "A Letter on the Michigan Third Party Conference," *Politics*, April 1944, 80–81.

33. Seymour Martin Lipset, *Agrarian Socialism: The Cooperative Commonwealth Federation in Saskatchewan: A Study in Political Sociology*, rev. ed. (Berkeley: University of California Press, 1971), 134–58.

34. See Lewis Corey, "Program for a New Party?" *Antioch Review* 4 (Fall 1944): 465–69; "Toward a Social Program and Action," *Antioch Review* 4 (Winter 1944–45): 633–35; "Toward a Liberal Program for Prosperity and Peace," *Antioch Review* 7 (Summer 1947): 291–304. See Michigan Commonwealth Federation brochure, *Democracy Aroused!! A Call to Organize*, in Daniel Bell's Files, Tamiment Library, New York.

35. "Interview with Daniel Bell, May 1972," in Dittberner, *The End of Ideology and American Social Thought*, 320.

36. "Summary of Discussion Held at Hotel New Yorker, December 1st, 1945, On Prospects for New Labor-Liberal Political Action," in Daniel Bell's Files, Tamiment Library; "Report on the Mid-West Exploratory Conference on Independent Political Action, Held at Madison, Wisconsin, Dec. 16, 1945," in Daniel Bell's Files; Letter, Corey to Bell, 23 November 1945, Bell's Files; letter, Bell to Corey, n.d., Corey Papers, Columbia University; letter, Corey to A. Philip Randolph, 23 November 1945, in Bell's Files.

37. See Bell interview, Socialist Movement Project, Oral History Research Office, Columbia University, New York; letter, Bell to Corey, n.d. [late 1945], Corey Papers; "Summary of the Conference of American Progressives Held at International House, Chicago, April 6–7, 1946," Socialist Party Papers, Duke University, Durham, N.C.

38. "Summary of the Conference of American Progressives"; Letter, Corey to Horace Fries, 15 December 1945, in Bell's Files; minutes of the National Educational Committee for a New Party, 5 October 1946, Detroit, in Bell's Files; *Ideas for a New Party* (pamphlet, National Educational Committee for a New Party, Chicago, 1946); "Ideas for a New Party: Provisional Declaration of Principles, National Educational Committee for a New Party—A Symposium," *Antioch Review* 6 (Winter 1946–47): 602–24, *Antioch Review* 7 (Spring 1947); 146–58, *Antioch Review* 7 (Summer 1947): 305–12; letter, Bell to Corey, n.d. [fall 1947], Corey Papers.

39. On their disagreements regarding "Ideas for a New Party," see letter, Corey to Bell, 10 August 1947, Corey Papers; letter, Bell to Macdonald, n.d. [fall 1946], Macdonald Papers.

40. Richard Polenberg, *War and Society: The United States 1941–1945* (Philadelphia: Lippincott, 1972), 2–3; letter, Bell to Corey, 24 April 1944, Corey Papers; Letter, Bell to Macdonald, n.d. [late 1945, early 1946], Macdonald Papers.

41. Lichtenstein, *Labor's War at Home*, 126.

42. At times in earlier years, Bell had evinced an interest in social-

psychological analysis as a complement of his focus on economic structure, though it came to the fore of his thinking after the war, as the theory of repressive organicism required an understanding of social conformism. Earlier, he had commented that Guenter Reimann's *Myth of the Total State*, for instance, was too preoccupied with economics. "The 'total' picture is not drawn," he wrote in 1941. "Slurred over are the ideological and psychological factors which feed the dynamism of Nazism and which provide the revolutionary and explosive twist of this new juggernaut. These are important considerations in an era of ideology." In a 1943 review of Robert Brady's *Business as a System of Power*, Bell claimed that the supposed origin of Nazism in the "synchronization of monopoly" was too "mechanical" a thesis, for it ignored the specific impact of party, masses, ideology, and imperialism. And in his 1944 essay on Hilferding and the Monopoly State, Bell defined fascism by the hegemony of a political party and mass movement autonomous of the economic class interests traditional to capitalist society.

Bell, "Myths and Might," Review of *The Myth of the Total State* by Guenter Reimann, *New Leader*, 13 December 1941, 2. Bell, "Business and Politics," Review of *Business as a System of Power* by Robert Brady, *Partisan Review* 10 (July–August 1943): 377–80.

43. Arendt, *The Origins of Totalitarianism* (1951; new ed., New York: Harcourt Brace Jovanovich, 1973), 348; also, on the "general desire for a fusion of classes" underlying the Nazi movement, see Pierre Ayçoberry, *The Nazi Question: An Essay on The Interpretations of National Socialism (1922–1975)* (New York: Pantheon Books, 1981), 74.

44. On the essential role played by "mass suggestion," George Orwell, quoted in Bernard Crick, *George Orwell: A Life* (New York: Penguin Books, 1982), 367.

45. Letter, Bell to Corey, 17 August 1945, Corey Papers.

46. On the labor project and the Frankfurt School, see Martin Jay, *The Dialectical Imagination: A History of the Frankfurt School and the Institute of Social Research, 1923–1950* (Boston: Little, Brown, 1973), 206, 224–26; Jay, "The Frankfurt School in Exile," *Perspectives in American History* 6 (1972): 359–60. "Jewish Problem in the American Trade Union Press," no. 9, February 1945, Tamiment Library, New York; "Interview with Daniel Bell, May 1972," in Dittberner, 316. On the rise of anti-Semitism in the late war years and the response of the major Jewish organizations, see Leonard Dinnerstein, "Anti-Semitism Exposed and Attacked, 1945–1950," *American Jewish History* 71 (September 1981): 134–49.

47. Bell, "The Face of Tomorrow," *Jewish Frontier*, June 1944, 15–20.

48. Ibid.

49. Bell, "The Political Lag of Commonwealth," *Politics*, May 1945, 142–43.

50. See "Editor's Note" introducing the series "New Roads in Politics," *Politics*, December 1945, 369. Dwight Macdonald, "The Root is Man," *Politics*, April 1946, 101–2.

51. Will Herberg, "Personalism against Totalitarianism," *Politics*, December 1945, 369–74; Paul Goodman, "Revolution, Sociolatry and War," *Politics*, De-

cember 1945, 376–80; Albert Votaw, "Toward a Personalist Socialist Philosophy," *Politics*, July 1946, 15–17.

52. Macdonald, "The Root is Man: Part Two," *Politics*, July 1946, 197.

53. Nicola Chiaromonte, "On the Kind of Socialism Called 'Scientific,'" *Politics*, February 1946, 33–44. Chiaromonte echoed Kierkegaard's purity of soul: "That one might 'always come home with one's eyes blackened'"—as Rosa Luxemburg said of those motivated solely by abstract ideals—"will be the normal price to pay for having firmly willed one thing."

54. H. Stuart Hughes, *The Obstructed Path: French Social Thought in the Years of Desperation, 1930–60* (New York: Harper and Row, 1968).

55. Macdonald, "The Root is Man: Part Two," *Politics*, July 1946, 210–14.

56. Irving Howe, "Intellectuals' Flight from Politics: A Discussion of a Contemporary Trend," *New International*, October 1947, 241–46. On Howe's editorial assistantship, see Howe, *A Margin of Hope: An Intellectual Autobiography* (New York: Harcourt Brace Jovanovich, 1982), 115–16. See David T. Bazelon, "New Roads and Old Footpaths," *Politics*, July 1946, 184–87. Other key Marxist critiques contributed to the series were Lewis Coser [Louis Clair], "Digging at the Roots, or Striking at the Branches?" *Politics*, October 1946, 323–28, and Irving Howe, "The 13th Disciple," *Politics*, October 1946, 329–35. On Bell's sympathy with Macdonald, letter, Bell to Macdonald, 28 January 1946, and Bell to Macdonald, n.d. [June 1946], Macdonald Papers.

57. Letters, Bell to Macdonald, n.d. [late 1945, early 1946], 28 January 1946, and n.d. [March-April 1947], Macdonald Papers. Even in the midst of his collaboration with the Socialist Party Bell wrote Socialist Party executive secretary Harry Fleischman, jestingly, "What's new in the world—things are rather dead here. Me—I'm losing my interest in politics, books, the world." Bell to Fleischman, 3 February 1946, Socialist Party Papers, Duke University.

58. Letter, Bell to Macdonald, 28 January 1946, Macdonald Papers. On Camus's differences with Sartre's notions of the free self-creation of personality, see William Barrett's discussion in *The Truants: Adventures Among the Intellectuals* (Garden City: Anchor Books, 1983), 113–23.

59. Letter, Bell to Macdonald, n.d. [June 1946], Macdonald Papers.

60. Weber, "Politics as a Vocation," in *From Max Weber*, 120.

61. Ibid.

62. Ibid., 121, 125.

63. Reinhold Niebuhr, *The Nature and Destiny of Man, volume 2: Human Destiny* (New York: Charles Scribner's Sons, 1943), 284.

64. Ibid.

65. Reinhold Niebuhr, *The Nature and Destiny of Man, volume 1: Human Nature* (New York: Charles Scribner's Sons, 1941), 297.

66. Letter, Bell to Macdonald, 28 January 1946, Macdonald Papers. Bell's notion of "commitments" as a kind of "institutional pull" appeared also in the work of Philip Selznick, whom Bell knew at City College. Selznick's book, *The TVA and the Grass Roots*, was a Michelsian analysis of a public enterprise that was intended to open broad vistas of democratic reform but instead adapted conservatively to the preexisting power brokers in its social environment, and

Selznick made "commitment" a key part of his terminology to denote functions of organizational structure that channel inputs, exert influences, incur
debts, and enforce responsibilities, thus binding an organization (or a social
system as a whole) to certain definite practices and effects. The concept of
"commitment" was intended to capture the paradoxes of social action, the
forces that turn intentions into adverse consequences. Selznick wrote:

> The sociologically significant source of unanticipated consequences in-
> herent in the organizational process may be summed up in the concept of
> 'commitment.' This term has been used throughout this study to focus
> attention upon the structural conditions which shape organizational be-
> havior. This is in line with the sociological directive, stated above, that
> constraints imposed by the system will be emphasized. A commitment in
> social action is an enforced line of action; it refers to decisions dictated by
> the force of circumstances with the result that free or scientific adjust-
> ment of means and ends is effectively limited.

Selznick wrote the book in 1946 and 1947 and acknowledged discussions with
Bell. Philip Selznick, *The TVA and the Grass Roots: A Study in the Sociology of Formal Organization* (Berkeley: University of California Press, 1949), 255, 185;
letter Selznick to Brick, 5 May 1982.

67. Bell, "'Grass Roots' for Big Cities," review of *Reveille for Radicals* by Saul
Alinsky, *Commentary*, March 1946, 92–94.

68. On "Parable of Alienation" as a "companion piece," Bell to Travers
Clement, n.d., American Labor Conference on International Affairs papers,
Tamiment Library, New York; Bell to Macdonald, Fall 1946, Macdonald Papers.

69. Bell, "A Parable of Alienation," *Jewish Frontier*, November 1946, 12–14.
See Max Horkheimer and Theodor Adorno, *Dialectic of Enlightenment* (New
York, 1944; New York: Seabury Press, 1972), 168–208.

70. Bell, "A Parable of Alienation," pp. 16–19.

71. In a 1950 essay, Murray Hausknecht, then a Columbia graduate student
in sociology, nicely captured the drift of Bell's argument under the rubric of
the "independent radical." This figure, Hausknecht wrote, was a political deviate two times over, first in the sense of rejecting the norms of the prevailing
political order, and second in repudiating the principal form of radical opposition to that order (namely, Marxism and the Leninist parties). By retain-
ing, even after they have left formal organizations, the radical values that first
attracted them to the organized revolutionary movement, "independent radicals" were left rootless or "anomic" individuals, their thought centered on the
dysfunctional traits of organization per se; in response, he said, they tended
to embrace "absolute" ethics as the anchor of action. Murray Hausknecht,
"The Independent Radical: A Sociological Study of Deviate Political Behavior" (Master's thesis, Columbia University, 1950).

72. Sidney Hook, *From Hegel to Marx: Studies in the Intellectual Development of
Karl Marx*, with a new introduction (Ann Arbor: University of Michigan Press,
1962), esp. 15–76 and 272–307, 1–9.

73. Bell, "Where the News Ends," *New Leader*, 22 August 1942, 8, 7.

74. Later, Bell reflected on different uses of "alienation," Marxist and existentialist: Daniel Bell, "The Debate on Alienation," in *Revisionism: Essays on the History of Marxist Ideas*, ed. Leopold Labedz (New York: Frederick A. Praeger, 1962), 195–211.

75. Interview with Daniel Bell, 20 April 1982.

76. Gershom Scholem, *On Jews and Judaism in Crisis: Selected Essays*, ed. Werner J. Dannhauser (New York: Schocken Books, 1976), 55.

77. For instance, letter, Bell to Macdonald, n.d. [1944?] Macdonald Papers, Yale University.

78. For discussions of alienation as a peculiarly Jewish trait, see Ben Halpern, "Letter to an Intellectual," *Jewish Frontier*, December 1946, 13–18; Nathan Glazer, "The 'Alienation' of Modern Man: Some Diagnoses of the Malady," *Commentary*, April 1947, 378–85; Arnold W. Green, "Why Americans Feel Insecure: The Sense of Alienation is Not Exclusively Jewish," *Commentary*, July 1948, 18–28. Richard Gillam cites C. Wright Mills's unpublished memoirs, *Tovarich*, where Mills commented on the sense of alienation that grew among young Jewish intellectuals in the 1940s. Mills suggested that this mood served a kind of Jewish chauvinism, while helping the intellectuals to find a place within the "great American celebration." Mills, quoted in Gillam, "C. Wright Mills: An Intellectual Biography" (Ph.D. diss., Stanford University, 1972), p. 278.

79. Salvador Giner, *Mass Society* (New York: Academic Press, 1976), pp. 160–61. On the influence of Arnold on *Scrutiny's* definition of the critic, see Francis Mulhern, *The Moment of "Scrutiny"* (London: Verso, 1981), 33–35.

80. Giner, 72–76, 86–87; Arendt, quoted in Daniel Bell, *The End of Ideology: On the Exhaustion of Political Ideas in the Fifties*, rev. ed. (New York: The Free Press, 1962), 25; Karl Mannheim, *Ideology and Utopia: An Introduction to the Sociology of Knowledge*, trans. Louis Wirth and Edward Shils (New York: Harcourt Brace, 1936), 160–61.

81. The slide in the 1930s from the modern tradition of the intellectual to the adoption of Leninist notions of leadership can be seen in the case of John Wheelwright, the radical New England poet who began his move to revolutionary socialism by calling for "a party of professional minds dedicated to the cause of national culture," which would combat the rule of business on behalf of the working masses. See Alan M. Wald, *The Revolutionary Imagination: The Poetry and Politics of John Wheelwright and Sherry Mangan* (Chapel Hill: University of North Carolina Press, 1983), 90; William Phillips, quoted in James B. Gilbert, *Writers and Partisans: A History of Literary Radicalism* (New York: John Wiley and Sons, 1968), 281. See Gilbert, *Writers and Partisans*, 253–82, 180–220, 234–52.

82. C. Wright Mills, "The Powerless People: The Role of the Intellectual in Society," *Politics*, April 1944, reprinted in *Power, Politics and People*, ed. Irving Louis Horowitz (New York: Ballantine Books, 1963), 292–304. Richard Gillam discusses Mills's conception of the intellectual in terms of Weber's two ethics, "C. Wright Mills: An Intellectual Biography," 233.

83. Dwight Macdonald used the concept of "responsibility" as Mills did, to mount an antibureaucratic critique, in his essay, "The Responsibility of Peoples," *Politics*, March 1945, 86–87, 92–93: "Modern society has become so tightly organized, so rationalized and routinized that it has the character of a mechanism that grinds on without human consciousness or control. . . . The scale and complexity of modern governmental organization, and the concentration of political power at the top, are such that the vast majority of the people are excluded from . . . participation. . . . The common people of the world are coming to have less and less control over the policies of 'their' governments, while at the same time they are being more and more closely identified with those governments. . . . As the common man's *moral* responsibility diminishes (assuming that the degree of moral responsibility is in direct proportion to the degree of freedom of choice) his *practical* responsibility increases. Not for many centuries have individuals been at once so powerless to influence what is done by the national collectivities to which they belong, and at the same time so generally held responsible for what is done by those collectives."

84. Bell, "The Quest for Order," *The Progressive*, 29 April 1946, 8.

85. Karl Jaspers, quoted in H. H. Gerth and C. Wright Mills, "Introduction," in *From Max Weber*, 26–27.

86. Bell, "The Economic Founding Fathers," review of *The Economic Mind in American Civilization* by Joseph Dorfman, *Commentary*, July 1946, 94.

87. See C. Wright Mills, "The Contribution of Sociology to Studies of Industrial Relations," in *Proceedings of the First Annual Meeting, Industrial Relations Research Association*, ed. Milton Derber (Urbana, Ill., 1949).

88. Letter, Bell to Macdonald, n.d. [June 1946], Macdonald Papers, Yale University.

89. Bell, "Adjusting Men to Machines: Social Scientists Explore the World of the Factory," *Commentary*, January 1947, 80, 87.

90. Ibid., 88.

91. Ibid., 86–87.

92. Bell, "Parables from Jewish Existence," review of *The Eternal Light* by Morton Wishegrad, *Commentary*, November 1947, 495–97; Bell, "Magazine Market Report: What Do the Masses Read?" *New Leader*, 22 May 1948, 8; Bell, "Marginal Notes on American Culture: The Invasion of Privacy," *New Leader*, 17 January 1948, 8.

93. Bell, "'Screening' Leaders in a Democracy: How Scientific is Personnel Testing?" *Commentary*, April 1948, 371, 374.

94. Ibid., 374–75.

95. Ibid., 375.

Chapter 4

1. On the significance of the Marshall Plan as a measure placating the liberal left in domestic politics, see Alonzo L. Hamby, *Beyond the New Deal: Harry S. Truman and American Liberalism* (New York: Columbia University Press, 1973), 185–86. In the summer of 1947, James Wechsler wrote, "Mr. Truman has

reached the crucial fork and turned unmistakably to the left." Abroad, Leon Blum was an example of a socialist leader who lambasted the Truman Doctrine but embraced the Marshall Plan, turning his fire on the Soviet Union for inhibiting reconstruction of a unified continent. See Blum, "Whose Fault?" *Modern Review* 1 (August 1947): 407–8. Socialist solicitude for the Marshall Plan, as opposed to the Truman Doctrine, is evident in the account by Julius Braunthal, secretary to the Socialist International from 1950 to 1956, in *History of the International: World Socialism 1943–1968*, trans. Peter Ford and Kenneth Mitchell (Boulder, Colo.: Westview Press, 1980), 145–46.

2. In his essay, "The Two Postwar Eras and the Conditions for Stability in Twentieth-Century Western Europe," Charles S. Maier cites State Department memoranda from the summer and fall of 1947:

> Despite the admitted difficulty in reconstructing a mass base for the socialists, by 1947–8, American policy makers, AFL emissaries, and European businessmen diligently encouraged the formation of social democratic unions in the Latin countries and pressed for the purge of Communist sympathizers from British, German, and American federations. The moderates of Force Ouvrière, the TUC, of the Italian Catholic union federation (CISL) became all the more essential as interlocutors for labor. "The trend in Europe is clearly toward the Left," noted one of the Department of State's leading European analysts shortly after tripartism collapsed. "I feel that we should try to keep it a non-communist Left and should support Social-Democratic governments." The axis of the politics of productivity thus had to fall right in the center of the labor movement: "politically speaking the break must come to the left of or at the very least in the middle of the [French] Socialist party. Translated into labor terms, the healthy elements of organized labor must be kept in the non-Communist camp. Otherwise the tiny production margin of the fragile French economy would vanish and the ensuing civil disturbances would take on the aspects of civil war."

"The Two Postwar Eras and the Conditions for Stability in Twentieth-Century Western Europe," *American Historical Review* 86 (April 1981): 346–47.

3. Michael J. Hogan, "American Marshall Planners and the Search for a European Neocapitalism," *American Historical Review* 90 (February 1985): 44–72.

4. See Job Leonard Dittberner, *The End of Ideology and American Social Thought: 1930–1960* (Ann Arbor, Mich.: UMI Research Press, 1979), 126–27. As Sidney Hook put it at the Berlin conference, in a clear attack on the neutralism of third-force socialists, "Instead of saying 'Neither-Nor' . . . we must recognize an 'Either-Or.'" Hook quoted in Richard H. Pells, *The Liberal Mind in a Conservative Age: American Intellectuals in the 1940s and 1950s* (New York: Harper and Row, 1985), 129.

5. Braunthal, *History of the International*, 38.

6. Richard F. Kuisel, *Capitalism and the State in Modern France: Renovation and Economic Management in the Twentieth Century* (Cambridge: Cambridge University Press, 1981), 157–271. On the welfare principle of mixed economy, Pierre

Mendès-France, former advocate of socialist planning, quoted in Kuisel, 252.

7. Adam Przeworski, "Social Democracy as a Historical Phenomenon," *New Left Review*, no. 122 (July/August 1980), 46–58.

8. Lipsitz, *Class and Culture*, 112–34.

9. Hogan, "American Marshall Planners," 59–60.

10. See David M. Gordon, Richard Edwards, and Michael Reich, *Segmented Work, Divided Workers: The Historical Transformation of Labor in the United States* (Cambridge: Cambridge University Press, 1982), esp. 165–227.

11. Socialist Party executive secretary Harry Fleischman wrote to Lewis Corey on October 18, 1948, about "get[ting] a new party really started" after the election: "The campaign has been coming along beautifully with good publicity and support snowballing. If we had anything like a decent campaign fund, we would get millions of votes. I mean that literally. As it is, we shall certainly get a better vote than we have had at any time since 1932." In fact, the vote total of 139,520, while almost twice that of 1944, was less than the 1936 returns of 187,500. This number in itself was a disastrous drop from the 903,000 Thomas won in 1932. See David Shannon, *The Socialist Party of America* (New York: Macmillan, 1955), 255; Bell, *Marxian Socialism in the United States* (Princeton: Princeton University Press, 1967), 157, 171. On the prospects for the disintegration of the Democratic Party as the basis for a left-liberal political realignment, see Alonzo Hamby *Beyond the New Deal*, 264–65. *The Progressive*, quoted in Hamby, 269.

12. Dwight Macdonald, "I Choose the West," reprinted in Macdonald, *Politics Past: Essays in Political Criticism* (New York: Viking Press, 1957), 197–200.

13. On Bell's assumption of the labor post at *Fortune*, see "Interview with Daniel Bell, May 1972," in Dittberner, *The End of Ideology and American Social Thought*, 323–34. Besides the appeal of returning to New York and writing regularly on labor, financial exigencies compelled Bell to take the *Fortune* post. Having to support his daughter and ex-wife, Bell had been working two jobs, teaching labor history at Roosevelt College in Chicago in addition to his duties at the University of Chicago. *Fortune* offered a salary of $12,000, three times his instructor's salary at the University of Chicago. The salary differential seemed "an interesting commentary on the scale of values of American life," he wrote Lewis Corey. Letters, Bell to Corey, 10 June 1948, and Corey to Bell, 14 June 1948, Lewis Corey papers, Columbia University, New York.

Still, Bell's initial decision to join *Fortune* was a bit hesitant. He wrote to Corey on June 10, 1948, "The step is not as drastic as it sounds, for the University was loath to leave me go and I have a year's leave of absence, officially voted, and I have an agreement with Fortune to terminate our contract any time after six months if things don't go satisfactorily." Still, "I am quite excited about the idea. I think it is a top journalistic job yet one that will give me time—and research help—to dig deep into the guts of the labor movement and the economy." Even into the spring and summer of 1949, Bell kept up a correspondence with his Chicago colleague Bert Hoselitz, who lobbied for a permanént University appointment for Bell but failed to elicit anything but the offer of an adjunct position. By the fall of 1949 Bell decided to stay in New

York. He had remarried, and his wife, Elaine Graham, had received a long-term fellowship in psychology at Yale. He also found that he was free of editorial interference at *Fortune*. Letters, Hoselitz to Bell, 2 April 1949, Bell to Hoselitz, 7 April 1949, Hoselitz to Bell, 24 May 1949, 18 June 1949, all in American Labor Conference on International Affairs papers, Tamiment Library, New York.

14. See Charles Maier, "The Two Postwar Eras," 345–46, and Charles Maier, "The Politics of Productivity: Foundations of American International Economic Policy after World War II," in *Between Power and Plenty: The Foreign Economic Policies of Advanced Industrial States*, ed. Peter Katzenstein (Madison: University of Wisconsin Press, 1978), 23–49.

15. Sidney Hook, "The Rebirth of Political Credulity, Sidney Hook Analyzes the Illusions of the Peace and the Realities of Power Politics," *New Leader*, 1 January 1944, 4–5.

16. Philip Rahv, "Disillusionment and Partial Answers," *Partisan Review* 15 (May 1948): 519–29, and Irving Howe, "How *Partisan Review* Goes to War: Stalinophobia on the Cultural Front," *New International*, April 1947, 109–11.

17. See Bell, "Inflation in Soviet Planned Economy," *New Leader*, 8 February 1947, 5, and "The Militarization of Industrial Life," *New Leader*, 1 March 1947, 6. Bell's 1947 thesis that Soviet-American strife was a vicious circle of self-fulfilling hypotheses has reemerged recently as a central argument of "post-revisionist" Cold War diplomatic history, as in William Taubman's *Stalin's American Policy: From Entente to Detente to Cold War* (New York: Norton 1982), and Robert Dallek, *The American Style of Foreign Policy: Cultural Politics and Foreign Affairs* (New York: Alfred A. Knopf, 1983).

18. Macdonald applauded Bell's intention. He responded,

> Good for you to break with the New Leader (especially as it was such a personal wrench) over their war-drums beating. Harold Rosenberg believes that the . . . PR-New Leader set is even more of a threat to decency and sanity on the left today than the Commies were in the 30s. I think this is exaggerated, but certainly the neurotic intensity with which those critics pursue a hate-Russia policy is making it easier for the black rightists to push the country still faster towards something damned unpleasant—as in the red purge now projected in govt offices.

Letters, Bell to Macdonald, n.d. [1947], Macdonald to Bell, 8 April [1947], Macdonald Papers, Yale University Library.

19. Daniel Bell, "Fatalism of the Left," *The Call*, 16 April 1947, 4.

20. "The Manifestoes of 'The Third Force,'" reprinted in André Malraux and James Burnham, *The Case for DeGaulle* (New York: Random House, 1948), pp. 75–87.

21. Interview with Lewis Coser, 17 April 1983. See Daniel Bell "*The Modern Review*: An Introduction and Appraisal," *Labor History* 9 (Fall 1968): 380–83. On Abramovitch's background, see introduction by Sidney Hook and author's preface in Abramovitch, *The Soviet Revolution 1917–1939* (New York: International Universities Press, Inc., 1962), and Leopold H. Haimson, ed., *The*

Mensheviks: From the Revolution of 1917 to the Second World War (Chicago: University of Chicago Press, 1974), xv–xvii, 240, 267, 269, 284, 321; for Abramovitch's definition of the journal's mission, see letter, Abramovitch to Sidney Hook, 20 February 1948, American Labor Conference on International Affairs (hereafter ALCIA) Papers, Tamiment Library, New York; for Clement and Coser's attempt to span the gap, see letter, Clement to Abramovitch, 15 January 1948, ALCIA papers.

22. In 1947, Bell published the following pieces in *The New Leader*: "Inflation in Soviet Planned Economy," February 8; "The Militarization of Industrial Life," March 1; "'The American Dream'—1947 Model: The Omissions of Walter Lippmann," March 29; "The Trend to Statism: Argentina as 'Zis'," May 3; "Arvin and Dinuba: A Case Study of Two Towns," May 31; "Alice in Wallaceland: The Theory of Amalgam," June 21; "Alice in Wallaceland: Topsy-Turvy and the UAW," October 18; "Global Dislocation as the Focus: Random Spokes on the Economic Wheel," November 8. In 1948, Bell published nine pieces in *The New Leader* under his own name or under his pseudonym Murray Everett. Letter, Bell to Clement, 2 June 1947, ALCIA papers. On the choice between different kinds of bureaucratic states, see letter, Bell to Macdonald, n.d. [June 1946], Macdonald Papers. On the virulence of Stalinist repression after 1945 and the early Cold War, see "Interview with Daniel Bell, May 1972," in Dittberner, 325–26, and Bell's contribution to "Liberal Anti-Communism Revisited: A Symposium," *Commentary*, September 1967, 38–39.

23. On Denicke's "idiosyncratic" political character, see Haimson, ed. *The Mensheviks*, xviii–xxi. Letter, Isaacs to Coser, 11 October 1947, ALCIA papers.

24. Harold Isaacs, "South Asia's Opportunity," *Modern Review* 1 (December 1947): 758–71.

25. Raphael Abramovitch, "From Socialist Utopia to Totalitarian Empire," *Modern Review* 1 (June 1947): 265; Abramovitch, "Can the Choice Be Evaded?" *Modern Review* 1 (December 1947): 772–74; Harold Isaacs, "The Question of Choices," *Modern Review* 2 (January 1948): 77–79; Abramovitch, "One Must Still Choose," *Modern Review* 2 (January 1948): 79–80. The editor's note introducing the second installment of the dispute stated: "The editors of *Modern Review* wish to make it clear that they have not associated themselves with either side in this debate. Allowing both points of view to be adequately expressed is in keeping with the open forum character of *Modern Review*." *Modern Review* 2 (January 1948): 77. On the intraeditorial wrangle that followed, see letter, Abramovitch to Hook, 20 February 1948, ALCIA papers. For Denicke's advocacy of U.S. Cold War policy, see Denicke, "Challenge of Soviet Conquest," *Modern Review* 1 (March 1947): 63–70.

26. Letter, Sidney Hook to Abramovitch, 15 March 1948, ALCIA papers. Letter, Bell to Corey, 21 July 1947, n.d. [1947], 4 November 1947, n.d. [1947–48], 9 February 1948, 10 June 1948, 23 June 1948, 13 July 1948, and Corey to Bell, 29 October 1947, 31 January 1948, 12 February 1948, 14 June 1948, all in Corey Papers.

27. When Bell suggested running an article on the protoexistentialist Rus-

sian religious thinkers Vladimir Soloviev and Leo Shestov, Abramovitch, who considered them nothing but backward presocialist figures, declared according to Bell, "Soloviev and Shestov? Why, we defeated them in 1902!" Bell, "*Modern Review*: An Introduction and Appraisal," 383.

28. "Towards a new 'Modern Review,'" five-page typescript dated 8 February 1949, ALCIA papers.

29. Letters, Bell to Richard Lowenthal, 28 March 1949, Bell to Milton Singer, 17 June 1949, Bell to J. F. Wolpert, 20 July 1949, ALCIA papers. See Milton B. Singer, "The Social Sciences," in *The Idea and Practice of General Education: An Account of the College of the University of Chicago* (Chicago: University of Chicago Press, 1950), 134–36.

30. Letters, Bell to "Nat," 23 February 1949, Bell to Philip Reiff, 24 February 1949 and 6 July 1949, ALCIA papers; Bell's handwritten notes, ALCIA papers. The ALCIA papers include a long string of suggestive letters from Bell to Reinhard Bendix, Gertrude Himmelfarb, Robert MacIver, Bruno Bettelheim, Paul Tillich, James T. Farrell, William Barrett, Seymour Martin Lipset, Bert Hoselitz, Hans Gerth, Irving Howe, Richard Hofstadter, Hannah Arendt, and others. On intellectual responsibility and exhaustion, see Bell to Paolo Milano, 17 February 1949, Selznick to Bell, n.d. [1949], Bell to Melvin Lasky, 9 June 1949, all in ALCIA papers. Bell later used the phrase, the "tyranny of psychology" in his essay on "Work and Its Discontents" to describe the manipulative style of "human relations" management techniques. See *The End of Ideology*, revised ed. (New York: The Free Press, 1962), p. 251.

31. "An Editorial Farewell," *Modern Review* 3 (January 1950), see Bell, "The *Modern Review*: An Introduction and Appraisal," 383: "Abramovitch had conceived of the magazine as providing a platform for himself and his group in international socialist affairs, particularly if a reconstituted Labor and Socialist International would ever achieve importance, and was less interested in a socio-philosophical journal. I found it hard to interest my friends in a socialist magazine. . . . The nineteen fifties was not a decade of vigorous political discussion. The demise of *Modern Review* was an early signal of that fact."

32. Letters, Bell to Hofstadter, 29 March 1949, and Hofstadter to Bell, 31 March 1949, ALCIA papers.

33. Bell, "The Political Lag of Commonwealth," *Politics*, May 1945, 143.

34. "Interview with Daniel Bell, 1972," in Dittberner, 321.

35. Bell, "America's Un-Marxist Revolution: Mr. Truman Embarks on a Politically Managed Economy," *Commentary*, March 1949, 207–9.

36. Bell, "America's Un-Marxist Revolution," 209–12.

37. For a lucid review of Weber on class, see Seymour Martin Lipset, "Issues in Social Class Analysis," in Lipset, *Revolution and Counterrevolution: Change and Persistence in Social Structure* (New York: Basic Books, 1968), 121–58.

38. Bell, "Has America a Ruling Class?" Review of *Strategy for Liberals: The Politics of the Mixed Economy* by Irwin Ross, *Commentary*, December 1949, 603–7.

39. Bert Hoselitz, "The Dynamics of Marxism: What Remains Valid," *Modern Review* 3, no. 1, 11–23.

40. Bell, "America's Un-Marxist Revolution," 209–12.

41. Ibid., 213–14.

42. Ibid., 208, 215.

43. Robert Wiebe, *The Search for Order 1877–1920* (New York: Hill and Wang, 1967).

44. Bell, "America's Un-Marxist Revolution," 215.

45. See Bell, "Business and Politics," review of *Business as a System of Power* by Robert Brady, *Partisan Review* 10 (July-August 1943): 377–80.

46. Bell's view of the reactionary thrust of the "small-town mind" resembles Talcott Parsons' argument that the fascist movement arose in Germany as part of a "fundamentalist" reaction against the forces of modernization disintegrating habitual relations of traditional community life. See Talcott Parsons, "Democracy and Social Structure in Pre-Nazi Germany" (1942) and "Some Sociological Aspects of the Fascist Movements" (1942), in Parsons, *Essays in Sociological Theory*, rev. ed. (New York: The Free Press, 1954), 104–41.

47. Bell, "Has America a Ruling Class?" 606–7.

48. David Riesman, in collaboration with Reuel Denney and Nathan Glazer, *The Lonely Crowd: A Study of the Changing American Character* (New Haven: Yale University Press, 1950), 238–70; David Riesman in collaboration with Nathan Glazer, *Faces in the Crowd: Individual Studies in Character and Politics* (New Haven: Yale University Press, 1952), 32–38. The amorphous and indeterminate character of power had also been a theme of the Frankfurt School, on whom Riesman relied (but, according to Adorno, vulgarized). Horkheimer and Adorno had written in *Dialectic of Enlightenment*, "Each individual is unable to penetrate the forest of cliques and institutions which, from the highest levels of command to the last professional rackets, ensure the boundless persistence of status." In a similar vein, they wrote, "The socially responsible elite is in any case much more difficult to define than other minorities. In the fog of relationships between property, possessions, ordinance and management it successfully escapes theoretical determination." Max Horkheimer and Theodor W. Adorno, *Dialectic of Enlightenment* (New York: Social Studies Association, 1944; trans. John Cumming, New York: Seabury Press, 1972), 38, 207. Martin Jay summed up the argument this way: "domination in what Marcuse was to popularize as 'one-dimensional' society seemed to exist without the conscious direction of dominators, whether economic or political. As a result, it appeared more sinister and invulnerable, and the chances for effective action to negate it even more remote." Martin Jay, *The Dialectical Imagination: A History of the Frankfurt School and the Institute of Social Research* (Boston: Little, Brown, 1973), 166. In his essay, "The Frankfurt School in Exile," *Perspectives in American History*, 6 (1972) 339–85. Jay upheld Adorno's charge against Riesman by suggesting that the Frankfurt critique of *mass culture* did not suppose that a *mass society*, in which power was really dispersed, actually existed: that is, presumably, remarks on the amorphousness of power referred not to the realities of power but the inability of the popular consciousness to penetrate the veil of power.

49. Bell, "Has America A Ruling Class?" 606–7.

50. Bell, "The Prospects of American Capitalism: Today's Economists' Somewhat Rosier View," review of *American Capitalism* by John Kenneth Galbraith, *Commentary*, December 1952, 603–12.

51. [Bell], "Labor and the Election," *Fortune*, December 1948, 191. The "Labor" column in *Fortune* was written by Bell though unsigned. Bell believed that among "professionals"—all those who worked in or with organized labor—it was well known that the voice behind the column was his. Interview with Daniel Bell, 10 December 1982. In the notes below, Bell's authorship of the Labor columns is indicated in brackets.

52. See W. L. Guttsman, *The German Social Democratic Party, 1875–1933: From Ghetto to Government* (London: George Allen and Unwin, 1981) 319.

53. [Bell], "The 'Old Look' Returns," *Fortune*, November 1948, 208–10.

54. J. B. S. Hardman, "Power-Accumulation Transcends 'Job Consciousness,'" *Labor and Nation* 7 (Winter 1951): 48.

55. Bell valued industrial peace above all. When strikes still occasionally grew violent, he asked, "How had such an anachronistic situation boiled up?" In such instances, he usually found "a thick streak of irrationality" that resurrected the practices of "nineteenth-century brass-knuckle labor warfare." In the social-democratic search for order, class struggle was not a route to socialism but a remnant of the chaos of unregulated capitalism. While Bell recoiled from labor violence, however, he was also a "conflict" theorist who recognized the strike as a normal expression of social and economic friction and as the legitimate means of testing strength between two parties as they jockeyed for positions in bargaining.

[Bell], "Anachronism at American Enka," *Fortune*, August 1950, 43; [Bell], "Back to the Jungle," *Fortune*, May 1950, 52–56.

56. Bell, "The Worker and His Civic Functions," *Monthly Labor Review* 71 (July 1950): 62–69; Bell, "Labor's Coming of Middle Age," *Fortune*, October 1951, 114; [Bell], "Subversive Wobblies," *Fortune*, July 1949, 154; Bell, "Language of Labor," *Fortune*, September 1951, 86.

57. Bell, "Spotty Book on Unions," *The Progressive*, 13 May 1946; [Bell], "Strategic Position," *Fortune*, June 1949, 183; "Labor's Coming of Middle Age," 138; [Bell], "Lewis' Apparent Heir," *Fortune*, May 1949, 190; [Bell], "Sociology of Fashion," *Fortune*, July 1952, 56; Bell, "Do Unions Raise Wages: The Illusion of the Wage-Price Spiral," *Fortune*, January 1951, 65; [Bell], "The Labor Economists," *Fortune*, December 1948, 198.

58. [Bell], "Toledo in a Storm," *Fortune*, January 1950, 146–48; [Bell], "Labor Notes," *Fortune*, February 1952, 66; [Bell], "The Fair Income Fund," *Fortune*, August 1949, 152; [Bell], "'Flash Strikes'," *Fortune*, April 1952, 55–56; Bell, "Do Unions Raise Wages?" 140; [Bell], "As Steel Goes . . . ," *Fortune*, October 1949, 191–92; [Bell], "Management's 'Prerogatives,'" *Fortune*, September 1949, 173; [Bell], "Turning Point: The Ford Contract Opens a New Phase in Drives for Security," *Fortune*, April 1949, 189–91.

59. Bell, "Taft-Hartley, Five Years After," *Fortune*, July 1952, 172.

60. [Bell], "Into the Political Vortex: American Labor Takes the Lead in

Democratic World Labor," *Fortune*, February 1950, 38–42; see also [Bell], "Let George Do It," *Fortune*, May 1951, 50; and [Bell], "The A.F. of L. Aids Labor Abroad," *Fortune*, July 1949, 154.

61. Bell, "Labor's Coming of Middle Age," 137–40; [Bell], "Labor on Capitol Hill," *Fortune*, March 1949, 177; [Bell], "Unions as Political 'Pros'?" *Fortune*, November 1948, 206.

62. [Bell], "Unions as Political 'Pros'?" 206; [Bell], "The Labor Economists," *Fortune*, December 1948, 198; Letter, Bell to James T. Farrell, 14 March 1949, ALCIA papers.

63. Bell, "Labor's Coming of Middle Age," 115; [Bell], "'Speed-up,'" *Fortune*, January 1949, 154; [Bell], "Labor Notes," *Fortune*, April 1952, 64; [Bell], "The Centralization of Power," *Fortune*, March 1950, 158.

64. [Bell], "Civil War in the C.I.O.," *Fortune*, November 1949, 206.

65. [Bell], "Mutiny at Ford," *Fortune*, August 1951, 43–44; [Bell], "Effective Morale," *Fortune*, August 1950, 48–50.

66. [Bell], "Industrial Relations," *Fortune*, February 1949, 171–73; [Bell], "Effective Morale," 46, 50.

67. [Bell], "Organizing—the Cream is Off," *Fortune*, April 1950, 51–54; Bell, "The Growth of American Unions (Comments before the Industrial Relations Research Association), December 14, 1954," in Daniel Bell's Files, Tamiment Library; Bell, "Labor's Coming of Middle Age," 114.

68. Bell, "Labor's Coming of Middle Age," 114.

69. Ibid., 144.

70. Bell, "Language of Labor," *Fortune*, September 1951, 210; Bell, "Do Unions Raise Wages?" *Fortune*, January 1951, 140; Bell, "Labor's Coming of Middle Age," 150.

71. [Bell], "I.L.G.W.U.," *Fortune*, June 1950, 34; Bell, "Labor's Coming of Middle Age," 149. From J. B. S. Hardman Bell borrowed the concept of "power accumulation" to define the social dynamic of unionism. For Hardman's presentation of his thesis, see J. B. S. Hardman, "Power-Accumulation Transcends 'Job Consciousness,'" *Labor and Nation* 7 (Winter 1951): 46–50.

72. Bell, "Labor's Coming of Middle Age," 150.

73. Bell had commenced work on the project in 1945, when he told Macdonald in a letter from Chicago that he intended to write an analysis of "the failure of the SP . . . in terms of failure in Symbolism." Letter, Bell to Macdonald, n.d. [fall 1945], Macdonald Papers. In fall 1946, Bell outlined what would be the essential themes of the study in a letter to Macdonald, n.d., Macdonald Papers: "I don't think the study will be dry, I hope to explore the question of the failure of socialism, to take root, the role of declasee middle-class [*sic*] who dominated the SP, the relation to the labor movement in a bureaucratized world and the ambiguity of political action for a party which seeks the complete overthrow of a system yet has to propose solutions for immediate issues raised within the system, the whole dilemma of Norman Thomas as a moral personality." In the summer of 1947 he was gathering Socialist Party documents, though the writing began in earnest only in 1949. Bell hoped to finish the work that summer, but he did not get a complete

manuscript to his Princeton editors, Stow Persons and Donald Egbert, until the spring of 1950; substantial revisions took months more. "Bell Writing Socialist History," *New Leader*, 21 June 1947; Letter, Bell to Stow Persons, 30 June 1949, ALCIA papers, Letter, Persons to Bell, 21 April 1950, Bell's Files.

74. Letter, Bell to Fleischman, 24 October 1947, Socialist Party Papers, Duke University. Bell had been a leading member of Independent Voters for Norman Thomas, a group chaired by James T. Farrell and including Erich Fromm, Sidney Hook, Harold Isaacs, C. Wright Mills, William Phillips, Philip Rahv, Meyer Schapiro, Edmund Wilson, and Bertram D. Wolfe, advertised in *The Call*, 29 October 1948, 2.

75. Daniel Bell, "The Background and Development of Marxian Socialism in the United States," in *Socialism and American Life*, ed. Stow Persons and Donald Egbert (Princeton: Princeton University Press, 1952), pp. 213–405; reprinted as *Marxian Socialism in the United States* (Princeton: Princeton University Press, 1967), 4–5, my emphasis.

76. Ibid., 5.

77. Bell, "American Socialists: What Now?" *Modern Review* 2 (January 1949): 346.

78. Bell, *The End of Ideology: On the Exhaustion of Political Ideas in the Fifties*, rev. ed. (New York: The Free Press, 1962), 278.

79. Bell, *Marxian Socialism*, 5, 9–11.

80. *Marxian Socialism*, 17–18, 20, 24, 25–29, 45–58, 51–52. See Bell, "The Political Lag of Commonwealth," *Politics*, May 1945, 139.

81. *Marxian Socialism*, 37, 43–44.

82. Ibid., 8, 55.

83. See David Herreshoff, *The Origins of American Marxism: From the Transcendentalists to De Leon* (New York: Monad Press, 1973), 106–72.

84. *Marxian Socialism*, 42, 57–59, 72, 84, 86–97, 116. See James Weinstein's argument that the party's opposition to the war had a significant base of support and that the party's collapse has to be credited, not to its anti-imperialism, but to official repression and the left-right split of 1919. James Weinstein, *The Decline of Socialism in America, 1912–1925* (New York: Monthly Review Press, 1967). Bell also emphasized the repression, xenophobia, and vigilantism which the war stirred and the Socialist Party suffered, *Marxian Socialism*, 117–18.

85. *Marxian Socialism*, 88, 180–82.

86. Ibid., 5.

87. Ibid., 5–6.

88. Daniel Bell interview, typescript, Socialist Movement Project, Oral History Research Office, Columbia University, 8–10.

89. Toller, quoted in Bell, "First Love and Early Sorrows," *Partisan Review* 48 (1981): 540.

90. For example, Lewis Corey wrote to Jim Cork, "We must find the means of making the moral and ethical values come alive as an integral part of libertarian socialism and which alone, I believe, can give it dynamic force," letter, Rand School Collection, Tamiment Library, New York.

91. *Marxian Socialism,* 13.

92. Posadovsky had asked, Bell originally wrote,

> whether the need for the exercise of absolute authority by the revolution-
> ary nucleus of the party might not prove incompatible with those funda-
> mental liberties to whose realization socialism was officially dedicated. He
> asked whether the basic minimum civil liberties—the "sacrosanctity of
> the person"—could be infringed and even violated if the party leadership
> so decided. Posadovsky was answered at that time by George Plekhanov,
> one of the founders of Russian Marxism, the teacher of Lenin, and at
> that time a leader of the Bolshevik faction. Speaking solemnly, "and with
> a splendid disregard for grammar, Plekhanov replied, *Salus revolutia su-
> prema lex.* Certainly, if the revolution demanded it, everything—democ-
> racy, liberty, the rights of the individual—must be sacrificed to it." (Quoted
> by Isaiah Berlin, "Political Ideas of the Twentieth Century," *Foreign Af-
> fairs,* April 1950) To this serene philosopher of Russian socialism, Posadov-
> sky's question must have seemed puerile. It smacked of neo-Kantianism
> with its emphasis on the abstract individual as an end in himself. Later,
> Plekhanov retreated from his position. But this retreat was a "weakness"
> in the man himself, not in his Marxism. Ethics, even Kautsky had said,
> was class-bound; what other position was tolerable if all moral judgments
> are rendered by "history" and if the proletariat is the class which stands
> on its "agenda"?

Draft, typescript, I–5 and I–6, in Daniel Bell's Files, Tamiment Library.
Bell published an article on the subject separately, "On the Trail of Posadovsky:
Who Was the Forgotten Russian Who Challenged Lenin Back in 1903?" *New
Leader,* 27 November 1950, 11–12.

93. Niebuhr, *The Nature and Destiny of Man, volume 2: The Destiny of Man*
(New York: Charles Scribner's Sons, 1943), 86.

94. Niebuhr, quoted in Paul Merkley, *Reinhold Niebuhr: A Political Account*
(Montreal: McGill-Queens University Press, 1975), 147.

95. Niebuhr, *The Nature and Destiny of Man, volume* 2, 124n.

96. Bell, "Parables From Jewish Existence," review of *The Eternal Light* by
Morton Wishegrad, *Commentary,* November 1947, 495–97.

97. Max Weber, "Politics as a Vocation," in *From Max Weber: Essays in Sociology,* ed. H. H. Gerth and C. Wright Mills (New York: Oxford University
Press, 1946), 121.

98. Bell, "American Socialists: What Now?" 347, my emphasis.

99. Letter, Bell to Thomas, 4 November 1947, Norman Thomas Papers,
New York Public Library, New York.

100. Weber, "Politics as a Vocation," 78.

101. On "real politics," Bell's notes on Norman Thomas's reminiscences, in
1982 Addendum to Daniel Bell Collection, Tamiment Library, New York.

102. Bell's notes on Debs, in 1982 Addendum to Daniel Bell Collection,
Tamiment Library.

103. *Marxian Socialism,* 189.

104. Ibid., 88.

105. Ibid., 90.

106. Ibid., 6–7.

107. Karl Mannheim, *Ideology and Utopia*, trans. Louis Wirth and Edward Shils (New York: Harcourt Brace, 1936), 211–19.

108. *Marxian Socialism*, 5.

109. Mannheim, 247, 251.

110. *Marxian Socialism*, 7.

111. Bell, *The End of Ideology*, 281–82.

112. Bell, "The World of Moloch," *Politics*, May 1944, 111–13.

113. *Marxian Socialism*, 5–6.

114. Ibid., 7.

115. Ibid., 7, 13.

116. Draft, typescript, in Daniel Bell's Files, Tamiment Library.

117. *Marxian Socialism*, 56–59, 93.

118. American Socialism rose with the Progressive tide, Bell pointed out in *Marxian Socialism*, and as he wrote elsewhere at this time, again in a quasi-Nietzschean vein:

> The progressive tradition, as most American movements of reform, have been products of middle-class morality and its typical hallmark, indignation. . . . Max Scheler once speculated that moral indignation, which he said was typical *only* of middle-class psychology, itself was disguised envy. It arose, he claimed out of a curbing of natural impulses, the foregoing of luxuries, the frugal present for the accumulative future—all giving rise to resentment. It leads, in Scheler's phrase to a spiritual "self-intoxication" based on the suppression of emotions.

Draft of review of Daniel Aaron's *Men of Good Hope*, in 1982 Addendum to Daniel Bell Collection, Tamiment Library.

119. *Marxian Socialism*, 10, 42.

120. Ibid., 102.

121. Ibid., 177–79.

122. Bell, "American Socialists: What Now?" 351–52, my emphasis.

123. Ibid., 351–52.

124. Ibid., 347, my emphasis.

125. Ibid., 353.

126. Bell, draft, typescript, 283, Daniel Bell's Files, Tamiment Library.

127. Hannah Arendt, *The Origins of Totalitarianism*, 372, 363.

128. Bell, "Utopian Nightmare," review of *1984* by George Orwell, *New Leader*, 25 June 1949, 8.

Chapter 5

1. "Ideology" was "a program of action derived from a mixture of facts and values," according to Raymond Aron, one of the proponents of the end-of-ideology doctrine. "Systematization was the keynote." Aron, "On the Proper Use of Ideologies," in *Culture and Its Creators: Essays in Honor of Edward Shils*,

ed. Joseph Ben-David and Terry Nichols Clark (Chicago: University of Chicago Press, 1977), 1.

2. Max Horkheimer, *Eclipse of Reason* (New York: Oxford University Press, 1947; New York: Continuum, 1974), 178.

3. Seymour Martin Lipset, "The End of Ideology and the Ideology of the Intellectuals," in *Culture and Its Creators*, 17–19, 34–35. Lipset, "Europe: The Politics of Collective Bargaining," in *Decline of Ideology?*, ed. Mostafa Rejai (New York: Aldine-Atherton, 1971) 85–86.

4. Daniel Bell, "Language of Labor," *Fortune*, September 1951, 211.

5. Daniel Bell, *The End of Ideology: On the Exhaustion of Political Ideas in the Fifties*, rev. ed. (New York: The Free Press, 1962), 302, 191.

6. See Oskar Lange and Fred M. Taylor, *On the Economic Theory of Socialism*, ed. Benjamin E. Lippincott (University of Minnesota Press, 1938); H. D. Dickinson, "Price Formation in a Socialist Community," *Economic Journal* 43 (June 1933): 237–50; A. P. Lerner, "Economic Theory and Socialist Economy," *Review of Economic Studies* 2 (October 1934): 51–61; Dickinson, *Economics of Socialism* (Oxford: Oxford University Press, 1939); Lerner, *The Economics of Control: Principles of Welfare Economics* (New York: Macmillan, 1944).

7. Karl Mannheim, *Ideology and Utopia: An Introduction to the Sociology of Knowledge*, trans. Louis Wirth and Edward Shils (New York: Harcourt Brace, 1936), 262.

8. Lukács had already recognized such a trend in the interwar years. He wrote:

> The economic theories now being developed no longer have a purely bourgeois base, as they did in the age of classical economics. . . . And the theories of war-economy and planned economies show that this tendency is becoming stronger. . . . There is no contradiction in the fact that simultaneously—say, from Bernstein onwards—a section of socialist theory came more and more strongly under bourgeois influence. . . . however this is to be judged from the standpoint of the proletariat, its meaning for the bourgeoisie is unmistakable: namely that it is incapable of defending its own position ideologically and with its own resources.

Georg Lukács, *History and Class Consciousness: Studies in Marxist Dialectics*, trans. Rodney Livingstone (Cambridge: The MIT Press, 1971), 227–28.

9. *The End of Ideology*, 44, 94.

10. Bell, *Marxian Socialism in the United States* (Princeton: Princeton University Press, 1967), 193.

11. Bell, *The Coming of Post-Industrial Society: A Venture in Social Forecasting* (New York: Basic Books, 1973, 1976), 380.

12. The proficiency of economic forecasting, for instance, seems to be declining, despite the growing sophistication of statistical techniques for making projections. See "Economists Missing the Mark: More Tools, Bigger Errors," *New York Times*, 12 December 1984, D1.

13. *The Coming of Post-Industrial Society*, xxv.

14. Ibid., xi, 343, 380.

15. Ibid., 37.

16. Ibid., x.

17. Ibid., xxi.

18. Ibid., 160, xiii, 113, 298.

19. Ibid., 481.

20. Ibid., 488.

21. Ibid., 378.

22. Ibid., 379n.

23. Ibid., 265.

24. Ibid., 350; in contrast, there is Weber's *Wertrationalität*, "the rationality of 'reason' whose ends are to be considered by themselves as valid, independent of means," Ibid., 365n.

25. Ibid., 365.

26. Ibid., 337.

27. Ibid., 298.

28. Ibid., 377.

29. Bell, "America's Un-Marxist Revolution: Mr. Truman Embarks on a Politically Managed Economy," *Commentary*, March 1949, 208.

30. Bell, *The Cultural Contradictions of Capitalism* (New York: Basic Books, 1976, 1978), 84.

31. Ibid., xxx.

32. Bell, *The Reforming of General Education: The Columbia College Experience in Its National Setting* (Garden City, N.Y.: Anchor Books, 1968), 151.

33. Bell, *Cultural Contradictions*, 111, 77, 71.

34. See Bell, "The Dispossessed—1962," in Bell, ed., *The Radical Right: The New American Right, Expanded and Updated* (Garden City, N.Y.: Doubleday, 1963), 12:

> What the right wing is fighting, in the shadow of Communism is essentially 'modernity'—that complex of attitudes that might be defined most simply as the belief in rational assessment, rather than established custom, for the evaluation of social change—and what it seeks to defend is its fading dominance, exercised once through the institutions of small-town America, over the control of social change. But it is precisely these established ways that a modernist America has been forced to call into question.

35. Bell, *Cultural Contradictions*, xxviii.

36. Ibid., 7, 20.

37. Ibid., 144.

38. In *The Reforming of General Education*, Bell remarked that "the university is no longer the citadel of the traditional mode . . . but an arena in which the critics once outside the Academy have . . . found a place—deservedly—within." He is, of course, talking of his own experience, as one who proudly held the standard of the "critic," a thinker forever apart. Bell, *The Reforming of General Education*, 151.

39. Bell, *Cultural Contradictions*, 118, 42.

40. Ibid., 120.

41. Ibid., 278.

42. Ibid., 84.

43. Jürgen Habermas, "Neo-Conservative Culture Criticism in the United States and West Germany: An Intellectual Movement in Two Political Cultures," *Telos*, no. 56 (Summer 1983): 75–89.

44. Lukács, *History and Class Consciousness*, 22.

45. See, for instance, Dennis Wrong, "Reflections on the End of Ideology," in *The End of Ideology Debate*, ed. Chaim I. Waxman (New York: Funk and Wagnalls, 1968), 116–25.

Bibliographic Note

The books and articles consulted in the writing of this study are cited at the relevant points in the notes.

The following periodicals were systematically reviewed and the following documentary collections consulted.

Periodicals

American Socialist Quarterly/Monthly, 1932–37
The New Leader, 1938–52
Socialist Review (Supplement to *The Call*), 1943–44
Politics, 1944–47
Modern Review, 1947–50
Fortune, 1948–52

Documentary Collections

Daniel Bell's Files, Tamiment Library, New York University, New York.
1982 Addendum to Daniel Bell Collection, Tamiment Library, New York University, New York.
American Labor Conference on International Affairs Records, 1939–50, Tamiment Library, New York University, New York.
Rand School of Social Science Records, 1901–56, Tamiment Library, New York University, New York.
Social Democratic Federation Records, 1933–56, Tamiment Library, New York University, New York.
Socialist Party Correspondence, 1902–47, Tamiment Library, New York University, New York.
Socialist Party Minutes, 1900–36, Tamiment Library, New York University, New York.
Socialist Party of America Papers, Manuscript Department, Duke University Library, Durham, North Carolina.

Lewis Corey Papers, Rare Book and Manuscript Library, Columbia University, New York.

Dwight Macdonald Papers, Yale University Library, New Haven, Connecticut.

Norman Thomas Papers, Rare Books and Manuscripts Division, The New York Public Library, Astor, Lenox, and Tilden Foundations, New York.

Socialist Movement Project, Oral History Research Office, Columbia University, New York.

Richard Hofstadter Project, Oral History Research Office, Columbia University, New York.

Index

COMPOSED BY G & S TYPESETTERS, INC., AUSTIN, TEXAS
MANUFACTURED BY BOOKCRAFTERS, CHELSEA, MICHIGAN
TEXT AND DISPLAY LINES ARE SET IN BASKERVILLE

Library of Congress Cataloging-in-Publication Data
Brick, Howard, 1953–
Daniel Bell and the decline of
intellectual radicalism.
(History of American thought and culture)
Bibliography: pp. 265–266.
Includes index.
1. Bell, Daniel.   2. Conservatism—United States.
3. Liberalism—United States.   I. Title.   II. Series.
H59.B42B75   1986   300'.92'4   85-40757
ISBN 0-299-10550-4